BITTER HARVEST

A Woman's Fury,
A Mother's Sacrifice

Ann Rule

timewarner
paperbacks

A *Time Warner* Paperback

First published in the United States in 1998
by Simon & Schuster, Inc.
First published in Great Britain in 1998
by Little, Brown and Company
This edition published in 1999 by Warner Books
Reprinted 2001
Reprinted by Time Warner Paperbacks in 2002

A CIP catalogue record for this book
is available from the British Library.

*Unless otherwise notes, all photographs
are from the author's collection.*

ISBN: 0 7515 2669 X

Typeset by M Rules
Printed and bound in Great Britain
by Clays Ltd, St Ives plc

Time Warner Paperbacks
An imprint of
Time Warner Books UK
Brettenham House
Lancaster Place
London WC2E 7EN

www.TimeWarnerBooks.co.uk

BITTER
HARVEST

Prologue

Sometimes the places where searing tragedies have happened are marked with visible scars. More often, when normalcy returns, only the most discerning eye or the most sensitive mind will know. This is the way the world is and must be; we cannot forever grieve over old wounds and ancient sorrows. New grass covers bare ground, and flowers come back in the springtime, no matter what has happened on the earth that nurtures them.

Prairie Village, Kansas, became one of those places where an unbearable, irredeemable tragedy occurred. Something terrible happened there on a windy October night in 1995, a catastrophe of such magnitude that it seemed that the street where it happened—Canterbury Court—could never recover, that no one living there could ever laugh again. And yet, when I walked along Canterbury Court long after the wildfire that had erupted there, I saw no sign that anything unusual had taken place on that quiet suburban street.

People who live in other parts of America often don't realize that there are *two* Kansas Citys, one on the easternmost border of Kansas and the other on the western edge of Missouri. If they were sisters and not cities, the former would be an independent cowgirl, and the latter a graceful patron of the arts. Natives of each state seem to differentiate between the two with no difficulty whatsoever; they call one KCK and one KCMO. However, two cities with the same name create much confusion for visitors. Kansas City, Missouri, with a population of 450,000, is three times as big as its Kansas counterpart. Ward Parkway, in Kansas City,

Missouri, is lined with beautifully landscaped homes and estates and has a proliferation of statues and fountains. Kansas City, Missouri, has opera and ballet companies, and quaintly restored shopping areas whose original glory days were sixty or seventy years ago. At Thanksgiving, thousands flock to the Country Club Plaza to see the tiny lights that outline the old stucco buildings turned on. Instantly, the picturesque plaza becomes a holiday wonderland. Residents in "KCMO" live "north of the river" or "south of the river"— meaning the mighty Missouri.

The Missouri-Kansas border—State Line Road—runs south from the confluence of the Kansas and the Missouri rivers where they become one: the Missouri. Indeed, in some areas the state line is the center of the Missouri River. Thousands of families live in the Johnson County, Kansas, suburbs of the metropolitan Kansas City area and commute to Missouri. Visitors to both cities fly into KCI, a shared airport on the Missouri side. The gift shops sell souvenirs of *Kansas*'s most famous—if fictional—characters: Dorothy, Toto, the Cowardly Lion, the Scarecrow, and the Tin Man, all the beloved players in *The Wizard of Oz*.

Johnson County is in Kansas; Jackson County is in Missouri. Johnson County has 430,000 residents and is one of the most sought-after areas for upwardly mobile families. The Shawnee Mission Parkway rolls west from Kansas City, Missouri, and intersects with I-35, which turns south—a feeder freeway to myriad communities with tree-lined streets and homes built for pocketbooks ranging from modest to sumptuous: Roeland Park, Leawood, Mission, Fairway, Mission Hills, Merriam, Shawnee, Prairie Village, Overland Park, and, some thirty miles down the line, Olathe, the Johnson County seat. Many of these towns actually straddle the state line; homes just across the street from each other are in different states. Police jurisdictions intermingle, as do fire departments' perimeters. More than in most areas, cooperation between agencies is essential.

Of all these suburbs, Prairie Village is probably one of

the most desirable (second only to posh Mission Hills), although its name scarcely describes its appearance. There is no prairie, and this is not a village but an upscale haven for professionals, with more doctors, lawyers, CEOs, and others with incomes well over $100,000 a year than almost any town in Kansas. Many of the houses in Prairie Village are "old money" classics of brick, built in the thirties or earlier. One small development, Canterbury, with its Canterbury Court and Canterbury Cul de Sac et al., is clearly "new money," its mansions expensive imitations of English Norman, baronial Georgian, and Frank Lloyd Wright modern. Canterbury Court opens, somewhat incongruously, onto busy West Seventy-fifth, with its smaller homes and apartment houses.

It is an orchid dropped among dandelions and daisies— exquisite but out of place. Few of Canterbury's privileged children go to public school; rather, they are driven to private schools like Pembroke Hill, whose tuition is prohibitive for the average working family. Schoolchildren who live one block on either side of Canterbury sometimes tease the "rich kids."

In the mid-nineties, every other house in the first block of Canterbury Court seemed to house a doctor—or two. Mom-and-pop docs, as it were. And for someone who had grown up in a working-class family in a rural town, one mansion on Canterbury Court marked the pinnacle of achievement. A three-floor, 5,000-square-foot house with a swimming pool, it was meant to be a house to mend a marriage, a perfect home to solidify a family torn apart—a place to begin anew. But as a dread scenario unfolded, it became a house of horror.

When I first stood in front of what once had been 7517 Canterbury Court (the numerals still visible on an elm tree), it was January and desperately cold. I found it almost impossible to imagine that sheets of fire had consumed the house, flames fanned by autumn winds until they were higher than the treetops. In deepest winter, the ground was frozen solid; the huge maples and elms were bare. Even the blue spruce trees drew into themselves against the cold. Only a copse of seven or eight fragile white birches seemed alive. Incredibly, they had survived despite the heat that caught them in a deadly embrace, searing their bark and curling their leaves. The spring rains might revive them.

Blizzards had come and gone, leaving a light dusting of snow over the brown grass and ice-hardened ridges made by some heavy vehicle driving through mud. I had to look closely to see that the small rocks at my feet were not rocks at all, but cinders, charred fragments plowed into the earth. That was all. There was no "For Sale" sign on the vacant lot, no yawning burned-out foundation, no blackened boards, no reminder of what had once been there. It was all gone— along with the hopes and dreams of the five human beings who had lived in the house that stood on this lonely place.

The neighbors' leaded windows and heavy doors were shut tightly against anyone with questions. They were as impenetrable as the houses' stone and brick façades. No one wanted to remember that windswept October night when there were screams and sirens and, finally, only the muted voices of firefighters moving with a kind of organized desperation.

By that time, there was no longer any need for haste.

When I revisited Prairie Village and Canterbury Court six months later—in July—the vacant spot between the two closest houses looked like a park. The grass was bright green and the trees made a canopy of leaves that cast long shadows on the lawn. There was nothing alive there, and that haunted me because, in the interval between visits, I had learned the details of what had happened nine months before. The adjacent houses seemed to have edged stealthily together as if to pretend that no structure ever stood between them—certainly nothing as massive as a stucco and fieldstone mansion with a four-car garage.

The children who lived in the neighboring houses woke

less frequently from their fiery, wild-eyed nightmares now that summer had come. Their parents turned away from reporters and gawkers; they had told what they had to tell in a court of law. They wanted only to regain the safe feeling Canterbury Court once offered. They wanted to forget.

But, of course, none of them can really forget. Not ever.

Part I

Degenerate Sons and Daughters,
Life is too strong for you—
It takes life to love life.

—EDGAR LEE MASTERS
Spoon River Anthology

Chapter 1

The wind had blown constantly that fall, but that wasn't unusual for Kansas. Most Kansans scarcely acknowledge the wind; however, on October 23, 1995, gusts were strong enough to scatter carefully piled mounds of leaves and make lights flicker on and off. Housewives set out candles and flashlights—just in case.

In Prairie Village, Dr. Debora Green went about all her usual errands. With three children to take care of, she practically needed a timetable to coordinate their activities. She would have welcomed a power outage so they could stay home, light faintly scented candles, and just talk to each other. Later that day, they were all back together in their beautiful new house on Canterbury Court: Debora; her son, Tim; and her daughters, Lissa* and Kelly. After supper they all went to bed in their separate rooms. Debora thought she had turned on the burglar alarm, and the smoke alarm was always set on "Ready."

Fire can erupt with a raucous explosion or be as furtive as a mouse skittering silently along a wall. It was after midnight when the wind coaxed out the first tongues of fire and blew them into billows of orange before all the sleeping neighbors on Canterbury Court even knew they were in danger. The magnificent homes were so close together that squirrels could leap from one yard's trees to those next door. And the roofs were made of picturesque wooden shakes, dry as bone from the long midwestern summer.

Debora Green was barely able to escape the flames that

---

*The names of some individuals have been changed. Such names are indicated by an asterisk (*) the first time each appears in the book.

engulfed her house. She rushed to her neighbors' house
and pounded on the door, pleading for someone to help
her save her children. Then she looked back at the fire and
her heart convulsed at what she saw. Silhouetted against the
glow in the sky, the small figure of a child scampered ahead
of flames that were already eating away at the beams of the
garage. As the child moved north, the roof just behind her
began to give way and cave in. The child—it was Lissa—
miraculously made her way up over the peak of the garage
roof and down the other side, where she perched precari-
ously on the edge of the disintegrating roof. In moments,
she would surely fall into the fire below and perish.

"Help me!" Lissa screamed. Even through the thick black
smoke, she had seen her mother standing by their neighbors' house. The little girl called again and again, her small
voice lost in the roar of the flames. Finally—as if Debora was
moving through quicksand—Lissa saw her mother head
toward her. She *saw* her! She was coming!

Lissa knew she would be all right now; her mother would
save her. Debora stood beneath the edge of the roof, her legs
spread wide and her feet planted firmly so that she would not
slip. She held her arms open and beckoned to Lissa to jump
down to her. But it was such a long way to the ground. For a
moment, Lissa hesitated—and then she looked over her
shoulder and saw that the garage roof was almost gone.

"Jump!" Debora ordered. "Jump! I'll catch you."

"I'm afraid. . . ."

"*Jump! Now!*" There was urgency in her mother's voice,
and something else, something that frightened Lissa more
than the fire.

Lissa obeyed. With her arms above her head and the heat
licking at her back, she leaped from the garage roof. But
Debora didn't catch her; her arms were not spread wide
enough, or maybe she was standing too far back from the
garage. Lissa crumpled to the ground at Debora's feet. But
the lawn was carpeted with a cushion of leaves and she was
not hurt.

Lissa felt safe now. She was with her mother. She didn't know how many houses were on fire, or if it was only *their* house. It seemed to her that the fire was everywhere, and the smell of smoke was also a taste of smoke in her mouth. Her mother led her toward their neighbors' house, and Lissa looked around for her brother and sister. Lights began to appear in windows up and down the block. She heard sirens far away, then coming closer and closer until they died out, whining, in front of the burning house. And in her head, she kept hearing a voice crying, "Help me! Help me!" She tried to tell her mother about that, but Debora seemed to be in shock. She said nothing. She did nothing. She was just standing there, looking at the fire.

Lissa didn't see her brother and sister and she began to scream for someone to save Tim and Kelly, someone to save Boomer and Russell, their dogs. Still her mother said nothing.

When Lissa saw a police car screech to a stop in front of the burning house and a policeman running toward them, she begged him to save her brother and sister. He listened to her screams and then ran by without even stopping. Lissa clung to her mother and looked up into her face for reassurance, but she saw no expression at all. Debora was transfixed by the fire. The two of them just stood there, braced against the wind that was turning their house into a raging inferno.

Debora had saved one of her children. Was it possible that the other two were trapped in the fire, unable to escape? It was every mother's nightmare. And it was happening to her.

Chapter 2

Havana, Illinois, is a small town like thousands of other farming communities in the Midwest. For most drivers traveling from Keokuk, Iowa, to Bloomington or Champaign,

Illinois, Havana is only a blur along State Highway 136 east
of Adair, Table Grove, Ipava, and Duncan Mills, west of San
Jose and Heyworth. Over the years, Havana's population
has remained at just over 4,000 citizens. It sits in historic
country, close to the birthplaces of both Carl Sandburg and
Wyatt Earp, and near a number of lakes and the Illinois
River. The Spoon River, immortalized by Edgar Lee Masters,
flows into the Illinois a few miles west of Havana. And, like
the characters in Masters's *Spoon River Anthology*, it has had
its share of grotesques, tragedies, triumphs, and human
frailties that spawn gossip, the vast majority of it of import
only to people living in Havana.

Joan (which she has always pronounced "Joanne") Purdy
and Robert Jones settled as newlyweds in Havana. They were
married very young; Joan was barely eighteen, and Bob was
a year younger. Their second daughter, Debora, would recall
that both her parents came from large families and that
each had been raised "in poverty."

Pretty and blond, Joan was a brilliant student and had
won a partial scholarship to Stephens College in Columbia,
Missouri. She *did* enter there as a freshman, even though
Bob Jones hadn't wanted her to go. Stephens is a presti-
gious women's college; many of Joan's fellow students were
wealthy, while she had to work to make up the difference
between her scholarship and the cost of tuition and room
and board. College girls in the late forties wore cashmere
sweaters with pearls and long skirts—sometimes so tight they
could hardly walk. The "New Look" was in, and girls who
wanted to be well-dressed had to toss out their entire
wardrobes and start over.

Joan Purdy couldn't afford to do that. She was an unsophisticated girl, she was homesick, she missed Bob, who was
still in high school, and she felt out of place with the far
more worldly coeds—"snooty girls"—at Stephens. It was,
perhaps, inevitable that she would soon drop out of college
and say yes to Bob's marriage proposal.

Bob was a handsome young man, as good-looking as

movie stars Guy Madison or Gene Barry, whom he closely resembled. His hair was almost black and naturally wavy, and he combed it back from his forehead. He wasn't a big man, no more than five feet eight inches or so, but he was muscular and tan.

The young couple were married on Halloween, 1948, and Joan's dreams of being a math teacher evaporated. She became pregnant almost immediately and gave birth to their first daughter, Pamela, in the hot summer of 1949. Her second baby came less than two years later: Debora (who was first called Deborah, then Debra, Debi, and Deb before she finally settled on a spelling that suited her) was born on February 28, 1951.

By all accounts, the Joneses' marriage was happy enough, despite their youth. Had Joan worked, she would probably have earned more than Bob did in the early years. But spouses didn't switch roles in the fifties, so Joan stayed home and kept house. The marriage lasted; they were still together as their golden anniversary approached.

Both Pamela and Debora were cute little girls. And both of them were exceptionally bright, but it was Debora who showed true genius. Her uncle Gordon Purdy, who lived in Minnesota, remembered that she taught herself to read at two and a half by poring over the newspaper. He was astounded to get a letter written by his toddler niece.

Some who knew her said that Joan resented giving up her education to marry Bob, and that she sometimes took her frustrations out on her daughters with verbal abuse. Perhaps. Maybe she only wanted them to succeed beyond anything she had ever accomplished. If she seemed resigned to her role as a mother and housewife, she nevertheless wanted her girls to go to college and have professions. When Joan found fault with either girl, it was usually because she had failed to study hard enough. Where Bob was easygoing, Joan could be almost obsessed with the idea that her daughters had to succeed. She would brook no criticism of them from anyone outside the family.

"Between my parents," Debora would say cautiously later on, "I think I would say my mother was the strongest—the one who made the decisions."

Joan was the serious parent, and Bob was fun—the parent who made jokes and played games with the girls. Joan demanded excellence and high grades, although the girls were both good students. Debora was, in truth, a lazy student, but it didn't matter; she was so smart she didn't have to exert herself, not even to make straight A's. If she heard it once, she heard it a thousand times: she was a genius.

Forever after, Debora would define herself in terms of her scholastic accomplishments and her intelligence. She would also judge others, perhaps unconsciously, by how smart they were and how well they did in their careers. Everything came so easily to her that she had little comprehension of her peers' problems in grasping reading and math. She was also agile and athletic, and a gifted musician.

Her father drove a Butternut Bread bakery truck and gradually moved up in the company. "We didn't have a lot of money," Debora recalled, "but we always had everything we needed."

Later, when asked about her childhood, Debora could not remember anything unusual, anything negative. It was almost as if her memory was blank. She described an idyllic existence, with no family dissonance. But, in fact, there was at least one unpleasant incident. Debora was very angry with her father when he came home drunk from a bowling tournament. It was late, but she was still up and she startled Bob as he was counting several hundred dollars he had won in the tournament. Furious, Debora bawled him out. Later, when she found out that he had always meant the money for her college fund, she was ashamed about what she said to him that night. She did not mention that in her recall of her young years, nor did she speak of the fact that she wet her bed until she was twelve.

Debora and Pam shared a room, and they got along well—as sisters do, with the normal squabbles. If Pam resented Debora's transcendent intellect, her sister wouldn't remember it. Debora took piano and violin lessons and excelled at both, continuing the piano lessons well into her college years.

Pam was perhaps prettier than her younger sister, her features softer and more feminine than Debora's. Pam's hair was almost as dark as her father's, and she was small-boned. Debora was more solid, but "square" rather than chubby; she was growing up to be a cute girl rather than a pretty one, given her round face and the slight bump on her nose. Her forehead protruded above her eyebrows, a feature that would become more pronounced as she grew older and that gave her a slightly masculine look. Moreover, she was something of a chameleon; all her life, her appearance and weight seemed to change and blur continually, so that even acquaintances sometimes failed to recognize her. One thing was constant, however: Debora's hair was wonderfully thick and wavy, a gingery-auburn color. She wore it long and hanging down her back, sometimes naturally wavy and sometimes absolutely straight.

The Joneses moved to Metamora, Illinois, a hamlet even smaller than Havana, when Pam was in her last year in high school. Debora spent her freshman and sophomore years in Metamora's small high school, where her academic excellence shone even brighter. But the family stayed in Metamora for only two years. Bob was moving up in the parent company, Roman Meal, and eventually stopped driving a bread route and became a district manager. The family moved to a house at 3122 North Sheridan Road in Peoria when Debora was about to begin her junior year. For most teenagers, that would have been an unfortunate time to move, and going from a high school in a little town of a few thousand to one in a city with almost 200,000 people would be terrifying. Not for Debora.

Asked if she had ever felt frightened inside even though she was capable of keeping up a fearless façade, Debora shook her head firmly. "I always felt confident," she remembered. "I always felt I could accomplish anything I set out to do. I was never scared—not until later. . . ."

"Debi" Jones rapidly became a popular member of the class of 1969 at Peoria High School. Even then, she had developed the wonderful sense of humor that drew people to her. Extraordinarily witty, she could turn anything into a joke—to the delight of her fellow students, and occasionally to the annoyance of her teachers.

The late sixties were turbulent years for teenagers, but Debora never wandered from the path she had set for herself—or, perhaps, that her mother had set for her. Harry Whitaker, who was the principal of Peoria High in the sixties, would remember her twenty-five years later as an outstanding student. "She seemed to follow all the rules. She didn't take drugs and she didn't drink. She was rather an aggressive girl," he commented. "You could tell she was going to be successful."

Debora had entered Peoria High in the 1967–68 year, and 1968 was the year of the Illinois Sesquicentennial, celebrating the 150th anniversary of the state's admission to the Union in 1818. "I remember we read *Spoon River Anthology* in English in my junior year," she said later. "It was part of Sesquicentennial." Although her intelligence was turned more toward science and math, Debora enjoyed reading Masters's work, and tended to choose epic books with historical links after that. She would always be a prodigious reader, able to lose herself in a novel so completely that the rest of the world faded away.

Debora was a cheerleader for Peoria High, served on the Student Council, and was a National Merit Scholar. The list of accomplishments after her name in the Peoria High yearbook, *The Crest*, was as lengthy as those found under top students' pictures in yearbooks all over America. She sang in the Concert Choir; she was a Music Accompanist, a member of the French Club, Music Workshops, Senior Services, and the *Crest* business staff. She was a superlative athlete as well, so much so that her steady boyfriend, Greg Short—who was on the varsity football and wrestling squads—wrote in her yearbook, "You know, it's really terrible going with someone who is by far more athletic than I. . . . But, you know, I think I like you more because I have to compete with you. It isn't fair, you being so darned talented . . . ."

Short, who went on to become a lieutenant in the Peoria Police Department, dated Debora for two years. They attended the proms together, posed for silly pictures that appeared in the yearbook, and were expected to stay together after high school. It would be fair to say that Greg Short was totally in love with Debora. He declared his devotion over and over in his yearbook "love letter."

Debora was the covaledictorian of Peoria High School in 1969. She and the other valedictorian, Scott Russell—now assistant superintendent of the Peoria School District—had perfect grade-point averages. Debora had never had less than an A in her life. She had scored close to a perfect 800 on both sections of the Scholastic Aptitude Test. She was headed for the University of Illinois.

Most of the scribbled messages in Debora's copy of *The Crest* referred to her intelligence: "To the girl who never studied in history but always managed an 'A'"; "You really are too smart for your pants. . . ."; "All the luck at college, but you don't need luck too much"; "To the laziest chemist in the class. For being so smart, you don't look it or act it. Go easy on the profs next year—you're so smart."

Debora did excel at the University of Illinois, but her grade-point average was no longer unblemished. She received her first B in college. Greg Short remembered how that affected her. "She perceived it as an abject failure . . . . She was very, very, disturbed by that. She was the smartest person I ever knew."

Debora continued to date Greg for the first quarter of college, but then the romance faded. "He wasn't nearly as smart as I was," she would say many years later. "He was just going to a community college or some small college—we drifted apart." The last time Greg talked to Debora was in 1971; she had moved on to a new phase of her life and he didn't fit in.

Debora was a natural at chemistry and had set her sights on becoming a chemical engineer. She had never had any particular pull toward medicine. "My mind works the way an engineer's does," she would explain. "But after I started in engineering, they told me there was a glut of engineers and I should consider another major. I chose chemistry—pre-med—and I graduated in three years."

Medical school is a challenge to the most dedicated, the most motivated students. Debora became a physician by default. Medicine had never been a passion or even a goal for her. She applied to the University of Chicago and the University of Kansas medical schools. Her grasp of chemistry was phenomenal, of course, but her scores were lower in other areas. "I didn't do that well on the medical aptitude tests," she would say later. "But I was accepted at both. I chose the University of Kansas Medical School."

KU is in Lawrence, midway between Kansas City and Topeka on the Kansas Turnpike with its medical school in Kansas City. It is the home of the famous Jayhawks basketball team, whose all-time star was Wilt Chamberlain, but Debora had little interest in the sport. She began medical school in the fall of 1972. She had picked KU because her parents were living in the Kansas City area. Bob Jones's rise through the ranks at Roman Meal necessitated regular transfers; for the moment, Debora's parents lived close to her.

She had chosen medicine, but Debora's heart was not really in it. When she was asked later, "Which profession did you *love?*" she answered immediately, "Oh—engineering! My mind is very mathematical, very organized." But she had decided to become a doctor. In the first of a number of coincidences that would lace her complicated life, one of her team of four medical students in anatomy class was a handsome, gentle young man named John Walker.* There was no romance between them, but they became good friends as they worked over the cadaver assigned to their foursome.

Debora recalled that she had no problem at all detaching herself from the humanity of the cadaver she and John dissected. "An autopsy is different," she explained. "That person has been alive recently. I didn't feel that way about the cadavers—but I always smelled of formaldehyde and I always felt greasy."

Her fellow medical students found Debora likable. Reginald Hall, a classmate, remembered her as studious and caring. "She was a very easy person to get along with," he said. "She always seemed very concerned about her patients and their well-being."

Debora finished medical school in three years, graduating with her M.D. on May 16, 1975. During her internship rotations, she found that she enjoyed emergency medicine most. She did her first residency in the ER at Truman Medical Center in Kansas City: "I really liked it—something was always happening." But after spending more time in emergency medicine, she was disappointed. "I found out that the biggest part of emergency medicine were patients who had earaches—or something that they should have had treated in an office call, but they waited too long and then showed up in the ER. It was boring."

Later, Debora would switch to oncology, cancer treatment. "I picked oncology," she said with a smile, "because I'm a 'people person'—I really like people. But oncology was so depressing because I cared so much about my patients, and yet I knew they were going to die."

Chapter 3

Debora had met and dated a fellow engineering student at the University of Illinois: Duane M. J. Green. Their relationship deepened, and they were married during her studies at the KU Medical School in Kansas City. It was a charming, if informal wedding. Debora was thin, almost willowy, and she looked very young and very lovely in her old-fashioned "pioneer" gown with a high collar and puffed sleeves. She wore a pinafore of white eyelet over the long pink cotton gown. Her beautiful hair, parted in the middle, fell straight and shining to her hips. Her matron of honor and only attendant was her sister, Pam, who wore a similar eyelet dress. They posed together after the ceremony, two sweet-faced young women beaming with happiness.

Duane was tall and thin, towering over Debora's five feet four inches. His sideburns and waxed handlebar mustache, de rigueur for the seventies, made him look almost as old-fashioned as she did. Bob and Joan Jones attended the wedding and it would seem that all Joan's dreams had come true. Her daughters were both married. Pam was interested in studying psychology and counseling; Debora was about to become a doctor and she was married to a handsome engineer who would soon have his Ph.D. The future couldn't have looked brighter.

Debora and Duane Green lived in an apartment at first, but after she graduated from med school in 1975, they moved to a house at 3110 Sterling Avenue in Independence, Missouri, so that Debora would be within reasonable commuting distance to her residency in the ER of the Truman Medical Center and Duane could be close to his job in Kansas City. But their marriage had been in trouble almost from the beginning. When asked what went wrong, Debora shrugged and said, "I'm not even sure why I married him, but I knew as soon as I did that we had absolutely no common interests. He was an engineer. That pretty much says it all. Engineers are boring and they don't communicate well."

Odd. Debora had aspired to be an engineer herself, but she had been forced to drop out of the program at the University of Illinois because there weren't enough jobs waiting. Now that she was a physician, she denigrated the engineering profession.

Duane and Debora separated in the late seventies; even before her divorce was final, Debora began what she described as a "hedonistic lifestyle." She was in her mid-twenties and had been in school since she was five. She had never traveled, never taken long vacations. Now, she did. "My friends and I would fly down to Guaymas or Belize or wherever and just do what we liked. . . . But part of me had a need to be grounded—to have a more secure life."

Though Debora had had long, monogamous relationships with men who cared deeply for her, in the months after she left Duane, she had numerous boyfriends. She had craved freedom. And she was probably as attractive as she had ever been—or would ever be—in her life. She was slender and her hair was perfectly cut so that it moved in bouncy waves when she tossed her head. Her wit was sharper than ever. She had friends who laughed with her, and she was totally competent as a senior resident in the emergency room of Truman Medical Center. She seemed to have boundless energy; she worked extra shifts to add to her considerable income. She bought a silver Jaguar XKE for $27,000 and zipped around Independence and Kansas City. Any man looking at her would have to notice how vibrant she was, how full of life. If there were less attractive aspects to her personality, they were not immediately apparent.

At least, not when Michael Farrar met her. Mike was a medical student, starting his senior year with an emergency room rotation at Truman Medical Center. Born in Lawrence, Kansas, and raised "north of the river" in Kansas City, Missouri, he was four years younger than Debora and considerably lower in the medical-education pecking order. He found her exciting. "She was an attractive woman—a thin, attractive woman," Mike later recalled. "She was obviously exceedingly bright. She was tremendously witty; everyone who knew her knew how witty she was. But she had kind of a sarcastic, biting wit. She was very funny."

Mike was drawn to Debora. And she noticed him. He was in his early twenties and around five foot ten; his facial features were as fine as hers were coarse. He was quite handsome, with dark hair worn in the long and curly style of the decade. He looked, if anything, younger than twenty. And, like Debora, Mike was extremely intelligent. "I got straight A's too," he said. "But I had to work very hard for them—Debora didn't. Everything academic came easily to her." Mike's parents expected him to get A's, and he had not disappointed them. But Debora was probably the smartest woman he had ever known.

In Mike Farrar, Debora perceived a stability she needed. Her "hedonistic" life left her as ungrounded as a balloon that has lost its tether, and she sensed that she needed a good, stable man to feel safe. Mike was brilliant; she knew he was going to be a very successful doctor. Speaking of him later, she did not say that she loved him. Rather, she said that he seemed to be a "good person," someone she could count on. Apparently, the lifestyle she had been enjoying had left her frightened and in need of an anchor. Or perhaps she sensed some deficiency, some weakness in herself and needed a strong man to bolster her.

Debora and Duane were separated, and he no longer lived in the house in Independence, so when she and Mike started to date, Debora didn't tell him that she was, technically at least, a married woman. At some point, Mike realized the truth, but she assured him that she was going to start divorce proceedings—and she did.

By December 1978, the marriage was legally over. It was, allegedly, an amicable divorce. Their attorney, Ronald Barker, said they had come to his office together and asked that he represent them both. However, although Duane was awarded the silver Jaguar in their divorce settlement, he would say many years later that he felt that he had been a convenience—that he'd helped pay Debora's way through college and med school, only to be dumped when she had no further need of him.

Mike Farrar met Duane Green only once; Duane stopped by the house in Independence in October 1978, when Mike was visiting. "He seemed like a nice guy," Mike remembered. "There were no problems with my meeting him. I didn't realize until later that he had actually lived in that house."

Looking back many years later, Mike tried to remember the early days of his relationship with Debora. Admittedly, he was seeing those days through the far end of a very dark tunnel; events in the interim had colored his recall. But he could not remember that theirs was ever a passionate coming together, or a matter of one seducing the other. Debora won him with her soaring intelligence and her wonderful sense of humor—and, Mike admitted, by the air of success that seemed a part of her. And just as she did not speak of loving him, he failed to mention that emotion as a component of their relationship.

"I was a twenty-three-year-old medical student living on ten bucks a week," Mike said. "I ate a lot of tuna fish. I have to admit that knowing Deb was going to start practicing and make seventy thousand dollars a year impressed me. I was going into my internship and I would be making $14,190 a year. Debora drove that Jag XKE and then she paid cash for a cherry-red Fiat Spyder. I hate to admit it, but I think it was all of those things about her that attracted me—her vitality, her wit, her success. Even so, I somehow knew she was very insecure.

"She felt threatened by my family's closeness. I have two sisters and my family is close. Her family was very cold. Her mother's personality was similar to Debora's. Her father, interestingly enough, was a very nice man—kind of a salesman type, garrulous. I always liked to play golf with him, took him to some football games. I thought he was a great guy."

One aspect of Debora's personality struck a dissonant note with Mike. "She was very volatile; she would fly off the handle and do things that were really embarrassing. I remember one time she got into an argument in a Kroger parking lot with two people who took the space we were headed for. Debora got out of the car and just gave them hell. I was shocked. I asked her, 'What are you *doing*?' But she walked with them all the way to the door—until, finally, the wife unloaded on Debora."

Mike was mortified. It would be the first of many times when Debora's rage at seemingly small slights would embarrass him.

Why Debora had such a propensity for sudden anger was puzzling. Her parents had not spoiled her, but her genetic gifts of talent and intelligence had always made her life so easy, and there were precious few things she wanted that she did not get. Perhaps that was why she behaved outrageously when anyone crossed her. She believed that she deserved to get what she wanted—whether it was a parking space or instant respect. She could not abide anyone who questioned her intelligence, or any glitch in plans that inconvenienced her.

Before their marriage, Mike and Debora lived together in a small apartment. Mike would also recall that their sex life was very low-key and that Debora seemed apathetic about a physical relationship. They were, of course, both working very hard and very long hours. It did not seem a serious problem to him—not then. Despite early warning signs, they were a committed couple, and although Mike entertained some doubts, they went ahead with plans to marry.

The wedding, on May 26, 1979, was far more lavish than Debora's first. This time, she wore a simple long-sleeved white sheath; her veil was a lace mantilla. Mike wore a gray shantung tuxedo with wide lapels, and a ruffled dress shirt. Debora had carried a single red rose at her first wedding; now, she held a cascading bouquet of pink roses and white carnations. Mike's sisters, Vicki and Karen, were her bridesmaids. They wore lovely pink dresses; the mothers and grandmothers of the bride and groom wore shades of pink.

But all was not as serene as it seemed in their wedding pictures, and Mike's wide grin hid his sense that he might have made a wrong choice. "Even as I walked down the aisle," he remembered, "I realized I was making a mistake."

Any number of brides and grooms experience wedding jitters, but Mike felt more than that. As they made wedding plans, he had seen more of Debora's moodiness and anger than ever before. She seemed to make no effort to fit into his family, and he knew his mother and sisters were worried by that. What he had first seen as Debora's insecurity and shyness, Mike had come to recognize as self-absorption. Her needs came first—always.

To his disappointment and frustration, Debora at first declined to make love with her new husband on their wedding night. "She wanted to read a book," Mike said. "Then I knew for sure I'd made a mistake." Although Debora finally gave in to Mike's wish to consummate their marriage, she did so reluctantly and with little enthusiasm. And then she went back to her book.

Mike tried to hope this was not a bad omen. "My parents had instilled in me that marriage was a commitment and you worked on it to make it right. . . . I really thought that over a period of time she would change."

Debora and Mike honeymooned in Tahiti for two weeks.

It was Debora who paid the $5,000 that the trip cost; Mike had precious little income at that point. They had planned to stop in San Francisco on their way home, but they were stranded in Tahiti after a tragic air disaster. On May 25, 275 people had perished in the crash of a DC-10 taking off from O'Hare International Airport in Chicago. "They shut all the DC-10s down the morning we were to come home," Mike remembered. "And Air New Zealand didn't have any other planes. So we had an extra five days there."

The extension of their honeymoon didn't thrill either newlywed. Theirs had not been a perfect honeymoon, or even a particularly happy one. If he had hoped that the atmosphere in Tahiti and the respite from their stressful careers would make his bride more responsive sexually, Mike was disappointed. Sex did not seem to matter to Debora one way or another. He wondered why she had married him. He was an impecunious intern; she was already in practice in emergency medicine. She didn't seem to love him, and she didn't like his family. She preferred reading novels to being intimate with him, and the vivacity that had first attracted him seemed to have disappeared completely.

Debora didn't even take Mike's name; she decided to keep her first husband's, for professional reasons. This seemed emblematic of the distance between her and Mike. Still, he kept hoping that somehow things would get better—if only with the passage of time.

Chapter 4

It was clear, early in their marriage, that Mike had a kind of self-control that Debora did not. This was probably because of his background. His father, William Farrar, was an inspector with the U.S. Food and Drug Administration and a colonel in the Air Force Reserves. Bill Farrar traveled two weeks out of every month. He figured that, over the years, he had been in every town in Kansas, Nebraska, and Iowa, checking food-processing plants, feedlots, and drug companies. Although Bill didn't enjoy his job much, the FDA willingly granted him time to fly for the Air Force Reserves, and he flew to the South Pacific, Guam, Midway, Panama, and Peru, among other exotic spots. It was Bill Farrar who imbued his son with a love of travel.

Mike's mother, Velma, a grade school teacher, was an attractive, patrician-looking woman who prided herself on her perfect figure. When it came to raising children, discipline was important to both Farrars. Duty and honor meant more than mere words, so Mike was not about to tell his parents that his marriage had turned out to be a huge disappointment. He could not imagine what they would say if he were to give up and seek a divorce so soon. He had hoped for a warm, loving wife. He got, instead, a woman whose mercurial moods kept him continually off guard.

Debora's predominant emotion seemed to be anger— anger at him. At first, Mike met Debora's outbursts of temper by fighting back. If she yelled at him, he initially tried to reason with her, then yelled back. Neither approach did any good. Their arguments followed a predictable course, its timing set by Debora. And when she was not angry, she was withdrawn, losing herself in a book.

Looking back, Mike struggled to bring forth some good memories. "In Debora's defense," he said slowly, "I don't want to say that my marriage was always unhappy. We had a number of things in common, besides medicine. We both liked to travel and we went on a number of very nice trips. I would never pretend that every moment of our marriage was horrible. The thing that was clearly lacking—always— was that affection, that caring, that intimacy, that was so clearly what I longed for." And he was the last to know why.

Debora's family was not in the picture much. Her sister, Pam, had been married several times, had borne a son, Isaac, in the mid-seventies. She later became a drug and alcohol counselor. Debora was scornful of Pam's profession.

Bob and Joan Jones were still relocating frequently as he

rose in the hierarchy of the Roman Meal bread company. Their somewhat nomadic life suited them. They bought a fifth-wheel camper and were constantly on the road, seeing America. They rarely visited Debora and Mike, and had fallen into a pattern of getting together only about every two years.

Mike was much closer to his parents and to his sisters, Vicki and Karen. But Debora seemed stilted and tense around her new husband's family. She had virtually nothing in common with her mother-in-law. Velma Farrar had a highly developed sense of fashion, and clothes seemed to matter to Debora not at all. Mike's sisters were slimmer and prettier than she was, and Debora's biting sense of humor, which charmed so many, missed the mark with the Farrars.

At first, it seemed to Mike that his mother tried to form a friendship with Debora and Debora held back. Later, he thought, Debora tried but his mother pulled away. Christmases would always be difficult, as they are in so many families, although Debora decorated trees, wrapped packages, and made an effort to be festive—particularly after their children were born.

Mike did his three-year residency in internal medicine at the University of Cincinnati. He stayed on for a fourth year, as chief medical resident, and was then awarded a three-year fellowship in cardiology. Altogether, he would spend seven years in advanced study before he entered practice as a heart specialist.

Debora, of course, moved to Ohio with Mike; she went into private practice in emergency medicine at Jewish Hospital. But she soon soured on emergency medicine, and she had a number of run-ins with other doctors—even supervising doctors—in the ER. "One time she called me," Mike said. "The patient had come in with a heart problem, and Debora told me she knew exactly what he needed. She called the attending physician, but the doctor didn't agree with her. She was absolutely outraged. . . . But the fact is that Debora was right."

Although Debora was often on target in diagnosing and recommending treatment, she was unpopular. Co-workers found her abrasive, autocratic, and difficult to work with. She lacked the tact to differ with them in a diplomatic way. Instead, she exploded with anger if anyone questioned her judgment. Moreover, the vast majority of cases presenting in the ER were mundane; consequently, they irritated her. Debora could not understand why patients waited so long before they sought medical help, letting minor earaches become raging infections, small scratches turn into cellulitis, and colds into pneumonia. Her bedside manner was more confrontational than comforting. She had always been disgusted with stupidity, and she saw so much of it in emergency medicine.

As part of her training for emergency medicine, Debora had done a rotation in internal medicine. While she and Mike lived in Cincinnati, she decided to switch to that field. Doing so would mean another residency, of course. Her husband was already in an internal medicine program, and through attrition, there were always vacancies at the end of the year.

"So she came and joined my residency. . . ." Mike recalled. "She and I were both second-year residents. We were both on call on the same nights, one of us at the V.A. hospital and one at the University of Cincinnati hospital. I can remember the very first night she was on call as a supervising resident. She had someone helping her, because she had been out of internal medicine for a while. But she called me up and was absolutely beside herself. She didn't know what to do; she didn't know where anything was. . . . I told her, 'Just *ask* someone. You're learning the ropes.' But Debora couldn't do that. She couldn't seem to admit that she needed help with all these things."

That puzzled Mike. When he first met Debora, she had appeared very self-confident, able to deal with anything that

came her way. Now, she was unsure of herself and hyper-
sensitive to criticism. And she continued to avoid Mike's
attempts at greater intimacy. She seemed either to be frightened by it or have no need for it; rather, she enjoyed solitary
pursuits, burying herself in books or playing solitaire. Later,
she played computer games designed for one person. Still,
when they went out with other people, she was the same
witty and vivacious person Mike had fallen in love with. He
figured that she was just apprehensive about trusting in marriage; she had been mistaken once and maybe she was afraid
she would fail again.

She had a tender side. She talked about wanting to help
people; she loved animals and adopted two cats—one a
huge white cat and the other a tiny black kitten. A photograph that Mike took during their first year in Cincinnati
reveals both his interests and Debora's; she is sitting at her
piano, holding her black kitten and white cat, while Mike's
first very modest wine collection of seven bottles is displayed
in an inexpensive wine rack on top of the piano.

Debora is slender and pretty in the photograph, but she
gives the camera lens only a half-smile. She and Mike had
been married for more than a year. She had a handsome
and brilliant young husband who wanted very much to love
her—but in the photo she seems sad, as if her world does
not suit her at all. Mike, an avid photographer, took hundreds of pictures of Debora over the years of their marriage,
and many of them caught an expression of deep unhappiness—as if Debora's mind and heart were far away.

Although Velma Farrar had her doubts about her new
daughter-in-law and was not particularly welcoming at first,
Mike's parents tried to draw Debora into the family. Their
efforts met with little success. One Christmas, the elder
Farrars drove from Kansas City to Cincinnati—six hundred
miles. Mike was still at the hospital when they arrived.
"Debora had been reading a book in the back room," he

recalled. "She came out, let them in, and then went back to the bedroom and continued to read."

At other times, too, Debora virtually ignored Mike's parents. On one such occasion, "I was on call," he said. "Debora got home from work and they were there at our apartment. She walked past them to the bedroom and they didn't see her again all night."

Clearly, Mike and Debora had a very different concept of family. Obviously, their principal common interest was medicine, and few professions demand as much in terms of time and commitment. It was relatively easy to overlook hollow spaces in their marriage, simply because they had so little time to contemplate them.

In retrospect, Debora and Mike seemed so mismatched that they might have been pieces from two different puzzles. Debora was a loner and as unpredictable as a caged tigress. She didn't like housework or care about neatness for its own sake. She was highly intelligent about *things* but had virtually no aptitude for dealing with human beings, a flaw that was subtly undermining her medical career. Mike—gregarious, punctilious, neat—was progressing rapidly at the University of Cincinnati's medical school, and higher-ups had their eyes on him. He was a passionate man, and his wife was disinterested in sex.

At the beginning of their relationship, it was Debora who had held the reins of power. She had been the resident about to go into practice, the laughing, witty woman in a cherry-red sports car, while Mike had been the poverty-stricken medical student. In Cincinnati, the balance of power at first became almost equal; then Mike's star rose while Debora's descended. But to an outsider looking in on them in 1980, they would have appeared to be a solid couple. With two M.D.'s in the family they could count on being wealthy. Mike was immersed in his medical training and loved what he was doing. Although his goals were entirely clear in his mind and Debora would change the focus of her career often, they seemed to have a workable marriage.

But then Debora began to have health problems, and Mike suspected she was taking drugs, either regularly or sporadically. "When I was an intern," he said later, "occasionally I would find these bottles of sedatives or narcotics . . . Dalmane and Valium, that kind of thing. Sometimes Tylenol Number 3 or Tylox or Percodan. I'd find them at home, but they would have some patient's name from the clinic at the hospital on them. It wasn't very often, but I would find them from time to time. I asked Deb about those, and she would say, 'Oh yeah—I picked that up when the patient brought his drugs in and I forgot to give it back to him.'"

At first, Mike wasn't much concerned. In that inner-city hospital, many patients were on "a jillion different medicines," which they commonly brought in in paper bags so that the residents could take inventory and keep track on the chart. It was within the realm of possibility that Debora could have found vials that had fallen on the floor or been left behind, and slipped them into the pocket of her lab coat.

"Anyway," Mike recalled, "I remember coming home one day and there was a gouge in the wall—with a big black mark. . . . Clearly one of our wrought-iron chairs had been knocked into the wall, and it was lying on the floor. I went into the bedroom and Debora was lying there. She was sick and complaining of a terrible headache and was just kind of out of it. I thought, '*What's* this?' She continued to complain about these headaches, and said she felt awful, and had all these problems."

Not only did Debora have excruciating headaches in the back of her head—an unusual site for a headache—but Mike was alarmed to see that she sometimes walked with a staggering gait, as if she was dizzy. Afraid that she might have a brain tumor, he took her in for a consultation with a neurologist at his own hospital.

Asked what health problems she had had recently, Debora mentioned that she had injured her wrist in a fall and had developed an infection so intractable that she'd had to have surgery to drain it. Mike agreed that her recovery from the wrist incident had been complicated.

After a series of tests, the neurologist diagnosed Debora as suffering from an unusual condition, cerebellar migraine. The cerebellum is located in the back of the brain and migraines in that area would account for Debora's headaches. She was given a prescription for beta blockers, drugs usually prescribed for high blood pressure.

"Ultimately," Mike recalled, "she did get better, so that's what I assumed it was. Later, with more incidents, I realized that she probably had some continuing pain in her wrist and was using these narcotics to ease it."

Debora Green had another affliction: she suffered chronically from insomnia. "She tried every way I know of to get [a good night's] sleep—and she never could," Mike said. "I think the sleeping pills were to let her get some rest. But, at the time, I believed her explanation that she had absentmindedly pocketed both the painkillers and the sleeping pills."

Although Mike and Debora used no birth control, Debora did not conceive for almost two years after their wedding—perhaps because their intercourse was so infrequent. But when Debora found she was pregnant, in the spring of 1981, she was very pleased—and so was Mike. Aside from their shared nearsightedness, they were perfect genetic specimens for producing exceptional children. Debora's IQ was 165, and Mike had tested at genius level. They were both healthy and attractive. A child born of their union would be smart, strong, and fair to look upon.

Timothy Farrar, born on January 20, 1982, was all those things. Debora had asked to have an epidural anesthetic, but her labor was overdue and had to be induced. Once the contractions started, Debora's cervix dilated so rapidly that there was no time to inject the numbing anesthetic—so Tim was born, perforce, by natural childbirth. Mike was in the delivery room and remembers being thrilled to have a son. Debora would also recall that her husband was beside himself with happiness at Tim's birth. The baby boy would have "Farrar" for his last name, as would all their children.

Debora was a good mother; she nursed her son and took a six-week maternity leave so that she could stay with him for the first month of his life. But she never intended to be a stay-at-home mother. She had worked right up to the end of her pregnancy and, having hired a warm-hearted Jamaican nanny to take care of Tim, she went back to school. She had received a fellowship to study hematology and oncology at the University of Cincinnati.

Tim's birth was unplanned, but welcome. Both Mike and Debora decided that they should have a second child within three years, so Debora's next pregnancy was a mutual decision. Lissa was born two days after Christmas, 1984. Once again, Debora had requested an epidural; but this time the anesthesiologists mistakenly gave her a spinal anesthetic, which often leaves the patient with a severe headache. Nevertheless, Debora was out of bed the next day and walked down to the nursery with two-year-old Tim so he could look at his new baby sister.

Tim would always be the child who most resembled Debora physically. He had her coloring, her features, her sturdy, square body. He was blond (his hair would later turn russet) and brown-eyed, full of beans and very masculine, but Lissa was a delicate elfin baby, dark-haired and petite, with her father's rounded forehead and fine features. Debora and Mike now had the perfect family: a little boy and a baby girl.

Again Debora went back to work almost immediately. Although she and Mike both had fellowships in internal medicine and were supposedly working the same hours, she was usually back at their apartment by four in the afternoon, while he worked three or four hours later. "She used to tell me that was because I was inefficient and I spent too much time stopping to talk to people," Mike recalled. "And part of that was true—but I just don't think she ever had a burning desire to excel. She never really wanted to be an excellent or outstanding doctor. Interestingly enough, here is a woman who is brilliant—and she had to take her oncology boards *twice*. Both times, she failed. She barely passed the internal medicine boards. Those *were* difficult tests, but if you're an American who goes to a university training program, who works hard and does a reasonable amount of study, you *should* be able to pass those. . . . She was just ill-prepared."

Mike rarely saw Debora studying medical books; she read only for pleasure. She went to classes and on rounds, and her keen mind made it possible for her to retain far more than most students—but it was not enough to pass her board exams.

The day the test results arrived was not a good one. Mike's letter said, "Congratulations! You have passed the boards for cardiovascular disease," while Debora's began, "We regret to inform you . . ."

Debora opened both envelopes and phoned Mike. She was angry and crying—in hysterics—and accused him of caring only about his own test scores. She blamed him for her failure: she'd had to take care of Tim and Lissa, she said, and hadn't had enough time to study. The truth was that both of them had cared for the babies until they were put down for the night, and that Mike then read medical books while Debora went upstairs with a novel.

Debora never passed either her hematology or oncology board examinations. That would not bar her from practicing in those specialties, but if patients checked, they would find she was not "board-certified." She seldom read literature on medical advances in her field, and she rarely attended seminars and conventions. Apparently she had no desire to mingle with her fellow oncologists.

In 1985, Mike had one more year of his cardiology fellowship in Cincinnati to complete, but Debora was finished. With their dependable nanny caring for Tim and Lissa, she started a private practice in oncology and hematology. Dealing with cancer patients requires both compassion and acceptance of what is often tragic beyond words. Most oncologists manage to maintain enough emotional distance to protect themselves, while still evincing true concern for their patients. Although Debora insisted that she chose her specialty because she loved people so much, both her husband and her co-workers were appalled at her indifferent approach to patients.

Again, Mike wondered why. "She had trouble dealing with patients," he recalled. "I can remember listening to her talking to a patient one night when she was on call. It was clear that the patient needed to go into the emergency room and that she would have to go in and check on her. Debora was very passive-aggressive with the patient—angry about the whole thing." Nurses, too, were puzzled by her behavior toward patients. One commented, "She was the strangest doctor I've ever worked with in my life." Another found her "cold" and "unfeeling."

Mike, however, was emerging as a "real superstar," according to a physician who worked with him in Cincinnati. "He was so good at everything. He showed unusual maturity. He related extremely well and had extremely good judgment, all of which marked him as someone who would be a superior cardiologist."

In the spring of 1986, he completed his fellowship and agreed to stay at the University of Cincinnati as an assistant professor at the medical school; he would also serve as medical director of the heart transplant unit. "But the chairman of cardiology resigned and they were bringing in new people," Mike said. "I wasn't sure what my future would be there." A physician friend in Kansas City, Missouri, invited Mike to join his partnership, so he and Debora decided to move back there rather than wait to see how things would shake out with the new regime at the university.

It was July 1, 1986, when they settled in Kansas City. Twelve twenty-four West Sixty-first Terrace, in an older, upscale neighborhood near the Country Club Church, was a beautiful house with stucco walls crisscrossed with heavy beams, and a brick façade with arched passageways that led into a side garden. After so many years of studying and deprivation, Debora and Mike brought their children home to the area where they had met and been married—the Kansas-Missouri border, where the wind blew all the time, a steady, almost comforting sound in the trees. It was, really, a whole new start. They both looked forward to their careers and to raising their two children. On West Sixty-first Terrace, children abounded and the neighbors were friendly. But the move meant leaving behind their nanny, who had been with Tim for four years and Lissa for two. Debora and Mike would have to interview applicants for child care in their home, and Debora did not go back to work until they found a new nanny.

Mike went into private practice with the group in KCMO, and Debora soon joined another group of physicians. They were on staff at many of the same hospitals and occasionally ran into each other during the day. Debora was thirty-five that summer, and Mike was thirty-one.

Mike's practice did very well, although he ultimately moved on to join another group of doctors. At the end of Debora's first year in her group, both she and Mike expected that she would be offered a partnership. That was medical protocol—but the offer didn't come. Such a slight is almost unheard-of.

"I knew what the reason was." Mike sighed. "She could not get along with patients—she drove them away. So she left that first practice in Kansas City at the end of the year, and went into private practice on her own."

*

But the doctors in her group practice may have had more serious reasons for not offering Debora a partnership. An old bugaboo raised its head soon after they moved to Kansas City. Mike noticed that once again Debora's gait was off-balance enough to make her stagger slightly, and her speech was sometimes slurred. And, though she had always written with flowing cursive letters so perfect they could have been used in a penmanship manual, Debora now began to scribble. A doctor she worked for called Mike and said, "Hey, what's wrong with our Debora? She's not being as attentive to details, and her writing has really deteriorated. What's going on?"

There were other signs. Mike's sister Karen was getting married and his whole family was thrilled with the new son-in-law. Debora had not been welcomed into his family with open arms and she began to complain that she was sick of hearing about Karen's wedding. "One night," Mike said, "she actually called my sister up and told her that we weren't coming . . . for the wedding, and she was pretty insulting and her speech was slurred and almost incoherent."

Debora had physical problems besides her wrist injury. Some years earlier, she had fallen while climbing stairs at the University of Cincinnati and somehow gotten a puncture wound in her knee. A stubborn infection developed; extremely painful, it required a ten-day hospitalization. Much like her wrist injury, the mysterious infection required draining by syringe several times a day. Antibiotics finally cured it, but Debora had had chronic pain in her knee ever since.

Now, with Debora behaving so bizarrely, Mike deduced what the problem was. His heart sank. She was using drugs again. He searched their house and found a drawer jammed with sleeping pills and painkillers—potent narcotics, including Tylox.

Mike told Debora that he had to talk to her alone. With the bedroom door closed so that neither Tim, Lissa, nor their nanny could hear, he silently lined up the narcotics vials on the dresser. For once, she did not shout at him.

There was no way she could explain having so many bottles of Tylox, prescribed to different names, none of them hers.

"My knee has been bothering me," she said weakly. "It's hard to keep on my feet without something to ease the pain."

"Debora, you can't *do* this," Mike said softly. "These prescriptions aren't for you—these are for your *patients*. They have bone pain, and you have a minor knee injury. I don't believe you're taking Tylox for pain—I'm afraid you're in trouble again."

After a long silence, Debora lifted her head. "You're right," she agreed. "I know I have to stop. And I will. I promise you."

"Are there any more of these?" Mike asked. Debora shook her head. He stared at her, drew a deep breath, and began to gather up the vials of pills and capsules. "I'm going to throw them out," he said. "I'm going to believe you when you say it won't happen again."

As far as Mike could tell, Debora kept her promise. Things got better for them after that, and he didn't notice any suspicious signs that Debora was using narcotics.

Rather than apply to join another group practice in Kansas City, Debora opened her own office, and having a one-woman practice seemed to work for her. She was on staff at St. Mary's Hospital. It wasn't a really busy hospital, and there weren't many doctors there covering oncology. For the first time since she had gotten her M.D., Debora didn't have other physicians looking over her shoulder or second-guessing how she treated her patients. Her quick temper and her confrontational behavior when she was questioned were, for a time, not an issue. She employed an answering service and hired a woman to do her billing.

"It really went pretty well for her," Mike said of Debora's solo practice, which lasted a little less than a year. "The problem was that St. Mary's closed. And then Debora got pregnant with Kelly. She was pretty upset about that."

Although Debora was thirty-seven, which is no longer

considered unusually late for childbearing, she and Mike
had assumed that there would be no more children. She was
shocked when, in May of 1988, she recognized the unmistakable symptoms of pregnancy. This, added to the closing
of the only hospital where she had felt comfortable, effectively ended her attempt to establish a private practice in
Kansas City.

Kelly was born almost exactly four years after Lissa—on
December 13, 1988. This time Debora got the epidural anesthetic she had chosen for each of her deliveries. All through
the labor, Mike stood beside Debora's bed, trying to comfort
her. He fed her ice chips, rubbed her back, and reached out
to hold her hand. But she brushed him away impatiently;
she didn't want him to touch her at all. They had been married nine years and this was their third baby, but Debora
seemed to resent Mike because she was delivering a child
she didn't want, a child who had interfered with the first successful practice she had ever had.

"She clearly didn't care if I was there or not," Mike said.
"It was kind of upsetting to me, because I thought that this
was something that we would always go through together."

Kelly turned out to be a special child, an unexpected gift,
a curly-haired blond pixie of a baby. And there was something more: she exuded love and seemed to have the
somber wisdom of an old soul. She was, her father would
judge, the most intelligent of the three children born to
him and Debora. Of course, it wasn't long before everyone
forgot she had begun as an unwelcome surprise. Both her
mother and her father adored her, and Tim and Lissa welcomed their baby sister.

Debora had always been an excellent mother to newborns
and toddlers. Mike was proud of her for that. She seemed to
enjoy them tremendously—and they her. There were always
special birthday cakes and parties. Debora taught them to
swim and saw that they had tennis lessons and dancing
lessons and that Tim started in sports early. She had great
ambition for her children.

If only their marriage could have grown as naturally as their children. But it didn't. Debora suspected that Mike was looking at other women, a concern that may not have been unfounded. One nurse who worked with Mike later recalled that Debora seemed obsessed with him and would follow him around to see what he was doing when he was away from her.

Even so, nothing changed at home. Debora either would not or could not control the tantrums brought on by frustration at delays and small annoyances. She had never been a homemaker and she was clearly not about to change. She and Mike had the children in common, but the physical side of their marriage, the intimate man-and-wife side, scarcely existed.

And while Debora had been able to lose her pregnancy pounds easily after Tim and Lissa's births, she found it difficult to get back to her normal weight after Kelly was born. She was discouraged by that, and by other small—but cumulative—blows to her self-esteem.

Chapter 5

One activity the family enjoyed together was traveling. Somehow, tensions eased once they got to their destinations. They had a time-share condo on Sanibel Island, off the western coast of Florida, and all five of them looked forward to their vacations there. They went to Alaska, British Columbia, Puerto Vallarta, Knott's Berry Farm, Hollywood, and Disneyland. They traveled to Cabo San Lucas, to the Alamo, took a real western wagon-train trip in the Flint Hills, and to Breckenridge, Colorado. Perhaps Debora and Mike were seeking an escape from their marriage. If things weren't good at home, maybe they could travel to some spot so exotic and so different that their marriage wouldn't matter.

Mike recalled that he and Debora and their children *did*

have a great time on vacations. The problem was getting there. "There were more scenes in airports than I can count," he said wearily. "I would absolutely cringe at the thought of traveling with Debora. When we *got* there, it was okay. But if the flights were delayed, if there was a change in schedule, she would become absolutely unglued. I can remember her chewing out people at the desk because planes were delayed because of storms."

On one trip to Sanibel Island, the airline announced that the flight would be delayed by storms in Dallas. Debora could not deal with the few hours' wait, despite Mike's argument that they would get to Sanibel even if they were a little late. It was a concept that Debora could not accept.

While other disappointed passengers murmured to each other, Debora began to shout at the airline representative at the desk. "We will never fly on this damn airline again!" she said loudly. "You are incompetent, ridiculous, and you have no consideration for the people who pay your salary!"

"Debora—" Mike said, trying to draw her away from the counter.

"My husband, *Dr.* Farrar, agrees with me," Debora said, pounding on the counter. "And *I* am *Dr.* Green. You are a very sorry excuse for an airline! Don't you agree, Michael?"

Mike could have cheerfully sunk through the floor as he felt scores of eyes watching them. He knew what was coming next: Debora was getting ready to use her extensive vocabulary of four-letter words.

"Michael, tell them what you think of this kind of lousy, stupid, fucking inefficiency!"

"Debora, they can't help it if there's a storm in Dallas," Mike said quietly, balancing Kelly in one arm and trying to hang on to Lissa with his other hand. Tim stood there quietly, staring at his mother as her face got redder and redder. "It isn't safe to fly," Mike said. "When it's safe, we'll fly. We'll get there."

Now Debora was furious with *him* because he wouldn't side with her against the airline. She blasted Mike with a few more vulgar epithets and then stomped off down the airport corridor.

"You'd see that over and over and over," Mike recalled. If planes were delayed, Debora would demand that he rent a car and *drive* them where they were going. Debora was a "perpetual pessimist" who always believed the worst. "You couldn't talk to her, you couldn't reason with her when something like that happened," Mike said. "She used absolutely vile, terrible language. It was embarrassing."

It was a paradox: Debora loved their vacations—yet made the trip itself hell. But once they reached Sanibel or the dude ranch or Disneyland—wherever they were headed—everything would smooth out; anyone looking at the hundreds of happy-family-on-vacation photographs that Mike took would have no hint that anything roiled beneath the surface.

Debora had her own version of their vacations: "Mike had everything planned from the time we got up until the time we went to bed. We were on a schedule. We couldn't relax. One year he couldn't go to Mexico with us and we had a wonderful time. We got up when we woke up and I asked the kids, 'Well, what should we do today?' We just did what we wanted, and we rested when we felt like it. It was so much better without him."

Mike didn't dispute Debora's complaint. "I did want to see everything there was to see," he said. He had been attracted to Debora because of her energy and the air of excitement about her; once married, she seemed to him to have little enthusiasm for anything.

Mike was working punishing hours in his cardiology practice, often leaving the house at six and coming home after eight or nine. When Debora was working, she was usually home by four or five. "Of course, societal mores dictated that she was the one who was home with the kids more," Mike said. "In her defense, she worked fewer hours because of that."

Mike was a perfectionist in many aspects of his life. Because he seemed able to compartmentalize his world and concentrate completely on whatever task was at hand, he expected that Debora could do the same. He liked schedules and well-planned trips, with no spur-of-the-moment flights of fancy. He felt most comfortable when he could control his environment and, in a sense, Debora and their three children were part of what he wanted to organize. But Debora was the most disorganized and chaotic woman he had ever known. Her sense of humor and her slapdash approach to life didn't mesh with Mike's need for order.

Debora's poor study habits, lack of social graces, sloppy housekeeping, and, finally, failure at the practice of medicine all disappointed Mike. It seemed almost as if she had decided that if she could not please him, she would *displease* him, would go out of her way to behave outrageously. Or perhaps she thought her rages were a way to control and manipulate him, to demonstrate her importance and superiority. But, in fact, she was allowing herself to become completely dependent upon Mike and their marriage for her support and survival.

Nevertheless, after Kelly's birth, Debora tried to reestablish her practice, going on staff at Trinity Hospital. The competition there was rough, particularly because the doctors who had failed to offer her a partnership were well established at Trinity. She failed to attract enough patients to warrant keeping her on staff. And so, in 1989, with her practice failing and her knee bothering her so much, she let her career go.

Mike encouraged her to do so. "She never really seemed to like being in practice, anyway," he said. "I would get these phone calls from her—and I was trying to do my work—and she would want to sit there and complain how bad things were for her. I would try to console her, tell her what to do. I thought she was depressed."

That was probably an accurate diagnosis, even though it came from a doctor whose specialty lay in the valves of the heart and not in the more ethereal workings of the psyche.

Something was tormenting Debora. Despite all her intelligence, she seemed unable to find anything good about her life—except for her children. And again she began to use drugs to escape.

By now, Mike easily recognized the signs. "She'd get this kind of funny look on her face, a funny smile, and a specific way she talked—and I could tell. I confronted her again and she denied it, multiple times."

It took a more concentrated search, but he finally found her cache of drugs. And this time, Mike surmised that Debora must be calling in prescriptions for her patients, then going to the pharmacy and picking the drugs up. Some of the narcotics were rigidly controlled substances, which she couldn't order by phone. Without knowing for sure how she was getting them, Mike assumed Debora was pretending to be the patient. In fact, she didn't really *have* any patients; all she had was a medical license. And if she were deeply involved in drugs, it would affect not only her career but his as well.

Mike could not bring himself to turn his own wife in. It would have meant the end of her life as a physician; it might even result in her going to prison. So once more, he talked to her about this seemingly insoluble problem.

"Debora," he said flatly, "you aren't just hiding drugs from me, and you aren't just harming yourself. You are breaking the law. Do you realize that this is a felony? You can lose your license. You can go to jail just like any junkie out there on the street. If you keep doing these things, somebody is going to catch you. And then what's going to happen to the kids?"

"I'm not like—" she protested.

"Yes, you are," Mike cut in. "In a way, you're worse. You're a *doctor*. You've heard what people say about doctors who get hooked on drugs. You've got to stop. Turning you in is the last thing in the world I want to do, but I swear I'll do it if I find one more of your hidden stashes. And you know I'll find them."

Debora looked horrified at the possibility that she might

go to jail and be separated from her children. It was as if the thought had never occurred to her before. But Mike left her no place to run and he accepted no excuse. She was going to bring them all down if she didn't stop taking drugs.

The warning seemed to be effective. Mike never again found vials of Tylox and other narcotics hidden under piles of underwear or in the back of a closet. As far as he could determine, she stopped her drug use after that.

But throughout their marriage, Debora had an inordinate number of accidents—the mysterious knee injury; a finger that became infected after she was bitten by a patient; the break in a tiny navicular bone in her wrist—an unusual injury, with subsequent complications. None of her injuries healed quickly and all of them required painkillers. Asked later if he ever suspected that Debora might have been deliberately injuring herself either to get attention or to obtain more painkillers, Mike seemed genuinely surprised at the idea. That his wife might have suffered from Munchausen's syndrome (self-injury to achieve attention or importance) had not occurred to him.

But at least her problems with pills had not carried over to other addictions. Debora never drank alcohol to excess. They went to wine-tasting parties, and Mike had his small wine cellar. They enjoyed a glass of wine or a gin-and-tonic at the end of the day—nothing more.

Debora tried another job, at the Missouri Patient Care Review Foundation. Again, she initially seemed to do very well working in peer review. The position offered regular hours, and Mike felt that she had a real knack for going through medical charts and spotting red flags. Rather than having someone hovering over her work and criticizing, she was now looking for troubling areas in other physicians' patient care. It was tedious and meticulous work, but it seemed a good fit for a woman who had once longed to be an engineer. There were rules and guidelines and familiar pathways to follow. If some other doctor whom she had never met veered from the guidelines, she took pleasure in spotting his or her failings.

"It sounded to me as if Debora was very successful," Mike said. "But she wasn't. *Her* reviews were being reviewed because, again, she was having trouble with people in the office. Ultimately, the Missouri Patient Care Review Foundation had to downsize and consolidate their regional offices to one office, down in Jefferson City. Debora told me that they were going to put her in charge of the whole operation there, but that she had turned the job down because my practice was here in Kansas City."

Mike would come to wonder if his wife was even offered the job in Jefferson City, but he could never substantiate his doubts. At any rate, Debora went on to do freelance work, reviewing Medicaid files sent to her by a number of states. This was something she could do at home and that left her free to drive her children to school and to ballet and sports practice. She did not have to deal with other people; her work was solitary.

Tim and Lissa were attending the very exclusive, very expensive Pembroke Hill school. Tim was playing soccer and hockey, and Lissa was taking ballet lessons. Kelly was only four, and there was plenty to do at home. But Debora took another job, working in an occupational medicine clinic. The man who hired her also contracted to oversee a number of emergency rooms, and Debora had known him for some time. But she had absolutely no training in occupational medicine, and her supervisor was notoriously difficult to work for.

"Ultimately, it didn't work," Mike remembered. "Debora said she was just going to do freelance reviews and stay home with the kids. I thought 'That's great. That's fine.' We didn't need the money, and if she's home with the kids, driving them around—maybe joining a country club and playing tennis—she'll be happy. As long as she's happy and not so stressed by work, maybe things will be better."

Debora did stay home and she did join a tennis club. She was the most devoted of mothers, always there for car pools and school visits, and to pick up Tim from soccer or hockey practice, Lissa from ballet lessons and Kelly from toddler tennis lessons. Some of the women in her social group described her as a wonderful mother, "very loving with her children. She did everything with her kids." But others found Debora somewhat abusive: when she sat on the sidelines of soccer matches, "she always bad-mouthed her kids," one mother said. "She would say, 'They are driving me *crazy*!' It made us really uncomfortable because it was so continuous."

Debora had a cleaning lady who came in once a week or so, but between times, the brick house on West Sixty-first inevitably became cluttered and dusty. Debora had never found housework interesting or necessary. It didn't bother the children if things were untidy, but it drove Mike nuts. He thrived on order.

Debora was still a licensed physician, but she had no practice and no regular job; and although her profession had never seemed to fulfill her (or even interest her that much), without it she had lost another piece of her identity. She had always been someone special—the best student in school, the wittiest resident in the ER, a doctor with her own practice. Now she had all the time in the world to read the stacks of novels she brought home from the library, time to play with her children, time to take care of the black Lab—Boomer—that the kids had begged for.

But some essence of Debora seemed to disappear in the early nineties. Few would deny that she had behaved bizarrely in the past, that her tantrums were shocking and uncalled-for, that she could be a pain to work with. But now, in an unkempt house, with the daily chores every mother faces, it was as if her outrageous behavior had brought her to a place that even she—with all her brilliance—could never truly have contemplated.

She wasn't remotely special anymore.

Something else about her had undergone a dramatic change: her appearance. Although there had been times before when she put on weight, she always took it off rapidly enough. Now she gained forty or fifty pounds, and her thighs and hips bulged beneath tight jeans. She was in her early forties now and looked five years older. In contrast, her husband, four years younger, looked to be in his early thirties. Debora cut her beautiful hair into an unflattering straight bob. She wore the thick glasses prescribed for her severe nearsightedness rather than the contact lenses she had once used. She wore no makeup, and her clothing was sloppy and unisex— T-shirts and jeans or shorts. It almost seemed as if she had given up. And if she had no insight into her own bizarre behavior, she could only blame someone else for her pain.

Mike had always been focused on his career, and, at the same time, determined to make his marriage work. He couldn't overlook Debora's behavior. He *had* to deal with her rages; she was in his face, yelling, stomping her feet. Sometimes she beat herself on the head with books, or beat on her thighs until she left bruises. Or, worse, she behaved the same way in a public place while their children cringed and strangers stared at her with a mixture of concern and curiosity. That behavior, her drug use, and the repeated problems she had had with her practice were clear evidence that Debora could not adjust to the world and its stresses the way other people did. But Mike didn't know why—or what he could do about it.

When he left home in the morning for rounds, it was a relief. He plunged himself into his career so completely that he didn't have to think about his marriage during the hours he was away. And he would not deny that he noticed other women—soft-voiced, blond, slender, seemingly compliant women—who would not shriek at him or stomp off in an hysterical fit of pique when life did not go smoothly. But Mike overlooked or failed to recognize that some of his wife's behavior was totally irrational, even dangerous. Or perhaps he simply repressed signals that were too alarming to deal with.

During the early nineties, despite his troubles with Debora, Mike remained true to his belief that a married man, a father, does not break his wedding vows. There are those who say that another woman—or man—cannot break up a good marriage. But then Mike and Debora did not have a good marriage, or even a vaguely workable one. He had married her when he was very young, and though he'd had an inkling that she had a harridan's temper, he had no idea how deep-seated her psychological problems were.

"I wanted my marriage to last," he later said with conviction. "Rather than contemplating an affair, I would have preferred to have my marriage somehow hold together, would have preferred to be at home with my children. I just wanted a marriage that would work."

At the same time, Mike wondered how he could go on in this joyless marriage with nothing to look forward to but complaints, fights, and recriminations. Debora demanded so much and gave so little in return. At times, she seemed to resent him—even hate him—for failing to give her what she wanted. In fact, Mike would have an affair with another woman. But he did not leave Debora. He stayed in their marriage.

Chapter 6

There was another sore eating away at Mike and Debora's marriage. Rather than recognizing that a boy needs to admire and respect his father, she enlisted their son, Tim, as her ally in her fights with her husband. When she was angry at Mike, she complained to Tim about it, speaking to him as if he were a little adult. Add to that the fact that Mike had himself been the only son and had always been expected to obey his parents without question, and he had a difficult time parenting Tim. Not surprisingly, the two had a less than perfect father-son relationship.

As Tim grew older, the gap between father and son grew wider. There were some good times, but they were fewer and fewer. Debora did not encourage Tim to obey Mike; rather, she seemed to delight in having the boy take her side in arguments. She treated Tim more like a brother than a son, unaware—or perhaps heedless—that she was fostering a devastating psychological situation in her family. Her priorities were all wrong, her perception skewed. Debora told all their children what a bad father Mike was, so that Lissa, particularly, began to side with her mother and brother. Kelly was such a sunny little girl—and still so young—that she loved her daddy without question.

Debora's manner of marital combat never changed. She yelled, screamed, stomped her feet, threw tantrums. At first Mike had shouted back at her, but he soon learned that only drove her to higher peaks of rage. So over the years he modified his response—he offered passive resistance and simply ignored her since it did no good at all to reason with her. Finally, he left the house when she was angry with him. Initially, he left for an hour or two. Later, it took a whole day for him to feel that he could go home and not be met with her accusations. Inevitably, Mike's short-term absences from his marriage lengthened until, by 1994, he was ready to walk away forever.

He felt he could no longer remain in the marriage and believed that all of them would be happier if he were to remove himself from the home. Maybe he *was* the odd man out, and the one who triggered anger and dissension in his family. He was depressed and hopeless in the twelfth year of his marriage, convinced now that things would never get better. "I hated to fail—I had never failed at anything," he said, "and I especially hated to fail in my marriage. But there was nothing else to try. I knew it would be terrible when I told Debora—and it was."

Once before, after five years of marriage, he had concluded that he and Debora would never be happy together, and he had almost asked for a divorce. But he had reconsidered—they had Tim and Lissa by then—and decided to work harder at making the marriage succeed. And it *was* work. Mike and Debora had managed to limp along for seven more years, using vacations and work to avoid the reality that they were two people going in opposite directions.

"The house was disheveled all the time," Mike would remember. "There was no attempt to keep it in order. There was no attempt to get the kids to try to follow rules, to keep their rooms cleaned up. There were no boundaries set for them . . . it was a pretty bad living situation. Obviously, any of us that have children know that a house is not going to be kept in perfect order—but it did concern me. . . . It was a bad example for the kids. You know, I think that there has to be some semblance of order in a house you live in."

Although Debora would say later that she was totally surprised when Mike asked for a divorce in January 1994, he believed she knew full well what was coming. She could not have missed seeing how unhappy he was, and she had told the women she played tennis with that her husband was cheating on her and she feared he might leave her.

In retrospect, Mike believed that Debora tried to forestall exactly the conversation he knew he had to initiate. Suddenly, she did a complete turnaround, which she was capable of if she wanted something badly enough. For two weeks, Debora was solicitous of Mike's needs, becoming—for those fourteen days—the ideal wife. However, the change came far too late. And Mike no longer trusted her motives.

Finally, he told her he was moving out and wanted a divorce. And as soon as Debora realized what he was saying, she turned and stomped down to the basement, shouting at the top of her lungs. Tim was in the family room watching television and Mike didn't want him drawn into their discussion. It was too late.

Debora grabbed whatever objects were closest and began to throw them around the room. Books and toys thudded against walls; lamps and knickknacks shattered. She was screaming incoherently and yelling at Tim, recruiting him to her side. "God damn," she shouted at her son. "Now *look* at what he's going to do. I've done so much for him—you know that—and now he's going to cheat us out of what is ours!"

Tim, twelve years old, looked at her, stricken, his face pale and fearful. Debora kept screaming at him as Mike tried to draw her aside. "We're going to lose all this!" she cried, sweeping her arms wide.

"Debora—*don't* . . ." Mike pleaded, but it was as if she didn't even hear him.

"Your father is cheating on me!" Debora shrieked. "He's going to leave us and we'll lose everything we have. I'll have to go back to work, and I don't know where we'll live. I don't know who will take care of you."

"Mom . . ." Tim said plaintively. "Mom—it'll be okay."

"No it won't!" she screamed, pounding her fists against her thighs. "Your father is going to take everything we have away from us because he doesn't love us."

The family room was a shambles, and Debora had worked herself into a frenzy. There was no point in Mike's trying to talk to her, nor would Tim let his father comfort him.

"It was awful," Mike said.

It *was* awful. But it only solidified his decision that he and Debora could no longer go on together. Continuing their farce of a marriage would only destroy their children.

He moved out of the house into an apartment in the Country Club Plaza. The name did not denote plush quarters; the area was an older neighborhood in Kansas City, Missouri, halfway between Mike's office and the street where Debora and the kids still lived in the brick house they had bought with such high expectations six years before.

Surprisingly, things did improve after Mike moved out. He talked to Debora almost every day. "Nothing had changed—I still supported them, of course," he said, "but I just wasn't there."

He took Tim, Lissa, and Kelly two or three times a week, and they had "pretty good times." Tim and Lissa were very angry with him at first, but he wasn't surprised at that. He was sure that Debora was talking to them as confidants and not as children bewildered by the breakup of their parents' marriage. Lissa, in particular, was furious with her father. It took her a long time to admit that her world had not really changed that much. She still had her ballet lessons, the same friends, the same school, and the same house; the kids had their beloved Lab, Boomer.

In fact, things seemed to be getting better all around, so much so that Mike even began to wonder if he and Debora might reconcile. He really did want to hold his marriage together, if they could avoid Debora's histrionics and temper tantrums. However, the one thing he could not see himself doing at that point was going to marriage counseling. "Debora wanted to go, but I knew I wouldn't open up—I couldn't see myself sitting there and opening up to a counselor and it wouldn't have done any good."

Even so, he and Debora began to talk about getting back together. She was calmer and it began to seem that they *could* somehow be together and raise their children without the anger and bitterness that had sullied every facet of their marriage. Mike became hopeful enough to tell Debora, "One of the things I'm unhappy about is that house. If we got back together, we would have to move out of that house. It's too small for us—it needs too much work."

Debora agreed at once. If they had more room, she felt, and if Mike could come home to a clean house without dozens of chores that needed to be done, their marriage would be so much better. She immediately began searching for more suitable houses and found the beautiful mansion on Canterbury Court in Prairie Village. Mike caught her enthusiasm and looked at the huge house with its six bedrooms, den, exercise room, pool—everything a family could ask for. He agreed that it seemed perfect, if somewhat expensive. It had gone on the market at something over $600,000. In California, it would have listed at $3 million. Even so, in Prairie Village, Kansas, $600,000 was a lot to pay for a home.

But the house had been empty for a while and the owner—who had built many of the luxurious houses in the Canterbury development—accepted Debora and Mike's bid of $400,000. They were getting a tremendous bargain.

Then Mike began to get cold feet. He had been swept up in Debora's fervor and in her promises that everything would be different. Now he realized that he had been rushed into a commitment that he didn't truly believe in. Nothing had really changed, except that they had been apart for four months. They had made no attempts or promises to reconcile, and once he signed the papers the real estate agent was rushing to prepare, he would be agreeing to pay almost half a million dollars for a second house, while he wasn't sure he could sell the house he already owned. Debora wasn't working—except for occasional case reviews—the children's school was expensive, and they had other debts, including payments and leases on several new vehicles. Mike made excellent money, but he felt as if they were running pell-mell into a hasty, ill-thought-out decision.

"I backed down," he admitted, "and, of course, everyone from the real estate agent to Debora and the kids were devastated. The realtor kept calling and asking me *why?* and I told her there were personal issues I didn't care to discuss."

Two or three days later, on a Sunday in May, 1994, Mike was working at the North Kansas City Hospital when he got a call from his answering service. "I got a stat call, which seemed odd since I was on second call," he remembered. "The doctor who was first up should have gotten the call. And then I knew something was wrong. I called the service and they said, 'Call your neighbor. Your house is on fire!'"

His neighbor on West Sixty-first Terrace was out of breath

and panicky. She said Mike's house was on fire. "I'm pretty sure that Debora and the kids aren't there—but I'm worried about Boomer," she said.

Mike had no way of knowing who was or wasn't inside his house. He ran to his car and raced home at "literally ninety miles an hour. There were seven fire trucks out in front, and an ambulance—which really shook me up—was parked on Ward Parkway. I ran out there through a huge crowd of people. There was smoke pouring out of the house, and water—but I couldn't see any flames."

Frantic, Mike called Debora on her cell phone and asked her where the kids were. Tim was playing in a soccer game, she said cheerfully, and she had the girls and Boomer in the car with her. When Mike told her the news, Debora hurried home and they watched firefighters mopping up the last of the blaze. She told Mike over and over how glad she was that she had given in to Tim's pleas to take Boomer with them. He would surely have died in the fire.

Although the family was safe, there was massive damage to the house. The fire had apparently started in the basement and raced up a laundry chute. Most of the basement was ashes, as was the kitchen. Flames had even reached Tim's room on the top floor before firefighters managed to put the fire out. The damage estimate was $80,000, almost half of the $205,000 they had originally paid for the house. But for Mike, the worst part was the time, which seemed endless, when he didn't know where his family was. He never wanted to live through such an experience again; the sight of the parked ambulance, waiting, perhaps, for one of his children, haunted him for weeks.

The Farrars' insurance company sent an arson investigator, who determined that the cause was a rather unusual electrical problem. The cord of a practically new dehumidifier had been wrapped around a copper water pipe so tightly that it had shorted through, apparently in three small areas. The pipe had gotten so hot that it had heated adjacent wood paneling to the burning point.

Mike discussed the fire with friends, one of whom said flatly, "She set it."

"What do you mean?" he asked, puzzled.

"Debora set it."

"*No . . .*" he said, disbelieving. "Of course she didn't set it."

"Believe what you like—but I'm telling you that Debora set that fire to make you come back."

Mike didn't buy that theory for a moment. Even if Debora *had* deliberately set fire to their house, she had no expertise in arson. He knew that arson investigators could spot an amateurish effort. He accepted the insurance company's opinion and figured his friend had an overactive imagination.

"I never really believed that Debora set that fire," he said later. "We had to board the house up, of course, and Debora and the kids had nowhere to live. They moved into my apartment. We were reconciled by the fire as much as anything. A day or two later, we put the bid back on the house on Canterbury Court. The owner asked for more earnest money this time—*quite* a bit more earnest money—but I didn't blame him."

Their mortgage insurance paid off the burned house. Almost everything Debora and Mike owned had been extensively damaged, too, if not by the flames then by smoke. Furniture, clothing, books, objets d'art. "We had *fifty-seven* pages of inventory," Mike recalled. "You don't realize what you own until you have a fire. We had to go through every room, every drawer. It took five months for us to go to stores, establish prices, replacement costs. They paid us about $48,000 on our possessions alone."

The insurance companies paid off without question, and Mike and Debora repaired the house and replaced their lost property. And they sold the Sixty-first Terrace house for $20,000 more than they had paid for it, so their plunge into the much more expensive estate-like home on Canterbury Court was not as financially ill-advised as Mike had feared.

Mike, Debora, and their family moved the few blocks to Canterbury Court. It took only five minutes to go from one house to the other, although the first was in Missouri and the second in Kansas. The whole family took a trip to Disney World; then, on the first day of summer, June 21, 1994, settled into 7517 Canterbury Court.

Where life had been bleak for Debora only a few months before, now things were looking up. Her husband had rejoined the family and they had a brand-new house—grander than anything she had ever dreamed of owning—new furniture, their own pool, a four-car garage. They had a red pickup truck and a Lexus—paid off with proceeds from the insurance—and Mike wanted to get a minivan to use on family vacations. "Debora didn't want that," he recalled. "She wanted a Toyota Land Cruiser, a $40,000 vehicle." Again, Mike capitulated. If it would make her happy, they would all benefit.

Mike felt optimistic about the future. Once he had committed himself to the new house and to a renewed and better marriage, he relaxed and enjoyed their second chance. He saw how beautiful their new home was, and he and Debora furnished the rooms to make them fit their needs exactly.

"Things had calmed down," he said of this period. "And they seemed better. In Debora's defense, I think she really tried to change. And I thought—initially—that I was happy. The house was certainly nice. It was a wonderful neighborhood. We had a swimming pool. The kids were happy with that."

Debora had never been an enthusiastic cook, usually plunking down a pot of something or other—simple midwestern stews or spaghetti—on the table, or sending out for fast food. But she tried to become more involved in the actual running of her wonderful new home. And she was there for her children and their activities, driving endless car pools, buying birthday cakes, cheering Tim on in soccer or hockey, encouraging Lissa's genuine promise as a ballerina. As far as all that went, Debora was a good mother. But too often she still failed to see the demarcation between mother and child in emotional disputes. It was almost as if she herself *was* a child.

But Debora was trying. She even made an effort to clean house, although she would later admit that she had a hard time getting her children in gear to pick up their rooms. "Tim is the smartest of my children," she said. "Kelly was next. Lissa will do whatever she needs to do to succeed— Tim and Kelly would do it if they felt like it. Tim's room was absolutely immaculate, like a drill sergeant was going to inspect it. Kelly's was a mess. One time, I told Tim I'd give him a new CD he wanted if he'd clean Kelly's room. He cleaned it—but Kelly lost all her possessions. He just picked everything up and threw it away!"

Mike tried to work shorter hours and spend more time with his family. He vowed that somehow his relationship with Debora would turn into a loving marriage and they would magically become a happy family. He was so eager for that to happen, in fact, that he made a promise to his children that he was not sure he could keep: he told them that he would never go away again, that they would be a family forever.

He would regret that promise for the rest of his life.

The "honeymoon phase" in the Canterbury Court house lasted only six months. After Christmas, all the old problems resurfaced. Mike summed it up accurately: "I made the mistake that so many people make—either they have a baby, or they buy a house, and they think that everything is going to change, that all the bad times will be left behind. But they never are."

Once again, Mike had to evaluate his marriage—his life. "It became clear to me that our relationship had not substantially improved. I still did not have any love for Debora, and I decided that I wanted a divorce."

As far as Mike could see, the new house was soon as messy

as the old house had been; Debora had little interest in keeping it in order, and order and neatness mattered tremendously to Mike. Even more, he longed for the passion he had never found in his marriage. Reconciliation or not, she was no more interested in their sex life than she had ever been. And she had become a heavy, unattractive woman who paid no attention to how she dressed. She had cut her beautiful hair even shorter and looked sloppy and rumpled most of the time. Mike could barely remember the slender resident in her expensive sports car, with her long hair flying in the wind. And although she was keeping a lid on her tendency toward violent histrionics, he still felt Debora was a powder keg waiting for a match.

Finally, Mike had come to believe that his role in their marriage was simply to give Debora status in their community and bring home a paycheck. When he had the time to visualize the life he longed for, it seemed he didn't want more than most men: a caring wife who appreciated his sexual interest in her; children who loved him; a clean house. But he had none of these things; he had only a steeper mortgage than he had before.

He wanted out—badly.

He did not, however, tell Debora of his decision; he dreaded a repeat of the scene in their old house. Besides, he, Debora, and Tim planned to go on a trip with a group from Pembroke Hill School that summer—a wonderful trip to the Amazon River and the Inca ruins in Peru. Mike knew perfectly well that if he told Debora beforehand that he wanted a divorce, all hell would break loose. "I thought it would make the trip miserable for us, and potentially miserable for the other people on the trip."

If the vacation in Peru went well, at least Tim would have memories of a last happy time with his mother and father together. So Mike kept his mouth shut. Knowing that eventually he would have to leave his marriage if he was to enjoy any happiness in life, he thought he could stay for another six months.

Chapter 7

The Kansas City area of the mid-1990s was, like so many other parts of America, caught somewhere in a time warp. Anyone with imagination could close his eyes and see the covered wagons rumbling west over the prairie, which is not flat at all, but faintly undulating. A century and a half ago, the population of Kansas City, Missouri, was measured in the dozens, but merchants there thrived when it became the jumping-off place for pioneers and the California gold rush. Then as now, the roads west were surrounded by trees where creatures with watching eyes scanned the plains below. In the summer, the hawks are hidden. In the winter, they perch, their feathers ruffled against the frigid wind, about a hundred yards apart, dark gray birds a foot tall or more. It is said they can spot a mouse running for cover a half-mile away. Farmers welcome them and they are beautiful to watch in flight, raptors that kill so they may survive.

Oaks, elms, and the Kansas state tree, the cottonwood, abound, but it is the paper-white trunks of the Osage orange tree that stand out, particularly when the rest of the vegetation is dormant. The wind is fiercely cold in the winter and hot and dry in the summer. Indeed, Kansas is named for the wind; the name comes from a Siouan Indian word meaning both "people of the south wind" and "smoky wind."

The towns along I–70 to Topeka and I–35 to Olathe spike off onto gridlike main thoroughfares dotted with every franchise in America. The parts of Olathe, the Johnson County seat, that were built when the century was new abound in wonderful wooden houses with sagging porches and lilacs in the dooryard. On the "other" side of I–35, the houses are closer together, and have no history before last year. Business seems to follow the new houses and the franchises,

but the sunflowers and zinnias crowding whitewashed fences
have more appeal to the soul and the senses.

The sun shines bright as fire in Kansas; even though every
twig, bush, and tree is a sere brownish gray in the middle of
March, the earth seems to come fully alive overnight in May,
as if answering a silent signal of nature.

The two Kansas Citys, population aside, are really small
towns where community involvement is concerned. People
know each other and there are many interconnections. The
Women's Exchange Club, which meets in an historic old
firehouse in Kansas City, Missouri, is representative of the
kind of mutual support that transcends age, occupation,
ethnicity, and personal wealth.

The medical communities on both sides of the Missouri
River are even more akin to small towns where gossip,
rumor, and scandal move with the speed of a snake in a
wheat field and, more often than not, are equally impossible
to trace. Many physicians are on staff at hospitals in both
states.

Celeste Walker* was a woman who would become the target
of many rumors, innuendoes, and outright lies. She was in
her early forties in 1995, but she scarcely looked it. She had
thick blond hair—streaked perhaps by the Kansas sun, perhaps by her beautician—green eyes, a deep tan, and the
taut figure of a woman who works out whether she feels like
it or not. Although she had not practiced for a decade, she
was a registered nurse. Her expertise was in recovery room
nursing and she had occasionally done psychiatric nursing.

Celeste had been married to Dr. John Walker for sixteen
years; they had two sons, Brett,* fourteen, and Dan,* ten.
The family lived in a sprawling split-level on a huge lot in
Overland Park, Kansas, one of the affluent suburbs south of
KCMO. John, an anesthesiologist at Shawnee Mission

Medical Center, was a handsome man with brown hair and eyes and a solemn, gentle manner. Of medium height and weight, he had worn a mustache for the last few years.

The Walkers' home was a monument to Celeste's creative and innovative style and it had a pool, a party room, and a dressing room in the backyard. Celeste's flower beds covered every other available square foot, and she knew the Latin name for every bloom. During the short but fierce Kansas summers, she virtually lived outdoors, gardening, swimming, or cooking for groups of friends. Celeste wore a bathing suit as often as she wore a dress. The more tanned she got, the deeper the blue-green of her eyes seemed, and she was, without question, a sensational-looking woman.

Celeste had an unquenchable and ebullient air, but the bubbly attitude she showed the world was a carefully constructed mask. Optimism had been—a long time ago, and down deep—her essential nature, but the many years of being married to John had knocked most of the joy out of her. Inside, she felt the desolate pain that every woman married to a clinically depressed man lives with. In almost two decades of marriage, Celeste had gone from hope to despair to acceptance. John was a good man, a kind man, but no matter how hard she tried, she could not make him happy. She could not even get him to admit that the *possibility* of happiness might exist.

Eventually, in order to survive, Celeste spent her days with her sons and with her many female friends, mostly in activities connected with Pembroke Hill School. She may have longed to be with a man who loved life as much as she did, a man who believed in the future—but she had never even come close to having an affair.

Celeste's sister and mother were both very much like herself—strong, fun, bright, and creative. Celeste's mother, in her seventies, was "going steady." Her sister lived in the deep woods of the Northwest, in a house she and her husband had built themselves. Both of them tried to bolster Celeste, to keep her spirits up and urge her to live her own life, to try to be happy even though John could find neither solace nor joy in his life.

Celeste and John had met in a surgical recovery room when he was checking on a patient. It was a romantic way to meet and she was impressed with him right away. "He was so smart. That man knew *everything*," she would remember. "You could ask him any medical question on any specialty. He had an unbelievable memory." She did not see the sadness that was an integral part of John. Maybe it wasn't there in the early days.

They were married on October 6, 1979, four and a half months after Debora Green and Michael Farrar. John was twenty-nine and Celeste was twenty-seven. Coincidentally, John was the same John Walker who had been on Debora's cadaver-dissection team in anatomy class at the University of Kansas Med School. They had been friends then, but had rarely, if ever, met since graduation.

The Walker marriage, much like the Farrar-Green marriage, proved early on to suffer from flawed communication, with the marital partners working at cross-purposes. "I thought when we got married, we loved each other," Celeste would write one day, trying to understand what had gone wrong. "But in the first few months, we found we had entirely different expectations. We both tried to make the marriage work, we had children, we built a life together." But as time went on, Celeste realized that her husband was becoming more and more depressed. It seemed that she fought harder to bring new life to their marriage than he did. "He just didn't have much energy—and just wanted to escape."

They managed to bumble along, somehow, until 1990. By then, they were both desperately unhappy; John said that he wanted to be out of the marriage. Still, when Celeste suggested that they separate, he balked. They went to a marriage counselor and things seemed to be better for a while—a very short while.

"That was the point," Celeste would remember, "where

John realized the marriage was a failure, and he felt that he had in some way failed also. He became more depressed as time went on and we had fewer mutual interests. There was little affection or closeness and we grew apart and much more distant from each other until we reached a point where we were more like roommates. John still was a good friend and a wonderful person. He was always sympathetic when I was sick or down. I respected him and valued his opinion—but we just couldn't connect on an intimate level."

Sometime in 1994, Celeste had accepted that she and John could not go on together. He had no interest in anything having to do with their home. When the roof leaked and the basement flooded, he simply walked away. "I confronted him," she remembered. "I said, 'Anybody else would be down there helping to clean up the basement and putting it back together, and getting the roof fixed and stop the leaking.'

"He said, 'Well, I figure all we have to do is have some damage repair. I really don't care. I figure I'll be gone in ten years anyway. You can't raise those boys by yourself so I'll stick around until Brett is in college and Dan is in high school, and then I'll be gone.'"

Celeste assumed that this meant he planned to divorce her in ten years. But, by then she would be over fifty; it would be difficult to find a job. Knowing that there was a stopwatch running on her marriage, she arranged to update her nursing skills. "I began to plan an independent life for myself," she said. "I had been out of the workforce for ten years, so I took a reentry course for nursing. I became stronger and more confident. John became more dependent and pessimistic about us, his ability to afford a divorce, the direction of health care in general."

Celeste agonized over her husband's ambivalence. He wanted to leave her; he didn't want to leave her. He would leave in a prescribed number of years. He didn't feel he could afford a divorce. From one week to the next, she didn't know where she stood. She didn't have a marriage;

she had a pendulum, and it sank lower with each swing.

And all the while Celeste grew more concerned about John's profound depression. "In December of 1994, he brought me a gun and told me to hide it—which I did." Frightened, Celeste made an appointment with a psychiatrist for her husband. John seemed to be descending from increasingly darker moods to a point where he himself feared he might commit suicide. He did go to about four sessions of therapy before dropping out.

Celeste's hope that John wasn't actually considering suicide was somewhat bolstered by the fact that he worked hard to keep himself in good physical shape. He exercised and talked about getting a bike that he could ride in the morning before he left for work. She tried to tell herself these weren't the activities of a man who wanted to die. But her experience in psychiatric nursing told her that John was in deep trouble emotionally.

She didn't know then that John was buying more and more life insurance—another policy with each devastating episode of depression. He seemed a good risk; he was healthy, and he had a wonderful career. The insurance he was accumulating didn't strike the underwriters as excessive.

When he was home, John was emotionally removed from Celeste, but he tried to be present for his sons. He watched television and took naps. He seemed to care even less about the house and didn't have the energy to fix things that needed repair. The kitchen floor needed replacing, but he wasn't interested. He was too tired, with the kind of absolute fatigue that is not alleviated by sleep, though he went to bed right after supper and slept through the night until it was time to go to work. Celeste felt that John was sleeping through their marriage, their lives.

The Walkers had moved in the same tight circle of close friends for twenty years, but now John told Celeste that he knew they weren't really *his* friends—they were hers, and they included him in their activities only because of her. He felt that none of them really cared about him. "That was so

far from the truth," she said, "but it showed how unconnected John felt to everyone in his life."

Celeste saw the Pembroke Hill School's summer 1995 Peru
trip as a chance to step back from her world and evaluate
where she and John were going. And she was excited about
the project: she thought it would be a wonderful time for
herself and her older son. Though John wasn't at all interested, he didn't mind if Celeste and Brett went.

Planning for the two-week trip got under way in the latter
part of 1994, and a number of parents signed up. They had
several meetings about what they should take, what clothing
they would need, what they hoped to see while they were
there, and even what health hazards they might face.

Even though they were all part of the medical community,
Celeste had never met Michael or Debora. Mike practiced
north of the river, in Missouri, while John's practice was on
the Kansas side. Celeste had been active in getting
Pembroke Hill families signed up for the Peru trip, but she
had never seen Mike before May 1995, at one of the Peru
trip meetings. "I was drawn to him," she said. "He had
energy and enthusiasm; he just had a spark about him."

Mike and another doctor would be in charge of providing
antibiotics and health information on the trip. As he did
with everything, Mike had carefully researched what bugs
and viruses might attack tourists in Peru. At the meeting, he
and the other physician argued briefly about what the best
medical protocol would be.

"After he left the meeting," Celeste remembered, "Mike
called me on the car phone and said he was going to call the
CDC [the federal Centers for Disease Control, in Atlanta] to
be sure we were all really protected—that we got the correct
shots, and that we took the right medicines and first-aid
equipment with us. I got off the phone and I thought,
'Gosh, this man is so different from John.' John never followed through on anything, and here's Mike Farrar calling

back right away to assure me that we would have what we needed in Peru."

Although they had a few business dealings about the trip by phone and mail, Celeste didn't see Mike again until they were on the Peru trip, six weeks later. She talked on the phone more with Debora, and it was Debora who had delivered the package of medicine to the Walker home.

The Pembroke Hill group left Kansas City on June 24, 1995. "Before I left for Peru," Celeste said, "we [she and John] decided we would both spend that two weeks being really honest with ourselves about where we wanted to go from here."

Things were also close to a watershed point between Mike and Debora. Tim had lost almost all respect for his father. One evening, mouthing off to Mike, he so angered his father that Mike picked up the thirteen-year-old and slammed him against a wall. Fortunately, Tim hit at a point between the studs, and the plasterboard buckled. He wasn't hurt, but Mike was horrified to think that he had literally put his own son through a wall. It didn't matter that Tim was a well-muscled young athlete and Mike was not particularly strong; it mattered that he was the father and he had lost control.

On two other occasions, father and son were angry enough at each other to wrestle. Debora did not step in to stop these confrontations; she only watched. The worst scene of all came on a late Mother's Day celebration, in May 1995. Debora's parents, Joan and Robert Jones, were visiting and the atmosphere was tense. Joan later described what happened that day:

"The plans were to take me out to dinner, a sort of combination Mother's Day/birthday. It wasn't really Mother's Day, as that day had to be reserved for Farrar's mother. Farrar went to work early as usual. Tim sat and had tea with us and told us all his plans and hopes. He seemed so grown up. He didn't know if he wanted to be a teaching tennis pro or a chef. He was really into cooking and wanted to go to cooking school and wanted a pasta maker for Christmas. He and grandpa played a lot of pool, and Tim told his grandpa the reason he was working so hard at lifting weights was to protect himself from the 'wimp' (one of the nicer names he called Farrar.)"

Joan was disappointed to find that the man she called Farrar was going to dinner with them. She felt that he didn't want to take her out and that he meant to spoil her evening by deliberately "starting in on Tim," harassing his son until he was in a rage.

"Farrar made Tim go [with the party] but every time Tim started to settle down, Farrar would say something to start him off again. . . . When we got to the restaurant Farrar wouldn't let Tim go in. . . . Tim came in and apologized and asked if he could have something to eat and Farrar actually got up and chased Tim from the restaurant."

The argument between Tim and Mike continued at home. Mike wouldn't deny that. But he did reject his mother-in-law's version of the rest of the evening's events.

"Tim was on the floor, and he called me a motherfucker," Mike said. "That was too much. I was pulling him into his room. It was dark, and he was flailing around, and he hit me. It was a lucky punch—but he broke my nose."

Hearing his mother-in-law's version of that evening, Mike was amazed. He had felt that Debora's parents agreed with him that Tim had gotten much too cocky, especially when they saw Mike's bloody nose. "I went downstairs after Tim was in bed and they said, 'Well, you put up with his behavior longer than *we* would have!'"

It was humiliating for Mike to have to go to a fellow physician the next morning to have his nose set, and to explain that his own son had done it in anger.

There was no question that Tim was a very unhappy teenager: he was being manipulated by his mother, who was lining up her children to be soldiers on her side of the family war; his father was angry and miserable; and he was just entering that stage of puberty when *every* kid is alternately shy and aggressive, unsure and a know-it-all.

*

Despite the tensions in the family, Debora, Mike, and Tim were still signed up for the Peru trip. (Lissa and Kelly would stay with relatives in the Kansas City area and in St. Louis.) Twenty parents and twenty children were slated to be on the trip for the first week; half of those planned to stay for the second. Most of the children were sixth-graders, a few fifth-graders. The adults were fortyish and professionals in their fields.

Mike and Debora planned to stay for both weeks of the tour, returning on July 6. The group flew from Kansas City to Atlanta on Delta Airlines, then continued south to Peru, where they would spend half their time in the jungle and half in the Andes Mountains. The jungle lodge where they spent their first few nights, though remote, was not primitive. There were "open air" double rooms and a dining hall. Afterward the tourists took a boat down the Amazon River to an even more remote camp.

Celeste Walker, her son Brett, and Carolyn Stafford, a teacher at Pembroke Hill, spent a lot of time together on the trip. Celeste could not help but feel a little wistful when she saw how Debora and Mike seemed to be together all the time; it would have been such a great trip if she had a husband who shared her love of travel and adventure. Debora and Mike struck Celeste as a perfect couple. She noticed that they always sat together on the buses, hiked together, and ate together. They seemed so devoted to each other.

Celeste had been surprised the first time she saw Debora: she had expected a thinner, prettier woman. On the trip, she wondered whether maybe Debora and Mike were such a tight couple *because* of their differences. They didn't look as if they belonged together. "Debora was pretty intimidating looking," Celeste said. "She was big—heavy. She was bigger than *he* was, and she had a really short haircut, boyish looking."

It was true; Debora's latest metamorphosis made her look quite masculine. Ever since she had started to work out of her home, she seemed oblivious to her appearance. In hot weather at home, she often wore a robe or muumuu all day; on the Peru trip, she wore faded old T-shirts and shorts. She didn't wear any makeup, but neither did any of the other tourists. Hiking up Machu Picchu wasn't the sort of activity that called for makeup.

Celeste had thought Mike handsome the first time she saw him, and she would later admit she was strongly attracted to him—but she had not the remotest notion that he saw her as anything more than another mother from Pembroke Hill School. That was just as well. Her life was too complicated as it was. She was a married woman, and she was a confused and miserable married woman. The last thing she needed was to become involved with another man. But she could not deny the longing she had felt for the past five years, the need to share her life with someone.

In Peru, Mike grew a beard and wore a wide-brimmed "Indiana Jones" hat to ward off the relentless sun. He seemed even better looking than Celeste remembered. He was still a take-charge kind of man, eager to start each day's hike or climb or boat ride. She could not help comparing him with John, who was so exhausted by a day's work in the operating room that he couldn't stay awake.

Celeste and Carolyn Stafford admired the way Debora and Mike discussed things in a calm, reasonable way. One day, they watched as the couple worked out who would pick up Lissa in St. Louis when they got home. It seemed to Carolyn and Celeste that the two had the perfect egalitarian marriage.

"He was going to go to St. Louis," Celeste said, "and she was going to take care of the stuff from the trip—and then Mike said, 'You know, I'm much better at doing the laundry, so why don't *you* go get Lissa, and I'll do the washing.' Carolyn and I just looked at each other in awe. Here was a married couple who could work things out without worrying about roles. They were both happy and we were impressed. This is what a good marriage is."

Or was it?

"They seemed very married," Celeste said later. The image that Debora and Mike presented to the world was of two people who were together so much they were almost joined at the hip. Of course, Celeste knew nothing about their separation less than a year earlier. The act they put on—if it *was* an act—was flawless.

Odd, then, that from the second or third day, Celeste had picked up on "weird vibes" from Debora: "She talked to everyone on the trip, but never to me. Every time she could, she excluded me from the conversation." Debora seemed jealous of her, so Celeste bent over backward never to be alone with Mike. And, as happily married as Debora and Mike seemed to be, there was an undercurrent that puzzled Celeste. Debora had everything—a solid marriage; an attentive husband—but sometimes she appeared to be on edge. And she seemed to go out of her way to ignore Celeste. Celeste watched to see if Debora was that way with anyone else, but no—the animosity was directed at her.

"We were on a bus once," Celeste said. "And Deb and Mike were sitting across from Carolyn and me. I remember being really careful that my knees didn't touch Mike's. I knew somehow that that would bother Deb."

Another time, Celeste found herself on a climb with Mike, a hike that Debora had passed on. "It was the day after Machu Picchu," she remembered, "and we were in Agua Caliente. A lot of people wanted to go shopping, and that's the last thing I wanted to do, so I suggested we go hiking. Michael and I went, and Brett and Tim went. We hiked together all the way up to the top of a waterfall and all the way back. Coming back up the railroad track to the hotel where everybody was waiting for the train, Brett and Tim were walking really fast. I was trying to catch up with them and I couldn't. It ended up that Mike and I came walking back together. It crossed my mind, 'This doesn't look good—Deb might think this is really weird.' But nothing had happened at all. I remember I deliberately put a lot of space between us as we came back to where they were all sitting on the patio. I felt guilty—but I had no reason to. It was perfectly innocent and the kids had been along." Still Debora stared at Celeste, and Celeste saw frank enmity in her eyes.

Nevertheless, Debora was the spark plug of the Peru tour and everybody liked her. Even Celeste considered her the hit of the trip: "Deb had the *best* sense of humor! She was the wittiest. She was hysterically funny—she is *so* smart. She could make connections between things that other people didn't get. Her jokes were always at someone's expense. I laughed so hard I was falling down—I couldn't even hike behind them, she was so funny. She was the best thing that could have happened to us on that trip."

But the Peru trip wasn't all fun. Mike had studied up on what diseases they might encounter and had done his best to see that no one suffered anything worse than "Montezuma's revenge," the travelers' diarrhea that is pretty standard for tourists in South America. "We all took malaria prophylaxis," he recalled, "and we had vaccinations for hepatitis A."

About 90 percent of the adults and three or four of the children developed fairly severe diarrhea in the first few days. Mike had taken along a good supply of the antibiotic Cipro to kill the bacteria that caused the fever and diarrhea and shorten the course of the illness from five to seven days to only thirty-six to forty-eight hours. The Cipro worked well, but even so, it took about forty-eight hours for the sufferers to recover. Mike himself suffered a bout; Celeste was knocked flat for two days, and she lost a night's sleep. But although the diarrhea was miserable, it was not life threatening. Once it was gone, it was gone; no one feared they would bring some terrible bug back home to Kansas City.

If Debora sensed Celeste's admiration for Mike, she didn't mention it. Celeste was the most attractive woman in the group, and she was an energetic hiker, while Debora's

weight and her bad knee made her less than enthusiastic
about some of the more vigorous climbs. The two women
had pleasant enough conversations with each other at first.
One day, on a riverboat, Celeste asked Debora why she was
no longer in practice. "She said she had to stop because she
needed to be with her kids," Celeste recalled. "But she had
an offer from someone to go into family practice. She said
she kept giving them reasons why she couldn't do that at the
time. I remember she said she was running out of excuses
not to go back to work. I'd been out of my nursing practice
for ten years, and I told her I thought the family practice
sounded great, that I missed nursing. I was longing to get
back in the mainstream. . . .

"But then later Mike told me that Deb was *always* going to
go into some different kind of practice."

Celeste was captivated by Mike, as much as she tried to
deny it. Except that they were both physicians, he was the
antithesis of her husband. Mike was so interested in everything, so full of life. Celeste envied Debora, having such a vital
man for a husband. One thing became apparent to Celeste in
Peru: she had laughed so much, had so much fun—and had
observed couples who actually enjoyed their marriages.
"While I was gone, I came to the truth that John and I were so
incompatible it would never be a satisfying marriage."

Unfortunately, John had come to the opposite conclusion: "John said it was worth trying again to salvage it."

It was the beginning of a strange and tragic summer.

Chapter 8

Although Celeste and Mike were nothing more than members of the same traveling group in Peru, they had felt a
tremendous magnetism between them. That wasn't surprising; they shared more than most people knew. Celeste and
Mike had the same energetic, optimistic nature. And they
had both stayed in their marriages for years after they

became convinced that there was no hope, comfort, or passion to be found there. Celeste had been faithful to John, but she longed for some intimacy in her life. And Mike had been faithful to Debora since they moved into the house on Canterbury Court, but he kept alive his decision that their reconciliation was a disaster. He had made a stupid mistake in going back.

The façade of togetherness that Mike and Debora had managed to maintain on the Peru trip cracked and fell away the second day they were home. True, in the conversation that had so impressed Celeste and Carolyn, they had calmly worked out the logistics of who would drive to St. Louis to get Lissa. Debora would go, while Mike stayed home to unpack and start doing laundry.

It was July 8 when Debora left for St. Louis. Leaving six-year-old Kelly alone in the house with a sleeping Tim, Mike went to see Celeste. Debora was furious. "We had brought some things home for her [Celeste] in our luggage, and he went over there—and left the children alone, left Kelly alone with no one to supervise her," she said tightly. And, she insisted, her husband wasted little time that day.

Mike did, in fact, go to Celeste's home in Overland Park that hot July 8 to deliver some souvenirs and artifacts of hers. "Everyone fit stuff into their suitcases where they could," Celeste said, "and we figured out what belonged to who later." She thought Mike might also have brought some photographs that he had had developed in a one-hour camera shop.

Whatever the reason for his visit, the end result was the same: on that day, in her home, Celeste and Mike began an affair. Mike had felt the same pull toward Celeste that she had toward him, although their behavior in Peru had been completely circumspect. They had never even spoken of how they felt, not until that moment; Celeste had assumed that Mike had no interest in her. But now, as Celeste showed him her backyard, it was apparent to both of them that they wanted more than friendship. "I could see it in his eyes, too," she said.

Their coming together as lovers immediately produced the need for secrecy and subterfuge—more so than most affairs. Those who had gone to Peru had become friends, and there would be parties and get-togethers all summer. Celeste and John and Debora and Mike would be thrown together frequently; it was not as though either had begun an affair with a stranger. It probably would have been better if they had.

Their affair was not a matter of stealing away to motels, although it *was* sexual. Nor did they see each other alone that much; they were lucky to meet two or three times a week. Even then, sometimes they just parked their cars and talked. "It wasn't often [that they met]," Celeste said. "He had to go home, and I had to be with my family. . . . Mostly, we just talked a lot." Their affair was one of sharing, of many, many phone calls to touch base, to hear kind words, to make quick promises that were almost impossible to keep. Within a matter of days, Mike had told Celeste that he found her the perfect woman, so beautiful, the woman he had been looking for. She had wanted to hear that for so long, it was easy for her to believe.

And Celeste would later say that she thought no one would ever have suspected that she and Mike were having an affair. "We were that discreet."

It wasn't easy. The Peru gang spent a lot of time together that summer of 1995. Kansas City's Fourth of July fireworks had been postponed because of inclement weather; now many of the travelers went to see the delayed show. "John was there, and my mother, and sons, and Mike and Deb. I'm not sure if Tim was," Celeste recalled. "And Carolyn and Laura Sutherland. . . . I really liked these people and so I called them and tried to get a bunch of them together for the fireworks."

Celeste threw an all-adult party on July 15, inviting Carolyn Stafford, Mike and Debora, and some other people from the trip. When it got dark, they showed slides of Peru in the backyard. Celeste had talked on the phone about it with both Debora and Mike.

On the last weekend of July, Celeste also threw a backyard barbecue and pool party, meant to be a trip reunion. Again, Mike and Debora came. Debora talked pleasantly enough to Celeste, who believed she had no idea that anything was going on.

There was no question that both Celeste and Mike wanted their fledgling affair to continue. The encouragement and affection—and, yes, the sexual fire—that Mike got from Celeste made his marriage seem all the more bleak in comparison. He had been waiting for seven months to tell Debora that their marriage wasn't working, that he truly wanted his freedom. He was desperate to be away from her, yet afraid of the scene he knew she would create.

Mike also worried about his children: what would become of them if he left Debora and moved out? But, he decided, they would be better off with a single parent, in a home where there was no arguing, than they were now. He would gladly be that custodial parent—if Debora would agree.

It was so hot that summer; the air was thick and still. When the wind blew, it was like a blast furnace, stirring up dirt devils in the dust. Gardens burst forth into bright flowers and the sunflowers bent under their own weight on ten-foot stalks. There were no flowers around 7517 Canterbury Court; Debora had never been interested in gardening. The trees that had been there when they moved in were enough. The kids enjoyed their pool, Mike went off to his office very early every morning and came home late, and Debora lay in bed reading.

Mike had vacillated for months, weighing his dread of another thirty or forty years with Debora against his almost equal dread of a "horrible divorce." They were not getting along, and they never would. It was as simple as that. Neither of them could heal unless they made a clean break and started to build separate lives.

Sometime in late July, Mike asked Debora for the second

time if she would give him a divorce. The result was a "terrible outburst," far worse than even he had expected. "It was . . . volatile behavior," he said, "screaming, a lot of profanity, hitting herself. It was awful."

Debora opposed the idea of a divorce, although she had no choice, really. She would not hear of their telling the children together, or of planning the best way to break the news to them. She was not going to let Mike walk away from the marriage looking like a man with a shred of decency; it was more important to punish him than to cushion the blow to their children. Just as she had done the first time, Debora told Tim, Lissa, and Kelly in her own way: a hysterical outburst designed to make the children detest their father. He had broken his promise to them, and he was leaving them all. Not surprisingly, Mike's older children hated him after that.

There was so much hate in that beautiful house on Canterbury Court. Debora hated Mike. He had come to detest her. Their children were carefully schooled to stand by their mother, the victim, and to revile their father.

But however much she hated him, Debora wanted to stay married to Mike—for many reasons, some probably too convoluted to understand. Possession was one, of course. Mike was *her* husband; she had viewed other women with suspicion long before he was guilty of infidelity. As the family of a highly respected, wealthy physician, she and the children had a place in society; without him, she feared losing that.

Perhaps most important to Debora was her dream that both Lissa and Kelly would be BOTARs (Belles of the American Royal). Kansas City has two "coming out" events, at which debutantes are introduced to society: one is the Jewel Ball, the other the American Royal, a horse and livestock show that lasts almost two weeks. There are several social activities during the celebration of the American Royal, but the BOTAR Ball is the most visible. About twenty young women are presented at the BOTAR Ball each year. They are the loveliest, most talented daughters of haute

Kansas City. Debora wanted Kelly and Lissa to join them. She wanted Tim to be a BOTAR escort.

If her children's home was broken, Debora was certain, they would lose their chance to move among the most sought-after young people in the area. *She* had never been a debutante—not in Peoria—nor a beauty queen. The kudos she received had all been for her superior intellect; she seemed, now, to be living through her "beautiful children," as she called them. She wanted them to move easily in the rarefied air of Kansas City society.

Most of all, Debora did not want to lose any more of her prestige and her self-esteem. Mike was a well-known and successful cardiologist and she was his wife. For all the bragging she had done about her intellectual brilliance, she was not a confident woman. A long time before, she had been the one who had money, far more money than Mike; now she was dependent upon him for everything. Quite simply, Debora had failed at everything from the practice of medicine to the most basic housekeeping. And now she was facing a failed marriage.

She buried herself in novels and books about bizarre crimes that summer, wasting her mind on escapist literature. She checked books out of the Johnson County Library and the Corinth Library in Prairie Village, usually eight or more at a time, and she bought numerous paperbacks. Her book selections were full of violence: *Blood Oath; Wedded to Crime: My Life in the Jewish Mafia; Amy Fisher: My Story; Blood Sister; Blood Games: a True Account of Family Murder; Bodies of Evidence; The Murder of Little Mary Phagan; Smoked: A True Story About the Kids Next Door; Final Justice*; and *Before He Wakes: a True Story of Money, Marriage, Sex and Murder*. Some of the books she chose were light novels—by Danielle Steel, for instance. Still, Debora seemed fixated on bloody murder—particularly within families—during the high summer of 1995.

There seemed no way to achieve a happy or even a civil ending to their marriage. Mike didn't move out; his children wanted him to stay, and he vacillated between desire and guilt. Debora moved to the guest bedroom on the lower level, which had its own private bath. That summer, she and Mike lived together in a wary, tight-lipped silence, as if in an armed camp.

There was another reason Mike didn't move out. Debora, who rarely had more than a glass of wine or a single high-ball, had suddenly begun to drink so heavily that he dared not leave the children with her at night. It was not unusual for her to drink a liter and a half of vodka or gin over a period of two days. Although there had been intervals when she was addicted to painkillers and sleeping pills, she had never been a heavy drinker. Now, with no practice and no hospital work to give her access to drugs, she was apparently filling the void with alcohol.

Debora's days took on a bizarre kind of order. Somehow, she drove her children to their lessons, their sports events, their friends' houses; then, once that was done, she closeted herself with a bottle of liquor and drank until she passed out. On some days she was too drunk to get out of bed. Once, Mike found her passed out on the basement floor. And her language was foul. Her remarkably high consumption of alcohol loosened her inhibitions so much that she made no effort whatsoever to watch what she said in front of Tim, Lissa, and Kelly.

Tim and Lissa wavered between begging Mike to stay and treating him with great hostility. They were angry at their mother, too, but their resentment was chiefly aimed at their dad. He had promised them that he would never leave, and now he was leaving. It did not matter to the children that his marriage had become unbearable, and he didn't even attempt to explain that to them. It did not matter that he would have taken them with him, gladly, if their mother had let him. Predictably, their behavior toward him deteriorated. They became defiant and repeated much of the language their mother used in her descriptions of him.

Kelly, only six, had always had a serenity that seemed to protect her from the storms erupting behind the stone façade of the wonderful house that was no longer a home. She clung to Boomer, the big Lab, or played outside with her friends. Lissa hovered nervously over her distraught mother, who was often sick with the "flu" and throwing up. And Tim was so angry, far too angry for a boy still six months from his fourteenth birthday.

No problems are absolutely insoluble; the challenge is always which solution will do the most good for the most people. The rancor that was thick in the house on Canterbury Court that summer kept the family at an impasse, and there seemed no way out. Mike had, at least for a time, an escape into his work, and occasionally with his lover. He was gone from home from early morning until early evening. Debora escaped into a bottle.

Tim and Lissa were highly intelligent children, and they quickly became the "parents," watching over Debora as she flung herself headlong into self-destruction. Although she claimed to love her children above everything else, she allowed her pain over the impending divorce to be an excuse to virtually ignore them.

Tim went off to camp, which left ten-year-old Lissa to handle things during the day at home. But she soon reached a point where she could not deal with her mother's behavior: One Friday afternoon in early August, Lissa couldn't get her mother to wake up. She was afraid that Debora was dead.

Sobbing, she called her father at the hospital about 4:30. "I asked to speak to her mother," Mike would recall, "but Debora apparently was unable to speak to me."

Mike headed for home at once, impatient in the Friday afternoon traffic. When he turned off Seventy-fifth onto Canterbury Court, he saw Lissa waiting anxiously at the edge of the cul-de-sac, watching for his car. She was very upset, and begged him to hurry to help Debora.

He followed her into the house. In the master bedroom,

he was shocked to find a scene of complete disarray. "Debora was completely nude except for a T-shirt or a kind of a chiffon top . . . lying face down," he remembered. "She was clearly drunk. There was a one-and-a-half-liter bottle of gin that was largely empty lying next to her."

Kelly was also home, of course; she, too, was sobbing. Neither of the little girls had been able to get their mother to respond. They weren't sure what was the matter with her; they had never seen her have the "flu" as badly as this.

On the way home, Mike had called his sister, Karen, who lived on the Missouri side of the state line, to tell her something was wrong and ask her to take the girls for the night. She had agreed instantly. With Debora alive and apparently well except for the fact that she was completely intoxicated, Mike scooped up his daughters and took them to their aunt's. It was now about six P.M.

Knowing that, at least, they were safe, he then hurried back to his house to see what he could do about Debora. He had told her—although he didn't know whether it registered—where he was going and asked her not to leave until he got back. "I really didn't expect her to go because I thought she'd be too drunk," he recalled.

But Debora wasn't in the master bedroom, and she didn't answer when he shouted her name. Worried, he looked in the garage and was grateful to see the Land Cruiser still there. At least, she wasn't out on the road someplace, a danger to herself and everyone else.

Filled with foreboding, Mike searched their huge house. On the lower level were a playroom, the bedroom Debora was using, an exercise room, a recreation room, and the room where he kept his wine collection. The kitchen, dining room, living room, music room, master bedroom, and den were on the main floor. A single staircase to the third floor went up from the foyer just inside the front door. The children's bedrooms and a computer room were up there, along with the children's bathroom.

It was an eerie search. Mike looked in closets, in crannies, behind shower curtains, his heart pounding. When he hadn't found his wife on the two lower levels, Mike went quietly up the carpeted stairs to the third floor. "I looked through every room in the house," he remembered. "I honestly expected to find her dead." He was afraid that Debora had hanged herself or cut her wrists. She could not have left the house on foot—the neighbors would have seen her—and she had been half-naked an hour and a half before. But she was nowhere to be found.

Mike didn't know whether he should call the police. If Debora had somehow gotten out of the house and was wandering around, the police would probably find her. If she was sleeping off her drunkenness someplace close, he didn't want to make things any worse than they already were. He didn't want to embarrass her. It had grown dark now, and he didn't know where to look for her next.

Mike paced through the huge house and searched the yard. Tired to the bone, he knew he couldn't sleep. As bad as things had become between them, he didn't want Debora to hurt herself or be hurt by someone else. He didn't want her humiliated. She was the mother of his children, and they had suffered enough already.

The phone rang and Mike leaped to answer it. It was Celeste. "I'm so glad you called," he said gratefully. He told her what had happened, and she was as mystified as he. The profound change, in a matter of weeks, from the witty woman who had kept everyone on the Peru trip laughing uproariously to this drunken harridan was more than Celeste could visualize. She realized what Mike had been living through, but she felt a little guilty: knowing Mike had asked for a divorce, she wondered if she was the cause of Debora's drunken disappearance.

After he hung up the phone, Mike tried to think where Debora might have gone. She had no friends. She had never seemed to need them. There were women she used to play tennis with, some mothers she knew casually from Pembroke Hill School, people she had met on their recent trip. But she had no one remotely like a confidante, no one she could call to pick her up to get her away from the house, no neighbor she might conceivably go to to spend the night with. Mike had no idea where she was. He circled the yard again, checked the shed where they kept the lawnmower and yard tools, looked inside the cars in the garage, and still found no sign of her.

With no place else to look, Mike lay down, although he knew he couldn't sleep. He jumped when the phone rang at eleven P.M. "Hello?"

"It's me. . . ." It was Debora. She didn't sound drunk.

"Where are you?"

"As if you cared."

"Debora," Mike said evenly, "tell me where you are and I'll come and get you."

"I'm at a friend's house."

"Whose house?"

"It doesn't matter. Someplace where I can think."

Before Mike could respond, the line went dead. It rang again immediately. It was Debora. "We have to talk," she said. "We never talk, Mike. How can we get a divorce if we never talk about it?"

"Where *are* you?"

"That's for me to know and you to find out."

She hung up on him again, only to call back the moment Mike set down the phone. He was relieved, but annoyed. She was someplace safe, apparently. She had a phone at her disposal. And she sounded completely sober, if argumentative.

"Debora," he said wearily, "why don't you come home, get some sleep, and we'll talk tomorrow?"

"What's the point? I don't trust you."

"Debora—"

The phone went dead again. Debora couldn't seem to make up her mind whether she was angry at him or wanted him to call off the divorce. She was talking in circles. And she seemed to be enjoying his concern, enjoying her power to cut him off.

The phone shrilled again, for the sixth or seventh time. Mike picked it up without saying anything.

"Mike, you think you have secrets, but you don't have any secrets. You're so stupid and transparent. I know everything about you—"

This time, Mike hung up the phone. And then he unplugged it. He was exhausted and he needed to get at least a few hours' sleep. Wherever Debora was, she was all right. In the blessed silence, he fell asleep almost immediately.

He woke at 5:30 and searched once more for Debora, thinking she might have come home. But she wasn't there. Earlier in the week, Mike had arranged to go birdwatching with a group of friends—including Celeste—and then have breakfast. He knew the children were all being cared for, and he knew that Debora had found someplace to stay the night. He needed to be with happy people, even if just for a little while.

He was home by nine. "Debora was there. She was sitting back in the dark den on the main floor—on the couch." Coming into the dim room from the bright sunshine, he saw only her outline.

"Where have you been?"

"I have been out wandering in the streets of Prairie Village," she said quietly, "hoping that someone would run over me with a car and kill me. That would solve everybody's problem, wouldn't it?"

"You know that's not true," Mike said. "I care about you; the kids care about you. Where did you really spend last night?"

She wouldn't tell him.

Mike realized he was seeing only a heightened version of her usual histrionics; she was like a child threatening a parent that she will do something she has no intention of doing. It would be weeks before she would finally admit to him that she had never left the house at all that Friday night. "She told me that all that time she had been hiding under the bed—or behind the bed—in the basement bedroom," Mike said. "There are two phones in the bar area. One is the children's line and one is our regular line. So she could easily have called from the children's line to our main phone number."

Mike had not thought to look *under* the beds when he searched for Debora; he had been so convinced that he would find her hanging, or bleeding, that he had been racing around the house to find her in time to cut her down or stop the flow of blood. He was chagrined when he finally learned that she had been playing a spooky game of hide-and-seek with him. He had to wonder if Debora had been as intoxicated as she seemed when he had rushed home from the hospital after Lissa's frantic call. She appeared to have the ability to seem passed-out drunk and then quite coherent within a very short time.

What Mike didn't realize until much later was that Debora had been listening in on Celeste's call that night. She had never trusted Celeste, and now her suspicions about Mike and Celeste had been confirmed.

Later, Debora would recall that she had done a good job taking care of Tim, Lissa, and Kelly that summer in spite of her drinking. "I always drove them where they needed to go," she explained. "I was home with them." Asked if she didn't feel that she had taken chances, driving them and their friends when she was intoxicated, she shrugged. "Nothing bad happened. If it had, it would have been better than what happened later."

Chapter 9

A few weeks after the late-July pool party at the Walkers', Debora and Mike hosted a similar party. Celeste would remember being shocked at the chances Mike now took in his own home, after they had always been so discreet. She was terrified that Debora might see him touch her. "He kissed me in the basement of their home. She could have seen us," Celeste said. "And, at our pool a week later, he put his arm around me when Lissa and Kelly were playing on the other side. It was as if he didn't care if Debora knew."

And perhaps he didn't care, anymore. Debora's overnight disappearance had terrified their little girls and left Mike frightened and enraged. Maybe he was angry enough to want to punish her. Or perhaps he felt that Debora would agree to a divorce if she understood he was in love with another woman. If that was his motive in being openly affectionate toward Celeste, it didn't work.

Debora was angry, too. She knew Mike was having an affair and she had begun to feel completely displaced, totally adrift. "He wanted the house," Debora said later. "He wanted to live in that beautiful house, and he wanted the children and me to live in a smaller, cheaper house. He just wanted to be rid of us. I couldn't have that."

"That wasn't even remotely true," Mike said when the accusation was relayed to him.

On Friday, August 11, Mike arrived home between six and 6:30. The rest of his family had already eaten, but Debora said she had saved a chicken salad sandwich in the refrigerator for him. He stood in the kitchen and talked to her while he ate it. Still worried about the children, he had not yet moved out. They continued to live in a stand-off.

The sandwich tasted slightly odd, and Mike commented to Debora that it was "a little bitter."

"We all had them—and nobody else's tasted funny," she said.

Maybe it was because the sandwich was cold, or perhaps it had taken on a taste from something else in the refrigerator. It was not so bitter that Mike stopped eating; the slightly off taste was very subtle. He was hungry and he ate the whole thing.

After dinner, he changed his clothes and he and Debora
went to the Ward Parkway Shopping Center, where they
both bought running shoes; then they picked up the children from their activities. Debora, who had said she was
going to start getting back in shape, chose not to jog that
night. Mike went for his usual run, but he didn't seem to
have any stamina. "When I got home that night, I felt sick,"
he would remember. "I was nauseated. Initially, I thought it
was probably from overexerting myself when I wasn't in ter-
rific shape. But shortly after that, I started vomiting. I
developed abdominal pain, diarrhea."

What he was suffering from felt like a twenty-four-hour
virus; the nausea and vomiting were "bothersome but not
terribly severe." He was on call that weekend at North
Kansas City Hospital, and he got up the next morning and
went to work. In fact, he worked all weekend, although the
nausea continued. "I remember I had to leave patients'
rooms several times—and I left the heart catheterization
laboratory because I was suddenly sick again—but I still
managed to work."

His illness lasted three or four days but he continued to
work. "I improved, but I still didn't feel great." Besides the
nausea and diarrhea, Mike had abdominal pain—not
cramping, but a "burning sensation."

Mike was concerned enough that he talked to a gas-
troenterologist. He had been back from Peru for about five
weeks and he wondered if he had contracted some tropical
disease. They decided to wait to see if his symptoms would
ease of their own accord, and Mike did feel better by the
end of the week.

"I saw him on Thursday," Celeste would recall. "We met
up near my house for ten minutes and I could see that he
was better—his vigor was back."

But later on Thursday night, Mike's symptoms returned,
with a vengeance. He became extremely ill, extremely fast.
The vomiting was "torrential," twenty or thirty episodes over
a few hours. And the diarrhea was worse than anything he

had experienced in Peru. "It was truly a miserable illness—it went on all night. I got up in the morning to try to get ready for work. And I was on my hands and knees vomiting in the shower."

Realizing that he would not be able to work that day—Friday, August 18—Mike called one of his partners to explain. Then he phoned his personal physician, Nick Szilagye, and talked to him. As a doctor himself, Mike knew he was severely dehydrated; after he described his symptoms, Szilagye recommended that he be admitted to the hospital that morning. Mike drove himself to the hospital, passing Celeste's house on the way. She got in the car and talked to him for a very short time: "He was throwing up when he tried to talk."

Mike spent a week in the hospital, his condition verging on critical. He spiked fevers frequently—101 to 102 degrees. To his fellow doctors' concern, he developed sepsis, an overwhelming infection caused by bacteria that invade the bloodstream, carrying an original infection to other areas of the body. Sometimes it is not initially apparent which organs the sepsis is affecting.

One day while he was hospitalized, Mike tried to take a shower; he was suddenly gripped with "shaking rigors," violent shivering. "I could not control it," he said, "and my back and legs hurt; it was almost like tetany [violent muscle spasms and convulsions]."

Mike's fever was 104.4 degrees. His blood pressure dropped alarmingly. His systolic pressure, the top number in blood pressure readings, was 65 to 70; the normal range is from 110 to 150. The diastolic reading when his heart was at rest was not detectable. He knew that he could die. "I was moved to the intermediate care unit and a central line was inserted into my subclavian vein, underneath the collarbone. It is used to give large amounts of fluids to critically ill patients."

Mike's blood was cultured for bacteria. *Streptococcus viridans* bacteria grew out of the cultures. A strep infection can cause fever and many of the other symptoms Mike suffered, but his doctors kept checking to be sure they had isolated every possibility. He endured numerous diagnostic tests: a flexible sigmoidoscopy, a colonoscopy, an upper GI endoscopy. His whole digestive system and his entire colon were checked. With the assaults on his lower colon from the diarrhea, a break in the lining could very well have let strep bacteria leak through. But, his physicians wondered, what might have started the gastrointestinal symptoms in the first place?

Celeste was afraid for Mike, so worried that she took a chance and visited him in the hospital. "But I didn't go alone; I got Carolyn to go with me, and other people we knew. I never saw Debora there—but I guess she found out I had gone to see him."

Gradually, Mike got better. He was released on August 25, and went home, actually hungry for the first time in a week. He even felt well enough to eat a spaghetti dinner that Debora brought him. But within three or four hours, he became "horrendously sick" again, with the same torrential vomiting and diarrhea. He was back in North Kansas City Hospital by eleven that night. Whether there was any reason behind the pattern or not, he noted that he had become desperately ill approximately every seven days—on a Friday, a Thursday, and then another Friday.

Whatever Mike had, diagnosing it was not easy. He was far too ill to be suffering from simple influenza. And cultures showed that the *Strep viridans* was no longer present. "That was curious to us all," he said later. Any number of doctors at the hospital where he himself practiced had been called in for consultations. Here was a young man, just forty, who had been in the best of health and now could barely exist outside a hospital. He was losing a tremendous amount of weight, and he was wretchedly sick.

One of the specialists called in was Dr. Beth Henry, an expert in infectious diseases. Good diagnosticians weigh lab tests and the patient's symptoms against what has been going on in his life, and Dr. Henry wondered what Mike had done in the month or so before his sudden illness that was different from his usual habits.

The obvious answer was the trip to Peru, where he might well have been exposed to disease, impure water, and insects. Mike had swum in the Amazon River and eaten exotic food that might have been prepared under less than sanitary conditions. Oddly, not one of the forty other people on the trip had been ill since their return. *Their* travelers' diarrhea had been unpleasant but had not lasted more than forty-eight hours. Mike had suffered the same symptoms as they—while they were all in Peru. Furthermore, he had been home in Kansas City for more than a month, feeling perfectly well. What was it, then, that made him so sick now?

Dr. Henry ultimately settled on two possible diagnoses for Mike's fever, intractable vomiting, and diarrhea: typhoid fever or a disease called tropical sprue (also known as gluten-sensitive enteropathy). But she was still puzzled because his symptoms didn't fit neatly within the parameters of either.

Neither typhoid nor sprue is necessarily fatal, although each *could* be if the patient remained dehydrated, with his electrolytes out of balance. The indwelling line in Mike's subclavian vein was working to rehydrate him with larger amounts of fluid than he could manage to keep down because of his persistent nausea. He received a twenty-one-day course of antibiotics that would take care of typhoid fever—if, indeed, that was what he had. And he was put on a gluten-free diet.

Meanwhile, Debora was also having a difficult time during the latter part of August. Not only was her husband ill with some mysterious malady, but her mother had phoned from El Paso, the Joneses' home base between trips around the country, to tell her daughter that she had been diagnosed with breast cancer. Her doctors had recommended a mastectomy. As a specialist in oncology, Debora was able to evaluate her mother's condition, and she assured Joan that her chances were good for long-term survival.

"I talked to Deb on the phone many times," Joan recalled. "And she talked to my doctor several times. Everything seemed normal in Kansas." Debora had told her parents that Mike was sick, but they evidently didn't know *how* sick; they hadn't seen him, and they weren't very concerned anyway. "We knew Farrar was sick," Joan said, "but were not surprised because he will eat anything no matter how gross, if he thinks it is 'native.' He is also a terrible 'boob' when he is ill, although he has absolutely no empathy for a patient's pain."

It was clear that Debora's parents—at least her mother— had no love for Mike. Joan had attributed to Mike the very uncaring response to patients that he had seen in Debora. But Debora knew that Mike was terribly ill; she had seen him go downhill rapidly. Perhaps, wanting to spare her mother worry, she avoided burdening her with the gravity of his condition. After all, Joan Jones was about to undergo surgery herself.

Debora's mother later said she was completely unaware that Mike was really sick that summer. She felt that he was putting on a show for sympathy, being a "boob" as usual.

By the end of August, Mike was skin and bones. Celeste was so frightened for him that she went to the hospital alone to visit, and seeing him frightened her more. She was a nurse and she had seen other patients near death. There was no longer any secret that they were having an affair. She loved him and she wanted him well. Whatever it took, she would do.

Debora told him he needed to be in his own home; he was too weak to take care of himself outside the hospital. Mike stayed at North Kansas City Hospital for five days this time. He was released on August 30. And, too debilitated to talk about separation or divorce, he went home.

Back in the Canterbury Court house, Debora was

solicitous and kind to him. She carried his meals to him so that he wouldn't have to come to the table.

On September 4, Labor Day, Mike had been home for five or six days from his second hospitalization in two weeks. He felt better—but weak—and he was sitting in their downstairs recreation room watching the Kansas City Chiefs game on the big-screen television set. Debora brought him a plate of ham and beans and cornbread, and he ate while he watched the game, appreciative of her thoughtfulness.

But later that evening, Mike felt the unmistakable, all too familiar symptoms—vomiting, diarrhea, and a terrible burning stomach pain. He had to be rushed back to the hospital. And this time he began to wonder if he was going to die from whatever it was he had. He couldn't work; he couldn't, apparently, survive outside the hospital.

Still in the hospital on September 9, Mike got a phone call from Lissa. She was very upset and crying, and from what she said, he knew that Debora was drinking again—so much that Tim and Lissa were frightened. Gathering all his strength, he asked Lissa to put Tim on the phone. "I told him to hide all the alcohol in the house, and to make sure that his mother was okay," Mike said. "I asked him to see that the girls got up to bed."

Tim promised to do as his father asked. And Mike lay back on his pillow, worrying about how he could make sure his children were safe. His sister Karen knew that Debora was drinking too much, but he had not told his parents. His mother had enough to worry about: both of *her* parents were terminally ill. He knew he would have to act, but he was just too sick to start making calls. He would have to count on Tim to take care of things at home. Tim loved his mother and his little sisters. He would have to be the man of the house on this night. In the morning, if things were no better, Mike would call Karen and his parents and ask them to take care of his children until he could get home.

Sweat beaded on Mike's forehead from the effort of talking to Tim and Lissa. He had lost thirty pounds, a fifth of his normal weight. What would become of his children if he didn't get better? He couldn't bear to think of that.

At home, Tim followed his father's orders, gathering up large bottles of gin and vodka and hiding them outside the house. His mother had passed out again, and his little sisters were frightened and tearful. He put them to bed and tried to reassure them, but he knew he couldn't very well hide *all* the alcohol; his father had hundreds of bottles of wine. And his mother knew where they were. She didn't like wine very much, but she might drink it when she couldn't find anything else.

Chapter 10

Celeste Walker had lived for a half dozen years with a man incapable of much more than mere survival, a man who went to work without enthusiasm and came home without joy. When she fell in love with Mike and began her first affair, she was incredibly vulnerable and naive. She saw a happy ending though common sense should have told her that there is no such thing as an affair that hurts no one.

John Walker marked his forty-fifth birthday in August 1995. One of his presents was a new bicycle. He showed as much enthusiasm as he could muster, but the truth was that his depression had become constant. His inner pain was almost palpable, obvious to everyone he worked and lived with. Celeste had tried for years to draw him out of his black funks, but nothing worked.

Now, Mike was ill and, she felt, in danger. He had told her how much he loved her, how much he needed her. "He said I was the love of his life," Celeste remembered. He was just out of the hospital for the second time and she was afraid he was going to die. When she saw him she barely recognized him: he was so thin and his eyes were so hollow looking. He *did* need her—and John quite obviously didn't. He had been telling her for years that he didn't need her, that he planned to leave her just as soon as the boys were well on their way in life.

That August, Celeste decided to tell John that she wanted a divorce and that they should separate. It was not a new idea; one or the other of them had brought it up often in the last few years. Celeste believed—or had convinced herself—that her being with John would not make him less depressed. In fact, he might be happier if they made the break now rather than delaying the inevitable.

John seemed to take her decision fairly well. He even consulted a divorce attorney, although Celeste would not know that until later, when she saw the lawyer's bill. She filed for divorce in late August, citing incompatibility.

John rented a house not far from the family home and began to move into it on Labor Day. Coincidentally, the house was owned by Mike Montgomery, one of Mike Farrar's partners. Dr. Montgomery was visiting Mike in the hospital when Celeste dropped by. She mentioned that she was getting a divorce and that her husband was looking for a nice small house to rent. Montgomery suggested his house, and John had looked at it and rented it on the spot.

A number of John's friends offered to help him move, but he insisted that he could manage by himself. He had made four trips with clothes to the new place, but most of his belongings were still at the house where Celeste and the boys would continue living.

"It was really tough for him," Celeste recalled. "He was *crying* as he went back and forth, back and forth. I offered to help. And then I said, 'Don't *do* this.'"

They had been married for sixteen years. There was no hurry for John to move out; Celeste begged him to take his time, to accept her help and the help of his friends. "He came back home on Labor Day," she recalled. And, perhaps to get through the memory, she used a term from psychiatric nursing. "He collapsed—he decompensated right in front of me. And I said, 'Don't do this, John . . . I know someone who can do the moving for you. You can have it done. Quit right now. Go on your fishing trip next week with your guys—and we'll do it while you're gone.'"

Celeste wanted to make things as easy for John as possible. But even as she tried to explain that he didn't have to do the physical work of moving out, he kept saying, "I can't do this. . . . I can't do this," and sobbing uncontrollably. "What I assumed he meant was that he couldn't move his things," Celeste said. "Later, I realized he meant he couldn't go on. He couldn't separate. He couldn't have a life without me."

John went to bed at four o'clock that afternoon. He woke at seven, watched television with Brett, ate a little bit of the dinner Celeste cooked, and then went back to bed. That wasn't unusual for him. For months, he had gone to work, watched TV, and gone to bed early. Lately, he had been in the habit of getting up early to ride his bike before he went to work, but on the morning of September 5, he didn't do that.

"I never saw him that morning," Celeste said quietly. "I jumped up and went upstairs to wake the boys, and when I came downstairs, John had left for work. He never said good-bye. He never said good morning to the boys. Nothing."

Celeste went about her usual weekday chores. She fed the boys, took care of her house, and then drove Brett to soccer practice. She and Dan did errands until it was time to pick Brett up.

She expected to see John at home after he finished work as usual. Their separation was in an embryonic stage; technically they still lived together, and John had no pots and pans or groceries yet. But by 6:30, he wasn't home, and he wasn't at work at Shawnee Mission Hospital, although Celeste learned his staff there had had a meeting that kept him a little later than usual. He wasn't at the golf course, and he wasn't at any of the friends' homes she called.

Out of ideas, Celeste called Janie, one of her best friends. "Maybe he's over at his new place," she said. "Maybe he's just reading the paper over there—having some quiet time alone. I think he has a phone there, but I don't know the number. I'll go over and check."

There was a long pause and then Janie said, "My dad killed himself. Don't you go over there alone. I have a terrible feeling."

Janie lived near the house John had rented. When Celeste got there, she was already standing in the driveway. They knocked and got no response. They tried the door; it was locked. They worked their way around the house, trying doors and windows, but they were all locked.

"John had taken me for a tour of the house a few days before," Celeste said, "so I knew about this letter-drop thing into the garage. I opened that and I could see a light in there. There were no windows in the garage so it was completely dark, except for this light. I kept staring at it—and my brain just wasn't computing. It wouldn't let me identify what I was seeing. It didn't make sense to me. *Finally*, I could *see* what I was seeing."

Celeste's subconscious mind had tried to keep her from recognizing what she was looking at. Her eyes saw the faded blue, pink, and tan checks of John's shirt, but her mind would not process that information. Finally, she realized that the little light she saw was the dome light of her husband's car. His head was thrown back and the light was shining down on his face.

He wasn't moving at all.

Frantic, Celeste and Janie raced around to the back, where the garage door lifted up, but it was locked tight. Celeste called 911 on her cell phone, screaming for help. Neither woman would remember exactly how they got into the garage, but somehow they did. "Janie practically wrecked the door," Celeste said, "but she got it up so we could get in."

Janie managed to drag John from his car onto the garage floor; there, three women fought to save his life: Celeste, Janie, and a doctor who lived next door. The doctor, who was

hugely pregnant, got down on the floor and tried to breathe
air into his lungs, but her own lungs were so compromised by
her pregnancy that she couldn't even manage to lift his
chest. Celeste pushed her out of the way and placed her own
mouth over her husband's. She willed him to live, and took
heart when she saw that his chest *did* rise and fall.

"The reason we all fought so hard was because we
thought there was time—he was still so warm," Celeste
would remember. They hadn't stopped to think that it was
105 degrees outside. It wasn't life that kept John warm, it
was the weather. "He had been dead a long time," Celeste
recalled sadly. "He had left work at four o'clock and it was
seven-thirty when we found him."

Although ultimately she had to accept that John was
beyond saving when she found him, Celeste refused to give
up. She insisted that he be admitted to the ER at Shawnee
Mission Medical Center, the hospital where he had administered anesthesia to hundreds of patients, where only that
morning he had helped to save lives. Gently, the staff there
told her that they could not admit a patient who had been
dead for hours—not even one of their own.

Sergeant Gary Hines of the Mission police had responded to
the 911 call. Most suicides in garages are by carbon monoxide poisoning. But Dr. John Walker was a skilled
anesthesiologist. When Hines arrived, he saw that the dead
man had IV tubing in his left arm that was attached to two
syringes. There was also a vial of some kind of medicine and
a sterile-water solution. The victim's shirt had been ripped
open down the front and his tan trousers unzipped and
pulled down a little. There were a few drops of blood on his
thighs and some staining on the pants themselves.

That wasn't suspicious; as the three women had prepared
to administer CPR, they would have torn and pulled at his
clothing and ripped the IV needles from his hand, spilling
the small amount of blood there. He would not have bled

after death. The police presumed that Dr. Walker would have known exactly how much of certain drugs it would take to kill him. Even so, an autopsy was ordered to determine the exact manner of his death.

There was one fact that only Celeste knew. John had carried a syringe of fentanyl with him always. She had found syringes in his jacket pockets and in his car. "It was like his ace in the hole, if things got too bad," she said. "I don't think he was abusing it; I think he just kept it close as his safety valve."

Fentanyl is a powerful painkiller, an opioid drug often used by anesthesiologists, but almost always in conjunction with assisted breathing because it tends to depress respiration. The speed with which it is introduced into the body is very important. Cases of sudden death from heart palpitations or tachycardia (racing heart), lack of oxygen, or severe electrolyte disturbance are not uncommon at doses of fentanyl over 25 milligrams. Fentanyl is also highly addictive. Mike was in the hospital when John Walker died, being treated for the fourth episode of the mysterious ailment that seemed to be bringing him closer and closer to death. Celeste couldn't bring herself to call and tell him about John. "When I was back home and I got myself together a little, I called Carolyn and asked her to tell Mike. She did. He called me and he was very sympathetic, very comforting. He kept telling me that it wasn't my fault. . . . But when Mike told Deb that John had killed himself, she got hysterical and started drinking. She called his sister Karen and told her, 'Celeste killed John.' She told her children that, too."

Later, a nurse who had been on the operating room team with John Walker the day he died remarked on his demeanor. "He was so sad that day, so depressed, that you could feel it. It was catching. I could barely bring myself to stand close to him and feel that much pain."

Chapter 11

One of Celeste Walker's relatives would insist that she heard John talking on the phone to Debora a day or two before Celeste found him dead in the garage of his rented house. If Debora had, in fact, told him of the affair between her husband and his wife, it would have been a powerful incentive for him to check out of his bleak life, particularly after Celeste chose that day or the next to ask him for a divorce. Debora would deny that any such conversation took place; Celeste believed that it did, that Debora was so jealous that she would have done anything to get back at her and Mike. Anyone who knew John at all well would have known how fragile he was. Debora had known him since medical school. To tell him about the affair, bluntly and in the vulgar terms she used to tell her own children, would have been an unbelievably cruel thing to do.

It was a ghastly time. John's mother, Kathryn Walker,* had left for a long-awaited trip to France the day he killed himself. She had no sooner landed in Paris than she was greeted with the news that her son was dead, an apparent suicide. She never left the airport, but caught the next plane back to the United States.

Kathryn Walker could not accept that her son had killed himself, even though other family members and his friends had said he was depressed. She admitted that John was "heartsick" about his divorce. "He did not realize anything until she filed," Kathryn would claim. "He said he made a terrible mistake by not going to Peru." She said that he had been thinking about the future. He was buying a new car and furniture. He had planned to go to Canada with six friends. Those, his mother insisted, were not the plans of a would-be suicide. Kathryn wanted to believe her son's death was an accident. Even murder would have been easier for her to accept—although she named no suspects.

Gossips said that Celeste wore too much makeup at John's funeral services, that her clothes were inappropriate, and that the first thing she said when she got home afterward was "Who's going to make the margaritas?" She was too merry a widow. "She laughed at his funeral," one woman said disapprovingly. "She acted as though she was at a cocktail party." But no one who knew Celeste would have been surprised by her behavior. She had long since learned to conceal her pain with laughter.

Gossips also said that Celeste had John's car detailed the day after his death, then billed his office for it. Some mean-spirited people would have pilloried her in the town square if they could have. They did not take into account the enormity of her horror when she looked through that mail slot into the garage. They did not know her well enough to know how she responded to an emotional blow. Celeste moved through the days following her discovery of John's body like an automaton. She had wanted to be free of her sad marriage—but not like this.

She had always expected that she and John would remain part of each other's lives, that they would consult on raising their two sons. The trouble with her marriage had never been that she didn't care about John. She *did* care, but she had exhausted every way she could think of to make him happy. Anyone who had seen her hysterically pleading with the ER staff at Shawnee Mission Medical Center to treat John, to save him—even though he had been dead for hours—could testify that she had wanted him to live.

But still there were rumors that Celeste had either killed her husband or deliberately driven him to suicide. "She got millions of dollars in insurance, you know," the rumor mongers said, hugely inflating the actual amount.

"The police investigated me," Celeste would admit frankly. "They questioned me, and they cleared me."

Question her they did—not once but several times. They asked her to account for every moment of September 5. She remembered most of the day well, but she could not remember whether she had bought her younger son ice cream or taken him to a video arcade while they waited for Brett to finish soccer practice. That day had been endless, full of sadness, worry, anxiety—and, finally, panic.

Celeste was not immediately eliminated as a suspect in her husband's sudden death. It took two autopsies to explain the cause of his death—precisely *because* he was an anesthesiologist, who knew the most effective way to stop his heart instantly.

Dr. Bonita J. Peterson performed the first autopsy, on the morning of September 6, 1995, approximately fifteen hours after John's death. She noted that Dr. Walker had an intravenous line in his left hand, attached to tubing with two interconnected syringes. "One was labeled as being Pentothal. An empty vial labeled pancuronium bromide (Pavulon) was also found in the car."

Dr. Peterson found two anatomic conditions: pulmonary congestion and edema; and mild coronary and aortic arteriosclerosis. The former was the immediate result of John's manner of death; the latter is common to almost all humans over the age of forty. It is the buildup of plaque—fat deposits—along arterial walls.

Dr. Peterson was not entirely sure of just how Dr. Walker had died. As she wrote in her report, her final comment was, "This is the puzzling case of a 45-year-old white man, an anesthesiologist who was found dead, hooked up to IV tubing connected to a Pentothal syringe. Sterile water and pancuronium were also present at the scene. Exhaustive toxicological examination failed to reveal Pentothal in the urine or blood, although Pentothal *was* present in the syringe. Examination for fentanyl was negative and potassium injection was also excluded. The specimens were taken by me personally to the toxicology laboratory on the day of collection . . . therefore, a mix-up of specimens is not a logical possibility. The death is an obvious suicide from the circumstances and sodium pentothal is still the most likely cause, even though, for unknown reasons, it cannot be confirmed in the body fluids."

John Walker had no drugs or alcohol in his system. He may have carried a syringe of fentanyl with him as security in case he was gripped by such overwhelming depression that he needed it. But he was not addicted to it; fentanyl was not present in his blood.

For experts, the disturbing finding of the first postmortem examination and the toxicology screen was that Walker, a skilled anesthesiologist, seemed to have carried out an unnecessarily agonizing suicide by using the intravenous fluids in the wrong sequence. Pancuronium, or Pavulon, paralyzes the muscles, so the patient cannot move—not even to breathe. Pentothal is truth serum; it brings on unconsciousness. Anesthesiologists use pancuronium to immobilize patients during surgery; with a mechanical ventilator, they then "breathe" for the patient. Pancuronium's effect lasts longer than the effect of pentothal. Why would Walker deliberately paralyze his lungs when he knew he would awaken from the pentothal and be aware that he was suffocating?

Could this mean that someone else had administered the two drugs, attempting to make murder look like suicide? That seemed very doubtful. No one would calmly submit to such a procedure, and there were no bruises, no signs of struggle at all, on John's body, save that the buttons had been ripped from his plaid shirt. That certainly had happened when his wife and the physician neighbor attempted CPR.

A second postmortem evaluation was ordered; it might be

weeks—or even months—before the questions about Walker's death were answered definitively. Until then, his widow was the subject of continuing gossip.

Dr. John Walker was dead; Dr. Michael Farrar had come very close to death, and was not out of the woods yet. Although he was released from North Kansas City Hospital on September 11, 1995, it was only with the proviso that he would have an intravenous-feeding setup at home.

Dr. Beth Henry, weighing all the known factors in Mike's curious illness, had come up with a best guess—that her patient had gluten-sensitive enteropathy. Every time he ate outside the hospital, he had to be readmitted with the same symptoms. "He was eventually placed on a very restricted gluten-free diet and also supplemented with IV nutrition."

For some reason, his doctors decided, Mike could not eat anything containing grain or certain other food products. "They put in a pik line," he would explain, "which is a special type of IV that went into the antecubital vein [the vein on the inner side of the arm, at the elbow] in order to give me intravenous feeding." Using this semipermanent line, Debora could attach the intravenous-feeding tube easily. An IV bag on a stand would hold a milklike substance; fat was added to it, along with multivitamins, which had to be injected directly into the bag. Debora kept the vials of vitamins in the rec room refrigerator downstairs.

Mike was a smart doctor. He had made the connection that he became ill every time he went home. He was not yet sure why. But it could have been the stress associated with being around Debora that made his symptoms flare. It could also have been that he was used to eating a blander diet in the hospital than he got at home.

Celeste and her friend Carolyn Stafford had a more sinister explanation: "They told me they were convinced that Debora was poisoning me." Mike scoffed at the idea. "I just couldn't imagine that she would do such a thing."

Celeste was suspicious enough to write down the date of every relapse and note every symptom. She would not be convinced that his illness was natural or accidental. But Mike continued to deny the possibility. He and Debora had certainly had their problems, but they weren't living in a soap opera or a mystery novel. He suspected that his doctors would probably commit him if he mentioned his friends' suspicions about poison. He said nothing.

Mike had weighed only 125 pounds—about as much as Tim—when he left the hospital on September 11, but he began to gain weight from the intravenous feeding. He had been ill, he was getting stronger, and he hoped to be able to go back to work soon. Mike had a new understanding of what some of his patients had undergone, and of the hopelessness of constant illness. If he ever got well enough to practice again, he knew he would be a better doctor—one with considerable empathy.

Although Debora was taking care of him, Mike knew that it was only a matter of time until he could move out and start divorce proceedings. He told her that he had not changed his mind about that.

Debora was still drinking a great deal and it was not unusual for her to pass out at night. And she was saying very disturbing things to Mike. "She said she wanted to die— that she couldn't live without me. That she wanted to commit suicide. She wanted somebody to kill her. And then she'd say she wanted me dead."

Mike had been home from his last hospital stay for about two weeks when his concern for Debora's state of mind drove him to another search of their home. He wanted to make sure that she didn't have something that she could take to commit suicide, some medication that she was hiding.

Tim, Lissa, and Kelly were back in school by September 24, the day Mike searched the house and found Debora's purse in the guest bedroom in the basement where she was sleeping. He didn't believe in invading someone else's privacy, but he was afraid of what Debora might do next. If she got out of control, *he* certainly wouldn't be able to stop her physically. Debora would never tell him how much she weighed, but he suspected that she now outweighed him by about fifty pounds.

When Mike opened the tote bag that Debora used as a purse, he found a collection more bizarre than he had envisioned in his wildest imagination.

There were around a dozen seed packets that were all the same. The picture on the packets showed some kind of luxuriant vine with multi-colored bronze and purplish leaves and bright-colored bristling berries or seeds. The leaves were somewhat like those of the marijuana plant. The packets were labeled "Castor Beans: (Ricinus commonis.)" They were the seeds of the castor-oil plant. Mike was more puzzled than anything else. What on earth was Debora doing with a purse full of seed packets? He had never seen her plant so much as a petunia.

In the tote bag was also a letter. It was in Debora's distinctive handwriting, and as Mike read it, the hair stood up on the back of his neck. He had read this very letter before, but then the text had been typed on a computer. "I left the house one day and when I walked out the front door," Mike remembered. "There was a letter sitting on the mailbox addressed to me. It said, 'Mike Farrar' on the envelope and those words were printed in pencil in what seemed to be a child's handwriting.

"And so I took the letter and read it and it was an anonymous letter from someone telling me that I should not divorce Debora, that she was a wonderful mother, hardworking for Pembroke Hill School, and that we had such a wonderful relationship."

The anonymous correspondent, who seemed to have been on the Peru trip, said that it would be devastating if he and Debora were to get divorced. Their children would be deprived of social activities in the future; the girls would never be BOTARs.

Recognizing the font they had on their computer, upstairs in the room next to Tim's, Mike had been suspicious. Who in his house had written this? One of the youngsters? Debora herself? He suspected Debora, because the phraseology and the arguments sounded like hers.

Now, in Debora's purse, he had found what appeared to be a "practice" letter in her handwriting. What a grotesquely childish thing for her to do. After years of arguments, did she really think that an anonymous letter was going to make him change his mind? But clearly she had worked hard over that anonymous letter, producing a handwritten draft and then typing it on the computer.

He looked at the seed packets again. And now he saw the warning: castor beans were extremely toxic and were not to be taken internally. He stared blankly at the seed packets. Was it possible that Debora, who insisted that she could make a better home for him if he would only stay, was thinking about landscaping? It seemed totally unlike her, but lately everything she did was unlike what she had done before, as if she were on a slowly revolving platform, showing a slightly new side of her self each time the mechanism moved. The only thing recognizable about Debora were her temper tantrums. Those she seemed unable to change.

Fishing deeper into the roomy bag, Mike came up with three empty vials of potassium chloride, along with three used syringes. Potassium chloride is a common substance— as common as salt (which it basically is). It can be both life-giving and life-threatening, depending on the dosage. It is given to people suffering from heat prostration or profuse vomiting, to reestablish electrolyte balance. But too much potassium can throw the heart into a fatal arrhythmia. When it is found in syringes, it is usually to be added to an IV line.

Mike's pik line hadn't worked very well. "It wouldn't run," he said, "so after three days, I asked my doctor to take it out and he did." But if Debora truly hated him enough, she could easily have killed him as he slept: all she had to do was inject the potassium chloride into the pik line. He would never have felt it. But she hadn't done that. As far as he knew, she had only kept the intravenous nutrients and the massive doses of vitamins flowing into his veins, just as his doctors had ordered.

With every reason now to be suspicious, Mike wondered if his wife had been injecting the potassium chloride into the nutrient bag at the same time she injected the multivitamins. She had always added the vitamins out of his sight, in the rec room. That would account for the three used potassium vials and syringes; she might have used them during the three days the pik line was in. But the potassium would have been too diluted in the bag to harm him.

Mike was feeling better; he was able to eat without vomiting now, and he was even gaining a little weight. Maybe he was imagining the worst. Maybe Debora hadn't meant the potassium chloride for him at all. She had been so abjectly miserable; maybe she meant to inject herself. She had said she wanted to die, had threatened to kill herself.

The castor beans were more of a mystery. Crumpled inside the tote-bag purse, Mike found a receipt from the Earl May Garden Center in Olathe, twenty minutes south of Prairie Village. The receipt, for several packets of seeds, was dated August 7, 1995.

Mike knew nothing at all about castor beans, but he planned to find out more. He put the seed packets, the used syringes, and the empty vials that had once held potassium chloride in a plastic bag and hid them in his closet.

Chapter 12

In the wake of John Walker's suicide, those who had been close to him tried to pull their lives into some kind of order. Celeste's sister, Jan Johnson,* flew to Kansas to help her.

During her visit, she had a very odd conversation with Mike. As Jan recalled later, Celeste took her to meet him at a park near her home. Jan did not approve of Celeste's affair with Mike, and she was prepared to dislike him. "I was against the whole thing," she said, "because it was based on dishonesty. There was no honor in it, and Celeste had told him the way I felt."

But Celeste believed in Mike. She had confided to Jan that he had told her she was "the love of his life," that he "loved her more than life itself."

Jan was dubious. "Maybe if he'd told you that after a year, I'd believe it," she said. "But, Celeste, he can't love you, he doesn't *know* you well enough to say that."

When they met in the park, Jan felt that Mike was trying to charm her. But she was not about to be charmed. And one thing that he said, an embarrassing gaffe, would stay with her forever. "He was telling us about this teenager named Jared* who had been on the Peru trip and how Jared's parents had divorced," Jan recalled. "And Mike said that Jared was willing to talk to Tim and let him know that life after divorce was okay—that Jared had been through this and survived. And then Mike said that he could ask Jared to talk to Celeste's boy Brett, too, about divorce, if she liked. And Celeste said, '*What?*' And then Mike said, 'Well, Brett *is* his name, isn't it?'"

Of course, what had shocked Jan and Celeste was that Mike had completely forgotten: Celeste's sons were not dealing with divorce—they were trying to cope with their father's suicide.

"Divorce?" Celeste asked, as Mike stared at her. "*Divorce?*"

"Oh, I'm so sorry," Mike said. "I wasn't thinking."

Jan believed that Mike had already forgotten that John was dead—that it was so unimportant to him, it had slipped his mind. When he apologized for his heedless suggestion, she didn't want to hear it. She wanted her sister away from Mike, even though Celeste was clearly infatuated with him.

But nothing Jan could say would dissuade Celeste. Mike needed her, and she needed him. They hoped to stay together with every force in the universe pulling them apart. They were trying to build a stable relationship on a crumbling foundation: John was dead, and Debora seemed to be going insane.

Mike was worried about the castor-bean packets he had found in Debora's purse. Finally, on Monday, September 25, he asked her why she had them.

"I'm going to plant them," she said.

"That's baloney, Deb. I don't believe that. You've never planted a seed in your life."

She turned away from him, dismissing the subject, but he wouldn't let it go. "Deb, what were you going to do with those seeds?"

"All right—if you have to know," she said. "I was going to use them to commit suicide."

Mike looked at his wife and wondered whether she was telling the truth. Things were getting so weird in their house; Debora was more out of control than he had ever seen her before. Nothing she did would really surprise him. But clearly they would never be able to get along; if either of them was to get back to normal, he knew he would have to leave the house.

Debora had told him over and over that she would not allow that, that she would kill herself first. And he was beginning to believe her. But it didn't have to be this way, he thought. They could separate and still take care of their children. And the kids loved Debora very much. He could not bear the thought of their losing their mother to suicide. He had seen the terrible anguish in Celeste's home after her husband took his life. Mike didn't want Tim, Lissa, and Kelly to suffer that way.

However, as the day progressed, Debora's behavior became *so* erratic, her drinking so heavy, that Mike realized he had to do something. He called the Menninger Clinic in Topeka, an hour's drive away, and asked about the steps involved in arranging for voluntary or involuntary commitment. If Debora didn't get some help to stop her downward spiral, he didn't know what would become of their family.

Throughout that Monday, the situation deteriorated rapidly. Debora was behaving like a madwoman. Mike finally, reluctantly, called the Prairie Village Police Department, told the operator that he had serious concerns about the mental health of his wife, and asked for help.

All working police officers will acknowledge that "mentally disturbed subject" is one of the most potentially dangerous calls that ever come over their radios. Next to it is "family beef." Police dread receiving these two calls because they have little information going in. Some mentally disturbed people are meek and noncombative; others are quite capable of killing the police who respond, and have no compunction about doing so. Family fights are almost as unpredictable.

Sergeant Wes Jordan of the Prairie Village Police Department was supervising patrol units in his sector during the evening shift on Monday night, and protocol for "mental" calls from the dispatcher dictated that a sergeant accompany the patrol units responding. The address given was 7517 Canterbury Court, not a neighborhood where police were called very often.

Jordan turned right off Seventy-fifth, following one of his men, Officer Kyle Shipps. It was 9:25 P.M. when they pulled up. A man stepped out of the impressive house as if he had been waiting for them. They learned that he was Dr. Michael Farrar. Two girls and a boy were in the entryway. "They were all huddled together there," Jordan recalled. "They were all shaken. There were a few tears also. [The man] was visibly shaken. He was upset about the whole situation."

The youngest child, a little blond girl about five or six, sobbed inconsolably while the older children tried to comfort her. This was the kind of call that good cops hate: seeing a family in such distress. It was the same whether they went to a hovel or a million-dollar house like this one.

Mike explained to the officers that he wanted to commit his wife and had made all the arrangements necessary for her admission to the Menninger Clinic. He told Sergeant Jordan and Officer Shipps that his wife had been threatening suicide and had been on a drinking binge for two or three days.

Standing there in the soaring entryway of the house, the two Prairie Village police officers exchanged glances, trying to figure out what to do. They had not seen the wife yet, but they had seen the frightened children. It was always worse when children had to observe a parent in trouble. Jordan's concern was about *where* the suicidal woman was. Was she about to come down the winding stairway with a gun or a knife? Or if she *was* suicidal, he didn't want her left alone for long.

"Where is she?" he asked Mike.

"She's in the back bedroom—down that hall," he directed.

The officers told Mike to stay with his weeping children in the entryway of the home while they checked on his wife. Then Jordan and Shipps walked toward the back bedroom, uncertain and a little anxious about what they would find.

Dr. Debora Green was there. The room was dimly lit but they could see that she was lying on her side, with her back to them, on top of the covers. Although she wore a T-shirt, it was pulled up and her underwear and buttocks were exposed. There was a strong odor of alcohol.

"Dr. Green? Dr. Green?" they said, and finally: *"Dr. Green!"* The woman on the bed rolled over and acknowledged their presence.

"I introduced myself," Jordan said. "She was aware that we were coming. I explained why we were there, what we were going to do while we were there."

"We told her we had responded to a complaint by her husband that apparently some comments had been made that he had interpreted as harmful," Shipps added. "And she said she was depressed over the divorce."

When Debora heard her husband's name, she suddenly became hostile and very profane. "She was calling him names," Shipps said. "The two that I can remember very clearly are 'asshole' and 'fuckhole.'"

The woman on the bed was screaming out the words as if she wanted her husband to hear her. Debora didn't argue with the officers themselves, however; all her animosity seemed to be directed toward Mike. Jordan left Shipps in the bedroom and went to talk briefly to Mike and his son. Shipps saw that Debora's personal address book lay open on a dresser. In it, she had written the Olathe Earl May Garden Center's address and phone number, and directions for how to get there. The notation meant nothing to Shipps, not then.

Mike had a psychiatrist from the Menninger Clinic on the line and Sergeant Jordan talked to him, meanwhile watching Mike. The man was crying. "He was upset," Jordan said. "It seemed to me when I was evaluating the situation it was taking a toll on him having to do this. He seemed pained what this had led to—what their marriage had led to."

Mike told the police sergeant that he had found what he believed to be a "suicide kit" and showed him the plastic bag with the packages of seeds, the vials of potassium chloride, and the syringes. "He was explaining to me what this chemical in the vials would do, once injected into your system, and how he feared that she was going to use this to kill herself," Jordan said. He was convinced by what he had seen that Debora Green's condition met his department's protocol for commitment; he felt sure that she represented a significant danger to herself or others.

Back in the master bedroom, Officer Shipps talked to Debora for forty-five minutes to an hour. It was one of the oddest conversations of his life. The woman on the bed was clearly very intelligent, but her vocabulary was that of a fishwife. She didn't seem to resent his presence, but she reviled her husband in a nonstop stream of invective.

While Jordan was convinced that they had to take Debora to a hospital for mental evaluation, he explained to Mike that the Prairie Village police could not take his wife to Menninger's—that hospital was too far out of their jurisdiction. They could take Dr. Green to a facility in the Kansas City area, but not beyond. "We told him that we would have to first transport her to Kansas University Medical Center, which was in Wyandotte County, for a psychiatric screening," Shipps recalled. "Based on the evidence of that, she would be transported elsewhere."

Debora didn't want to go to the hospital. She saw no necessity for that. Yes, she was intoxicated, but she was in her own home, and she was *not* suicidal. "I have three beautiful children here," she said, "and I don't want to do anything to leave them." Nevertheless, she cooperated in getting ready to go, pulling on a pair of sweatpants and a jacket. And the officers gave her an opportunity to say good-bye to her children.

Shipps looked away from the poignant scene of six-year-old Kelly trying to comb her mother's hair so that she would look nice going to the hospital. "They were all talking among themselves. I don't remember the exact words," Shipps recalled, "but it was something to the effect that Dr. Green made the statement, 'This is all just happening because of your father.'" Tim, Lissa, and Kelly weren't crying as much now, although they were still upset and confused.

Shipps drove Debora to KU Medical Center, where she had once been on staff; Mike called his sister and asked her to come stay with the children so he could follow Debora to the hospital. He called his mother, too, letting her know for the first time how terrible his marriage had become. He was crying as he did so. Karen Beal, Mike's sister, hurried over. His parents arrived later to spend the night.

Dr. Pam McCoy worked in the ER at the University of Kansas Medical Center. She had been there part-time for five years;

since the previous May, she'd had a full-time post as an ER physician and a professor in emergency medicine. The emergency room at KU was an extremely busy facility, and Dr. McCoy's students had an opportunity to do hands-on treatment of myriad cases.

On September 25, Dr. McCoy was working the three P.M.–eleven P.M. shift. She was just about to go off-duty when an ER nurse stopped her. "They said there was a physician who did not want to be signed in to the emergency department, didn't want to be seen, who was in the custody of the police," Dr. McCoy said. "They wanted me to go talk to her." Surprised, and not knowing what to expect, she walked out to the police car and saw a disheveled woman who looked familiar. "It was Dr. Debora Green," she said. "She and I had been colleagues at another hospital I had worked at—at Trinity Lutheran."

Dr. McCoy introduced herself, explaining that she had been married since they last saw each other. Her maiden name had been McVey; as she told Debora, she had changed it only slightly to McCoy. Then she asked Debora the most pressing question: Why had she been brought in?

Debora seemed embarrassed and said, "Oh, great. Here's somebody I *know.*"

Dr. McCoy explained that patient confidentiality applied to everyone; Debora didn't have to worry about her privacy. She noted a strong odor of alcohol, but she could not say that Debora was drunk. At least, her speech didn't seem slurred. And when she got out of the patrol car, she didn't have the characteristic "ataxic gait" of someone completely drunk.

"I asked her again why she had been brought in," Dr. McCoy recalled. "And she told me that her husband, Mike Farrar, was accusing her of being a drunk and was trying to frame her into looking like she was crazy and a drunk. . . . She said she had drunk a half a bottle of wine."

Debora appeared to Dr. McCoy to be stressed and having a "rough time. I mean, she just looked *bad.*" She knew that women—particularly women doctors—who are going out usually make much more effort to look presentable. Kelly's attempt to neaten her mother's hair hadn't succeeded; Debora's thick wavy hair was a mess.

Dr. McCoy was in a sticky situation. Debora was telling her that her husband wanted a divorce, and that he was having an affair with some "bitch." He'd called the cops on her; she was upset and embarrassed because she didn't want to be admitted to KU. She was sure her husband was trying to make her look as if she were crazy.

Dr. McCoy asked Shipps if he had actually seen Debora behaving in an overtly homicidal or suicidal manner, and he admitted he had not. He had relied on Dr. Farrar's statements. He said Farrar would be arriving as soon as he could find someone to care for their children.

Dr. McCoy began asking Debora the standard questions used to screen potential psychiatric patients: Did she know her name, the date, the time, who the president was? She did. "I asked her if she was going to harm herself, and she said, 'Absolutely not!' I asked her if she was going to hurt anybody else and she said, 'No.' And so my assessment at that time was I was in the middle of one very ugly domestic dispute."

Dr. McCoy was trying to be fair and empathetic. "I was looking at her and thinking, 'Well, if *I* was in this situation, I would be very upset if my husband had called the police and said, "My wife's a lunatic, come take her to the hospital."'"

Debora appeared rational; Dr. McCoy, doing her best to make a valid assessment, asked Debora if she would come in and see the psychiatrist on call. She thought that after that Debora would probably be able to go home. "I did not think she would be a committable patient."

Debora agreed to go in. The two women were in the entrance to the ER when Mike arrived. And as he began to walk toward Dr. McCoy, Debora's whole demeanor changed. She became extremely agitated and approached her husband in what could only be called a menacing manner. "She kind of spit at him," Pam McCoy said. "And called him a fuckhole." McCoy was stunned at the sudden change in her patient. Debora looked as though she was about to physically attack her husband. Dr. McCoy quickly stepped forward and grabbed her arms, hoping to stop a fight in the ER.

"She was very angry," Dr. McCoy said. "She called him a fuckhole—which I remember very clearly since I hadn't heard that expression before—and then she said, 'You're going to get these kids over our dead bodies.'"

For a moment the trio of doctors froze in the entryway to the ER. They all knew one another—at least, Dr. McCoy had *thought* she knew Debora. She looked at Mike and was struck by how "very thin, very pale, ill-appearing, very anxious, very distraught" he seemed.

Debora's words hung in the air. "You're going to get these kids over our dead bodies. . . ."

Chapter 13

Doing their best to avoid open warfare in the ER waiting room, Dr. McCoy and Officer Shipps moved Debora off to one side, assuming that she would wait there to have a consultation with one of the psychiatrists on duty. Debora had begged not to be treated like a mental patient forced into the hospital.

Because she knew there were two sides in any domestic dispute, Dr. McCoy sat down with Mike and asked him what was going on. The events he related were bizarre and outlandish. He told her that he was seeking a divorce and that Debora had become more and more upset, agitated, and angry. "He said that she was drinking large bottles of alcohol at a sitting, was becoming very despondent—wouldn't get out of bed for days at a time."

When Mike told her about Debora's hiding under the bed all night and secreting used syringes and empty vials and packets of castor beans in her purse, Dr. McCoy became more alarmed. Debora had been disheveled and embarrassed, certainly, but she had seemed on the safe side of normal—until she saw her husband. And then she had become a spitting, frothing creature consumed by a maniacal temper.

Mike handed the bag of seed packets, syringes, and potassium chloride vials to Dr. McCoy. There was also a small bottle of Adriamycin, a cancer drug. She looked through the bag but was still doubtful. "Honestly, I kind of thought he was sort of pushing this suicidal thing," she said. "An oncologist *would* have—or may have—chemotherapeutic agents around. Potassium chloride *is* something you could kill yourself with, although it's not all that uncommon for a physician to have it as an additive that you put in IVs, especially if someone's been vomiting a lot." Of course, at that point, Dr. McCoy didn't know that Debora had not been in her oncology practice for several years.

Later, when she asked her about the packets of castor beans, Debora laughed harshly. "Well, for heaven's sakes," she said, "you can't even buy plant seeds anymore without somebody saying something about it!" Dr. McCoy's own mother grew castor beans as an ornamental plant. "To commit *suicide* with a castor bean would be a very unusual way to do that," the doctor thought. "I couldn't imagine why anybody would do that."

Still trying to be fair, Dr. McCoy reevaluated her two fellow physicians. They were both upset, but there was a difference. Debora was angry and full of rage; Mike seemed more anxious, worried, nervous. She knew she needed to talk to a third party—maybe a neighbor or an in-law. Mike said the only person who might know something about his wife's recent behavior was their son, Tim. Debora had been housebound so much that the only one competent to evaluate what had been going on was their son.

Working long after her shift was over, Dr. McCoy dialed the number Mike gave her. An older-sounding woman—Mike's mother—answered: Tim was in bed and she hated to wake him up.

"Well, it's kind of important," Dr. McCoy said. "I really need to talk to him."

She waited while the woman went to Tim's room and woke him. And then she asked the boy, "What's been going on with your mom?"

Tim sounded young but intelligent. He also seemed to want to phrase his answers in a way that would not be a betrayal of his mother. Finally, he sighed and said, "She's been very sad and very upset lately. . . . She hasn't gotten out of bed for several days—just been laying around. She's been drinking a lot." He had been hiding bottles from her because she was drinking whole bottles of liquor, "the big kind, you know, that you get from the wholesale club."

Dr. McCoy thanked Tim and told him to go back to bed, he didn't have to worry about anything that night. She had her answers. From the honest words of a child, she had learned that Debora was showing signs of serious depression. Her hiding in the basement, her despondency, and her drinking so much that she didn't get out of bed for days all indicated that she was probably seriously disturbed. This was much more than Debora had admitted to her. "And so I thought that Dr. Green was, in fact, going to need care," Dr. McCoy said, a little bemused that Debora had managed to maintain such a reasonable façade that she herself had been fooled.

Dr. McCoy walked back to the cubicle near the ER waiting room where she had left Debora. She felt she had convinced her patient that it would look better for her in any divorce proceedings if she were cooperative now—if she agreed to talk to the psychiatrist. "It would make her look like she was . . . an okay person—that she wasn't the crazy person her husband was trying to make her out to be."

Dr. McCoy was startled to find Debora gone. At first, she thought she might have gone to the bathroom, or outside for a cigarette. Growing more and more concerned, she searched the bathrooms, the patient rooms, the whole ER wing. But she didn't find Debora. And now she felt really worried and guilty, because she had tried to save Debora's pride and had not asked for a police officer to guard her. Dr. McCoy had believed her fellow doctor, believed that she was eminently sane and in control of herself, believed that the odor of alcohol had come from a mere half-bottle of wine.

After an exhaustive search, Dr. McCoy conceded that Debora was clearly not inside the hospital. She summoned the KU security force and asked them to begin a search for a woman in her forties, wearing sweats, with uncombed hair, and on foot.

And then Dr. McCoy jotted down several pages of notes about the startling events of the evening. At the very least, she suspected she might be called as a witness in what promised to be an ugly divorce. She was angry at herself because she had overestimated Debora's truthfulness, and she wanted to reconstruct their encounter from the moment she was called to the driveway to deal with a recalcitrant patient to the time she realized that Debora had "eloped" from the ER. She was very worried about Debora and hated to think of her wandering around Johnson County and the suburbs of Kansas City after midnight in her condition.

She was afraid that Debora had gone off somewhere to kill herself.

Mike Farrar and Officer Shipps sat together in the ER waiting room, watching as people with all manner of injuries and illnesses came in. It was familiar territory for both. Mike had done his turn as a resident in the ER in Cincinnati, and Shipps had brought in scores of people in distress of one kind or another. Shipps would write in his follow-up report of this incident that Dr. Debora Green was initially "drunk, profane, bizarre—but cooperative." He needed a formal statement about the reason for Mike's complaint hours before; Mike wrote one out and signed it. Both men expected to be in the ER until dawn. They believed that Debora had been taken for a prescreening by a psychiatrist about 11:30; it might be a long time before she was officially admitted.

But when Mike and Shipps saw Dr. McCoy's expression, they knew something was wrong.

The Prairie Village police radio put out a "want" on Dr. Debora Green. Shipps cruised along the area between the hospital and the house on Canterbury Court for an hour and a half. And eventually, Debora was spotted—miles away from the hospital, in Prairie Village, apparently headed for home. She was returned to the ER at the Kansas University Medical Center, although she insisted to Shipps that she was only walking home so she could go to sleep. She had been asleep when they disturbed her, and she had intended to go home and get a night's rest. Shipps characterized her demeanor at this point as vacillating between "calm" and "irate."

Once back in the ER waiting room, Shipps sat with Debora and kept a close eye on her. She was no longer pretending that everything was fine with her. She no longer claimed that she was being railroaded by her husband. As Shipps watched, her demeanor rapidly disintegrated into a temper tantrum like those Mike had long been familiar with. "Committals in general take quite a bit of time," Shipps would comment. And his patient/prisoner was becoming extremely frustrated by the delays. In fact, the woman was coming apart before his eyes. "You know," she said. "You're really starting to piss me off. . . . *This* could really make me suicidal."

Finally, Debora was interviewed by the psychiatrist on duty, who felt that she definitely should be committed for a mental evaluation. She could have stayed at KU, but Mike had already arranged for her admission to the Menninger Clinic. An ambulance transported her toward Topeka, through the toll plazas of the Kansas Turnpike, past the Topeka Correctional Institute for Women, and along the northern leg of the beltway that edges Topeka. Just beyond the governor's mansion, the Menninger Clinic property sprawls at the west end of Topeka.

Menninger's is actually a huge complex that resembles the stately homes of a royal family rather than a mental hospital. Its elegant gray buildings are situated far back from the frontage road, set among trees and shrubs on rolling land. Menninger's has been—and continues to be—a preferred retreat for the wealthy and famous whose minds and willpower have become fragile.

Once there, Debora voluntarily committed herself; and because she had agreed to be evaluated and treated, she could also leave at any time, whenever she decided she was ready to go.

It was six A.M., and it had been a long, hard night for everyone concerned, when Officer Shipps left the ER and went off-duty. He had with him the statement from Dr. Michael Farrar and the sealed bag of the suspect items Mike had given him: the syringes, the potassium chloride vials, the bottle of Adriamycin, and eight packets of castor beans. Whatever Dr. Debora Green had intended doing with this strange assortment of items, they would now be held in an evidence locker at the Prairie Village Police Department.

Mike went home to sleep, secure for the moment in the knowledge that Debora would be evaluated and treated at Menninger's. Beyond her obvious depression and her violent reactions to frustration, there might be something else that he had been too close to see.

While Debora was away, Mike took care of their children. Because of his illness, he had not worked since August 18; now he welcomed the chance to stay home with Tim, Lissa, and Kelly. It was a serene, happy time. He and the children got along better than ever before. And without Debora there to whip them into a froth of anger and competition, even his relationship with Tim improved.

It was Mike who combed Kelly's hair when she needed to look nice for her school picture. Her thick blond curls made it a daunting task for a clumsy father. He finally twisted her hair into a bun, but it was an attractive bun: Mike had bought a book on children's hairstyles to be sure he did it right. Kelly's pictures turned out beautifully.

The days they spent alone together were the calm after a violent storm. The night of Debora's commitment had been so distressing for all of them, and the weeks leading up to it had been horrendous. Tim, who was the eldest child of an alcoholic and whose father was often away, had taken on the role of the man of the house. He had done much of the cooking and watched over his sisters. Although he liked to cook and he loved his sisters, he was an angry boy.

With Debora away and being treated for her rage and depression, her family's constant apprehension, which had come to seem almost normal, began to diminish. Those days were, of course, only an island of tranquillity. Although Mike wasn't sure when Debora would come home, come home she would. And then he would have to leave. They could never again live together. He hoped they could find a modicum of peace apart.

Mike was in touch with Celeste often, more by phone than in person. Taking care of three children didn't leave much time for an affair. Celeste needed him; John had been dead for only three weeks, and she and her sons were grieving. Mike's children, too, were upset. And after Debora's commitment, the lovers were caught up in a faster-spinning whirlwind of vicious gossip.

Celeste had sent Brett and Dan back to school right after John's funeral; she thought it would be better for them to jump right in, rather than delay facing their peers. Some people criticized that. When she visited Mike in the hospital only days after John's suicide, the news quickly made the

rounds of the medical community in both Johnson and
Jackson counties.

Celeste was the main topic at cocktail parties and picnics
alike. Some maintained that she was pretty and "ditzy, but
didn't have a mean bone in her body"; others said she was a
manipulative seductress who could make a man do anything
she wanted, even have his wife committed. She was, of
course, neither. She was alone for the first time in almost
twenty years, and she clung to Mike. Debilitated by his
violent illness and facing the prospect of a messy divorce, he
was not a very strong support.

At Menninger's, Debora was diagnosed with a "major bipolar depression with suicidal impulses" and started on
medications: Prozac (an antidepressant), Tranxene (an anti-
anxiety medication), and Klonopin (which calms the
nervous system, much as Valium does, but is long-acting
enough to be taken just once a day). After four days, however, she signed herself out. Asked why, she would later say,
"I am so forceful that people do what I want. I told my psychiatrist that I wanted to leave. And I did."

The medications Debora was taking for her depression
were definitely not to be mixed with alcohol. To do so would
produce a synergistic effect, greatly enhancing the potency
of each substance, perhaps to fatal levels. Debora assured
her psychiatrist that she would not drink while she was on
her "meds."

While Debora was away, Mike had come to an almost
unthinkable realization. He had puzzled over the packets of
castor beans; when he gave them to Officer Shipps, he had
held one packet back so he could do a bit more research.
The directions said, "Plant in early spring," so why would
Debora have the seeds in September? The packet also
warned that castor beans were very toxic. Some of Mike's

friends had bombarded him with the opinion that Debora was trying to poison him, pointing out that he always got better in the hospital, then became ill again when he came home. But Mike had resisted their reasoning. It was too ugly to think that Debora hated him enough to kill him in such a tortuous way. And, too, if the poisoning theory was true, didn't he look stupid to have continued to eat the food Debora cooked for him?

But the fact remained that he had become violently ill each time he returned home from the hospital. He could not explain this away. As most people do when they become terribly nauseated after eating, he remembered precisely what he had eaten before each incident: a chicken salad sandwich; spaghetti; ham and beans and cornbread. Each time, Debora had served him separately, rather than calling him to the table to eat with the family. And each time the food had tasted slightly bitter. He had explained that away, thinking his illness had probably thrown his taste off. But while he still denied the possibility that his own wife would deliberately try to poison him as too far-fetched to be believed, he had to know more.

Mike could find nothing about castor-bean poisoning in his edition of *Harrison's Principles of Internal Medicine*, but Celeste had a copy of an earlier edition that discussed the topic. As he pored over the old textbook, Mike's neck prickled. It wasn't the bean itself that was so potentially deadly; it was the core. Freed from its protective hard coating, the inside of the castor bean could be ground into a substance known as ricin.

Mike went to North Kansas City Hospital and asked the librarian to search for articles and tracts that mentioned castor-bean or ricin poisoning. As he learned, opinions varied on how dangerous castor beans were. The articles cited a number of case histories of patients—some of them children—who had swallowed the hard beans whole or after chewing them. The vast majority not only survived, but were hardly ill at all. However, cases had also been found in which, despite heroic efforts on the part of their physicians, patients who had eaten castor beans died within three to twelve days. Chillingly, the symptoms of castor-bean poisoning were much like those of tropical sprue.

Mike found a reference to the doyenne of mystery writers, Agatha Christie. Christie's 1929 book *Partners in Crime* included the story "The House of the Lurking Death," which featured a murder by poisoning—and the poison was ricin. Mike wondered if Christie's book had been included in Debora's extensive reading of mysteries and true crime.

Remarking that "Ricin is reputed to be one of the most toxic naturally occurring substances . . . ," one text on poisonous plants listed the results of ingesting the center of the castor bean: "Symptoms of poisoning may not appear for several hours—or even for a few days . . . [They include] burning of the mouth and throat, nausea, vomiting, severe stomach pains, diarrhea (sometimes containing blood and mucus), thirst, prostration, shock from massive fluid and electrolyte loss, headache, dizziness, lethargy, impaired vision, possible rapid heartbeat and convulsions." To Mike, those horrific symptoms were all too familiar.

The *North Carolina Medical Journal* had published a paper on castor beans, "The Baddest Seed—Ricin Poisoning." In it, Dr. Robert B. Mack, a professor of pediatrics, minced no words. "This plant may be the most dangerous plant grown in the United States . . . [;] probably *all* parts of the plant are toxic, but the seeds appear to contain the largest amount of toxin—*ricin*. . . . Milligram for milligram, ricin is thought to be one of the top two or three deadliest poisons available."

Again and again in various articles and books, Mike read about the fatal potential of ricin ingestion. There is no antidote: treatment is aimed at the symptoms, to ameliorate the effects of dehydration, shock, and acute renal failure. Mike had suffered most of the symptoms listed, but unlike the patients in the case histories, who had endured only one episode of ricin poisoning, he had suffered three. The evidence seemed overwhelming. Mike was now certain that Debora had poisoned him at least three times.

Opinions varied on just how big a dose of ricin it took to kill a human being, but a 1983 paper in *Human Toxicology* estimated that the "lethal dose in man is one milligram per kilogram. This approximately corresponds to eight ingested seeds." Mike had no idea how many seeds he might have ingested. Debora had had almost a dozen packets of them in her purse, which meant she must have used others to poison him. Mike wondered how you ground up castor beans. Perhaps in a coffee grinder? A food processor? The granular fragments could easily have been mixed with spaghetti sauce or ham and beans.

Mike took the journal articles to the doctors who were treating him and they had to agree that, given the circumstances and the symptoms, he could well have been poisoned. Tests were possible to detect the presence of antibodies to ricin in his bloodstream. But they might not give a definitive answer. It would take a while for antibodies to form, and it had only been a few weeks since his last episode of illness.

Faced with the painful realization that his wife had poisoned him, Mike tried to understand her motives. Was it possible that she wanted him to stay in their marriage so desperately that she intended only to make him too sick to leave? Maybe she had never meant to kill him. Maybe she had only wanted him to depend on her to take care of him. As far as Mike could tell, he had not been poisoned since his last hospital release, even though Debora could easily have tampered with his intravenous feedings.

Whatever her motivations had been, Mike was now certain that Debora had been the cause of his repeated attacks. And one thing, at least, was obvious; if he intended to survive, he had to move out of the house after she came home.

He was surprised when she returned after only four days, seeming tremendously improved. Nevertheless, he packed a bag and left. He said nothing to Debora about his belief that she had tried to poison him; he would wait until he saw the results of the antibody tests.

It was the first week of October. Mike stayed with his parents for two or three nights, then moved into the Georgetown Apartments in Merriam, Kansas, only a ten-minute drive from his estranged wife and their youngsters. He would be close by and the children could stay with him on weekends.

Mike was concerned about the children's psychological well-being. "Whenever I was home," he said, "the situation was so volatile—Debora was saying horrible things to the kids in front of me, and I thought if I was out of the house it was clearly better for the kids."

But Mike was not worried about any *physical* danger to Tim, Lissa, and Kelly. If she hated him, Debora loved them. There was no question of that in his mind.

Part II

Seeds in a dry pod, tick, tick, tick,
Tick, tick, tick, what little iambics,
While Homer and Whitman roared in the pines!

—EDGAR LEE MASTERS
Spoon River Anthology

The venom clamors of a jealous woman
Poison more deadly than a mad dog's tooth

—WILLIAM SHAKESPEARE
King Richard III

Chapter 14

Ellen Ryan had her master's degree in social work and a doctorate in jurisprudence. Like Debora Green, she was an extremely intelligent woman. And like her, she was familiar with the medical community in the Kansas City area; Ellen had been married for two decades to a physician. The man she now called her significant other was both a physician and an attorney, and Ellen and her ex-husband had joint custody of four children, ranging from ten to sixteen years old.

At forty-seven, Ellen was a very attractive woman, whose strong face was spattered with freckles and framed by thick brown hair. In court, she dressed like an attorney; given her choice, she wore sweats and sneakers. With her partner, Ellen P. Aisenbrey, she ran a family-law practice and their offices were welcoming and modest, full of pictures and paintings of children. That was in keeping with Ellen's chief concern. Having been raised by her grandparents, she understood the bewilderment of children whose families have broken up and reassembled in different forms. Although she was an unfailingly optimistic woman, she had seen a great deal of pain in the clients who came to her and she willingly reached out to help, more than most lawyers. But she was, after all, part attorney and part social worker.

"If at all possible," she would explain, "I try to take an approach so that a couple can get through a divorce and be able to start over again. They're not going to destroy each other—they're going to be able to go ahead and parent their children together when it's over. I have joint custody myself and I tend to have a personal preference for that. At the same time, it's very important that we all play by the rules, ethically and legally. If my clients need to have an aggressive defense, then I will defend them aggressively as long as it's within the rules."

For the wives—and husbands, for that matter—whom she represented, Ellen could be a fierce advocate. She believed in a fair distribution of family assets, and she was adept at finding those assets. She was not so much a feminist as a humanist.

One of Ellen's most recent clients was a doctor trying to decide whether to file for a friendly divorce or take an aggressive approach. A very sad man, he was hoping to have joint custody of his two sons. Ellen had tried to help him find a place to live. But as it turned out, her client never went through a divorce at all. And Ellen was still reeling from the staggering fact that he had committed suicide. Although she had not discussed the tragedy with anyone but her significant other and no one else knew that he had come to see her, her client had been Dr. John Walker. The public records of Walker's estate included a bill for her legal services.

Ellen had expected John Walker to be able to move along with his life after the initial pain of divorce. Through a physician acquaintance, he had found a house to rent, and he had paid ahead on the lease. He'd had utilities and a phone installed. And then, suddenly, he was dead—a suicide, in what originally seemed to be questionable circumstances. "I said to myself [about John Walker]—I *still* say to myself"— "'There must be some logical explanation. This does not happen in real life.'" Ellen sighed.

She would pursue the results of the postmortem on Dr. John Walker and the subsequent evaluations of the drugs he had used and the order in which he had used them until, finally, there was a "logical explanation." But Ellen had no idea that there was any connection between John Walker and the woman who had scheduled an appointment in the last week of September. The woman's name was Dr. Debora Green.

*

Initially, Ellen Ryan was surprised by Dr. Green's appearance. "I went to the lobby to see Deb Green," Ellen said. "She looked kind of disheveled. . . . She had on a sweatshirt that was kind of dirty. Her hair was kind of messy."

Clearly, Debora did not want to be in the office of a divorce attorney, and she was quite nervous. "I brought her back to my office," Ellen said, "and she told me that her husband wanted a divorce. She also told me that she had been hanging out with a friend of hers for most of the summer—John Walker—whom she had gone to medical school with."

Ellen was not sure what the relationship between Debora and John might have been. She was only mildly surprised that they knew each other; after all, they were both doctors. But then Debora went on to explain about the trip to South America; her husband, she said, had been "hanging out" with John Walker's wife. She said that she and her husband had spent a lot of time during the past few months over at the Walkers'—as a family—and now John had ended up dead. "You know," Debora confided, "he wasn't suicidal."

Ellen had been listening to Debora's story without comment. Now, she fought to keep her expression bland. Was this woman before her implying that her husband had somehow been involved in John Walker's death? Of all the attorneys Debora could have come to, why had she chosen Ellen—Walker's attorney? She had been terribly upset by his suicide—if it was a suicide. It gave her chills to be listening to a woman who claimed she had been close to him during the days before his death.

"I could see that there was some kind of linkage," Ellen recalled. "I didn't understand it all then, and I cannot tell you what it was now. I know I will go to my deathbed and not understand, probably."

Ellen saw another potential problem, beyond "Deb" Green's connection to John Walker. (She would call her Deb almost from the beginning.) Debora said she and her husband, Michael, had been represented in the spring of 1995 by a lawyer Ellen knew—Norman Beal—to do some estate planning. At that time, their luxurious home in Canterbury Court had been transferred into a trust, the Debora Green Trust.

Usually, if an attorney has represented a client, the attorney does not go against that client in an adversarial situation later, unless the client waives his or her rights. Ellen would learn that Debora, without benefit of counsel, *had* waived her right not to have to face in the divorce action a lawyer who had once been her own attorney. Norman Beal (no relation to Mike's sister's husband) would be representing Mike in his divorce action against Debora. Ellen knew he was an ethical attorney, but he would, of course, have superior knowledge about the family finances since he had helped Mike and Debora plan their estate only months before.

Debora didn't understand that Norman Beal's representing Mike could be construed as a possible conflict of interest. Mike wanted to use Beal; he trusted him and they had a history. When Ellen would question this, Mike grew angry—although, in the future, theirs was to be a remarkably civilized business relationship. But in the beginning, Mike had allegedly threatened Debora, saying that if she didn't agree to his using Norman Beal he would hire a "nut-cutter attorney" who could take everything she owned away from her. In the end, both Debora and Ellen were completely comfortable with Norman Beal representing Mike.

It was quickly apparent that Debora was completely unsophisticated about finances. "That put up a red flag for me in terms of how I was going to protect her," Ellen said. And from the outset, she found Debora almost childlike. She didn't seem aware that the house was in her name, in a trust. She dressed like a messy child and was often vague. She didn't want a divorce and she didn't know how to handle money. Ellen wasn't aware of Debora's recent trip to Menninger's or that she had been out only a few days. She didn't know that Debora had a drinking problem. And she certainly didn't know about her new client's ferocious temper. She was seeing an entirely different person from the one others had encountered. And it was apparent that this person was alone and lost. She needed help, and Ellen agreed to handle her divorce, including the financial settlement.

Johnson County, Kansas, has strict guidelines on spousal and child support, based on the husband's (or wife's) ability to pay. "I find the money," Ellen explained confidently. And when she toted up what Mike was worth and submitted a figure based on the Johnson County guidelines, she fully expected a protest from Norman Beal.

Her knowledge of Mike's alleged response came, however, from Debora. She called Ellen constantly, nervous and frightened, telling her attorney how furious Mike was, how he wasn't going to pay support or look after her and the children. Debora kept asking, "What am I going to *do?*" Ellen felt sorry for her.

"Well, look, Deb," she said soothingly, "he's *going* to pay. They all do that in Johnson County when they see their guideline amounts. Don't worry about it. Everybody's going to adjust, and we'll just kind of move on."

In fact, Debora and Mike did seem to be adjusting and moving on. Debora was definitely bitter about the upcoming divorce and her husband's affair with Celeste, but she was far less violent and profane. With Mike living in an apartment and Debora in the house on Canterbury Court, the children were spared any more family conflict. Mike hadn't wanted any more pets. But now that he was gone, Debora adopted a greyhound through a program that found homes for racing dogs that were too old or too slow to compete and would otherwise be put down. She named the thin, nervous dog Russell.

The kids were back in school, Tim was playing soccer, and Debora was thrilled when Lissa won the role of Clara in the State Ballet of Missouri holiday production of *The*

Nutcracker Suite. Kelly wasn't left out; she would have a role as an angel. Although she was still "pre-ballet," she was tall for her age and graceful, and she followed directions perfectly.

Mike invited the children to spend weekends or portions of the weekends at his apartment, and sometimes they came. Tim and Lissa were still angry at him for leaving after he had promised to stay. And there were occasions when they called their mother to come and take them home. But Mike made a determined effort to be at Tim's soccer matches and hockey games, to prove to his son that he *did* care about him, and that while he was divorcing their mother, he still wanted to be part of his children's lives. Debora was, if not pleasant, at least civil to Mike when he came to the house. But he always refused anything to eat.

A week or so passed and Ellen was optimistic about Debora's progress. She was dressing better, her hair was combed, she looked better all the way around, and she seemed to be getting a grip on her life. She told Ellen she had been so impressed with the Menninger Clinic that she planned to apply for a residency there, in psychiatry. She explained that she and Tim were very close—that she understood adolescent problems well and cared a great deal about teenagers. She had pretty much decided to become a psychiatrist specializing in counseling teenagers.

If anyone thought it odd that a woman who was not yet a month past her own voluntary commitment for mental illness should be considering a residency in psychiatry, no one said so. Three months earlier, Debora had told Celeste Walker that she planned to start a practice in family medicine. Of course, she had already been an ER physician and an oncologist.

There was still much that Ellen did not know about Debora, but she was confident that she was pulling out of her despondency. She was especially concerned that Debora's children were faring well. No one had mentioned "one word" to her about any conceivable danger to them. "That's significant," Ellen said, "because I am one of the few lawyers in the metropolitan area who has included in their retainer agreement the right to withdraw from any divorce case if I think things are not being done in the best interest of the child."

Because of her background in social work, Ellen knew exactly what steps to take to get a child out of an injurious home environment *immediately* if the need arose. She never had reason to think that Tim, Lissa, and Kelly were in a precarious situation. Her own children, who were approximately the same age, liked Debora, who often called Ellen at home. It was also clear that Tim's friends were devoted to his mother—that she was a mom who always showed up for soccer, hockey, and school projects. Kids were welcome in her home, and she didn't fuss at them for making a mess. An immaculate house didn't matter to her.

"Deb had gone from being real angry and bitter and scared she could never start over again," Ellen said, "to talking about joint custody. She wanted to do her residency at Menninger's, a week-on week-off program. She wanted Mike to share the kids, but she didn't think he would. Deb said he only had a two-bedroom apartment and 'He won't help me with the kids—he's never helped me with the kids.'"

Ellen reassured her, saying that more often than not people change after divorce, and they *do* want to spend time with their children. And she was right. Mike was asking for joint custody and was looking forward to it. Debora was vehement, however, when she told Ellen that Tim hated his father and would never live with him. "But that's part of the process," Ellen said later. "At the beginning of every divorce, people are very polarized, so you have to take things with a grain of salt."

As for Mike, he believed that his children were doing well with Debora in her post-Menninger's state of mind. He had lived through seventeen years of histrionics, insults, tantrums, sullen silences, and accusations. But Debora had always been a caring mother, except for her verbal assaults in front of the children and the last days of her drunken near comas, when they had looked after her. Mike felt hopeful that things were going to be all right. He believed that she might try to harm him again—he had betrayed her, at least in her opinion—but he had no reason to doubt her love for their children.

In truth, Debora lived through her children, far more than most women do; she had always been proud of their accomplishments, their activities, their physical beauty, and their soaring IQ's. They were the friends she didn't have; they were her excuse for giving up her medical practice. They provided the love and acceptance that she seemed unable to receive in sufficient quantity from anyone else. She did not see her parents often, her sister lived far away and had different interests, and her husband was in love with another woman. That was why she spent so much time with her children. She vowed that Lissa and Kelly would grow up to be BOTARs despite the divorce. Debora was ecstatic about Lissa's starring role in the upcoming Christmas ballet. And Tim, the child who looked so much like her and who had inherited her brains, would be her protector.

Meanwhile, Mike was struggling to regain his strength and put his life back in order. He had come so close to dying, and he was still very thin. In the second and third weeks of October, he tentatively went back to his practice, working short hours with limited activity and not taking calls. Although he was feeling better and putting on a little weight, his recovery from whatever his illness had been— tropical sprue or typhoid fever or ricin poisoning—was very slow. He hadn't really worked since August 18; now he hoped to ease back into his practice. Perhaps he would be able to handle full-time work by the first of November.

*

Ellen Ryan was trying hard to help Debora grow stronger and more independent. She knew now about Debora's short stay at Menninger's, but she didn't know any details. "I had no communication with Deb's psychiatrist and knew none of her previous history, because that was confidential information. I was working only with the information I was able to pick up. Deb still looked a little bit rumpled but she was getting 'put together.' She was on meds, she had regular psychiatric care. She seemed to be doing well—except that they were fighting about the money."

One unusual feature of Ellen's practice was the CPA on staff— "to help me track the money, to help me figure out settlements and taxes. I have a lot of women like Deb who can't even sit down and think about putting together their discovery [the part of litigation when each side must reveal pertinent facts]. I can do that for them. At the same time, we work to get them able to stand on their own two feet."

Debora had absolutely no idea how much she was spending in a week, and Ellen's CPA planned to go to the Canterbury Court house to try to establish what Debora would need in the way of support. Debora didn't know what she owned, what Mike owned, or what their expenses were. Someone had always paid the bills, and since Mike had gone into practice, she had always had enough money to buy everything she wanted for the children, the house, and herself. Now her divorce attorney and her CPA were trying to help her start to focus on budgeting, to envision what her life was going to be like down the line.

"Deb was doing great with that. No problem. And we were trying to figure out what was in the marital estate—Deb had no idea about that either.

"It wasn't because she was a woman," Ellen hastened to add. "I've represented men with wonderful jobs and incredibly high IQ's who don't know how much their mortgage is or how much groceries cost. I can do that in my office without shaming them or embarrassing them."

On October 19, 1995, Ellen's CPA sat at the dining room

table with Debora, working on the concept of budgeting. "Deb made little stacks of bills. '*This* is a mortgage. *This* is insurance. . . .' That's how we kind of start," Ellen said, recalling the many wealthy women she had taught to manage their own finances.

Ellen's CPA reported that Debora seemed in very good spirits and appeared to understand that from now on, she would have to figure out her own bills and plan ahead to pay them. She had even talked enthusiastically about her planned residency in adolescent psychiatry.

In fact, everything seemed to be going well. But there were aspects of Debora's life that Ellen knew nothing about. She had never smelled alcohol on her client's breath. She was unaware that drinking had ever been a problem. And she still had no clue about the vitriolic fury Debora was capable of. To Ellen, her client was a frightened, incompetent, childlike woman who was doing her best to start a new life. Although she knew Debora had to be very intelligent to get through med school, she had no idea how truly brilliant she was. Ellen would have been shocked to see a picture of a young, slender, vibrant, smiling Debora.

The woman Ellen saw so frequently those first weeks of October was overweight, poorly dressed, and had an unflattering haircut. She spent all her time with her children or wrapped up in a book. Ellen felt sorry for Debora and vowed to help her find a happier way to live. What was going on behind Debora's façade of an unattractive, abandoned, anxious child was a secret, a secret so completely masked that Ellen did not even realize it existed.

Chapter 15

October is an enchanting time in the Midwest. The humid, baking summer dwindles and nights are cooler. The leaves turn and the air smells sweetly acrid as they are burned. Planting season is over and the petunias and geraniums grow straggly and wilted, while the sunflowers bend their heads and go to seed for next year.

Debora had told Ellen and the CPA that she was willing to take over her own life, and they believed her. Ellen felt confident enough that Debora was going to make it through her divorce in good shape that she went to Vermont for a week's vacation in mid-October. She was unaware of ominous signs in the house on Canterbury Court.

Mike, however, saw that Debora was beginning to deteriorate. Although he had never seen her as intoxicated as on the night Officer Shipps took her to the emergency room, she was drinking again.

And her old anger was bubbling to the surface. It didn't matter that she had a lawyer fighting for her rights and that she could expect a most comfortable income while she pursued another specialty. It didn't matter that Mike was helping her by often taking the children on weekends. Debora simply could not deal with the fact that her husband was involved with Celeste Walker. She had mentioned their affair to Ellen in an oddly old-fashioned way: "There's another woman who's set her cap for my husband." But she had said this almost casually, even with humor, and Ellen did not read the fury beneath the words.

Any normal woman would be angry and jealous. But Debora refused to recognize that her marriage was moribund before the trip to Peru, and that the entrance of Celeste had been the kiss of death to any hope of reconciliation. Because Debora was so adept at wit and sarcasm and turning a smiling face to the world when she wanted to, no one saw the first trickles of danger that were beginning to escape from her carefully dammed-up rage.

But she did express her anger to her son. "Celeste leads your father around by his penis," she fumed to Tim.

However inappropriate that was as a remark from mother to teenage son, it may have been accurate; Mike and Celeste were enjoying an intense physical affair. It had been a long time since either had been so consumed and they were both running away from sorrow and depression and acrimony. Their affair was still only three months old, and Mike had been desperately ill for much of that time. But in the autumn of 1995 they were together as often as they could be. Debora was aware of that and rubbed her children's noses in it, urging them to hate their father.

She tried out different scenarios on Mike. She told him that he was the fool, not she. She confessed to having had two affairs herself when they were back in Cincinnati and laughed as she said that he had never suspected a thing. Another day, she told him that she had decided to become a missionary in some distant country and would not be able to take the children with her. He would have complete responsibility for them. Mike would have been glad if that were true, but he suspected it was only a ploy to keep him off balance. Indeed, the next day, Debora was back to her plans to go to Menninger's and become a psychiatrist.

Nevertheless, Mike asked Carolyn Stafford, his friend and Celeste's from the Peru trip, if she would consider moving into a wing of the house on Canterbury Court. She was a teacher at Pembroke Hill and he trusted her. If Debora *did* decide to leave them all, Mike knew he would need someone to be with his children while he worked. Carolyn said she would consider such an arrangement.

On Saturday, October 21, Mike attended one of Tim's soccer matches. Tim was equally good at soccer and hockey, and Mike was proud of him. But an odd thing happened while he was watching from the sidelines. Debora walked over to him, carrying a cup of something. She smiled and said, "Here, Tim made this cappuccino for you. Be a good father and drink it."

Mike stared at the thermos cup she held out as if it were a snake. When Debora put it in his hand, he pushed it away. "No, you have it," he said.

She shook her head. "I've already had one."

Mike's stomach churned at the very thought of eating or drinking anything Debora offered him and he watched her walk back to her Land Cruiser with the cup. Later, he cursed himself for not keeping the damn stuff and having it tested.

All three children were to spend that night with Mike, but the older two ended up calling their mother to come get them. Mike felt discouraged sometimes, but he believed that, in time, he would be able to prove to his children that he was a good father rather than the monster Debora made him out to be. At least now their mother wasn't screaming epithets at him in front of them. But her campaign to undermine him continued. After he went to a "Renaissance Fair" with some of the people from the Peru trip, including Celeste, Debora told the children, "You know, your father's sleeping with three of those women."

It was hideous to hear her talk to his children in that vulgar way. He *was* sexually intimate with Celeste, but certainly not with anyone else, and the relationship was not a subject for the children's ears. Debora didn't care. She never censored herself in front of the children—especially if she was insulting him.

Six-year-old Kelly was the only one of the children who didn't have a grudge against Mike. On Saturday, October 21, she stayed at her father's apartment after Tim and Lissa left. She knew he was upset because her brother and sister had gone home. "She understood everything," Mike said, remembering the wisdom of a little girl who was only in the first grade. "She put her hand on my arm and said, 'Don't worry, Daddy. It's going to be okay. Everything will be okay. *I* know that you didn't sleep with all those women.'"

On Sunday, Mike drove Kelly home and found the house empty. He would not have left her there alone in any case, and he had to drive back to Merriam because Kelly had forgotten some of her things. As Mike was backing his Lexus out of his driveway, Dr. Mary Forman, his next-door neighbor to the north, came running up to the car. She needed to talk to him, she said. She seemed disturbed about something, but she definitely didn't want to discuss it in the driveway, and in front of Kelly.

"I took her phone number," Mike recalled, "and told her I would call her that night or the next day. Kelly and I drove back to my apartment to get her things, and then I took her back home." When he pulled up the second time, Debora was home. He left Kelly and drove away.

Drs. Mary and John Forman had lived next door to 7517 Canterbury Court since 1989. John Forman was a thoracic surgeon, and Mary was not currently practicing medicine because they had four children, the first aged eleven, the second nine, and eight-year-old twins. The children all went to Pembroke Hill School, as did the Jurden children, who lived on the other side of Mike and Debora's new house. Initially, the Formans had looked forward to having another mom-and-pop doctor family right next door, but after Mike and Debora had moved in a year before, they had not socialized much with them—even though their children were almost the same ages. Somehow, their differences outweighed their commonalities.

Mary Forman had been worried about Debora's children for some time, but she was really disturbed by a discovery her son had made that weekend. John Forman and his son had been raking leaves on the south side of their house, and the eleven-year-old asked his father if he had read "the letter." Forman didn't know what he was talking about. "He took me outside," Forman said, "and showed me one page of a letter. He was having a little trouble with words like 'adultery.'"

Forman soon found the rest of the letter. Its two pages had been left on a pile of leaves; they were neither damp nor soiled. It was as if someone had meant the Formans to read them. Forman found the letter as strange as anything he'd ever seen. It accused Mike Farrar and Celeste Walker of "moral indiscretion" and, in Forman's words, "praised Debora Green as a paragon of virtue. And it dealt with some adult issues that we didn't think he [their son] ought to be reading."

The Formans had no way of knowing, of course, that Mike had found a similar letter near his own front door a few weeks earlier. His suspicion that Debora had written it was confirmed when he found a handwritten draft of the letter in her purse. But Mike was used to his wife's manipulations, and had dismissed the letter as one more game.

That Sunday afternoon, October 22, Mary Forman told Mike about the letter someone had left on top of the leaf pile in their yard. That letter was addressed to Dr. Richard Hibschman, the headmaster of Pembroke Hill School; like the other, it listed the virtues of Debora Green and mentioned how much she had done for the school. It said it would be a shame if she and her husband should be divorced because they were a perfect couple. Mary promised to mail Mike the letter.

In truth, several parents of Pembroke Hill students were troubled by the situation in Debora's home. She could not hide her fumbling speech or the odor of alcohol on her breath, even though she felt fully competent, she would say later, to care for her children and drive them and their friends to school events. One neighbor had seen Kelly locked out of the house, crying, after ten at night. And Tim and Lissa had been fighting outside, long after they should have been in bed.

Mike had seen the deterioration, too, and he begged Debora to arrange counseling for the children to help them deal with their anger. She said she would make an appointment. As for the house, he gave up on it. Their beautiful home was, he said, a "shambles." There were food wrappers and clothes scattered all over the carpet. The dogs and the kids had free rein of the whole house, and with no one asking them to pick up, they didn't. Only Tim's room was meticulously neat, as always.

And Debora was definitely drinking again. Mike could tell by the way she slurred her words ever so slightly. She was good at hiding it, but after living with her for sixteen years, he knew her speech patterns as well as his own.

Mike had done quite well working short hours for the past two weeks, but he was more tired than he had expected to be, so he decided to take a week's vacation. It began on Monday, October 23.

That afternoon, he went to Celeste's house; they talked for a while, then went jogging. Mike wanted to get back in shape, and this was the first time since his illness that he'd tried to exercise. "It was a terrible day to go jogging for the first time," he recalled. "It was blustery and windy and cold." But he made an attempt, telling himself that he would grow stronger with every day he got out and ran. Celeste could easily have run circles around him that day, but she forced herself to match his pace.

At five, Mike went back to his apartment, showered, and changed clothes. He was due to pick Tim and Kelly up at 6:40. Tim had a hockey game, Debora had an appointment with her psychiatrist, and Lissa had ballet practice, so Mike had offered to take his oldest child and his youngest for the evening.

He drove Tim to his hockey game; Kelly enjoyed coming along to watch. She was a happy little girl, always in a good mood despite the tension that had sizzled around her for most of her six years.

The hockey game was over shortly before 8:30. As Mike drove Tim and Kelly home, they were all laughing and happy. Tim had played a great game. It must have been about a quarter to nine, Mike figured, when they arrived at 7517 Canterbury Court. He hesitated, wondering if he should knock or just follow his kids in. He decided to walk in behind them. Lissa and Debora were in the kitchen. Lissa was doing her homework and Debora was taking some

Kentucky Fried Chicken out of the oven where she had been reheating it.

Mike didn't stay long, probably not more than five or ten minutes. It was awkward being there. No one asked him to sit down and Debora pretty much ignored him. He asked Lissa how ballet was going and about school, and she answered him in short, clipped phrases. "Oh, she was cool," he remembered. "You know, she was still angry with me about things. She was cool—but not particularly rude."

Tim bounded up the staircase to the children's wing to take a shower, but Kelly sat down at the table to eat dinner. Except that Mike no longer lived there, everything seemed normal. Debora often served fast food, and the children certainly didn't mind. Kelly chewed on a drumstick and grinned at her dad.

Mike picked up a stack of mail and shuffled through it, removing the letters and bills addressed to him.

"And then I left. . . ."

In a sense, life is a series of curtains closing, shutting off the last act so smoothly and silently that we seldom realize we have moved out of one scene into another. Mike said good night and walked out the front door of his house, past the white birches near the entrance. They were bending and dancing in the wind, but he didn't notice them. Celeste had asked him to come for dinner after he took Tim and Kelly home, so he headed toward Overland Park. It wasn't far, only one village west of Prairie Village.

Shortly after nine, Mike was sitting down to dinner with Celeste and her two sons. He had left his old world and entered what he thought would be his new one, although he fully expected to be a frequent visitor in both for decades.

Mike could not help but notice how different things were at Celeste's home. Although it was not nearly as opulent as the Canterbury Court house, it was immaculate and exquisitely decorated. Every room had some special touch that was pure Celeste. The main bathroom was black with gold leaf, a spectacular bathroom. Celeste said she'd had a lot of fun designing it.

The dining room was homier. A huge photograph of Celeste, John, Brett, and Dan hung on one wall. Celeste never even considered taking down this portrait of what appeared to be a loving, handsome family. The boys needed to remember their father, to know that even if it was not meant to last forever, their family had mattered.

John had been dead for only six and a half weeks, and now Mike was eating supper with his widow and sons. Celeste, a wonderful cook who enjoyed being in the kitchen, had made twice-baked potatoes and stuffed pork chops. She was as different from Debora as she could possibly be; Mike thought that someday soon all the old wounds would heal.

After dinner, Mike and Celeste and her sons sat in the living room and watched Monday night football. Brett and Dan went up to bed later; since Celeste had to get up early to drive her sons to school the next day, Mike planned to leave for his apartment in Merriam about 10:30 or 11. But while he was still at Celeste's, he was paged. A cardiologist was used to pages at odd times. Mike glanced at his watch and saw that it was 10:35. The number on the display read 555-7262. He recognized it, of course. It was the number at the Canterbury Court house—the main number.

"So I called the number, and Debora answered. I said, 'You paged. What do you want?' And she said, 'No, I didn't page you.'"

Mike said someone had called from the house. Debora suggested that one of the children might have called him, but hastened to add, "They're all asleep. Do you want me to go wake them up?"

"No," he answered. "I can't imagine that they would page me at this time of night."

He hung up, puzzled, then he figured that Debora just wanted to know where he was and with whom. Five minutes later, his pager beeped again, another call from the

Canterbury Court number. "This time," Mike said, "Debora told me that she had talked to her attorney and that they felt it would be fine for me to use [Norman Beal]."

That was welcome news. Debora had promised to get back to Mike about that by Monday, and she had waited until Monday was almost over before she called him.

"She asked me what I was doing," Mike recalled. "I told her I was out with friends having dinner."

It was familiar behavior. Debora had called his pager or his phone repeatedly over the last weeks, asking him the same question. Sometimes, she called in the middle of the night, and as soon as he answered, she would hang up. He knew it was Debora: he had Caller I.D. on his phone.

About 11:15 Mike left and headed for his apartment. It was only a ten-minute drive. He was almost home when Debora paged him again. He decided to call her back from his home phone.

He suspected that she was drinking. The first time they had spoken, she sounded completely sober. The second time, they had a longer conversation and he detected a slight slurring in her speech. When Mike called her from his apartment at approximately 11:40, he was sure she was drinking: "She had a very typical speech pattern when she used drugs or when she drank too much alcohol."

He was very angry at this. They seemed to have moved away from the terrible summer just past, and now . . . "I basically was concerned that she was reverting to the same sort of behavior that she showed before she had gone to Menninger's," Mike said. "She was still seeing a psychiatrist, she was alone with the kids, and I *was* angry that she was drinking heavily again. She needed to take care of the kids."

Mike's anger crept up from deep inside. Now he said things to his estranged wife that he had swallowed for a long time. He pointed out that it was almost midnight; he told her he knew she was drinking, she wouldn't let him live any kind of normal life, she was calling him continually. "I told her I was angry with her," he remembered. "That she needed to buckle down and take care of the kids. I told her that there were some parents at the school who had noticed her behavior and poor parenting and were considering calling Social Services. I told her that she needed to get her act in gear, to get all of this taken care of."

As he exploded into the telephone, Mike remembered that he had almost died. Debora had poisoned him deliberately, he was sure. He had meant not to say anything that would tilt her any more off center, but he continued his litany of accusations. "I told her I thought she was crazy. I told her I thought she needed continued psychiatric care. I told her I knew she was poisoning me, and I told her I was going to try to take the kids away from her."

Mike was shouting by now, and Debora was furious, yelling back. Later, he didn't remember which of them had hung up on the other.

The apartment was quiet, but their hateful conversation still rang in his head. He stood at the table, thumbing through his mail, trying to quiet his breathing.

Five minutes later, the phone rang again. Wearily, Mike picked it up. Debora seemed surprised to hear his voice. "Oh," she said, "I didn't know you were home. I thought you were still out driving around. I really did not want to talk to you. I just wanted to leave a message on the machine. And since you're home, I'm not going to say anything."

She hung up.

She was playing games again, Mike thought. It wasn't that they had never argued before; their arguments were legendary. But Mike regretted mentioning the poison, and he really didn't want to take the children away from her—only, Debora *had* to shape up. She was a forty-four-year-old woman and she was behaving like a spoiled child. He was too upset to try to sleep, so he went downstairs and began working on a TV console he had partially assembled earlier in the day.

At about 12:30, the phone rang again, as Mike had half expected it would. Resignedly, he picked up the phone, but it wasn't Debora. It was Dr. Mary Forman, who only yesterday had told him about Debora's latest bizarre letter. Before Mike could speak, Mary shouted something, something that took him a moment or two to understand: "*Your house is on fire! There are fire trucks everywhere! Your wife is a fucking arsonist!*"

"*What did you say?*" he asked.

Numbly, Mike heard her repeat the same words again. He hung up the phone and ran toward the vehicle that was parked the closest, his pickup truck.

Chapter 16

Prairie Village's annual homicide rate is almost negligible; usually the police department has no murders to investigate at all. Some years, they have one. Prairie Village is close to Kansas City—which has one of the highest homicide rates in the United States—but it is an island of tranquillity. The vast majority of its 25,000 people do not resort to violence.

Miriam Russell had worked as a dispatcher for the Prairie Village Police Department for three and a half years. Before that, she dispatched for a decade for the Kansas City, Missouri, police. She knew her job, and, more than that, she had developed a certain intuitive sense about the calls. All 911 calls in Prairie Village came directly into Russell's communications unit, whether the caller needed emergency medical assistance, the police, or the fire department.

Russell's shift had begun at 10:30 P.M. on Monday night, October 23, and she would work until 6:30 A.M., October 24. She had been on duty for just under two hours when the 911 line lit up at 12:21 A.M.

"The call came in," she remembered, "but all I could hear was heavy breathing. I asked the caller if I could help them—what type of problem they had—and then the phone was disconnected. Based on my experience, I decided that there *was* some kind of distress with this caller, and it was not a routine 911 hang-up call."

Prairie Village has an extended 911 service, which gives the address where a call originates. Russell glanced at the readout and saw that the hang-up call had come from a "Farrar Residence, 7517 Canterbury Court." Something told her to treat it as an emergency. "I 'toned' the call," she said. "That lets the officers know that we've got an emergency call that's about to be broadcast. I sent two cars—red lights and sirens—to the residence."

The first two Prairie Village officers she dispatched were Sergeant Steve Hunter and Officer Larry Lamb. Hunter was less than half a mile from the house; at that time of night, with lights and siren, he arrived in two minutes. It was now 12:24 A.M.

As he turned off Seventy-fifth, Hunter saw the trouble immediately. An orange glow illuminated the night at the rear of a huge house with a two-story stone entry.

Hunter radioed Miriam Russell to get the fire department rolling, then leaped from his patrol car and ran toward the burning house. As he loped across the driveway of the house just north of the fire, he saw a child and a woman, both in nightclothes, standing barefoot. The little girl was nearly hysterical.

"My brother and sister are in the house!" she cried. "They're trapped! Please don't let them die! Please save them! Please don't let them die!"

The woman, who appeared to be in her forties, stood quietly, saying nothing.

Sergeant Hunter shouted into the radio transmitter he wore on his shoulder, alerting Miriam Russell once more: "We have people trapped in the house!" He wondered if anyone besides the two children might be inside the burning house, and he asked the little girl, "Where's Mom?"

The woman finally spoke. "Well," she said, "*I'm* Mom."

Hunter had precious little time to ponder her strangely detached manner, but it stayed with him as he ran toward the burning house. The woman had seemed very calm, very cool—as if she had no connection at all to what was happening.

The front of the house looked to be uninvolved in the fire at this point, and Hunter had noticed that the front door was closed. When he ran around to the rear of the house— the east side—he was shocked: "I was met with an intense wall of fire shooting out from both the lower level and the upper level of the house."

It was impossible to get in that way. He scrambled for the north end of the house. The first door he came to was hot and smoke was coming through the cracks. Not willing to give up, Hunter raced around to the front door and at that point, he noted gratefully that two backup cars had arrived. "I was going to try to make entry into the front door," he said. "But [when I was] approximately twenty feet from the front door, the door seemed to be—like *vacuumed* in or sucked into the house. . . . It fell in."

As hopeless as he felt, Hunter kept trying. There had to be some way to get to the children trapped inside. He saw another door, which appeared to lead into the multi-car garage. He tried to break its glass window with the butt of his flashlight. But the glass was too thick.

The blaze was being fanned by a stiff wind—Hunter had never seen a fire move so fast. As the flames roared in their ears, he and the other officers raced around the house, trying to find a way in. Hunter had been on the scene less than five minutes and already, he thought, the house was fully involved. Reluctantly, he ordered Corporal Curt Winn, Officer John Jagow, and Officer Larry Lamb not to try to go in.

Now they heard the fire sirens. Maybe, with the fire department's equipment, someone might still get in, in time to bring out the brother and sister the little girl had begged Hunter to save.

He wondered how *she* had gotten out. And the mother: How had *she* escaped the flames?

*

Drs. John and Mary Forman had been sound asleep
shortly after midnight on that blustery Monday night
when they were awakened by their dog's frantic barking.
They heard their doorbell ringing and someone rapping
on their side door. Waking more quickly than her husband, Mary Forman urged him to get up and answer the
door. He led the way down the stairs and, still drowsy,
opened the door without deactivating their burglar alarm.
The alarm, designed to automatically call a monitoring
service that would notify police and fire personnel, began
to blare.

Debora Green stood at the Formans' side entrance. She
wore some kind of nightgown or muumuu. Her hair was
very wet, and it looked uncombed, as if she had only run her
fingers through it or towel-dried it.

"*Call 111!*" Debora cried. "My house is on fire. My children are in there." Again and again, she asked John Forman
to call, not *911*, but *111*.

From the door on the south side of the Formans' house,
the view was of their neighbors' four-car garage. John and
Mary could see flames above the top of the garage. John
immediately grabbed the closest phone and called 911 to
report the fire, stressing that three children were still inside
the burning house. At the same time, Mary Forman called
911 from her car phone.

When John Forman returned to the door, Debora wasn't
there. It was easy to lose track of someone in the chaos of a
fire, their barking dog, and the blaring burglary alarm.
Forman noted the strong winds and, knowing how vulnerable their own shake roof was to fire, he fully expected their
house to go up next. He and Mary ran to wake their four
children and piled them into John's car. He hurriedly
backed it out of the garage and moved it to a safe spot.
Then Mary Forman called Mike from her car phone and
told him his house was on fire.

The first police car—Steve Hunter's—had turned in to
their cul de sac during John Forman's call to 911. He was

surprised at the quick response. He didn't know, then, that someone had already called.

Other neighbors were getting their children out, just as the Formans had, and moving their cars from their garages to Seventy-fifth. The houses on Canterbury Court were huge, but they were built on relatively small lots with many trees. It was possible that the whole street could go up in flames, just as complete neighborhoods are turned to ashes in California fires. The wind blew heedlessly, making everything worse.

Meanwhile, although no one saw her but Debora, Lissa had somehow managed to climb out of the window of her room at the front of the house and make her way over the peak of the garage. The next time the Formans saw Debora, she had Lissa with her, and it was Lissa who was screaming at a policeman to save her brother and sister while her mother stood there as expressionless as a statue.

It took Mike only ten minutes to reach 7517 Canterbury Court. When he arrived there were fire trucks, police cars, and emergency vehicles everywhere. "I could see smoke and flames coming out of the house from Seventy-fifth Street," he recalled. "I talked to a firefighter briefly and asked him where I should park, and I parked up on Seventy-fifth Street in front of a police cruiser."

Mike ran from his truck past the corner house and then the Formans', until he was standing in his own front yard. There were three policemen there; soon, they all had to back off because of the tremendous heat.

Perhaps because the mind blocks out terrible realities, it did not occur to Mike that anyone was *in* the house. He worried instead about how he was going to get clothes for his children to wear because it looked as though everything they owned was going up in flames. "I thought of all the other hassles of a fire because I knew what it was like—we'd been through a fire before." That fire had happened only eighteen months ago. Then, too, it had been a neighbor who called him and shouted, "Your house is on fire!"

Where would they all live now?

Mike had grabbed his mobile phone when he ran from his car, and now he called Celeste and told her that his house was burning. Later, he relived that moment, shaking his head at how well he had blocked out the worst possible scenario. "I said to Celeste, 'I'll bet Deb set it on fire.' It never even crossed my mind that the kids would be in any danger. I assumed they would be out." If Debora had set the last fire—which he strongly suspected now—she had been very careful to keep the children, and even Boomer, the Labrador, safely out of harm's way.

Mike told Steve Hunter that he was the owner of the house that was burning. Hunter took his arm and walked him back toward Seventy-fifth Street.

"Where are my kids?" Mike asked, looking around at the crowd that had gathered, trying to find their familiar faces. He wondered where his children had been taken. They would be cold in only their pajamas. "He didn't answer me," Mike said softly. "And so I knew right away that something was wrong. I asked him again, and by that time we were at a police cruiser and he pointed inside the police cruiser and he said, 'Your wife, Debora, and one of your daughters is in there. The other two children are in the house.'"

Mike let out a primal scream of pain and rage. He pulled away from Hunter and looked back at his house. The October wind was whipping the flames above the treetops. Tim and Kelly were inside that inferno. That could not be. He had been with them only a few hours ago, and they had been happy and laughing. He could not imagine that they could survive the awesome flames, which made a sound unlike anything he had ever heard. He *knew*—but he didn't want to ask anyone whether what he feared was true. He didn't want to hear the answer.

Slowly, Mike turned to Debora. "What have you done this time?"

She didn't answer. She only stared straight ahead as she sat in the police car.

Maurice Mott is now the battalion chief of Consolidated Fire District No. 2 of northeast Johnson County, in charge of twenty firefighters and three fire stations. Altogether, District 2 serves nine cities. On October 24, 1995, Mott was a captain assigned to Station Number 2 in Prairie Village. He and his firefighters worked twenty-four-hour shifts, from eight in the morning until eight the next morning.

The tones sounded in Station Number 2 shortly before 12:25 A.M. Mott's ladder company rolled out of the garage in moments. En route, they learned that two people were believed to be trapped in the house, and they went even faster. They were on the scene of the Canterbury Court fire at 12:31. Six minutes.

In firefighting, everything happens at warp speed. The battalion chief is the incident commander, sizing up the situation, deciding whether to call in more help, considering his water supply options, assigning men to tasks. "When we pulled up," Mott said, "our driver was our pump operator so he got the water. I had two firefighters with me. . . . They pulled a hand line and approached the front door."

Fire hoses come in different diameters, some far too heavy for firefighters to carry by hand. Indeed, firefighters designate the seriousness of a fire not only by the number of alarms sounded, but by the diameter of the hoses needed to fight it—"a two-and-a-half-inch fire," a "one-and-three-quarter-inch fire." This was obviously a two-and-a-half-inch fire. But Mott's men could carry the hand line, and the next truck would bring the monitor, which looks a great deal like a cannon. Up to three hoses feed into it, and it can bombard a fire with 1,000 gallons of water a minute.

Seeing that theirs was the first company on the scene, Mott shouted assignments and then took off on his own. Preserving life is the number one priority of any firefighter.

The front door faced west, but Mott first headed south and talked to a Prairie Village police officer. It was not a real conversation; it was a matter of shouting information as Mott ran by. "He [the officer] said he had been to an intrusion alarm at this house in the past," Mott would recall, "and he felt there was a downstairs bedroom on the south end of the house." That might mean there was some hope. The house appeared to have three levels. The upper floor was burning fiercely; the main floor showed fire; but the basement level might still provide shelter.

Mott could only hope that the cop's information was correct, and that the two people trapped inside were in that basement bedroom. At the front of the house, flames were shooting out the windows above the door and showing through at least half of the roof. When Mott reached the south side, he could see the back of the house. "I saw fire from the gutter line to the ridge. . . . I saw fire blowing out of the back [east side] of the house and extending to a wood deck on the back of this house and a railing. That was on fire from the fire blowing out."

It would be too late for anyone trapped upstairs in the north end of the house. Mott could not make his way across the backyard at all, even though the swimming pool was there. The billowing flames and intense heat barred his way. "I radioed 'Command' and advised him I had fifty percent involvement," Mott said.

Every other firefighter on the scene was busy with his own assignment. Mott commandeered the police officer to follow him to the ladder truck to get a ladder and an ax. They ran to the south side of the house. It was the only hope: Mott didn't see any fire through the windows at the south end. He climbed the ladder to a second-floor window and used the ladder to break it. Wearing an air tank, he leaned the top half of his body into the room, which he now saw was a bathroom. He could just make out the outline of a tub.

Three times, he yelled, *"Fire Department!"*

"I got no response," he said. "I left the ladder at that window and came down to this window [at ground level at the southeast corner] and broke it out with my ax." And again, he leaned his upper body into the room beyond. He could see perhaps two feet into the room; everything beyond was obscured by smoke. Again, he called out. Again, there was no answer.

The two men broke the southwest window and Mott grabbed handfuls of the vertical blinds hanging there, pulling them loose, tossing them out on the lawn. He noted that though they had burned spots they weren't smoking.

Mott could not go in alone: firefighters must work in pairs, for their own safety. He ran to the command post and signaled a newly arrived crew to come with him. He and the three men who followed him had their turnout gear: helmets, coats, gloves, boots, air packs—everything possible to protect them against the raging fire.

Mott broke the group into two-man teams. "I directed the two other firefighters to go into the [main floor] window. I told them not to go too far because of the overhead fire." Then he asked the remaining firefighter, Wayne Harder, to help him search the ground level. Harder was from another department. Mott had never seen him before; he might never see him again. Good firefighters are trained so well in the basic rules of rescue and survival that they know what to do. For these tense minutes, Mott and Harder would be responsible for each other's lives as they felt their way through rooms whose ceilings might drop on them at any moment.

They entered through the window where the blinds had been and dropped to the floor to crawl on their hands and knees. "We search by feel . . . through years of training," Mott explained. "We listen to fire crackling and we feel our way around the house. . . . To keep our bearings, we search to the right—so no matter how many rooms we have—closets, bathrooms, kitchens—if we continue to go to the right, eventually we'll end up back at the place where we made entry."

Mott and Harder could do nothing about the blaze itself: they had no firefighting equipment. They were hoping to save lives. In each room, they looked in closets, under beds, under tables. They moved through what was obviously a bedroom, sweeping the floor with their arms spread wide. They found no one. They were trying to buy time, and it was too awkward to crawl. They risked getting up off their hands and knees and walked in a bent-over shuffle.

The next room was a recreation room. Again, they found no one. They moved on to a hallway and came to a closed door. Mott opened it—to find a wall of fire. "I could see through the floor joists to the first floor of the residence," Mott said. There was nothing they could do here, with the fire blazing above all the way to the roof. Mott closed the door.

In what was obviously a playroom, they found only piles of toys and dress-up clothes. They entered a room with a pool table, but they didn't stay long. The ceiling fell in on them. Sheetrock, insulation, and boards let go and knocked Mott and Harder to their knees. Their time to find someone alive had run out. Their time to stay alive themselves was about to do the same.

After committing what he had seen inside to memory, Mott knew that they could be the next victims if they didn't get out of there. "We had done our jobs." In the dark, working to the right, they found the room where they had entered the house. Outside, they rejoined the other pair, who had worked their way in past the bathroom one floor up. They had not found anyone either.

Next the four men searched the garage. There was one car visible there and they still had faint hopes of finding the children—even one child—alive. But there was no one in the car or under it.

One of the assisting fire companies had set up a monitor hose in the neighbors' yard and water cascaded over the burning house. The firefighters had almost accepted the fact that the two children in the house were beyond saving, but Mott didn't want to give up. There was a walkway entry to the house from the garage that ended with two steps up to a locked door. When Mott and his men kicked the lock open, the door felt "spongy."

But there was nothing on the other side but "fall-down"— material from an upper floor that had dropped when the ceiling burned through. As much as Mott and his men wanted to get in the house, it was not possible through this route. Sheetrock, light fixtures, insulation—all had tumbled down and kept them from opening the door.

It was obvious now that the northern part of the house, particularly the upper portion, had suffered the most destruction. The firefighters feared the missing children might be up there. That was the children's wing, according to officers who had been called to the house before, and if that was true, any hope the firefighters had of saving the two missing children was futile by the time they arrived on the scene.

The fire was "tapped" —put out—at about 1:45 A.M., although the firefighters would remain on the scene all night.

No one knew yet what had caused this disaster, but the house had gone up so rapidly that arson had to be considered. Detectives Gary Baker and Trish Campbell of the Prairie Village police were called at their homes and told to come directly to the fire scene. Detective Sergeant Greg Burnetta and Detective Rod Smith were asked to report to the Prairie Village police station and stand by to question witnesses.

At what had been a lovely home at 7517 Canterbury Court, police and firefighters continued their work as the heedless wind blew. It would be hours before the ruined house cooled enough for them to go in and look for the bodies of Tim and Kelly Farrar. And it might be days before teams of detectives and arson investigators could identify the cause of the fire.

Chapter 17

Young though she was, Lissa held no more hope than her father about the fate of Tim and Kelly. While she was being treated by paramedics for smoke inhalation in the fire department ambulance, Mike and Lissa had a tragic conversation. "She looked at me," Mike recalled, "and she said, 'Dad, they're dead, aren't they?' I had to tell her, 'Yes, Lissa—I'm afraid they are.'"

Mike, Debora, and Lissa were transported to the Prairie Village Police Department in the early morning hours of October 24, 1995. Lissa waited in one room with Mike's parents, twisting her hands nervously, her face stained with tears and smoke. Mike and Debora were taken to separate rooms.

Mike would wait by himself for several hours. It was a terrible time to be alone, but the detectives wanted to question Debora first. He tried not to think about Tim and Kelly. Maybe there would be good news, although any rational being who had gazed into that hell of fire that had been a house would have a hard time being optimistic.

Detective Gary Baker had arrived at the fire scene shortly after 2:30 A.M. He would report back to headquarters as soon as there was any definitive word. At about three, the firefighters signaled that they had found a body. Baker had called Rod Smith to tell him that, and then called back almost immediately to say that it was one of the dogs—a greyhound.

Debora, still barefoot and wearing a dark rose cotton nightgown with a white collar and cuffs and a whimsical pattern of white sheep, was taken to a basement office in the police department. Here she would be interviewed by Detective

Sergeant Greg Burnetta and Detective Rod Smith. This
interview, and, indeed, all the other interviews connected to
the investigation would be videotaped so that every word,
inflection, and emotion would be available for reevaluation.
The video camera is a remarkably effective new tool available to forensic science.

Although the Prairie Village police have since moved to
new headquarters, in October 1995 the department was
housed in a rather outdated facility next door. The best
room for talking with Debora had painted cement-block
walls and a linoleum floor, all of the same bland, pale celery
color. There was a folding table—the kind families buy for
reunions—and some vinyl and metal folding chairs. The
room was not soundproof; and occasionally far-off tele-
phones and distant officers' voices could be heard.

It was one minute after four A.M. on Tuesday morning,
October 24, when Rod Smith started the tape rolling. He
and Greg Burnetta knew virtually nothing about the cause
of the fire that had struck Debora's home. They had been
wakened and summoned to headquarters to try to make
some sense of an embryonic case.

Burnetta and Smith did know that reports from
Canterbury Court were pessimistic about the chance that
Debora's son and younger daughter had survived. A
number of fire companies had been called out to fight the
blaze; this usually indicated that a residence was fully
involved. So the two detectives were somewhat startled to
find Debora talkative, even cheerful. Although there was a
slight odor of alcohol about her, she did not seem
intoxicated.

She was not an attractive woman. Stocky, with heavy,
almost masculine shoulders, she appeared to be in her mid-
forties, yet she perched in her chair with one leg tucked
under her in an almost childlike posture. She shifted her
position frequently; from time to time, she rubbed her feet
and picked at her toes. She wasn't crying, nor did she look
as if she had been crying.

Burnetta and Smith sat at one end of the fake-wood conference table, while Debora sat on a long side and turned
her head to the right toward them. Burnetta was dressed in
a striped white dress shirt, tie, and trousers; Smith wore
jeans, a sweatshirt that read "Kansas," athletic shoes, and a
baseball cap. Their roles quickly became apparent. It was
Smith who made small talk with Debora, while Burnetta
only occasionally asked questions, instead bending his head
over a yellow legal pad and taking copious notes.

"What we're going to talk about," Smith said, "is the
house fire at your house—"

"Which, by the way," Debora interrupted, "is the fire out?"

The detectives told her, truthfully, that they had not been
there yet.

"You're not under arrest," Smith said. "You're free to
leave anytime you want."

Debora was affable, but she asked, "Who are you guys?"

Burnetta and Smith introduced themselves and
explained their roles. She nodded agreeably. "I'm just curious," she said, and laughed. "I didn't know whether you
were the police or the fire department."

Debora's voice was very nasal, as if she had a cold, but her
affect was that of a woman completely comfortable in her
environment, and she seemed anxious to talk. She gave long,
convoluted answers to every question the detectives asked.

Asked if she was under the influence of alcohol or any
drugs, Debora said firmly, "No. I had *a* drink earlier tonight.
One. Maybe one and a half. Barely. I'm fuzzy on time
tonight because I can't remember what time I went to bed—
but I'd say between nine-thirty and ten-thirty. I had about a
drink and a half at dinnertime, and they were not strong to
begin with. I drank about half of the second one and then
just turned the light off and went to sleep."

Later, Debora said she had gone to her room, the master
bedroom on the south end of the main floor, where she
read and perhaps dozed. She thought Tim had gone to bed
at ten, but some noise had wakened her around eleven and

she went out to the kitchen. He was there, getting something to eat. They had said good night and gone to their own rooms at opposite ends of the house.

"And that's the last I saw of any of them," Debora said. "I turned my lamp off somewhere around eleven-thirty. . . . I did have a conversation with my husband on the phone sometime during the evening. It must have been ten or ten-thirty. He called me and asked me, 'What did you want?' He said someone had paged him. I told him, 'I did not page you, and to the best of my knowledge the kids are asleep. If you want, I'll go up and check.'"

She had found no one awake, she said. Burnetta noted all the discrepancies in times.

Debora told Smith and Burnetta that she was taking Prozac—20 milligrams a day—and that the last dose she had taken was at ten on Monday morning, fourteen hours before the fire. She recalled that she had been wakened from a sound sleep by a blaring noise. She said she assumed that her house had both a burglar and a fire alarm. "The alarm signal that woke me was nothing I recognized, and when I went to the panel in my room and tried to shut it off, it didn't do anything."

Debora said she was used to the burglar alarm going off; it had done so several times recently because she had two big dogs that set off the motion detector. But this sound was entirely different. "I thought I'd heard every noise it knew how to make—but this was a new one."

She had tried three or four times to shut the alarm off at the control panel with no success. "So I opened the door to the hall—and it was just filled with smoke. It scared me, so I found the key that's always on my bookshelf."

Debora explained that she had to unlock the deadbolt on her bedroom door from the inside in order to step out onto the deck along the back of the house. "I left that way. As I went around the corner to inform the neighbors to call 911, that's when I heard Tim on the intercom by the pool deck— he used to be my thirteen-year-old."

Debora spoke in a steady stream-of-consciousness style, and she was apparently unaware that she had just referred to Tim in the past tense. She hurriedly explained that Tim had lost so many keys that he was quite used to going in and out of his window by means of the second-floor roof. "He must have done that thirty times."

Debora had heard his voice on the intercom, but hadn't seen him. She didn't explain why she had not looked up toward his voice, but only listened to the intercom box attached to the wall of their house, by the back deck. "He said, 'Mom, what shall I do?' I said, 'Tim, wait where you are and I'm going to call 911 to come and save you,' and he said, 'Well, should I get one of the girls and try to come out?' I said 'No'—which, I'm sure, was the kiss of death."

Her words were chilling, but her inflection was matter-of-fact, even chatty. Debora could not recall the last time she had talked to Tim. She mentioned often that she was still "fuzzy" on time. She did remember running to the Formans' and asking them to call 911. "But I have a feeling someone else had called, because by the time they understood what I was saying, the trucks had started to arrive."

Debora did not say why she had not simply dialed 911 from the phone in her own bedroom or whether she had even lifted the phone to see if there was a dial tone.

After Dr. Forman had left her at his side door to call for help, Debora remembered, she turned around and saw "my ten-year-old on the garage roof. Lissa's afraid of heights," she remarked. "She's afraid of pretty much everything. I said, 'Jump!' and she said, 'No, I can't do it,' and I said, 'You *will*! Jump to me now.' And she jumped—and I missed her totally. I'm sure she'll never trust anybody. And she fell down right at my feet, but she was not hurt. But I'm sure that's the only reason we have Lissa alive."

When Rod Smith asked Debora to go over the afternoon and evening before the fire in as much detail as she could, Debora recalled the day virtually minute by minute. She had picked her children up from their Pembroke Hill schools at three P.M. on Monday. "They all go to Pembroke Hill," she said, speaking so fast that it was hard to make out her words. "At least, the living ones do."

Again Smith and Burnetta noted that Debora was referring to her children in the past tense. But she continued her recitation without pause. She said that after she got them home from separate schools in the Pembroke Hill system, she took Lissa to buy two pairs of shoes. "Then we went home, and I gave everyone small assignments of chores to get done, and they did them, and then they were watching *Saved by the Bell* or one of those shows until the point that Lissa and I had to leave.

"We had one of those typical nights. I had a psychiatrist's appointment at five-forty-five, and Lissa, the ten-year-old, had a ballet class from six to seven-thirty, and Tim had a hockey game at seven-fifteen, which left Kelly at loose ends."

Debora said she had left Tim and Kelly home alone, waiting for Mike, who was to pick them up at 6:40. He brought them home about nine, "give or take five or ten minutes. And they had their typical good home-cooked meal of Kentucky Fried Chicken. And [the girls] then went to bed. But Tim was up until about eleven. I talked to him for quite a while in the kitchen."

They had discussed Tim's hockey game, which had gone extremely well. Rod Smith asked if he was a goalie, and she shook her head. "He's not a goalie—he played goalie for two or three years, though."

Asked about the status of her marriage, Debora answered vaguely. "I'm not even sure anything's been filed, but we *are* signing . . . in the process of divorce." She said that her two older children were very angry with their father. "In fact," she remarked, "later today—at one-thirty—I have an appointment with a counselor to talk about what to do with the kids, before they go in to see him."

Debora said the counseling would be for her and her three children because her husband had never been a major part of their lives. She was concerned about Tim and Lissa, while Kelly seemed to be taking the divorce fairly well.

She told Smith and Burnetta that Mike was a cardiologist, and she listed her own varied medical specialties, saying that she had stopped practicing at the "suggestion—really the *coercion*—of my husband, who wanted me to stay home and be a mom. I even retired my license. A big deal in *my* life the last couple of weeks has been 'What am *I* going to do? Now.' Because my life is changing whether I like it or not. So what I've decided I want to do is I want to do a psych residency, which will be a whole new deal for me . . . to live life the way I want."

Her words rushed on, faster than Greg Burnetta could possibly write them down. He did his best, but he was glad that the video camera was catching them, too. There was scarcely a second's pause between one of Debora's thoughts and the next, and yet she seemed entirely rational—except for her references to Tim and Kelly in both the past and the present tense.

One thing was patently clear: Debora harbored intense rage toward her estranged husband. She apparently found fault with almost everything he did. She recalled that the weekend just past had been chaotic because she had to pick up Tim from his father's apartment when he called wanting to come home, and then return for Lissa at midnight because she had heard her paternal grandmother and other relatives talking about her mother. "She was very upset and very angry," Debora said, "because she was hearing her father and her grandmother talking about what a slob her mother was and how she couldn't keep the house clean and how Lissa had no social skills because *'she'* [Debora] had no social skills."

Debora told Smith and Burnetta that she had promised her children she would always come and get them if they found themselves, at their father's apartment, in a situation that they just couldn't handle. Then she elaborated on her appointment with the counselor. The therapy was intended only for her children and their feelings toward their father.

"We always said it was just the three kids and me, and they really didn't care if he was there, but they were tired of listening to his crap. So they're angry."

Asked about her own feelings, Debora chuckled as she said, "I haven't been particularly upset—or really even terribly emotionally involved. That's not quite the truth. I felt a tremendous sense of relief when he moved out, which surprised him because he thought I'd be *devastated.*"

With virtually no prompting from Smith or Burnetta, Debora leaped continually from one aspect of her life to another. The Prairie Village investigators noted that most of her conversation revolved around *her* feelings and *her* plans. Once more, she told them of her intention to become a psychiatrist, and of her hope that she would be accepted into a fellowship or residency at Menninger's. She wondered aloud how she could get back and forth to Topeka and still be sure someone could pick up her children—who would, of course, remain in the Pembroke Hill school system.

Debora returned again and again to her contention that all three of her children hated their father. "Tim has come to that incredible level of respect," she said, laughing, "where he says, 'Fuck you!' to his dad. And Lissa's beginning to do it, too."

Burnetta deliberately averted his face so that Debora could read no expression there. Smith, playing the easygoing partner, grinned at her, although he was taken aback by the raw hatred she seemed to feel for her husband. She was clearly delighted that her children had come to a point where they shared her feelings, where they shouted, "Fuck you!," at their father.

It was obvious, too, that, in Debora's mind, the children were wholly hers. The videotape rolled on, with only a word or two from Rod Smith or Greg Burnetta.

Debora seemed to have forgotten—or repressed—the sight of her house in flames. She explained that Lissa had been very excited Monday because she had won the role of Clara in *The Nutcracker Suite.* That had been her goal since she began taking ballet lessons in 1991, when she was only six. "She already had ten and a half hours of ballet a week to begin with," Debora said. "And last weekend she got thirty extra hours—so she was pretty tired."

One very effective interrogation technique is to ask the same questions two or three times in slightly different ways. Any small incongruities will pop to the surface with each flawed retelling. When Rod Smith again asked her to recall the previous evening, Debora repeated herself in precise detail.

When Mike brought Tim and Kelly home from the hockey game, she said, "I was kind of surprised to see that he had just walked into the house—because we reached a point a few weeks ago when I kind of demanded to have all my keys and garage door openers back and he refused to give them to me." She had not had her locks changed. "I just let it go, but I thought we had worked it out that he was not to be there unless he was invited. I was walking down the hall toward the kitchen and glanced over to my left to the entryway, and he had come in with Kelly."

Debora said she had ignored her husband while he flipped through his mail. "I guess he got bored and left," she said, estimating the time at nine P.M.

Debora's ceaseless monologue was bizarre, but Burnetta and Smith were not psychiatrists. They didn't know if she was talking so fast because she didn't want to think about the fire, or if she simply enjoyed having a rapt audience. Nor did they know if she was trying to present herself as a good mother and show them what a rotten father Mike was. She was clearly not drunk, nor did she seem to be under the influence of medication. Her memory for minutiae was perfect. She was so sure of times and places that she might have been reading out of an appointment book. And the two investigators most certainly did not know the motivation behind her barrage of words. They simply sat and listened.

Debora described the layout of her entire house, ending with the children's wing on the upper floor at the north end. There were four bedrooms and two bathrooms in that wing. "They go up there and *stay* up there," she said, laughing again, "because I don't want to see their mess! They share it with the dogs."

Usually, the two dogs slept with Debora, but on Monday Boomer and Russell had discovered a bag of coffee beans, dragged it out into the living room, ripped it up, and eaten countless beans. "So I said, 'These dogs are not going to sleep again for a hundred years, so they're not sleeping with *me* tonight,' so each of the girls took a dog. Kelly took Boomer, the Lab, and Lissa took Russell."

Then Debora performed another erratic leap. "He's been so odd lately," she said, referring to Mike and their phone conversations that night. "I said, 'No, I'm not going to talk to you tonight. I'm just not interested . . .' And then I hung up. And then I remembered something."

She said she knew he was on his way home to his apartment in his truck, so she had called him. For a moment, she could not recall why—oh, yes. It was about their attorneys. She said Mike had been "really snotty" because she had taken too long deciding if she would accept Norman Beal, who had been *their* attorney, as Mike's divorce lawyer. She said he had warned her a few days before that if she didn't make up her mind, he would go out and get "a real nut-cutter attorney." He had reverted to that refrain last night, she said, so she hung up on him. She had read for perhaps five minutes. After that, she went to sleep until the cacophony of some alarm had wakened her.

"You probably talked to him last at about what time?" Smith asked.

"Maybe eleven-twenty-five, eleven-thirty," Debora said.

In the predawn hours of Tuesday morning, Gary Baker waited on the lawn at 7517 Canterbury Court with Sergeant Steve Hunter and Detective Trish Campbell. Most of the neighbors had finally gone to bed. Some families, like the

Formans, were nervous about sleeping so close to the fire
and had accepted the hospitality of neighbors further away.
Except for some stubborn hot spots, the fire was out. But the
wind still blew and it smelled of ashes and cinders and
smoke.

Baker looked up to see one of the firefighters beckoning
to him. The house had finally cooled enough to enable him
to go in and assess the damage. Given a choice, he would
have preferred to walk in the other direction. He didn't
want to see what waited inside.

The first body was about fifteen or twenty feet directly
beyond the front door. From where Baker stood, he could
see that an iron bed frame and springs had apparently
dropped from an upper story and come to rest on the joists
of the room in front of him. Just to the left of that pile of
springs and iron posts lay a badly burned human body. He
could not be certain who it was, but from its size he judged
it was the missing teenage boy. The body had landed on the
charred joists of the living room floor below his bedroom.
The investigators would have to saw the joists in two in order
to remove it.

Next the firefighters led Baker into what appeared to be
the kitchen. They told him it was unsafe to try to get to the
second story via the staircase; he would have to climb a
ladder propped up in the kitchen closet. Baker climbed up
the ladder until he could see into the room above. It was
clearly a child's room. When his eyes adjusted to the light,
he saw the body of a small girl lying on her back in her
bottom bunk, the covers pulled up to her waist. There were
no signs that she had struggled at all. She and the big black
Lab beneath her bed had been overcome by smoke and had
died of carbon monoxide poisoning, in their sleep. Baker
felt some slight relief at learning that Kelly Farrar had never
awakened. And yet this was the sight hardest for him to bear:
"It took me a long time to get Kelly out of my mind."

The house was a burned-out shell. Furniture had actually
vaporized; windows had been blown out; walls had disap-

peared. Everything above the basement was damaged or missing. Baker could stand on the joists where a hardwood floor had once gleamed and look up at the dawning sky above. He and his fellow detectives would work eighty hours of overtime over the next two weeks to find out what had led to the horrible deaths of two children and their pets in that inferno.

"And every night," Baker would say, "the first thing I did when I got home was hug my kids."

Chapter 18

Back at the Prairie Village police station, Debora had not yet asked about Tim and Kelly. Nor had she asked where Lissa was. She just talked on and on and on.

Rod Smith led the conversation back to the window of time before and during the fire. He wanted to know exactly what time Debora had talked to Mike when he called to ask who had paged him.

It was after all the children had gone to bed, Debora said, but before Tim got back up and went to the kitchen around eleven. "Tim wanders," she said, chuckling.

"So you said you went upstairs to see if they had called?" Smith asked.

"I just peeked in the doors and saw nobody was awake. Even the dogs were sleeping. I just assumed that if anybody had called, it must not be important—it wasn't worth bothering about." She had paged Mike to tell him the children were asleep.

Debora said she had spoken to her husband a third time. "And then I called him again because I figured he's up and he's on his car phone. I was just calling to make sure he got that message from the lawyer. . . . That was probably no more than five minutes after he called me."

"How long did that conversation last?"

"Probably five minutes."

"You had a discussion that was pretty calm?"

"No." She laughed. "It was pretty apathetic."

"He say where he was at?"

"He just said he was on his way home in the truck. When I asked him earlier—when I paged him—he said he was 'out with friends.'"

"You lost me at one point," Smith drawled easily.

"I'm sure." Debora laughed. "I lost myself at several points."

"He called you about ten-thirty—"

"Right—whenever that was."

"There had been an earlier conversation when he called you about the lawyers?"

"I think that was yesterday when he called me."

Debora explained again that she and Mike had used the same attorney for the trust fund and for estate planning. "And then he got this wild hair and decided he wanted a divorce. And I said it seems to me there's a *major* conflict of interest." She told the detectives about the waiver she had finally signed, and how her lawyer had "an absolute fit" to learn that, and then had gone off to Vermont on a vacation and "left everything up in the air." But the attorney—Ellen Ryan—had come back from vacation and said she had no real objection to Norman Beal as Mike's lawyer. And *that*, Debora said, was why she had phoned her husband in his truck.

Debora clearly wanted the detectives to be aware that she was totally uninterested in the details of her pending divorce; she said it was only in the beginning stages, and no temporary support had been set up. "I don't even think there's been a paycheck [for Mike] since all this started. There's enough money in all the accounts just to live on for now."

The interview in the stark, pale room had gone on for nearly an hour and Debora still had not asked about her children.

She said she had talked to Mike for only five minutes in the call she made to his truck, about the attorneys. "I was really tired."

"What woke you up?" Smith asked, coming back to the vital times from another direction.

". . . It was more of a buzzer sound, not an alarm sound—no, there *was* an alarm type sound along with the buzzer. . . . There's a panel in my room, one by the front door, and one by the garage door. In fact," she said, "they're probably registering right now whatever set off the alarm—I just didn't think to look at it. I just tried to get it to shut off."

"What time did that wake you up?" Smith asked.

Debora wasn't much help. "Whenever. Maybe twelve-fifteen? It seems as if everything telescoped pretty close together. But I—honest to God—have no idea when the alarm went off. I didn't look at a clock. It could have been as early as midnight, or as late as twelve-thirty."

She agreed that it couldn't have been very long after she had gone to bed. At first, she had told them she went to bed between 9:30 and 10:30; then she decided it was after 11:30.

"So what did you do when you woke up?" Smith asked.

Debora repeated her story of struggling to turn off the alarm, of opening the hall door. "It was *really* full of smoke, so I turned around and closed the door." She unlocked the door to the deck and went outside. "And that's when I told Tim to wait. He was talking into the intercom in his room to the speakers on the pool deck. He was fairly calm but I could tell he was nervous."

Tim had said, "Mom, what should I do?"

"'Stay where you are,' I said. 'And stay calm, and I'll call 911 and they'll come rescue you.' And he said, 'Shall I get out?' and I said, 'Why don't you go figure out where Kelly is?'"

"Kelly?"

"She's my six-year-old." Debora had a tendency to refer to her children by their ages rather than their names, and she never said "*our* children"; it was always "*my* children."

Somewhere, far back in the inner rooms of the police station, a phone rang. It seemed to bring Debora back to the reason why they were talking. For the first time, her voice lost its perky, humorous tone; there was a quaver in it as she said, "And I know that if Tim or Kelly—either one—had made it, we'd know by now."

Smith and Burnetta didn't know, not for sure. Smith quickly asked Debora another question, the ages of all her children. She responded quickly, perhaps afraid herself of what might have happened to them.

"No," she answered to Smith's next question, another repeat, "I didn't think of calling 911 in my room. It never entered my mind. When I opened the door, there was so much smoke. It was very acrid-smelling and -tasting—and I closed the door quickly, trying to make sure that I didn't get a whole lot of smoke in my room . . . and I went across the room and had a little trouble finding the opening. And I think I got a little scared. I think I thought, 'God, I'm going to asphyxiate right now. . . .' so when I got the door open, all I thought of was getting out."

But she had told Tim to wait, and finally said, "If you feel like you *have* to do something, go find Kelly." ("She's on the same half of the hall he is," Debora explained.)

"Did you see Tim?"

"No, I just talked to him. If I had backed away from the house and looked up, I might have been able to see him."

"Could you see fire?"

"The back of my house is pretty much all glass. And I could see the full length of the hall inside with a few interruptions. Looking in the front hall from the pool deck, I could see flames, and I started to hear glass explosions. I couldn't tell what was exploding, but glass was starting to explode pretty vigorously."

Greg Burnetta had stepped out of the room, leaving Rod Smith to keep the conversation going. He asked Debora if she had any power outages on Monday because of the high winds. She replied that they had lost power around three, but only enough to cause "brownouts." Still, she believed the power had gone off for a while because her clocks were flashing when she brought the children home from school at 4:20.

The wind had been "fierce"; Debora told Smith she had actually hoped they would lose power, because she loved the smell of burning vanilla candles. "We could not find either a cigarette lighter or matches, so nothing got lit," she said, laughing again.

Smith and Debora were obviously tap-dancing around possible causes for a fire. "What about the food you cooked?" he asked.

"When I brought the stuff home from Kentucky Fried Chicken, I put it in the oven on Low. When they all got home and were ready to eat, I took that food out and turned it off. So I didn't forget and leave anything on in the kitchen," Debora assured him. "At least, not that I know of." She laughed. "Wouldn't be the first time if I had—that's for sure."

"How many staircases going upstairs?" Smith asked.

"One. It goes up and down."

Burnetta walked back into the room and sat down without saying anything. Debora asked again about what was happening at her house. Her voice dropped and her questions were more insistent now.

"Honestly, I don't know," Smith said. "I haven't been down there. The fire department's still down there. I don't know enough about the fire to tell you what could happen—I haven't been in contact with anybody down there. For all I know, they could be at the hospital."

For the first time, there was a bite in Debora's voice, a tinge of anger. "If someone had taken my kids to the hospital, wouldn't they notify us?"

Smith was stalling. Debora knew that. Probably all of the people sitting around the table knew it. Once the two detectives found out for sure that Kelly and Tim Farrar were dead, the interview would almost certainly come to a halt. And it was desperately important to Burnetta and Smith to get as much information as possible from this bizarrely cheerful woman first. They had a "hinky" feeling about this case. They had told Debora that she could stop the interview at any time, but she showed no interest in doing that. She seemed almost to enjoy talking to them.

"Well," Smith said, making a Freudian slip, "in the heat of the moment, the first thing they're going to do is probably get the kids to the hospital. I would think they'd get them medical attention first."

"Yeah," Debora said, and asked for a glass of water.

To quiet some storm that seemed to be brewing behind Debora's still-calm façade, Smith asked her her birthdate, her phone number, the children's birthdays—the easy questions. She told him of her parents in El Paso, her sister in Louisville.

They made small talk about birthdays in December, so close to Christmas. Both Kelly and Lissa had December birthdays. Debora's voice was not as confident now, and she seemed to be listening for other voices.

"When you were in bed," Smith asked, "did you hear anything as far as noise?"

That was a question Debora could deal with. "Now that you mention it," she said, "two days last week, I heard two people running in my yard between two-thirty and three in the morning. They sounded like they were probably young. It was such an odd hour that it was probably kids. And I thought maybe it was pumpkin-smashing stuff, but my pumpkins were still fine the next day. And my dogs are both such coma dogs. I don't even think either one of them noticed. . . . One night they [the footsteps] were in my backyard—in the pool area. It was just something I noticed, and I thought, 'Should I start to be worried about this?' I was afraid they might be going to break through my back windows . . . but it was only two days, and I never heard anything more."

"No problem with anybody?"

"No."

"Your kids?"

"They don't even bicker with the neighbors. They don't know them well enough."

Lieutenant Terry Young, a detective, walked into the room; Burnetta introduced her to Debora and said Young would get her some warmer clothing.

"When are we going to get some information?" Debora asked.

"I don't know," Burnetta said. "I'll try to do some checking."

Debora went with Lieutenant Young but would agree only to put on some socks and athletic shoes. She walked back to the interview room still wearing her pink nightgown.

It was 5:30 Tuesday morning when Burnetta approached her with the news she had been both expecting and dreading. Gary Baker had called to verify that her oldest child and her youngest were dead. Breaking such news is the worst job any police officer ever has to do.

"Both the other children are deceased," Burnetta said quietly.

"Oh Jesus Christ!" Debora cried. "I should have let my— I should have let Tim come out when he wanted to! Jesus fucking Christ!"

For just a moment, Debora dropped her head to her arms on the table. Smith and Burnetta stood by, trying to offer sympathy, but she did not want it. "Oh God," she said tearfully. "Beautiful Tim and beautiful Kelly are both *dead?*"

And then Debora's demeanor changed, in an instant, to rage. "Jesus Christ! Did they make any attempt at all to save 'em? *I* saved one of the kids. I could have gotten the second one out and didn't. I'll never forgive myself for that. . . ."

There was a strange flatness in her inflection. The words themselves were right, but she sounded as if she were reading the lines. There had been, perhaps, thirty seconds of tears, violent rage and swearing, and then accusations at both the firefighters and herself. But the tone was so very odd.

The detectives suggested that they take a break, but Debora would have none of it. "No. *No.* I'm not taking any more breaks. If you have any more information, I want to know it. I've been sitting here for almost four hours. Okay. Where are the kids?"

"They're in the house," Smith said.

Debora was up and pacing now. "All right. Then I want to be taken back to the house."

Lieutenant Young asked Debora to change from her nightgown into other clothes; this made her angrier. And then, very softly, she asked, "Does my husband know?"

"We'll be talking to him shortly."

"I want to go back to my house," Debora said imperiously. "I want to go back and see my babies. They're dead. You all let them lay there dead for four hours without even letting me know. I'm not going to wait another five or six hours until everybody gets their acts together. I want to go back now."

"Well, we can't do that now," Smith told her, his voice hushed in the face of this complete change from a garrulous, friendly woman to a raging shrew.

"Then I want to know where those kids are being taken," Debora shouted, "because I want to be with them!"

"We'll find out," Smith said.

"'We'll find out,'" she said in a singsong. "I've heard that for four hours."

"I'm sorry," Smith said. "But they just can't rush in there just now—"

"No, of course they can't. There might be somebody still alive."

"They've checked . . . unfortunately."

"God damn it! That thirteen-year-old was alive. He asked me if he could leave that house. . . . This is pathetic!" Debora was building up a head of steam. "Not only is it pathetic the way it was handled. It's pathetic what you guys have done to me. It's pathetic! It's inhuman. It's cold."

"Debora," Burnetta said, "we haven't had any more information than what you've had."

"I can't believe nobody went over there with a cellular phone. I can't believe someone couldn't have gotten some information from someone. This is the most disjointed setup I've ever had to deal with," Debora said witheringly. And then she changed the subject. "I would love to see my husband—even though we're getting a divorce—because he and I will be the only ones who can share in the mammoth grief. But I can't do that. I can't go to my home. I can't see my dead children. I can't see my husband. You people are pathetic."

There was no placating her, whatever they said, so Greg Burnetta asked again if she would change her clothing.

"*Why?*"

"Well, quite frankly," he said slowly, "we'd like to have that clothing to have it tested for a lab report."

"Oh," she said sarcastically. "You don't think it's going to have smoke smells?" Debora stalked to a small room off the interview room and Burnetta asked her to wait for the lieutenant. "What do you think?" she shouted. "I'm going out the window? This is pathetic, truly pathetic. You people need to rethink your policies and you need to enter into your equation possible family members of deceased people. I would never, *never*, treat anyone as much like an animal as you have treated me tonight."

They were still trying to reason with Debora, still trying to be considerate and not allow her shocking outburst to make them respond in kind. Rod Smith asked her gently, "Would you have wanted us to come here and tell you that your children were dead and then find out that they weren't?"

Debora insisted that the Prairie Village police had known her children were dead all along. But they had not seen her burning house. And *she* had. She had watched it blaze from the Formans' driveway, and told Officer Steve Hunter, "I'm Mom" in a remarkably calm voice. If anyone in that room had firsthand knowledge of how much of the Canterbury Court home had been involved in fire, Debora herself did.

She raged on and on at them. "I cannot fucking believe that my two kids are dead. I want to go where my children are going, and it does not take two hours to find out where that is."

Although she was a physician, Debora knew as little as any other civilian about crime scene investigations. Greg

Burnetta and Rod Smith knew that the children's bodies might remain in the house for many hours until the scene was thoroughly "worked" by both detectives and arson investigators. Meanwhile no one but official personnel would be allowed in. Besides, their own pity for this angry woman made them want to spare her the sight of her dead children in a charred and crumbling shell of a house.

Although she kept demanding to see her children, most of all, Debora wanted to be with Mike. "Jesus Christ!" she shouted. "There are two people here that care about what happened. So why can't *we* be together? But apparently you don't have compassion for anyone else. . . . *I* want to tell him. *I want to tell my husband that our babies are dead.*"

Chapter 19

The detectives were certainly not going to allow Debora to talk to Mike before they themselves did. They were already uneasy about this case. They had never seen anyone react to the dread news of a family fatality as Debora did. Her behavior baffled them. At this point, Greg Burnetta had no idea what her husband would be like. Would his affect be as skewed as his wife's? Debora had continually characterized Mike as a thoughtless, selfish womanizer who cared nothing for his children. Was she only reacting like any woman scorned—or was he the SOB that she described?

Burnetta was about to find out. And he wanted to make his own assessment of Mike Farrar, without any preconceived notions. But more than that, he wanted to verify or refute the time line and other information that Debora had given him. He did not want the two parents comparing notes, and that was why they had been kept apart throughout the night.

Already, the Kansas City television and radio reporters were on the trail of a major news story. One of Mike's partners

was driving into the office for their Tuesday morning cor-
porate meeting shortly before six A.M. when he heard the
news bulletin about a disastrous fire on Canterbury Court in
Prairie Village. The bulletin gave no names, but said only
that two fatalities had been reported. His partner paged
Mike at once, but Mike didn't have time to call him back.
He had just been summoned to the interview room.

This had been the longest night any of the principals—
police or family—had ever known. It was 6:20 A.M. when Mike
was brought downstairs to be interviewed. Sergeant Wes
Jordan—one of the two officers who had come to the house
when Debora was taken to the hospital on September 25—
was with him. Jordan was a big, soft-spoken cop. His dark eyes
mirrored Mike's agony. Jordan remembered the troubled boy
and the little blond girl who had tried to comb her mother's
hair so she would look "nice" when he took her away.

Jordan led Mike into the same celery-colored interview
area where Debora had been questioned. Mike had on jeans
and a multicolored sweater, the clothes he had worn to
Tim's hockey game. He was very thin and pale.

Burnetta could see immediately that Mike's demeanor
was diametrically opposed to his wife's. His eyes were red
from crying and it was clearly taking everything he had to
keep himself together. He was braced for whatever terrible
news they had to tell him.

Burnetta introduced himself. "Mike, I'm Greg Burnetta.
It's a shame to have to meet you under these circumstances.
Go ahead and have a seat."

Burnetta explained that he had been called at home to
come in and talk to Debora. Mike nodded; the two officers
shifted uncomfortably in their seats.

"Are you up-to-date on the most current information?"
Burnetta asked.

"I haven't heard anything," Mike answered, his voice weak
with dread.

"I wish I didn't have to tell you this—but your two kids are
dead."

Mike's whole body sagged. "I knew it," he said. "I knew it as soon as I got there—when they told me they weren't out. Did you find them, at least?" His voice was trembling.

"The firemen found the bodies," Burnetta said, "and some of our police officers are present at the house."

At this point, Burnetta and Jordan stepped out of the room for a few minutes, sensing that Mike needed time alone. While Burnetta and Rod Smith had attempted to comfort Debora when she got the awful news and been rebuffed by her rage, Burnetta knew that men usually reacted differently; they needed space to absorb their pain in privacy.

Mike, still watched by the mindless eye of the video camera, sat alone. He sighed deeply, covered his eyes with his hands, and cried softly. It seemed hours before Jordan and Burnetta came back, but only three minutes had passed.

"I wish there was some way I could make you feel better," Jordan said.

"I know," Mike said. "I've told enough people their loved ones were dead to know how bad they feel." And of course he had. As a cardiologist, he had had to explain so many times that a heart was too worn out or too flawed to keep beating. He had seen relatives' faces turn white, seen their mouths protest, and then seen them come to a single awful moment when they accepted that what seemed unbearable had, somehow, to be borne.

Now, it was his turn.

Burnetta handed Mike a white paper cup of coffee, and he held it in both hands as if the warmth might help.

Jordan reminded Mike of the last time they had sat together at dawn, and of how he had made it through the terrible scene on Canterbury Court. "That was a pretty unpleasant task at your house when we had to take your children's mom away. But they did pretty well."

"I know." Mike nodded, clearly anxious to fill the stark room with words. "I know. And they did fine when she was gone, too."

Burnetta, seeing how close Mike was to breaking down, hurried ahead with the basic questions, the easy questions. Mike gave his birthdate—March 3, 1955—his office address, his pager number.

Other parts of the station house were moving into daytime mode. The aroma of coffee filtered into the interview room; garbled-sounding radio messages crackled, and occasionally someone laughed, as if the world had not ended after all.

Mike did quite well until the room grew silent, hushes that somehow were louder than their conversation. And then either Jordan or Burnetta began to ask questions, many designed solely to keep the devastated man in front of them focused. Jordan wondered when it was that he and officer Kyle Shipps had been summoned to the Farrar-Green home. "How long ago was that? Three weeks?"

"Yeah, I think—about three weeks," Mike said weakly.

In truth, it had been exactly four. So much had happened in those four weeks.

Burnetta now suggested the ominous possibility that each of the three men had already considered. He asked if Debora might have started the fire, if she might have to be considered a suspect.

"I think it's a likely possibility," Mike said. "She's been mentally unstable, drinking, severely depressed." He told Burnetta about her four-day commitment at the Menninger Clinic. He said it was so strange, the way she had suddenly started drinking heavily. He had never known her to drink like that before. He himself could come up with no real answers.

"I could never talk to her psychiatrist," Mike said. "I could only deal with the social worker at Menninger's as an intermediary. When I saw that Debora had started to drink again—after Menninger's—I confronted her. She denied it, denied it, denied it. I reported my concerns to the social worker."

Mike said he'd been certain, the night before, that his wife was drunk. "She has a very characteristic pattern of

speaking. Clearly, to my eyes she was drinking. I suppose
it's conceivable that she was drunk enough and drugged
enough that she left a burner on. I have to tell you she's
done some odd things."

He told Burnetta about their first house fire, only eighteen
months before. That, too, had occurred after he had moved
out. They had talked of reconciliation before that first fire,
and had put a bid on the Canterbury Court house. "But I
realized that was just like having a baby when a couple is
having a problem, and I withdrew the offer," Mike said. "Two
days later our house burned. The arson inspectors couldn't
find a cause, but the insurance company did. They said it was
a wire wound around a pipe too tightly. Anyway, we all moved
into my apartment together, and we resubmitted our bid on
the house—the house that burned tonight."

Mike shared one characteristic with Debora; he spoke
very rapidly. However, he stayed on track and his answers
were responsive to Burnetta's questions. Unlike Debora, he
was not enjoying himself as he talked about family secrets.
He was finally saying things out loud that had haunted him
for months.

"Some of my friends were convinced that Debora burned
our first house down to get me back," he said. "At the time
I thought it was absurd. I didn't think she could outsmart
the investigators. But I will tell you that this woman is a brilliant woman. She is *brilliant*. She reads avidly—who knows
what she reads about."

Mike told Burnetta that his marriage had been deterio-
rating badly over the last six months. He had known he was
going to ask for a divorce when they came back from Peru.
It was inevitable. "In late July, I asked her for a divorce, and
things started getting weirder," he said. "It was more than
the bad behavior and swearing I was used to. All her emotions were laid wide open to the kids."

Wes Jordan sat silently, nodding slightly from time to
time. He had seen Debora lose control the night of
September 25.

"And then I got sick," Mike continued. "I was in the hospital for a total of three weeks—I was admitted three times starting with August eighteenth. There was no diagnosis. I had a number of specialists. It was a serious illness. There was one point in time where I damn near died. I was critically ill—more so than I realized at the time."

That was easy for Burnetta and Jordan to believe. Mike was pale, slight, and fragile-looking. Although he was close to six feet tall, he couldn't have weighed more than 130 pounds.

"Each time I went back in the hospital," Mike said, "I had eaten a meal at home that had kind of a bitter taste. But I thought, 'That's nuts—crazy—nuts.' And then I went through her purse, and I found the packets of castor beans."

Mike turned toward Jordan. "I saved one package and I gave you all the rest. I started thinking about it. I found an old internal medicine textbook—the seventh edition of *Harrison's Principles of Internal Medicine*—and I looked up the symptoms and they all fit: nausea, vomiting, diarrhea, low blood pressure. Then I went to the North Kansas City Hospital library and had them do a literature search." He had asked that any articles turned up by the search be mailed to Celeste Walker's address; he didn't want Debora to open the mail and learn what he was up to.

"Honest to God"—Mike shook his head as he spoke—"when I started reading [the articles], I started shaking. I found out that even the KGB had used castor beans—ricin—to eliminate people. The problem is, unless you do a toxicology screen at the time of the illness, you can't get the diagnosis. It's impossible to get a diagnosis now."

Mike also told Burnetta and Jordan about the mysterious letters that had been left on his porch and in the neighbors' yard. He knew Debora's turns of phrase and he recognized the same font as their own computer. "That threw me for a loop," he said. "I confronted her, and finally she admitted it."

The letter the Formans had found was addressed to the headmaster of Pembroke Hill School. Mike said that he had been asked to give a presentation about their Peru trip at the school, and the letter said the school shouldn't let someone with such low morals, someone who would betray his wife, speak to its students.

Surreptitiously, Burnetta glanced at his notes. Only two hours ago, Debora had said, "I haven't been particularly upset—or really even terribly emotionally involved. That's not quite the truth. I felt a tremendous sense of relief when he moved out, which surprised him because he thought I'd be *devastated.*" One of them was either lying or glossing over some facts, Burnetta thought. But that certainly wasn't unheard-of in messy divorces.

Mike began to describe the last six months of what sounded like a hellish marriage. Debora had done "just strange things. She told me she was going to Africa to do missionary work. And then she said she had been accepted at Louisville for a psychiatric residency and that all the arrangements had been made. I checked our phone bill. She hadn't made one call to Louisville. It was all made up.

"The house was absolutely in shambles. There were food wrappers all over every floor. There were clothes strewn about. You know how messy a house can be with three kids, but this was far more than that."

Greg Burnetta, tired as he was, was fascinated. Debora had painted quite a different picture of herself and her marriage. She had described her husband as totally uninvolved, coldly uninterested, and herself as a warm, loving mother who skillfully handled everything to do with her children. She had insisted that neither she nor her children needed Mike.

Mike began talking even faster now, as if under terrible pressure to finally get the story out. The planned visit from the kids to his apartment on the weekend just past had culminated in another screaming fight. Tim and Lissa had never come to his apartment at all. "Debora was screaming at Tim, and Tim was screaming at her." He ended up taking only Kelly. And after that, the neighbors told him that Tim had locked Lissa outside. She was banging on the door and screaming.

Sighing, Mike said that Debora had become totally dysfunctional. "She's been very concerned about the money. I don't know if she would have considered this [arson] for insurance. I have to admit that last time, we came out ahead. They replaced all our furniture and everything we lost. It was all new, and they wrote us a big check. I don't know if that fire was an insurance issue, or meant to scare me, or was so they would move in with me again. But I certainly think she's capable of setting a fire."

Mike gave his version of the debate over lawyers: Debora had delayed and delayed, even about getting an attorney for herself. Then she did everything she could to ignore the divorce. Yes, he had told her that he'd get a tough lawyer if he had to. He was tired of waiting.

Burnetta noted that Mike's recall of the family's activities on the evening of the fire corresponded exactly with what Debora had told him. Mike said that Debora hadn't seemed agitated or upset when he brought Tim and Kelly home from the hockey game. He thought she might have been slightly under the influence of her tranquilizers. He had stayed only a few minutes, while she got food out of the oven and fed the children.

Yes, he had called her between 10:30 and eleven to ask why she had paged him. She said it must have been one of the children. "The kids often page me—but not that late."

"Five minutes later, she called you back?" Burnetta asked.

"Right. I had told her it wasn't necessary to see if the kids had called me. But she called back and said they were all asleep. And then she paged me again as I was pulling into my street."

Burnetta looked up sharply. "And how long would it take you to get home? You left at nine and got home at eleven?"

"No, I was at a friend's house," Mike said. "I probably got home at eleven. Debora paged me at eleven-fifteen. I called her back [from my apartment]. I was angry with her. She

was really drunk. Her speech was slurred. I was *very* angry
with her. I told her she needed to class up her act, pull her
life together, clean the house, give the kids some boundaries. I told her that people were talking about her. She
wanted to know *who* and I wouldn't tell her. But people *were*
talking about her. People were concerned enough that they
were considering calling Social Services. I told her people
knew about this—that this wasn't something she could
hide."

With Debora already irrational and explosive, Burnetta
wondered, had Mike's angry accusations pushed her into
outright madness?

Whenever Mike wasn't speaking, he sighed heavily. The
reality of what had happened to Tim and Kelly caught up
with him; again and again, he nearly sobbed.

"Has Debora ever threatened to do anything—harm
anyone?" Burnetta asked.

Mike shook his head. "No, never. Except for all those
weird stories about getting a job and leaving for Africa. She
never threatened anything as far as harm to the house or
the kids. Part of the problem is she has *no* friends—no one
she talks to. She used to have some tennis friends, but not
anymore. She has no support system. All she has is her psychiatrist and her attorney. So she talked to the kids like you
would talk to one of your friends if you had a problem. She
said absolutely vile, horrible things to the kids."

Mike sighed. "She would tell them I was out 'fucking
three women' or I 'went to Peru and ran around with my
dick hanging out chasing other women.' She gave the kids
specific names [of women]. It was absolutely crazy. *Crazy*. I
have grown close to these people from Peru because of all
this, and some of them have their own set of problems."

Like his interviewers, Mike had questions to ask. He
wanted to know where his children had been found, and
who had searched for them. Who was looking for the cause
of the fire?

"There's been no good search of the house yet by the

state fire marshal," Burnetta said. "They're going to be looking for signs of foul play."

"I understand," Mike said quietly. "But I hope it's an accidental fire." It was clear he meant that sincerely but held little belief that it would turn out that way. His voice was suffused with tears as he said, "Tell me one thing—one more time. *Where* was Tim?"

Both Burnetta and Jordan shifted uncomfortably, and Burnetta answered cautiously, "To the best of our knowledge—it's hearsay to hearsay to hearsay . . ."

They didn't want to tell him. Jordan put in that it would be better for them not to guess, that they should wait until they were sure.

"You'll be able to leave with your mother and father and Lissa," Burnetta said. "But don't go back to the house."

"No . . . no, I won't."

"There's someone from the district attorney's office working with us. They will probably want an autopsy."

"I understand," Mike said, but had to ask, "Were they . . . were they badly burned?"

In almost every human life, there are times of incredible sorrow, sorrow that brings such desolation to the soul that any possibility of future happiness disappears. The three men who sat in that austere room had been part of too many of those moments of crisis. Police and firefighters and doctors live on the edge of other people's tragedies, striving always to maintain some kind of balance.

Now, Wes Jordan and Greg Burnetta struggled to give Mike some small scrap of information that might ease his mind—without resorting to deception. They told him, truthfully, that Kelly had not been burned. "Not at all. We think she died in her sleep of smoke inhalation."

"Oh, really?" Mike said. And the two investigators heard a slight sense of relief in his voice. They had given him a tiny benefaction in the midst of this horror.

Mike was doing what everyone in bereavement does, trying to find something solid to hold on to in order to regain his balance. "You know," he said. "You know, I've had a good life. This is the first true tragedy of my life. My parents, my sisters, my kids are healthy—" And he choked up again, remembering.

Women usually handle grief more easily, able to reach out and hug, to cry unashamedly. Mike was crying, and the two tough cops who were obviously bleeding for him had not the faintest notion how to help.

"Are you a religious man, Mike?" Jordan asked.

"No, I'm not a religious man."

"I wish there was just something we could do for you," Jordan said quietly.

The counter on the police videotape read 6:58 A.M. Burnetta and Jordan left the interview room for a few moments. Mike was alone, waiting for the policemen to come back and trying not to cry, heaving shuddering sighs.

When Burnetta returned, he told Mike that they would need to have his clothes. "So you can be eliminated as a suspect," he said.

Mike understood: if the fire had been arson, he would be considered a suspect, just as Debora would. But it was obvious that this was the first time the idea had occurred to him. "Sure. Sure," he said.

He told the two detectives that he had been at Celeste's house for dinner, that he had had two beers, that they had talked. He did not tell them that he and Celeste were having an affair, and they did not ask. It seemed to have no bearing on the fire.

"What time did you leave Celeste's house?" Burnetta asked.

"Between eleven and eleven-fifteen. I was there when Debora paged me the first two times. I don't have those pages—I erase my pages out of habit. The only ones on there now are the one from the alarm company and a page from my partner." Mike, too, was off on his time by ten or fifteen minutes. Last night it hadn't seemed important.

While Burnetta went to arrange for a change of clothes, Jordan and Mike talked quietly. And a disturbing thought hit Mike. "What are they going to do with Deb? *I* can't take her."

"Tell me, did the dogs get in the coffee beans?" Jordan asked, changing the subject.

Mike nodded. Tim had told him about that. As chaotic as the house had become, it didn't surprise him.

"What will happen to her today?" Mike persisted, wondering where Debora would go. There was no house anymore. She had no friends. Her family was far away.

"You, your mom and dad, and Lissa will be released," Jordan said.

"Where is Deb going to go if she's released?" Mike asked again. "I can't take her in my apartment. I'd be afraid."

Then Mike began to speak of his loss and his fears. "Poor Lissa. Goddamn! Two siblings that died in the fire. And maybe her mother . . . God, how can her life ever be normal?"

"She heard Tim," Jordan said softly. "She heard him calling for help."

"Oh, God. I know. I know." And Mike started to sob quietly. "Tim was so angry, so confused. But he was still participating in sports. He's a strong kid. The coach came up to me afterward and complimented Tim. The poor guy. He never had a chance. Poor Kelly. And I'm so thankful I went to the game. I missed part of it because I promised Kelly I'd go get some shoes for her."

Mike was beginning to come out of his shock a little, and he was trying to find answers. "I lived with this woman for *seventeen years*," he said. "I knew she had trouble in her interpersonal relationships—some problems with her personality. Basically, I thought she was a reasonably good mother. She got the kids involved in so many things. Lissa's going to be Clara in *The Nutcracker*. Kelly was going to be an angel. Tim was doing so well in his soccer and hockey. Kelly told me everything would be okay. She said, 'Mom and Lissa and Tim think you're chasing those women from Peru, but I know it's not true.'"

Sighing deeply, Wes Jordan told Mike that he would have to start thinking about funerals. "We'll need to know where the children are to be taken."

"Who should I call?"

"Find out who you want. Sit down with your mom and dad and make a decision."

"Oh, my God."

But thinking about funeral arrangements gave Mike something to do. He had always been a man who made lists, who planned things out to the smallest detail. This was not something he had ever expected to do, but he reached for the phone book that sat nearby and turned to the yellow pages.

"I'll have to call the social worker at Menninger's," he said more to himself than to Jordan, "and have her tell Deb's psychiatrist. I should call the school. I need to call her parents—the problem is, I don't know their number. Maybe she should call her parents?"

Time seemed to move sluggishly. Jordan didn't ask any more questions. He and Mike just talked. They spoke about how hard the wind had blown that night and how lucky it was that every house along the cul de sac hadn't gone up in flames.

"Our officers tried to get in," Jordan said.

"I know."

"But, you know, even when they were trying, it was already too late. It's an absolute miracle your little girl got out. The good Lord never gives you anything you can't handle." Jordan kept talking, trying to help. "I've seen some very bad things—and I know you have, too, as a doctor—but it's hard to understand."

Mike nodded. "When I think I've got problems, I hear about theirs."

"Well, today's your turn. *You've* got big problems today."

Mike was fighting so hard not to cry. The big cop was trying so hard to help.

Finally, Mike had to ask the question that kept bubbling up to the surface of his mind. "What if she *did* do this?

Would it be second-degree murder?"

"You see, we have to match three things," Jordan said after a long hesitation. "What you tell us. What she tells us. The crime scene—if it *is* a crime scene. Those all have to match. If we don't have a match, then something's the matter. It doesn't get any worse than that. It would be premeditated. That's why we're treating it very, very seriously."

"At least I'm sure Tim did not suffer long," Mike said.

"No."

"With all that smoke . . ."

"He would have passed out."

"Poor Tim," Mike said, his voice breaking. "He was so strong. I was going to get him into counseling. If we could just get him to control his anger. My grandfather died this week. He was eighty-six years old. He was healthy until he was eighty-six and a half. He just developed cancer the last three months. He lived a great life. His funeral was Saturday."

It was 7:26 on Tuesday morning. Still waiting to change his clothes, Mike tried to concentrate on the yellow pages listings of funeral homes. Only thirteen hours before, he had picked up Tim and Kelly for the game. Only ten hours before, he had had the last glimpse he would ever have of his son as Tim ran up the stairs to take a shower. His last look at Kelly was while she ate Kentucky Fried Chicken and grinned at him.

He wondered if he had said good-bye.

It wasn't nine A.M. yet when Mike returned to the Georgetown Apartments, where he had been living less than a month. His apartment sat a few feet from a frontage road that paralleled I–35. There was a little garden in back, and a sunken living room, but the apartment was a far cry from the house that now lay in ashes a few miles away.

His phone rang in mid-morning: the Prairie Village police were going to release Debora, but they didn't know quite what to do with her. She had nowhere to go. "She had no clothes, no money, no anything," Mike recalled.

Taking care of Debora had become a central part of Mike's life in the last two or three years. The private side of their marriage was no longer even a semblance of a partnership; now he was the caretaker and she was a child consumed by tantrums. And despite his grief, his anger, his frank fear of her, Mike could not in good conscience see Debora turned out onto the streets. He knew that she would not be able to cope.

Although he believed absolutely that Debora had poisoned him, Mike was mystified about her motivation. He was afraid of her—but he had trouble believing that she would deliberately harm the children who had sustained her. And the police investigation had barely begun. No one yet knew for sure what had caused the fire that had killed their two children.

It was less than giving Debora the benefit of the doubt, and more than most men might have done, but Mike told the police to bring her to his apartment. He would see that she had someplace to stay.

When she arrived, Debora expected to remain with her husband—after all, he had taken her and the children in after the fire on West Sixty-first Terrace.

"I told her absolutely not," Mike said. "I couldn't live with her again. I told her that I would lend her the truck, get her some cash, and give her a cell phone."

The most money Mike could get quickly—from an automatic teller machine—was $300, and he gave that to Debora. He let her use his apartment phone to make calls. He told her to be sure that she called her parents, and then find a friend she could stay with. Perhaps this was cruel—he knew she had no close friends—but he could no longer bear to be responsible for her. Their marriage was not merely broken—it was shattered, pulverized, reduced, like their home, to ashes.

After Debora had driven away, Mike called Norman Beal.

"He was concerned about Lissa's welfare, and I was concerned about Lissa's welfare," Mike said. "So I went down to his office and talked about what to do, and I filed for divorce and asked for custody of Lissa."

Lissa was staying with his parents. After filing for divorce, Mike went there, and slept for the first time in thirty hours.

Chapter 20

Johnson County District Attorney Paul Morrison came from a workingman's family. There were no lawyers or law enforcement officers in his background. His father was a railroad man most of his life, on the Santa Fe line. And after that he worked for an oil company. "I come from a real blue-collar family," Morrison said. "Farmers and railroaders. My father really pushed me hard to go to school and try to make something of myself. I was the first adult male in my family to go to college, in fact."

Way back when he was thirteen or fourteen, Morrison had toyed with the idea of being a lawyer, because he liked to argue and he questioned everything. "I'm sure," he said with a laugh, "that I was really annoying to my parents."

Morrison's ambition to practice law lasted until he got into college. Then he found that police work seemed more appealing. He wanted to be a detective. "But I realized that everybody can't be Sherlock Holmes, and I'd have to work my way up to a detective's spot. The idea of spending all those years in a police car . . . I thought there had to be an easier way to get involved in solving crimes, and that renewed my interest in law school with the idea of being a prosecutor, and *only* being a prosecutor. I tried to tailor everything I did in law school to that end."

The role of a county prosecutor in the State of Kansas up until three decades or so ago was usually filled by a lawyer who was the least experienced and least skilled. The newest lawyer around would be tapped for the job. It was his "turn."

However, that philosophy changed radically in the sixties; now, attorneys who aspired to become prosecutors faced stiff competition. Suddenly, the cream of the crop of criminal lawyers wanted to be district attorneys. This was, of course, a boon for the citizens of Kansas, and bad news for defendants.

Morrison knew that when he graduated from law school in 1980 it would be difficult to get a job with the Johnson County prosecutor. To improve his chances, he began getting experience while he was still in law school. He interned at two or three prosecutors' offices in rural counties under the Kansas Student Practice Act and was working as a student prosecutor almost full-time by his third year of law school. "I'd handled several hundred misdemeanor cases and I'd tried several jury trials," he recalled.

Morrison had made sure he had substantial experience to offer Johnson County when he graduated, and he was hired by then-District Attorney Dennis Moore as one of his ten assistant district attorneys. Morrison served as an ADA for eight years. With his wife's encouragement, he ran for district attorney of Johnson County in 1988, when Dennis Moore decided not to seek a fourth term. Morrison won both primary and general elections despite a long, difficult campaign in which his former boss supported his Democratic opponent. Basically apolitical, Morrison ran as a Republican. His biggest detractors came from the religious right in Johnson County, who found the moderate Morrison too radical.

Standing close to six feet, lean and full of energy, Morrison looked and sounded like pure Kansas. With his thick mustache, chiseled features, and icy blue-green eyes that could pinion a witness in their gaze, he could well have been a lawman a hundred years ago in the town of his birth: Dodge City, Kansas. His voice was a deep baritone, laced with a natural Kansas drawl. He was an individual. Where most men were fascinated with organized sports, he was a fan of the oddities in the sports world: lumberjack contests, log rolling, tree climbing. Probably his chief passion was keeping track of Alaska's Iditarod dogsled races.

Morrison's most publicized case was that of Richard Grissom, Jr., a case in which he faced criminal-defense attorney Kevin Moriarty. Grissom was, according to Morrison, "the closest thing to a serial killer to ever come around here." (For some reason, such killers prowl the coastal parts of America; there are very few documented serial killers in the heartland.)

Richard Grissom, Jr., was half-Korean and half-black. The Grissoms, an Army family stationed in Korea, had adopted him through a Korean orphanage when he was four. Up to the time he was adopted, he had survived on his own in the rough streets of Seoul. Perhaps those early horrors had marked him forever.

The Grissoms took Rich Junior back to America—first to California, and then, when they were transferred, to Fort Leavenworth, Kansas. Rich Junior was a beautiful child and grew to be a handsome young man, who—much like Andrew Cunanan—could fit into any race or culture he chose. But he brought his adoptive parents only pain, and he cast a pall over their name.

Rich ran away from home in 1979, when he was sixteen. He headed for Lansing, Kansas, in the middle of a blizzard. Seeking warmth, he broke into the basement of an elderly woman's house. The woman heard someone downstairs, and when she investigated, Rich confronted her and beat her to death. "He was tried as a juvenile," Morrison recalled, "and he was sent to a youth center in Topeka. They let him out after four years. He did penny-ante crimes for three or four years, some of them in Olathe."

By 1989, Rich seemed to have reinvented himself. He was a professional racquetball player, and he had the beauty and grace of a "Michelangelo. Perfect-looking individual," Morrison said. "He was a chameleon. He could change his appearance at will. He could look like a white yuppie; he could look like a black rapper with cornrowed hair. But he could also look as though he was from the Far East or Hawaii or a Wall Street brokerage firm. He was a phenomenal athlete and owned a commercial painting business. But he was also robbing apartments throughout Johnson County."

Over a two-week period, Rich murdered three young women. "We never found the bodies," Morrison said. "But we tried him in a four-week trial and we got him convicted. We made it through a cornucopia of circumstantial and physical evidence. We had a task force going for months, and we ended up with hair from his head and a few of his pubic hairs in two victims' beds. We found a little, tiny spot of blood in the trunk of one of the victims' rental cars. We did reverse maternity/paternity DNA with her parents and established it was her blood. He was taking these ladies around and draining their ATMs before he killed them. With one of them, we got ATM pictures. . . ."

Eight years later, the sadness Morrison felt about Grissom's victims was obvious. "You couldn't even look at those pictures without getting a lump in your throat. These were the last pictures of this girl alive, and she was all disheveled. In one, she was crying. Just a hell of a case."

For a time, after Grissom, the fledgling D.A. believed that he had already tried his most complex case—that he would never again find a defendant who demanded almost more than he, his staff, and the police investigators could give. "I thought that that early in my career my biggest challenge was already behind me," he said later. The Grissom case had, in fact, produced a landmark verdict, and also spawned a book: *Suddenly Gone*, written by an ex-FBI agent.

Paul Morrison and his wife, Joyce, had a good marriage, but, given their career choices, it wasn't always easy. Many prosecutors are tempted to give in to the blandishments of the media and appear on television. Morrison had never been interested in publicity. When he was preparing and trying a case, Morrison would have been gratified if reporters just went away. He gave only the interviews he felt were absolutely necessary to let the public know the most basic facts about any case he was working on. Joyce's highly successful career was, ironically, in the media: she was an assignment editor for Channel 5 News in Kansas City.

In 1995, the Morrisons had been married for sixteen years, and they had long since worked out the problems inherent in a marriage where one partner had inside information on some of the biggest crime stories to hit Kansas, and the other was a dedicated news seeker. He didn't tell. She didn't ask. That is not to say there hadn't been times when he wanted to tell her just a little bit, and when she wanted to ask him a lot of questions. But their careers and their marriage were definitely in separate compartments.

The Morrisons had three children, who were almost exactly the age of the Farrar children at the time of the fire. Mary Amanda was fourteen, Drew was twelve, and Cole was seven.

Prosecutor Claire McCaskill of Jackson County, Missouri, praised Paul Morrison for his wariness about being seduced by the press. She cited a number of high-profile cases—including the O. J. Simpson trial—that were blown all out of proportion by prosecutors who chose publicity over the matter at hand. "Paul has always been regarded by his peers as a prosecutor's prosecutor," McCaskill said. "He believes in a public policy role when it comes to pushing for things like changes in how domestic violence cases should be pursued. But when he has a specific case, he is low-key and to the point."

Although Morrison had handled administrative duties in the Johnson County D.A.'s office since January 1989, he still managed to try a number of cases himself. "If I couldn't try cases," he said, "I wouldn't like doing this job."

Nor did he want to try what he called "gold-plate cases" in which there were no complexities, no real challenges. After a hundred felony trials, including twenty murder trials, he looked for the cases that would test his skill the most, the ones in which a guilty verdict was not a sure thing.

*

Morrison was awakened early on the morning of October 24 by a call from the Prairie Village Police Department. He was about to be plunged into a case as convoluted as any he had ever encountered, one that would come to make the Grissom case look almost prosaic. The Grissom task force had searched for physical evidence; the new case would raise questions not only about physical evidence but about the cunning and shocking aberrance of a human mind.

That morning, Paul Morrison and Rick Guinn, one of his assistant district attorneys, viewed the blackened shell of the house on Canterbury Court and were amazed that anyone had gotten out of it alive.

Later that day, they attended the postmortem examinations of Kelly and Tim Farrar, performed by Assistant Coroner Jill Gould. Kelly's was the more difficult for Morrison to watch. She was such a little girl, and she seemed only to be sleeping as she lay on the autopsy table. Tim had suffered such terrible burns. They were mostly postmortem. Until he breathed in the overheated air and died, he had fought to stay alive. Neither child had wounds beyond the damage done by poison gas and fire. That was important to know: they had been alive when the fire erupted.

Chapter 21

Ellen Ryan had just returned from her Vermont vacation and was back at work beginning the week of October 23. She hadn't been at all concerned about leaving Debora.

"Dr. Miguel Stamati [Debora's therapist] said she was in very, very good spirits," Ellen remembered. "She was talking about plans for the kids. She wanted to make the adjustment so they could spend more time with their dad, and she wanted to be able to make that relationship better. I think, in many ways, for self-preservation—because she wanted to do a residency. But also, she was just sort of moving on away from the divorce. She was angry still with him, and that would come up periodically. She said he was going through some kind of midlife crisis, buying this red truck and all. But she was really kind of moving on with her life."

Ellen had no idea that Debora was drinking heavily again and that she was not nearly as sanguine about being on her own as she seemed. Ellen was in court Tuesday morning; she had been too busy to read the paper or turn on the news. When she got back to the office, she picked up her voice-mail messages.

One was from Debora Green. "Deb said, 'Ellen, something very terrible has happened. There was a fire and my children are dead. This is terrible. Lissa is with her dad and I'm afraid she is in danger. You've got to call me. Something very bad has happened.'" Debora left the number of the motel where she was staying.

Ellen stood there, stunned. "All of a sudden, I have three people dead in seven weeks," she said. "I *knew* John Walker was dead. I didn't know if these kids were dead or not. I wondered if she was psychotic." She called her partner in to hear Debora's frantic message. "I don't know if she's psychotic," Ellen said. "I don't know what's going on."

She had thought her client was doing great. She hadn't seen a sign of trouble, but the message was too weird to be true. "I called the Prairie Village Police Department, anonymously," Ellen recalled, "and I said, 'By any chance was there a fire in Prairie Village last night, with two children dead?' And the dispatcher said, 'Yes, ma'am.'"

What Debora said was true, although Ellen could hardly believe it. How much more agony was her client going to have to suffer?

Then Dr. Stamati called. He had just learned that Tim and Kelly were dead. They had to find Debora, he said, or there might be even more tragedy. Ellen assured him that she would find Debora, who had said she was at the American Inn north of the river. Ellen dialed that number and asked to be connected with her client's room.

Debora answered. "I said, 'Deb, what *has* happened?' and

she said again, 'My children are dead. There was a terrible
fire. My children are dead.' And then she kept asking me,
'Ellen, is it possible for someone to survive this? I don't
think I'm going to survive this. What's going to happen to
Lissa? How is this going to affect her? What am I going to
do, Ellen? What am I going to do?'"

Ellen told Debora to stay right where she was and she
would come to get her. Like the psychiatrist, Ellen was afraid
that Debora was suicidal; someone had to be with her right
away. Still not knowing any of the details of the fire, Ellen
ran for her car and headed for the American Inn. "I made
the decision to go alone," she said. "I just didn't know what
I was going to be seeing. I wanted to preserve attorney-client
privilege if I needed to."

But before Ellen left her office, she called ex-D.A. Dennis
Moore, now a top defense attorney at the firm Moriarty,
Erker & Moore of Overland Park. She had worked with
Moore before; he was a good lawyer, he was ethical, and she
trusted him. "I said, 'Dennis, remember that one case I took
for you that time? Guess what? I've got a big problem. . . .'"She paused, wondering how to explain what she
wanted.

"Get to the bottom line," Moore urged. "Get to the
bottom line, Ellen."

She told him about the big fire in Prairie Village and the
two dead children. Moore knew exactly what she was talking
about, of course—it was all over the papers, television, and
the radio. He had not expected her to call about *that*. He
had expected that Ellen wanted help with one of the child
molestation cases that often accompanied ugly divorces.

"But there's more, Dennis," Ellen went on. "You've known
me a long time, and you know I'm not crazy. I'm not making
things up." She told him how John Walker had hired her for
a divorce, only to end up a suicide a few weeks later. Then
Debora Green had come to her—and now two of Debora's
children had died violently. "I know this story sounds unbelievably bizarre, and I don't know what to do. You've got to

help me figure out what to do. I've got these three people who are dead, all in seven weeks."

"Don't worry about it," Moore said. "Let's bring her in."

"I *will* bring her in—if she's still alive," Ellen said. "And if she's still alive, I'll make sure she doesn't kill herself."

"Fine. I'll be there for you when you need me," Moore promised.

When Ellen arrived at the American Inn, she realized she didn't know which room was Debora's. She told the manager that she had a client who had just lost her children, and that she needed to find her right away. "She took me to the room and I went in," Ellen recalled. "Deb was in the room. She had on clothes I guess they'd given her in the jail—some brown stretch pants—and she was out of it. She had a bottle of booze next to her, some clear fluid. I don't drink hard liquor, so I don't know what it was, but it was a big bottle."

Debora was talking on the phone. Finally managing to get her to hang up, Ellen asked, "What is going on, Deb? Tell me what happened."

"My babies are dead. My babies are dead," Debora repeated over and over in a singsong litany of grief. And then she would vanish into her mind somewhere; she spoke, but what she said made no sense at all. Periodically, she leaned toward her attorney and asked, "Ellen, are my babies still dead? Ellen, are they dead?"

"Yes, the babies are dead," Ellen answered gently. "The babies are gone, and I am so sorry, Deb."

Ellen began to search the room. She had four children of her own who needed her, and she still didn't know whether her client was psychotic, drunk, dangerous, or delusional. She was looking for a weapon, or for drugs that Debora might have overdosed on. The situation was almost hallucinatory; Ellen herself felt a little like Alice Through the Looking Glass as she searched in the closet and peered under the bed.

Then she noticed fresh blood on Debora's pillow. She
couldn't see any wounds, but wondered if she was
hemorrhaging from her gastrointestinal system after drinking so much.

"I couldn't put her in the car to take her anyplace," Ellen
remembered, "because in the state she was in, I was afraid
she might jump out on the freeway. So I called the
paramedics."

Firefighter-paramedics Mark Fuller and Marvin Landes out
of District 1 of the North Kansas City Fire Department
responded to the emergency call: "Ambulance requested
American Inn, nature unknown," at 2:17 in the afternoon
with sirens wide open. "We run 'hot,'" Landes said, explaining that they always raced to the scene when they had no
idea what the problem was.

When they arrived at the American Inn, followed by a
pumper truck, they found two police officers in the hallway, waiting to lead them to the person in trouble. They
didn't know if they were about to see a heart attack or a suicide attempt—they had no specifics at all. Landes, with
thirty-three years on the fire department, loped ahead.

What he and Fuller found was a woman lying crosswise on
one of the beds with her face to the wall. She was crying and
very distraught. Another woman in the room introduced
herself as the patient's attorney. She said she was worried
because her client might have suffered a GI bleed; she
thought the woman belonged in a hospital.

Mark Fuller rounded the corner, carrying his airway bag
and a heart monitor. Landes was already trying to assess the
situation. Fuller heard a scrap of conversation that startled
him. He thought he heard the woman on the bed say, "I
killed my babies. . . ."

Marv Landes was having trouble getting Debora to coop-
erate. To find out if she had hemorrhaged from the mouth
or lower intestine, he asked her whether the blood had been

bright red or like coffee grounds, and she kept answering "No."

Scanning the room, Fuller saw a large amount of money lying on one of the end tables, and a huge bottle of gin on the nightstand. It was, he said, a 1.75-liter bottle. Someone had drunk or poured out enough to bring the liquid level below the neck and two fingers down into the wide part of the bottle. A cell phone lay between the room's two beds.

The sobbing woman wasn't really responding to the paramedics. She said, "My beautiful babies are gone. . . ." At that point, Fuller saw the woman's attorney step forward and say, "You still have one baby left. You must be there for her."

That seemed to snap the woman on the bed back to some kind of reality, and Fuller heard her say, "Okay, tell me what I'm supposed to say and I will say it."

The paramedics had no idea whom they were evaluating until her attorney said softly, "This is Debora Green, the lady with the house fire."

Ellen wanted Debora transported to Shawnee Mission Hospital, but they were in the catchment area of North Kansas City Hospital, where Dr. Michael Farrar was on staff. The paramedics could not take her to another hospital.

"I didn't know at that time if her husband had done this and was setting her up," Ellen said, recalling her own confusion. "Deb was perfect for a setup, because she was so out of it. I didn't know if they'd be nice to her there. I made a decision not to send her to North Kansas City Hospital."

Fuller and Landes had both heard the woman say what sounded like "Oh, I killed my poor babies." But only once. Thereafter, Debora chanted rhythmically, "Oh, my poor babies. Oh, my poor babies." After that, she asked her attorney to tell her what to say. However, they did not record this information in their report that day. Nor did they discuss it with anyone until they were interviewed by investigators a few days later.

*

Although Ellen was an attorney, she knew the local medical communities well; her ex-husband was on staff at Shawnee Mission Hospital. Whatever had happened, Ellen felt compassion for her client; Debora seemed to be crumbling before her eyes. "I knew the psychiatrists at Shawnee Mission—I knew they would be *kind* to her there," she said. "I wanted to get her adequate medical care and to have people be kind to her while I was sorting all this out."

Ellen asked the police officers standing by to call their dispatcher and ask for an ambulance. She took responsibility for any charges connected with getting a private ambulance. Next, she called her ex-husband and asked him to meet her in the ER, to help get Debora admitted. She also called Dennis Moore; he, too, met her and Debora, whom Ellen had transported by a MAST ambulance to the hospital.

"The longer Debora was in the ER, the worse she got," Ellen said. "She was babbling incoherent words. She said people were talking to her from China. Then I took Dennis in to meet her. She was out of it, but I said, 'Deb, this is Dennis Moore. I've called him in on the case because it's possible that a crime has been committed and I don't understand what's happened.' She didn't understand any of that. She looked at Dennis and said the same thing. She said, 'Are my babies dead? Are my babies still dead?'"

Whether Debora had suffered a psychotic break or whether she was a very, very good actress, she convinced the ER staff at Shawnee Mission Hospital. Ellen knew Debora had to be signed in, but she herself didn't want to do it in case of a possible conflict of interest. By this time, Debora didn't seem to know her own name, and a staff psychiatrist answered Ellen's call.

"I told him I had a client who was in no condition to defend herself," Ellen said, "that I didn't want her going up on the floor or being questioned until I had figured out what was happening."

With his help, Debora was admitted to Shawnee Mission Hospital. She was, for the moment, safe from questioning and protected from harming herself.

Chapter 22

Fire Marshal Jeff Hudson was a tall, good-looking man with black hair. His posture was so ramrod straight that he had an almost military bearing in his Shawnee, Kansas, Fire Department uniform: dark trousers, white shirt with four gold stars over his right breast pocket, a gold badge over his left, and the American flag on his right sleeve. His voice was soft but deep, and full of concern. "I always try to get something positive out of something negative—but this has been a tough one—totally senseless."

In 1995, Hudson was president of the Kansas chapter of the International Association of Arson Investigators. He had investigated more than a thousand suspicious fires, and after more than two decades with the Shawnee department, he probably knew as much about fighting fires and finding out who or what started those fires as any professional in America. He clearly loved his job. And there was a basic humanity about him, an unspoken wish that somehow there would be no more tragic fires.

Whenever he heard the "tones" in the Shawnee firehouse, or sirens in the night, Hudson's mind went immediately to the thought that someone might be in danger. In the middle of the night of October 23–24, home and off-duty, he heard the cacophony of sirens and hoped no lives were at risk. It sounded like a big fire, with a number of departments responding. That might well mean Hudson would be involved—if not that night, then soon.

Jeff Hudson was a founding member of the Eastern Kansas Multi-Agency Task Force. He and others in law enforcement and fire departments saw the need for such a group effort in the mid-eighties. "We worked for about a year getting the task force set up," Hudson said. "And then we went to the attorney general's office with our paperwork and our mutual-aid agreement signed by cities in Leavenworth, Wyandotte, and Johnson counties."

Included in the task force were people from the federal Bureau of Alcohol, Tobacco and Firearms (ATF), the Kansas Bureau of Investigation (KBI), and local law enforcement and fire departments. The concept worked well for a number of reasons. In the city of Shawnee, with a population of around 38,000, "doing fire investigations rests with me," Hudson said. "And there's only one of me. If we have a large loss or a loss with multiple deaths, that's a lot of work for one person. With the task force, we have a lot of help to draw from. It's like that bottomless cup of coffee; you can get equipment and people on the scene in a hurry. We have so much talent and experience on a scene in a few short hours."

Consolidated Fire District No. 2 provided fire protection for several communities in Johnson County, including Prairie Village. Gary Lamons, the fire marshal of District 2, knew that they were dealing with a suspicious blaze. At nine that Tuesday morning, October 24, he called Jeff Hudson and asked for help in activating the task force.

"I suggested he contact Dave Plummer in Olathe, who was on the board of directors in our area," Hudson said.

The task force was called out, and by late morning that day, a team including Hudson reported to 7517 Canterbury Court in Prairie Village. Lamons briefed the men and women who showed up about when the fire had occurred and the events surrounding it. He told them that two children had died and that the medical examiner had already been there to oversee the removal of the victims' bodies so that autopsies could be performed.

Now the task force would do its own autopsy on the ruined house.

Gary Lamons would be the investigative officer in charge of the task force; he would assign duties to other arson experts on the team, which included Dennis Craynor and John Mattox. Nancy Thomas from the Kansas state fire marshal's office was there with her "sniffer dog," Avon, a golden Labrador. Just as some dogs are trained to use their keen sense of smell to find heroin, marijuana, and cocaine, Avon could detect the presence of accelerants at a fire scene. Thomas worked Avon every day to keep her focused on her "job." When Avon detected an accelerant, she sat down and put her nose to the spot. Thomas would say, "Show me. Show me," and Avon earned her mistress's praise *and* her supper for that day. At a fire scene, Avon went in first. And every time she "hit" on an accelerant odor, Thomas put down a flag so the evidence technicians would know where to gather samples.

Some members of the task force would do the photography and videotaping, some would collect evidence, some would interview witnesses, and some would serve on the "origin and cause" team, led by Don Watkins, an investigator with the Kansas state fire marshal's office.

Jeff Hudson was one of the half-dozen experts assigned to the origin and cause team. He was—and is—a detective, just as much as a police homicide detective is, but he looked for clues in a different way. "It is really so simple," he said of investigative work that is anything but simple. "We work from the least amount of damage back to the most amount of damage. Through doing that the same way every time, you can put everything back together and reconstruct the scene."

Arson investigators sift through layers and layers of debris and fall-down until they come to a place where they figuratively look the arsonist in the eye and know how a fire started. Usually, they begin by walking around the structure to assess the damage and see which areas are most affected. Next, they move through the inside, where again their trained eyes find the areas with least damage and those with the worst. They determine where they are going to begin removing debris. They look at burn patterns—at the telltale

black "V's" that give up secrets to arson investigators,
although a layperson could not begin to understand them.
To the untrained eye, charred wood and piles of ashes look
like only that; to an arson expert, they are vital clues.

"We begin to remove the debris," Hudson explained, "by
layering down through the damage until we get down to
floor level. We photograph as we go along, we draw dia-
grams as we go along. We want to remove the top portion of
the structure first—the uppermost portion that fell in. We
will remove that layer. It might be part of the roof material
that's on top of the pile of debris. Then we'll look at what's
underneath that layer, and we'll get down to floor level. If
we're on a second floor, we will go next to the ceiling of the
room below, and then we'll get down to the contents of the
room, and on down to *that* floor level."

All the while, as they sift through debris, arson experts are
looking for burn patterns on walls, on floors. They can tell
whether a fire was fast-burning or slow-burning. They can
tell whether it burned low or high in a room, whether it
burned up or down. Given certain conditions, they can even
determine the direction a fire has traveled. Fire tends, usually, to burn *up* from its point of origin; it burns down only
when it has consumed everything above it.

An accidental fire has only one point of origin; a fire set
deliberately may have several. Gary Lamons's team had an
enormous job in front of them, one that would take not
hours, but days. The Farrar-Green house had been close to
5,000 square feet of luxurious living space on three separate
levels. And it had been almost totally destroyed.

The first thing to strike Jeff Hudson was that, although the
front of the house certainly showed evidence of fire damage,
there was almost nothing left of the rear (or east side) of the
residence. The railings around the main floor's rear decks
were a good eight to ten feet from the wall of windows and
sliding glass doors, but they had been charred black by

flames blasting out of what had been the living room or "great room."

The origin and cause team began their investigation on the ground floor, because it was the least damaged. This was significant to Hudson because many of the most common sources of accidental fires are in basement areas. "In the back part of this basement storage area," he said, "there appeared to be two water heaters and a gas furnace. To the right, there were two electrical panels. They were all ruled out as the cause of this fire. There was a second gas furnace near the fitness room." That furnace checked out, too. Moreover, the house had underground utility lines which would have been unaffected by Monday's wind storm.

Moving south in the basement level, Hudson's team came to the workout or fitness room. The weight machine, treadmill, and other exercise equipment were all in fairly good shape. However, the investigators could look up through the ceiling joists that had once supported the living room floor. Directly above that, there had been another room: a bedroom. A section of the ceiling beams of the fitness room was gone, sawed through. Hudson's team knew why, of course. In order to remove Tim Farrar's body for autopsy, the medical examiner had asked members of the engine company to remove the joists he had fallen on.

The fire had begun to burn down into the fitness room; the drywall was intact, even to the paint on the walls, but there was soot and charring at the top of the walls. The heat had come from above as the living room was completely destroyed. The fitness room was excluded as a point of origin of the fire. However, the floor of the room was deep in fall-down, some of which had come from two stories up— from Tim's bedroom. Parts of his bed and his furniture still hung from the floor joists of the living room.

Photographing and bagging evidence as they went, Hudson and his crew entered the recreation room, where the ceiling had fallen in on Maurice Mott and Wayne Harder as they searched for survivors. There was a pool table in the center of the room; there was a television set. The ceiling had fallen in not so much because of fire, as from the weight of water from firefighters' hoses. Hudson was satisfied that the fire had not started here.

Next there was a family room with a fireplace, a big-screen TV, a large wet bar with a refrigerator, bookcases, and racks of videotapes. This room, too, was basically intact. Two bar stools were still pulled up to the bar. However, Hudson noticed, some carpet next to one of the stools had been burned. It had melted in an irregular pattern, and then the fire had gone out because the carpet had been pretreated with retardant.

And there was no reason for the carpet to burn, not unless someone had tried to start a fire there. The ceiling overhead was unscarred by smoke or flames; the walls were intact. This was an unconnected fire: to arson experts, a red flag.

The guest bedroom, where Maurice Mott had crawled through the window in his desperate search to find Tim and Kelly, looked almost normal. The king-sized bed was neatly made up. There was a bathroom there, too, equally untouched. However, the vertical blinds that Mott had ripped out had burn marks on them, burn marks for which there was no explanation except that someone had tried to set them on fire.

Another unconnected fire.

The basement level was not where the main fire had begun. Even the family's 700-bottle wine collection, stored in the unfinished north end, was intact.

Satisfied that they had not yet located the source—or sources—of the huge conflagration of Monday night, Hudson moved his crew to the main floor. Their work here was more dangerous; the structure had been weakened by the heat and flames, and what floor was left could buckle at any moment.

Months later, Hudson could still diagram the house on Canterbury Court from memory. The foyer just inside the front door was two stories high, flanked by stone. It faced the living room, which was straight ahead and one step down. The single stairway to the children's upstairs wing was to the left of the foyer. Farther to the left, there had been a formal dining room, and beyond that a breakfast area, a huge kitchen, and a laundry room. To the right of the foyer, the main hallway of the house led to the music room, a guest bathroom, the den, and the master suite to the left. Hudson found out later that by shutting and locking three doors, it was possible to virtually seal off the den and master suite on the south end of the main floor with its master bath and jacuzzi.

There was extensive damage on the main floor, but not so extensive that an appalling discovery could be hidden: Hudson spotted "pour patterns" where someone had spread accelerants on the floors.

The foyer's floor had been expensive tile, giving way to the central hallway's solid oak. The stairs leading up to the children's wing had been carpeted. Hudson was working without emotion at this point. He could not risk feelings; he was going on training, experience, and intuition. He examined the amorphous patches he detected on the floor and the stairs. A flammable liquid had soaked into the carpeted stairs; the treads had burned so vigorously that the flames had "rolled" underneath the treads to burn the risers, some of which had actually burned through.

Climbing the stairs carefully, Hudson discovered that the landing at the top had been drenched so completely with some accelerant that it must have gone up in a wall of fire. Now, in the aftermath of the inferno, that landing was unstable and riddled with burned-out sections. Hudson shook his head in disbelief. An unseen hand had effectively blocked any escape for three sleeping children and their two dogs.

When Mike and Debora moved into this house, they had used the insurance settlement from the earlier fire to purchase almost all new furniture. The formal dining room had been beautiful, with a large oak dining room table and twelve chairs. A very expensive oriental rug had covered the floor, and a china cabinet stood along one wall. But the couple rarely, if ever, entertained there. They had invited fellow Peru tourists over, but those guests had stayed in the recreation room and near the pool.

Hudson, of course, had never seen the dining room as it had been. He could tell where the china cabinet had stood, but the table had been reduced to rubble. It was possible to stand on the floor—it was much more stable than that of the music room—but the floor was about all that was left.

Removing debris by layering down, Hudson and his team found pieces of furniture so small that they were identifiable only as "wood." There was no way to say how big the dining room table had once been. There was no sign at all of the rug. And when they got down to the bottom, they found a tongue-and-groove wood floor. Some intensely flammable liquid had pooled in the center of the room, charring the wood deeply in a flowing irregular pattern.

The breakfast area had the same pour patterns and a closet in the kitchen area had been destroyed. Looking up, the arson investigators saw that it was directly below Kelly's room. One by one they climbed up on a ladder, which was the only way to reach Kelly's room now, and they saw where she had lain. There was a pale child-sized outline on the smoke-stained bedclothes. In all likelihood, Kelly had gone to sleep and never awakened as deadly carbon monoxide and smoke filled her room. This was just as well, because she had had no way to escape.

The living room, with its window walls and sliding glass doors overlooking the back deck and the pool, had no floor at all, and every room leading back toward the master bedroom showed signs of isolated charring or low uneven burning where flammable liquid had been poured. With Avon leading them excitedly, her nose to the floor, and Nancy Thomas setting flag after flag after flag, the investigators moved down the long hall.

In the study, a couch against one wall was burned but recognizable, while an oak rolltop desk had burned so

Popular, brilliant, and very witty, "Debi" Jones graduated as covaledictorian from Peoria High School in 1969 and sailed through pre-med studies at the University of Illinois.

Debora married Duane Green in 1974, while she was at the University of Kansas Medical School and he was working toward his Ph.D. in engineering at the University of Illinois.

Robert and Joan Jones posed proudly with their daughter Debora in May 1975, the day she was awarded her medical degree.

Separated from her husband, Debora was a senior resident in emergency medicine at the Truman Medical Center in Kansas City when Michael Farrar, four years her junior and still in medical school, fell in love with her.

Debora and Mike at their lavish wedding reception in May 1979. Both dedicated and caring doctors, they were looking forward to a happy and prosperous future together.

Before she and Mike started a family, Debora showered affection on her pets.

Debora and Mike with their firstborn, Timothy, in their apartment in Cincinnati, August 1983

Tim Farrar, aged three and a half, was extremely bright and would grow to become very protective of his mother.

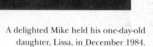

A delighted Mike held his one-day-old daughter, Lissa, in December 1984.

Debora, a devoted mother, always made special occasions of the holidays and her children's birthdays.

Lissa, four, and Tim, six, were thrilled by their new baby sister, Kelly, born in December 1988.

A formal portrait of Lissa, Tim, and Kelly in 1989

Though their marriage was beginning to show signs of strain, Debora and Mike always had a good time together on family vacations, here with Kelly on Sanibel Island, Florida.

Debora took her children to Mexico without Mike in the early 1990s. By then she had given up her medical practice and no longer resembled the vibrant, slender woman he had fallen in love with.

Kelly playing with Boomer in her room. They were almost always together.

Fire—later ruled accidental—gutted Debora and Mike's house in Kansas City, Missouri, in 1994, shortly after Mike asked for a divorce.

Reconciled and determined to keep their family together, Mike and Debora bought a luxurious new house on Canterbury Court in Prairie Village, Kansas.

Debora (third from left), Tim (to her left), and Mike (fourth from right) posed with a group of Pembroke Hill School parents on a trip to Peru in the summer of 1995. The trip marked the end of their marriage and the beginning of Mike's near-fatal illness.

Fire, fanned by a fierce Kansas wind, engulfed Mike and Debora's house on Canterbury Court the night of October 23–24, 1995.

Debora escaped the raging inferno through the glass door from the master bedroom to the outside deck.

Lissa climbed out of her third-story bedroom window, scrambled across the garage roof, and, at her mother's command, jumped toward Debora's outstretched arms. Unfortunately, Debora failed to catch her.

The third floor where the children slept was totally destroyed. Kelly and Boomer were asphyxiated in her room before the fire reached them. Tim's badly burned body was found in the charred ruins of the house.

The massive stone entryway was virtually all that remained of the front of the house. Firefighters and police investigators immediately suspected arson because the destruction was so great.

Avon, the sniffer dog, trained to detect accelerants

Johnson County Court House Square in Olathe, Kansas, where reporters and other observers flocked in January 1996 to watch an incredible case unfold

District Attorney Paul Morrison of Johnson County thought he had already prosecuted his most sensational case—until he met Dr. Mike Farrar and Dr. Debora Green.

Assistant District Attorney Rick Guinn joined Paul Morrison in investigating the tragic deaths of Tim and Lissa Farrar and the fire that destroyed their home.

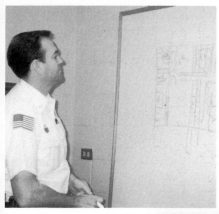

Jeff Hudson, the fire marshal of Shawnee, Kansas, drew a floor plan of Mike and Debora's house to show where the fire had started and how it had spread.

Attorney Ellen Ryan had no idea what a complicated series of tragedies she would encounter when she agreed to represent Debora in her divorce.

Detective Rod Smith of the Prairie Village Police Department interviewed Debora and Mike in the early-morning hours after the fire when they learned that two of their children were dead. Was it a tragic accident, or arson and murder?

Prairie Village Detective Gary Baker was only one of the homicide detectives assigned to investigate this very puzzling case.

The investigation complete, D.A. Paul Morrison led the prosecution team in a preliminary hearing to determine whether there was enough evidence to bring the defendant to trial.

DAVE KAUP

Johnson Country District Court Judge Peter Ruddick presided over the hearing that could lead to a full-scale trial and a sentence of death.

DAVE KAUP

Former Johnson County D.A. Dennis Moore (right) and his co-counsel, Kevin Moriarty (left), argued that their client, Dr. Debora Green (center), was not guilty of an unspeakable crime: setting the fire that killed her own children.

Dr. Mike Farrar, a scar from recent brain surgery clearly evident on his forehead, testified for hours at the preliminary hearing, detailing the shocking circumstances of his marriage and the cause of his mysterious illness.

Debora rarely showed emotion at the preliminary hearing until the prosecution introduced into evidence photographs of her children who had perished in the fire.

DAVE KAUP

The monument that holds the ashes of Tim and Kelly Farrar, victims of a towering rage and compulsive desire for revenge

FARRAR

TIMOTHY SCOTT
JANUARY 20, 1982
OCTOBER 24, 1995

KELLY CHRISTINE
DECEMBER 15, 1986
OCTOBER 24, 1995

Mike and Lissa, on a trip to Mexico in March 1996, began the painful process of healing and the reconstruction of strong and loving father–daughter ties.

completely that it had collapsed in on itself. Accelerant had to have been splashed over it for it to have crumbled into ashes. The carpeted floor had heat damage and was discolored. However, one section of carpet was missing completely, and, once again, Hudson saw the telltale pooling or puddling outlines.

From the door of the study, they could look directly across to the master bedroom and see the end of a bed. Fall-down covered the bottom of the door, holding it firmly in the position it had been in during the fire. Open.

What the origin and cause team members had found was clear evidence of arson. The proliferation of pour patterns and the heavy charring in certain areas were strong indicators for arson experts. Starting at the north end of the main floor, someone had saturated the dining room and kitchen floors with accelerant. The heavy soaking of the stairway carpet leading to the children's rooms could have been nothing less than a deliberate attempt to kill them; once the flames had exploded the children had no way out. This arsonist was also a murderer.

Not satisfied, the fire starter had gone on to spread accelerant in the living room and music room, and then down the central hall all the way to the door of the bedroom where Debora said she had been sleeping. Had that, too, been a murder attempt? But the bedroom had not burned, although, curiously, the investigators found evidence of still another unconnected fire close by. In the bathroom off the master bedroom, a drawer in the double-sink vanity was charred. The rest of the bathroom was intact.

Hudson didn't care what accelerant had been used. "I don't know what it was," he said, "and I don't care, because it doesn't matter. There are many, many substances that will burn like that . . ." And there were: gasoline, lighter fluid, kerosene, charcoal lighter, even gin or vodka will make flames race through a house. Nor did Hudson know how much accelerant had been used in the house on Canterbury Court. "This is only conjecture," he would say cautiously, "because I can't be precise. I'd venture to say that it was less than ten gallons and more than three gallons."

Obviously, someone had wanted to make sure the fire destroyed that house.

There were now scores of photographs of the house, and hours of videotape. Some showed the house as it was burning; others were a room-by-room record of what the fire had done to it. The pour patterns stood out distinctly, outlining exactly where the liquid accelerant had hit the tile and oak floors. In some photographs, Avon, the sniffer dog, stood poised, immobile, like the hunting dog she was. She had found what she was trained to find: accelerant.

Two of the pictures that the designated photographer, Ted McIntosh, took of the fire damage were truly ironic. They showed two books, intact but singed around the edges: *Necessary Lies* and *Nobody Gets Out of Here Alive*. Detective Gary Baker had found the latter lying on the floor in front of the wet bar in the basement recreation room. The words of the title were emblazoned on a red cover. He had been summoned by firefighters to see the bodies of Kelly and Tim when he spotted the book. "It gave me a chill," he remembered.

The arson investigation confirmed what police and firefighters had suspected from the beginning: the Prairie Village Police Department was confronting a criminal case. Or, rather, there was a series of cases, and they were far too convoluted for a relatively small police department to handle alone. While Prairie Village is not often the scene of a homicide, it now looked as though there might well have been *two* homicides attributable to arson. And then there was John Walker's suicide, only six weeks before the fatal fire, and the suspected multiple poisonings of Mike Farrar.

On October 26, two days after the deadly fire, the Prairie Village Police Department asked that the Metro Squad be activated. This, too, was a task force, but one oriented to death investigation rather than arson. Designed to aid police departments in the Kansas City area, it was comprised of detectives and police officers from many jurisdictions who had attended a four-day training session on death investigation. Officers who had completed this class and another on the workings of the Metro Squad had their names added to the list of available backup detectives.

When Prairie Village requested help in the Farrar-Green case, the Metro Squad board placed calls to police departments in both Kansas and Missouri asking for trained officers who were available to work on the case. Twenty-one investigators responded. Prairie Village detectives worked alongside the Metro Squad investigators, paired up with men and women who had expertise in various aspects of death investigation. A TIPS Hotline was set up so that anyone with information about the fire could call it in—anonymously, if need be.

Lieutenant Mark Kessler of the Overland Park police was designated the Metro Squad officer in charge, while Lieutenant Gary Pruitt of the Prairie Village Police Department was the lead officer, who would hand out the "lead cards" to detectives to follow up. Rumors and tips were already pouring in to the hotline. Tom Robinson of the Kansas City, Missouri, Police Department served as the press officer—an extremely stressful job in this case. The AP wires had carried the story of the mysterious fire, and even *The New York Times* had reported it.

Usually, the Metro Squad was activated for a set number of days. But if leads kept coming in on a case, the requesting department could ask for an extension. The investigation of this case would be a little like a military operation: the battalion facing the heaviest barrage could call for backup troops. Chief Charles Grover of the Prairie Village Police Department was gratified by the response from the Metro Squad. Gary Baker, Rod Smith, and Greg Burnetta would keep working on the case, but they would have all the help they needed.

Chapter 23

By Wednesday, October 25, Debora was coherent, but now she was asking Ellen Ryan the questions that Ellen had asked her the night before. "She told me, 'There has been a fire,'" Ellen said. "'What has happened? How could this happen? How could there have been a fire? What's going on?'"

"Deb," Ellen answered, "they think the fire may have been arson."

"*Arson?*" Debora gasped. "Who would want to do this to my family?"

"Well, we don't know for sure yet, Deb," Ellen said. "But we have to look at that."

"Do you think Tim was fighting with someone?"

"I don't know," Ellen said, puzzled by the question. She had no idea who might have wanted to set fire to Debora and Mike's house.

When Joan and Bob Jones learned that two of their grandchildren had perished in a fire, they set out immediately from El Paso, Texas, and drove straight through; it took them twenty hours to reach Kansas City. They were naturally very upset, but they were completely shocked when they saw Debora. They had spoken to her on the phone often since Joan's diagnosis of breast cancer, but they had not seen her for five months. In that brief period, she had metamorphosed into someone who didn't look at all like their daughter, their brilliant valedictorian, their med school graduate, the slender young mother of their grandchildren. Yes, she had put on a little weight in the last few years, but they had never seen her so bloated. Her sister Pam, who had not seen Debora in years, was stunned at how different she looked.

"We don't recognize our daughter," the Joneses said to Ellen. "Something has happened to her. What's wrong with her? She's swollen up like a balloon—her face doesn't even look like her."

Ellen could only shake her head in sympathy and bewilderment. She had seen Debora go from a frowzy, ill-kempt, dependent woman, to an angry, vindictive woman, to a competent optimistic woman, to a babbling psychotic, and, now, to a coherent, questioning, normal-seeming person.

Who *was* Debora Green? Even her own attorney didn't really know. There were so many ramifications of the disasters that had befallen John and Celeste Walker and Mike and Debora. Ellen became accustomed to prefacing almost every opening discussion with someone about the intermingled cases with a standard warning: "You know me. You know I'm not crazy—but this is going to sound really weird."

And weird it was. Ellen, too, was asking herself if John Walker's suicide, Debora's and Mike's divorce, and, now, the fatal fire on Canterbury Court were isolated tragedies or whether there was some arcane connection between them. When she looked at a photograph of a laughing group of tourists at the highest point of some far-off Peruvian mountain range, it was hard to believe that three and a half months later two of the families pictured there would be destroyed and the rest would be asking bewildered questions.

Shortly after 2:30 in the afternoon of October 26, two days after the fatal fire in her home, Lissa was interviewed. Winsomely pretty, with her dark hair pulled back in a ballerina's bun, she was a remarkably poised little girl. She wore a long-sleeved gray sweater, and betrayed her anxiety only by occasionally pulling its sleeves down so far that she seemed to have no hands at all. She spoke in the present tense about her family and her home. It was still too soon for a ten-year-old girl to truly accept that both her brother and sister were gone, and that her home was in ashes.

Lissa sat at the interview table and nodded politely when Gary Baker introduced himself. This was a meeting that Baker had both been looking forward to, as a detective, and dreading, as the father of small children. "I made a promise to Lissa in the very beginning," he recalled. "I told her that I would never lie to her, even though she might not like to hear some of the true things I would tell her. And I kept my promise to her—always."

Sitting in on the interview were a task force investigator—Dennis Craynor of the Kansas City, Kansas, Fire Department—and a Metro Squad detective—Roger Denton of the Grandview Police Department. Denton and Baker had been paired for the duration of this investigation.

Baker asked Lissa if she remembered talking to him on the night of the fire. She nodded. She was a very dignified little girl, who didn't seem at all intimidated at the prospect of being questioned by three men. She sipped daintily from a can of pop as she answered their questions. It was apparent that they were bending over backward not to bring up anything that might upset her any more than they had to.

Baker asked Lissa to recall the night of the fire for them, and she said she had awakened either to the smell of smoke or to the sound of the smoke alarm. She had fallen asleep with the light on, so she had been able to see smoke curling under her door and from every corner of her room. "I had no idea what was going on," she said. "I opened my door and I yelled, 'Tim!' I heard him across the hall, and he was yelling, 'Please! Please . . .'"

Lissa could not see Tim because there was so much black smoke in the hallway. She closed her door and went to the phone and called 911, but there was so much noise in the house from the alarms that she couldn't hear anything on the other end. So she had hung up. "And I was afraid my room was going to blow up on me, so I pushed the window out and crawled out."

Looking at pictures of the house that took up most of the front page of the Kansas City *Star*, Lissa pointed out the window through which she had escaped onto the roof of the garage. Because the flames were close behind her, she'd had to climb up over the peak of the roof and down on the back side of the garage. She had seen her mother in the Formans' yard and called out to her, but she said her mother hadn't heard her at first.

"My mother was terribly upset," she said firmly. "Really upset. She said, 'Where are you? Where are you?'"

When Debora had finally spotted Lissa, she came over to stand directly below where her daughter clung to the roof and told her to jump, promising to catch her. Lissa said she had jumped from the roof and hit the ground. "But I wasn't really hurt," she hastened to add. "A minute later the police came."

Lissa said that she and her mom were "very cold" and they got into a police car to warm up. "Two minutes later, my father came," she said primly. "He was kind of rude to my mom. He said, 'Deb, Deb, what did you do?' and she said, 'What do you mean what did I do?' She was very upset."

Lissa was the only person who recalled that Debora was upset on the night of the fire. She was adamant that her mother had been frantic. "She was crying and really sad," Lissa told the investigators. "She said, 'My babies are in there and they're going to die.' I saw her reach out to hug Mary Forman and Mary pushed her away, and wouldn't hug her back."

Lissa said that later she had gone to a neighbor's house, used the bathroom, and gotten some warm clothes. Then she had waited in a "van," her term for the paramedics' ambulance.

"This was all pretty scary, wasn't it?" Baker asked.

Lissa nodded her head, watchful, waiting for his questions.

Baker, Denton, and Craynor asked her about which alarm she had heard first. She was quite sure it had been the smoke alarm. "It went 'beep-beep-beep.'" She knew the difference between that and the burglar alarm—she had heard

them both before. At some point during the fire, she had
heard two separate alarms, the smoke alarm *and* the break-
in warning.

No, Lissa said, she had not seen any flames, only the thick
black smoke curling right through the walls of her room
and obscuring her view of the hall when she looked for Tim.
She said her room faced the front of the house, while Kelly's
and Tim's faced the back and looked down on the pool.

Carefully, Baker asked Lissa how things had been around
their house lately.

"Well, my father moved out . . . after school started," she
said. "My mom wanted to be a divorced couple that got
along really well. My dad was really rude to her. My father
didn't get along with her very well. He blamed her for
things. He told her she wasn't a good role model. But she
was a good role model. I really loved her. I thought she was
a good role model."

"In what way?"

"She was very smart, very caring, very kind to everyone,
very nice to everyone. If we got in trouble, we had to apologize very nicely."

Lissa said that her mother disciplined them by removing privileges. Yes, Debora had gotten along well with Tim.
"If she had problems with him, she told him she was the
boss," Lissa said. "She would threaten to send him to military school. But we had a really good relationship all
together."

It was remarkable. In a family whose emotions had spun
completely out of control, this ten-year-old was very mature
and well-spoken. She paused before she answered, and she
was clearly struggling to present her mother as a wonderful,
well-adjusted person. Apparently all of the children had
banded together to protect Debora from a world she could
not cope with. Baker remembered hearing how little Kelly
had combed her mother's hair before Debora was taken to
the hospital.

Of her father, Lissa would say only that he was often

"rude." She viewed her mother as a victim, a vulnerable person who had been unfairly maligned and betrayed—and, of course, that was exactly how Debora viewed herself.

But, no, Lissa said in answer to an investigator's question, her parents had not argued the night of the fire. Everything had been normal. Her father had come in to look at his mail, but he had not said anything "rude" to her mother on Monday night. Lissa recalled that earlier her mother had taken a Jacuzzi and was wearing her "red robe with the white sheep" on it when her father brought Tim and Kelly home. She and her brother and sister had eaten, but her mother had not. "I think she still had the flu."

Lissa thought her father had left about 9:30. "I went to bed after he left. I usually go to bed at nine-thirty or ten and read or do homework until I go to sleep."

Baker asked Lissa if her mother and father drank alcohol, and she said, "Sometimes. At special times. But only wine or champagne." But then, reluctantly, she acknowledged that once her mother had been drinking gin because she "got really sad because of my dad. But it was only a bottle, but it was all in a week." She wavered. "*Maybe* it was more than a bottle. . . ."

Lissa said that her mother had been embarrassed to visit Pembroke Hill School because of rumors that she had been drinking heavily. "My dad told everyone at school," she said. "Once I didn't get my homework done, and my teacher said that was okay because she knew things were difficult at my house. That was awful."

When she was asked again about the burglar alarm, Lissa's response proved she had been adept at programming it: "'47211' is the code to turn it off. I mean, the code is '4721' and then you punch '1' for off." She didn't know what all the lights meant, but she knew that if the alarm sounded, the security company would call the house and one of the family had to give another code, "4663." If whoever answered the phone didn't do that, the police would come. She and Tim both knew the codes; Lissa wasn't sure whether Kelly knew how to work the alarm. They always set the alarm when they left the house. At night, when they were staying in, they pressed "3." "My brother set off the motion detector at night, sometimes," Lissa said, "when he'd get up and go downstairs."

There were two phone lines into their house, Lissa said; she and her brother and sister each had a phone in their rooms. Both phone lines came into their computer's modem. The children's phone line was also wired into the basement and the laundry room. She said that her family had two safes behind a hidden door in the den closet; they kept their photographs there.

Did the family keep the house locked all the time? Lissa explained that they locked the exterior doors at night. They had to have a key to get out. Most of the keys were kept in a basket in the kitchen, but her mother's was on a shelf in the master bedroom. It fit both the front door and the glass door from the master bedroom to the deck. "We have a maid who cleans—Wendy—but she doesn't have a key," Lissa said.

The detectives asked how the intercom worked. People inside the house, Lissa said, could push a button to call to the intercom box mounted on the rear of the house, but there was no button on the outside to talk back. The person inside had to press the "listen" button and wait for the person outside to respond.

Craynor asked where they kept matches. Lissa was firm as she said she had never seen matches in their house. Never.

"You know," she said quietly, "Tim was always out on the roof. I don't know why he didn't jump."

Although Lissa betrayed no strain on her little pansy-shaped face and her eyes were dry, she had once more worked her hands completely into her sleeves and clasped the cuffs of her sweater with her fingers so that her hands had disappeared.

When the men sitting around the table asked if her mother had close friends, Lissa nodded vigorously. She had a lot of close friends. Lissa named several women, mothers of her friends. She said Debora used to play tennis often, but she didn't play much anymore. "Because she had the flu, and she was vomiting a lot."

Lissa knew about her mother's Monday appointments with Dr. Stamati, and about the pills she took. "I don't know what they are but they have Dr. Stamati's name on them."

When asked about her parents' separation, Lissa said frankly, "My brother doesn't like my dad for leaving. I am kind of mad at him too because my mom's so sad."

Lissa spoke about their pet dogs, but, again, she held back her emotions. She had not been able to save them any more than she could help her brother and sister. When she went to bed Monday night, she took Russell, their new greyhound, into her room. She wasn't sure whose turn it had been to have Boomer. She thought Tim, but then she thought it was probably Kelly. If Kelly had Boomer, her door would have been closed. This tied in with what the arson investigators discovered; Kelly's door was closed, but the flames had burned through the center panel. Boomer's body was found under Kelly's bed.

The three investigators needed answers to certain questions, but they hesitated to ask them of this little girl directly. They asked her who cut the grass at her house; she said she had cut it the last time, but usually her mother did. They kept a can of gasoline in the shed. They had two charcoal grills; the new one was on the deck and the other one was downstairs. Lissa said that Tim and her father were usually the ones who cooked on them.

The interview with Lissa lasted about forty-five minutes. "If we need to talk to you again," Baker said, "would it be all right with you?"

"I have ballet practice every night," Lissa said seriously. "And I'll be in rehearsal this weekend."

"We'll be sure to work around that," Baker said with a smile, relieved that, for Lissa at least, her world was continuing. "We'll probably talk to you tomorrow in the daytime if we need to."

"That would be all right," she said solemnly.

Baker did not delude himself about the effort it had taken for Lissa to talk about the awful night when her house and half her family disappeared in flames. He also knew that "tomorrow" was the day her brother and sister would be eulogized at their double funeral. He hoped mightily that he would not have to talk to Lissa again.

Chapter 24

Tim and Kelly Farrar's joint funeral was held on October 27, 1995, at the Village Presbyterian Church. Mike had made most of the arrangements, but both families attended. Family and friends and the funeral home staff were shocked by Debora's behavior in the narthex before the service started. She was very angry and made no effort to lower her voice.

"She was rude and she was mean," one funeral home representative recalled. "I've never seen anyone behave that way at a funeral, even though people are often in shock and grieving. She complained about some part of the arrangements she didn't like—Dr. Farrar had taken care of almost everything—and she swore at me over one detail or another. Everything we did was wrong in her eyes.

"Her parents were there, and her sister, and they were very nice people. They came up and said, 'Debora, don't yell at him. It wasn't his decision,' and she lashed out at them. I remember she used the 'F' word. She said 'I don't need any more of this shit. Shut the fuck up. You can go back home.' They were very kind to her, but she was so mean to everyone."

The two families, torn apart by tragedy, tried to present a united front. The Joneses sat in the front row of the main sanctuary, and the Farrars in the row behind them. "My parents and I sat directly behind Debora and Lissa," Mike remembered. During one of the songs Mike had chosen,

Debora stuck her finger in her mouth and pretended to gag.

The Reverend Ralph Clark, Mike's boyhood friend all through school and Boy Scouts, who had officiated at his wedding to Debora, conducted the funeral service. As he began, "Two days ago, when Bill Farrar called and asked me to be here today . . ." Debora turned around and snarled at her father-in-law, "Thanks, asshole." She spoke under her breath, but loud enough for everyone nearby to hear.

More than 300 mourners attended the heartbreaking and tense service. Lissa sobbed throughout, the enormity and finality of what had happened perhaps clear to her for the first time. One observer who was not related to the family commented that Debora was on a "roller coaster of emotions." As he watched, she would greet people joyously and laugh, as if at a social event. "The next minute, it looked as if she were trying to show sadness—but it didn't ring true."

Celeste Walker was at the funeral, and so were many of the friends from the summer trip to Peru. Ellen Ryan attended, still disturbed and puzzled by the unfolding of so many calamities in so short a time. Ellen didn't see the mean or rude side of Debora. She did notice that a number of Tim's friends came up and hugged her, that the children seemed to love her. Every time Ellen thought she had a fix on Debora, she discovered some new aspect of her client's personality. "You know," she would say a long time later, "I think I really thought of her as a child, as a little baby who needed to be held and comforted. She seemed so lost and so confused."

Ellen was very concerned about Lissa; she was only a little girl, but she was carrying the weight of the world on her frail shoulders. She had been her mother's keeper for so long that she couldn't easily abdicate her responsibility. Lissa worried about Debora constantly.

Ellen desperately needed to talk to Debora, and she didn't want to do it in front of Lissa. But she found it almost impossible to separate the child from her mother. Lissa was Debora's shadow, clinging to her side, trying to look after her. It was as if Lissa sensed a certain weakness in her mother, as if she knew Debora was incapable of dealing with the world.

"I didn't talk to Lissa about the case," Ellen remembered. "I don't involve children in a divorce. A lot of lawyers bring the kids in and ask them a bunch of questions. I won't do that." But she did want to reassure Lissa that everything would be all right. "I will take care of your mother," she said kneeling down to talk to the child. "I promise you that I will take care of your mother. That's my job, and your job is to be a little girl. I *want* you to be a little girl."

Lissa studied Ellen's face for a long time, and then she nodded. She seemed to have relaxed, if only a little.

The investigators sent representatives to the double funeral; they observed the crowd casually but carefully.

At the Highland Park Cemetery, on the Kansas side of the state line, Mike ordered a huge marble monument that would hold the urns with his dead children's ashes. His maternal grandparents had just been buried there, and many other Farrar relatives rested in the same cemetery. On the tablelike top of the monument, the name Farrar stood out in bronze letters. Beneath that, two bronze plaques read, "Timothy Scott: January 20, 1982–October 24, 1995," and "Kelly Christine: December 13, 1988–October 24, 1995." On the other side of the massive marker, there was a poem that has helped many families deal with loss.

> Do not stand at my grave and weep
>   I am not here; I do not sleep.
> I am a thousand winds that blow,
>   I am the diamond's gilt on snow.
> I am the sunlight on ripened grain.
>   I am the gentle autumn's rain.

When you awake in the morning's hush,
I am the swift uplifting rush
of quiet birds in circled flight.
I am the soft stars that shine in the night.
Do not stand at my grave and cry,
I am not here. I did not die.

Etched into the shining slab of bronze were snowflakes, wind, rain, the moon and stars, circling birds, and wheat against a setting sun.

Mike had to remind himself often that his last evening with his son had been a good one. It was a small comfort he could cling to: they had shared the joy of Tim's glory on the ice rink. For the first time in a good while, they had been together as a father and son should be. When Mike saw Tim's hockey coach, Jon Baskind, at the funeral, he said, "My greatest memory is of Tim playing that Monday."

Tom Deacy had coached Tim in soccer since the third grade. "He was very determined," he recalled. "He practiced certain soccer skills at home. He was far and away better than most of the other kids." Tim never wanted to waste time at practice. "He would be one of the first ones to say, 'Let's get back to doing what we were doing. . . .' I felt like he was a pit bull on a tether sometimes," Deacy said, "but he was a clean player."

Tim had been the same way as a hockey player. Jon Baskind had high praise for the boy he had seen grow from a little boy to a muscular teenager. "The neat thing about Tim was his intensity and his willingness to do anything to help his team win," Baskind said. "He singlehandedly won one game. He had three goals and three assists. He was a coach's dream."

Although Mike and Debora had taken hundreds of pictures of their children from birth up until a few weeks before the fire, they feared their photographs were lost.

Fortunately, they were found intact in one of the two safes Mike had had installed; they were being kept by the Johnson County district attorney's office for the time being. They smelled of char, and tiny particles of soot clung to them, but all of the good memories that had been committed to film were salvageable. The rest of Mike and Debora's world was in shambles.

Mike had remembered the safes the day after the fire; one held documents, wills, and some money—perhaps $500. The other held the photographs and family mementos. As it turned out, when the ashes had finally cooled, the fireproof safes were among the very few items in the house that survived the flames.

Where would Lissa live? Both her parents loved her, but her mother was an emotional wreck and Lissa had voiced her anger at her father for leaving them and for being "rude" to her mother. Everyone was concerned for her well-being, and a court finally decided that she would live with her paternal grandparents, and Karen Beal, Mike's sister, helped as much as she could. Debora would be allowed to visit Lissa—but, the order decreed, they must be supervised whenever they were together.

Joan and Robert Jones were with Debora almost constantly; she was seeing her psychiatrist and her behavior seemed to have leveled out. The question of visitation was a hard call to make. But Lissa had been through far too much already. To cut her off abruptly from the mother she loved would have been too cruel. And if the continuing investigation absolved Debora, it would be terrible to have kept her from her one living child. Debora was allowed to accompany Lissa to her ballet practice; Lissa would continue in her role as Clara in the Christmas Ballet. She would also have visits with Debora, as long as her maternal grandparents were present.

If there was one person whom everyone wanted to protect from further harm, it was Lissa. Her mother and father, both sets of grandparents, her aunts and uncles, and the investigators all made sure that she could fulfill her dream of dancing in *The Nutcracker Suite*. Whatever quarrels various factions had with one another, they would not let old resentments interfere with Lissa's life. The fact that she was alive at all was a miracle; seeing her graceful tour jetés and her slender figure on point gave everyone hope who cared about her.

Ellen Ryan worried about Lissa's physical safety, but she didn't know which parent was the one to watch. She knew Debora was a suspect, but Ellen considered Mike a suspect, too; she was troubled because there were no restrictions on his visits with Lissa. But there was nothing she could do about that. With the police watching both parents, she hoped that Lissa would be safe.

Ellen was a pragmatist. She made sure that Mike would continue the court-ordered payments of $5,400 a month to Debora. That was the amount listed in papers filed in Mike's divorce action against Debora. Out of that, Debora was expected to make a $3,400 monthly mortgage payment on a house that no longer existed.

Debora and her parents adamantly insisted that she had had nothing to do with the fire and instructed Ellen orally and in writing to do whatever she had to do to find out who had set it. Ellen promised them that she intended to do just that. But as the days passed, she began to realize that there was a good chance that Debora would be arrested, and she started stockpiling Debora's money for bail if that should happen.

When Ellen warned Debora that she might be arrested, Debora looked perplexed. "I didn't do this, Ellen," she said, "so *why* would I be arrested?"

Ellen usually ended up saying, "Just let me do what I do best. I explained to you in the beginning that I'm pretty good with money. I'm real careful with money."

Ellen got permission from Mike and his attorney to divide

up the Farrar-Green IRAs, and she took as much money as she could from the marital estate so that Debora would not be left without resources. She opened a separate bank account in Debora's name only, so that if she was arrested, Ellen would be able to draw on it to help her. Debora was basically helpless with money, and she might need it to pay for her defense against a murder charge.

And all the while, Debora looked at her lawyer uncomprehendingly. Ellen was being overly concerned, she said. Why should she have a defense when she was totally innocent? But Ellen had felt the wind change, and she knew that her client was being watched very, very carefully. If Debora was going to deny that she was in danger, someone had to look out for her. Ellen had two priorities. The first was Lissa; Lissa's life had to turn out all right, no matter how much she had already lost. Her second priority was Debora; if she could not protect herself, someone had to take care of her.

Debora was staying with her parents in a motel, but they were looking for something less transient. Debora was having a rough time; she could not sleep, often staying awake for twenty-four hours at a stretch. When, out of sheer exhaustion, she did fall asleep, she managed only a few hours. She dreamed, always, she said, of happy times with her children. As for awakening, she likened it to facing the terrible truth all over again: her children were gone. Meanwhile, her parents were exhausted because they couldn't sleep if she couldn't sleep. Joan had recently suffered a stroke and undergone breast surgery, and she needed her rest.

Ellen was kept busy seeing that Debora had the proper medications and care; it was she who arranged Lissa's visits. In a way, Ellen felt as if she were looking after not one little girl but two. She could not believe that Debora had started the fire, but she didn't know who else might have done it. If Debora *had* burned down her own house, Ellen was convinced that she was unaware that she had.

*

Meanwhile, Prairie Village detectives under Chief Charles Grover, along with the Metro Squad and the arson task force, continued to quietly investigate the fatal fire. As any good detective knows, in an unexplained death, you look first at murder, second at suicide, third at accident, and at natural causes only as a last resort. "Early on," Grover would tell reporters later, "we decided to investigate it as a homicide, hoping it would be a fire of natural causes and everything would be fine. It didn't turn out that way."

It would be some time before the origin and cause team from the task force would publicly announce its conclusions about how the fire had started in the Farrar-Green house. Many team members, however, had formed strong private opinions. As for the public at large, rarely would there be such divergent opinions about the guilt or innocence of a suspect. Perhaps it was the crime itself—the murder of one's own children—that evoked such partisan stances. Husbands kill wives. Wives kill husbands. Lovers kill lovers. But we want to believe that mothers protect their young; they do not set fire to them in a Medea-like rage.

Grieving friends and curiosity seekers got as close as they could to the blackened ruins; at 7517 Canterbury, only the stone arch over what had been a front door, and the massive stone fireplace, seemed solid. The yellow crime scene tape held them far back from the actual property. Many people left flowers—red roses and florists' pastel bouquets that seemed incongruous next to the brilliant autumn foliage.

Life continued on Canterbury Court, but it was a different kind of life. The many children who lived there were forced to deal with sudden, violent death far sooner than they should have been. The friends of both dead children had difficulty coping with the concept that Tim and Kelly had been there one day and dead the next. They had been welcome at Debora's home, and nobody cared if they were noisy or made a mess. If this could happen to Kelly and Tim, something bad could happen to *them* too. All humans come to ponder our own mortality, but usually such reflections intrude on our serenity when we have grown older.

The parents on Canterbury Court shut their doors to the media and closed their blinds to the public. This was not a neighborhood where anyone relished being featured on the nightly news, giving opinions on those who had died or speculating on what had caused the fire. Although Canterbury Court was not a gated community, it was—or, rather, it had been—a kind of oasis, whose gardens and trees and houses with fenced yards seemed to keep the rest of the world away. The doctors and lawyers and other highly paid professionals who lived there had to deal with illness and death and legal woes during their workaday lives. They hated to see scandal invade their haven. But there was such intense interest in the third house from the corner that Canterbury residents saw their street on television almost every night. Even the tabloid television shows sent scouts.

It was possible to close doors and turn away reporters, but it was not possible to ignore the charred skeleton of 7517. The house was not only an ugly and grim reminder, it was dangerous. The roof was gone from the north end where Kelly, Lissa, and Tim had slept. The powerful stream of water from the monitor had knocked down the roof beams. Now, it looked as if a strong wind could topple some of the walls, as indeed it could. The neighbors were anxious to have the house torn down as soon as possible, but of course that could not be done until the detectives and the arson investigators had finished.

Once they had, Ellen Ryan began to receive calls from the Farrar-Greens' neighbors and their lawyers, asking her to expedite the razing of the burned house. "It made me kind of angry," she recalled. "They said their children were sensitive and upset by the memories that burned house brought back. But I kept thinking, 'Why didn't somebody call earlier? Why couldn't someone have called for help for those three sensitive children who had lived there?' Maybe none of it would have had to happen."

Rumors ran rampant throughout the legal and medical communities, and the fire was talked about by almost everyone who read a paper or watched television news in the Kansas City area. The case was the main topic of discussion in an ever widening circle. No one really believed that the fire was accidental, and stories—most of them apocryphal—circulated continually.

Mike's relationship with Celeste Walker was suddenly common knowledge. It would probably have been prudent for them to stay away from each other in the aftermath of the fire, but they were so in need of comfort. Their lives were in upheaval and they seemed able to find some surcease from the horror when they were together. They had fallen in love to escape from moribund marriages; they could never have foreseen what chaos lay ahead. If John had lived and Debora had not retreated into alcoholic oblivion, it is quite possible that their affair would have died of its own weight. Now, despite public opinion, they clung together.

Celeste went with Mike one day to the ruin of his house. He had been given permission to enter the basement level and remove his wine collection. Someone alerted the media, and suddenly the house was surrounded by reporters and cameramen. Celeste was able to duck out a side door and escape through the backyard, but Mike appeared on all the evening news shows. It would have been a coup for the cameras if the lovers had been caught together with their arms full of expensive wine bottles, but they were spared that additional embarrassment.

Mike was not well. His last hospitalization had ended on September 11, six weeks before the fire, and he had never again had the agonizing symptoms that had sent him to North Kansas City Hospital three times. But he was weak and ill. He couldn't jog; sometimes he couldn't walk very far without great fatigue. He couldn't work. A little more than two months before, when he was hospitalized for his curious but violent illness, Mike had developed sepsis, an overwhelming infection, which had almost killed him. Bacteria had leaked into his bloodstream and, once loose, could invade any organ in his body.

"Bacteria gain access to the bloodstream," Dr. Beth Henry, the specialist on Mike's case, explained, "and that's a 'cascade' where the body produces protein substances that cause a tremendous reaction in the system. Typically, when we have bacteria in the bloodstream, we always get concerned about the possibility of it landing on a heart valve."

Mike didn't realize it at the time, but he had developed bacterial endocarditis—an infection of the heart valves. Heart damage was the major danger, but a clump of material could easily break away from the little nodule of bacteria on the mitral valve and flow through the arterial system to his brain. The doctors at North Kansas City Hospital had treated him— one of their own—with extreme caution, doing more than a dozen blood cultures to look for bacteria after Mike's first bout with sepsis. They had found none, but they knew there was a strong possibility that he might develop sepsis again.

And, indeed, that was what was happening to him. Mike's bouts with life-threatening illness were not over. He believed he knew now what had caused his problems originally— packets of castor beans like the ones he had found in his wife's purse. The Prairie Village police investigators had them now. If necessary, they would go to the FBI lab, whose criminalists were said to have had some success in isolating ricin antibodies in a human being.

Although they hadn't seen their younger daughter often during her adult life, Joan and Bob Jones cared about her and were prepared to stay in the Kansas City area as long as Debora needed them. They had to find a place for the three of them to live, and, Debora hoped, where Lissa could stay

with them at least part of the time. Not surprisingly, land-
lords were not anxious to rent to a woman who was suspected
of burning down her own house—not once but twice. But
finally, the Joneses rented an efficiency apartment in one of
the chain hotels, the kind where everything from dishes to
toasters to coffeepots is provided. There they would live with
Debora, waiting for whatever happened next. Lissa was still
staying with Mike's parents, and all of them wanted to make
her life as normal as possible. Debora especially wanted her
to continue practicing for her role of Clara in the ballet.

On October 27, three days after the fire, Fire Marshal Gary
Lamons of Fire District No. 2, who was the spokesman for the
task force, informed the Johnson County district attorney—
Paul Morrison—and the Prairie Village police that his
investigative team believed the cause of the deadly blaze to be
arson, and that the fire, or rather, fires, inside the house had
been started with an accelerant. The question now was who
had set fire to 7517 Canterbury Court. The members of the
investigative team had to be careful to avoid letting tunnel
vision cloud their peripheral sight. Debora Green was the
most bizarre and obvious suspect, but Celeste Walker and
Michael Farrar were still suspects, too, and they knew it.

Mike believed that Debora had poisoned him, but he
could scarcely bear the thought that she had deliberately
killed their two children. The night of the fire, when he
knew they were trapped in the flames, he had confronted
her and said, "What have you done now?" But he had
uttered those words at the height of his despair and panic.
He had lived with Debora for eighteen years; he had
thought he knew her. And whatever her flaws as a wife, he
had believed that she truly loved their children.

Debora had told the police about a group of people who
ran through her yard at least twice in the middle of the
night, only days before the fire. She thought they might
have had a grudge against someone in her house—perhaps
Tim. But she also envisioned a much more diabolical plot.
"Who had everything to gain?" she asked rhetorically.

"Celeste. Celeste wanted my husband, and the only thing in the way of their being together were her husband, me, and my children. With me and the children gone, Michael wouldn't even have to pay child support. Well, John is dead, and Celeste has three million dollars' worth of insurance, and I almost died and so did Lissa. You figure it out."

Rod Smith and Gary Baker spent a lot of time canvassing the Canterbury Court neighborhood, and talking with friends and associates of Mike, Debora, and their children. Both had Metro Squad partners. Smith's was Detective Bob Leever from the Overland Park Police Department; Baker was paired up with Roger Denton of the Grandview Police Department. No one had been arrested for the arson murders of Kelly and Tim Farrar, although Debora Green's name remained the one being whispered the loudest.

Fire Marshal Jeff Hudson had said he didn't really care what accelerant had been used to set a fire that would fully involve the huge Farrar-Green home within mere minutes. Any house has the wherewithal. Most families have gasoline for lawnmowers and weed-eaters, fluid to ignite charcoal briquets, kerosene, lighter fluid, turpentine, alcohol. Hudson was quite sure it had not been gasoline; the cobwebs on the metal gas cans in the shed were still attached to the shed walls when he and his team checked. But it wasn't nearly as important to know *what* flammable liquid had been used as it was to know *that* it had been used.

Amateur arsonists have no idea how dangerous accelerant-fed fires can be. As they pour the "trailer" throughout a house, many of them light the last drop, fully expecting that they will have time to get out before the fire erupts. Depending on the amount of accelerant used, an instant explosion often slams doors shut and traps the arsonist himself in a ball of fire. Even those who do escape virtually unscathed rarely get away scot-free. They leave a blueprint of exactly what they did. That was what the fire-setter in the house on Canterbury Court had done. And the task force suggested to the Prairie Village detectives that the person who had set the fire might have burns or singed hair from the fire flash.

Both Mike and Debora had given the clothing they were wearing on the night of October 23–24 to the police for testing: Debora's hot-pink nightie with the sheep pattern and Mike's shoes, socks, jeans, and gray wool sweater with the multicolored pattern. Bill Chapin, the crime lab officer for Johnson County, packaged the clothing and sent it to the Alcohol, Tobacco and Firearms laboratory to be tested. None of the clothing had tested positive for accelerants.

Next, the detectives wanted hair samples. Mike willingly allowed clumps of hair to be clipped from the front and sides of his head, so that they might be tested for singed ends. But Debora had been so angry with Rod Smith and Greg Burnetta at the end of their first interview, they doubted that she would give them a hair sample voluntarily. They obtained a search warrant, and on the afternoon of her children's funeral, while she was in a meeting in Dennis Moore's office, they walked in, slapped down the warrant, and demanded the samples. Moore was very angry at them for surprising Debora that way. She, too, was indignant, and once again told Smith and Burnetta what she thought of them. She assured them that no search warrant had been necessary; she would gladly have given them strands of her hair.

However, something about Debora's hair had apparently made her nervous. She had canceled her regular appointment with her usual stylist the day after the fire—Tuesday. That was understandable. But on Thursday, October 26, she and her mother went to another beauty shop, in the Jones Store in Prairie Village, and there a stranger cut her hair. "But it looked terrible," she said, "and I had to get it cut again." So, after the funeral, she had gone back to her regular hairstylist for yet another haircut.

Using a scanning electron microscope, forensic chemist

Gary Dirks of the Johnson County Criminalistics Laboratory found that despite her haircuts, a number of hairs from the front and side areas of Debora's head showed significant singeing. This information was passed on to the district attorney's office.

When would Debora's hair have been so close to the flames that it was singed? She had told detectives several times that she had opened her bedroom door, peeked out into the hall, and closed the door at once because of the suffocating black smoke. She had then gone immediately to get the key to open the glass door that led from the master bedroom to the back deck. Although flames were belching from the other windows and doors in the rear of the house by the time firefighters arrived, Debora hadn't mentioned seeing exterior flames while she was talking to Tim on the intercom mounted on the wall next to the glass doors. She had gone directly to the house next door, where the Formans had been puzzled to see that her hair was soaking wet. Debora *had* gone back to the garage where Lissa huddled on the edge of the roof, afraid to jump. But there was no fire there; if there had been, Lissa would have been burned.

Chapter 25

Debora had begged Ellen Ryan to find out who had set fire to her home and killed her children. She had flung down the gauntlet and asked authorities to "figure out" what she suggested was obvious. And, indeed, there were any number of people trying "to figure it out": the Prairie Village Police Department; the Eastern Kansas Multi-Agency Task Force; the Metro Squad; Ellen Ryan and Dennis Moore; and Johnson County District Attorney Paul Morrison and his assistant D.A. Rick Guinn.

Early-morning meetings to brainstorm and to compare notes on progress in the case were held every day at the Prairie Village Police Department. Morrison and Guinn attended to make sure they were up to speed with all new developments. If someone was arrested, the resulting trial would be unlike any eastern Kansas had ever seen.

Both Moore and Morrison had long familiarity with media interest in their cases, but neither had seen anything like the present frenzy, which grew daily as the investigation of the fire on Canterbury Court continued. Every aspect of the probe was being kept under wraps; that fact undoubtedly added to its fascination.

Ellen wanted the investigative team to be aware of her client's suspicions about John Walker's suicide and the ongoing affair between his widow and her husband. Morrison's office was already familiar with that facet of the case. For every tip that came in suggesting Celeste Walker had killed her husband for his insurance money, another maintained that Debora had driven John Walker to suicide with her constant phone calls trying to enlist his help in breaking up the relationship between her husband and his wife. One source, extremely close to the Walkers, said that Debora had called John not once but *three times* the day before he died.

Some tipsters claimed that Mike was a faithless husband who cared nothing for his children, but his closest associates had nothing but praise for him. "I think highly of him as a doctor," said one nurse, a woman who had worked with both Debora and Mike. "She *never* talked about her husband and children in a loving way." Other associates said that Mike's family had been very important to him. "Probably the biggest thing was he told stories of his children and he showed pictures of his children," one said. "It gave everyone a connection with him. I felt like I knew these children."

Adultery, suicide, poisoning, arson, murder—these were enough to make the media salivate. But Morrison kept a tight lid on what he already knew. For all his news producer wife learned about the case from him, she might as well have been married to a plumber.

*

There were still many, many loose ends to weave into the case. And until that was accomplished, no arrest warrant could be issued. Among the mysteries was the matter of the castor beans. There was no proof that it was Debora who had poisoned Mike with them; indeed, the Prairie Village detectives had only Mike's word that he had found them in her tote-bag purse. In order to absolutely connect Debora to the seed packets, it would be necessary to prove that she had bought them, whether in person or by mail.

A great deal of detective work is boring and routine, even if the case itself is interesting. To find one possibly essential bit of information, detectives have to plow through door-to-door canvassing, make endless phone calls, and listen to "witnesses" who really have no information at all, but only theories.

The Prairie Village detectives had to find which garden store in the Kansas City area had sold the castor beans and to whom. The label read "Earl May," the name of a chain of midwestern garden stores with headquarters in Shenandoah, Iowa, and at least a half dozen branches in the Kansas City region. Earl May Garden Centers sold fertilizers, planters, hoses, and all manner of gardening equipment, as well as pet supplies. And they carried over 600 different kinds of seeds, from the most common to the truly exotic.

Officer Kyle Shipps had seen the address of the Olathe Earl May store in Debora's address book on September 25, while he waited for her to dress for her trip to the hospital. Although detectives believed she might have bought castor beans there—perhaps in late July or early August, before Mike first became ill—they hadn't been able to find proof. No one at the Olathe store remembered her.

Leighann Stahl had worked for the Earl May stores for five years, beginning in Lincoln, Nebraska, and then transferring to a store in the Gladstone area, in a Kansas City, Missouri, suburb north of the river. Her store manager, Steve Ogden, received a call from a detective around Halloween who asked whether anyone in his store recalled selling a dozen or so packets of castor beans. Although Ogden didn't remember such a sale, he said they did carry castor beans in season; he promised to ask his clerks if they remembered such a sale. At that moment, Leighann Stahl walked in—and in reply to Ogden's question, she said that *she* had sold a large order of castor beans about a month before.

Stahl said that one of the other clerks had put a request for the beans on her desk in late September, after a woman had called to ask if the store had any castor beans on hand. They did not, but the clerk said they could try to order them.

There was a good reason why Earl May had no castor beans in September: smart merchandising. The castor bean is an ornamental annual that gardeners sow in the spring. The plant is fast-growing but short-lived. "They're large," Stahl explained. "They get anywhere from six to ten feet tall, depending on the site. They're used usually for quick cover and they have a kind of tropical appearance to them. [But] they'll die off with a freeze, so you plant them in the spring and they grow up very rapidly. Within a few weeks' time, you can have a two- or three-foot plant. People plant them as a screen along a fence line."

In Kansas and Missouri, the planting time for castor beans would be around April 15 to May 1. Leighann Stahl had never heard of anyone buying castor beans in the fall. When she saw the request for ten packets, Stahl hadn't even bothered calling the four other Earl May stores in the area; they wouldn't have any in stock, either. The only way to fill the order would be to get the seeds directly from the warehouse in Shenandoah.

About a week after Stahl placed the order, a woman called to ask whether the seeds had come in. "I told her I had them up at the front register, waiting for her," Stahl said. The woman asked for directions and told Stahl the town she lived in, but Stahl, who was new to the area, now couldn't remember anything more than that the customer said she was coming from "south of the river." Stahl had told her she could give her directions from I–35 but wasn't familiar with anything beyond that.

"She said that she would be up later to pick up the seeds." And later that day, sometime in mid-afternoon, the woman did come in and buy the ten packets of castor beans. She explained that she needed them for a school project— either for herself or for one of her children, Stahl couldn't remember which. But the explanation made sense to her; the woman certainly couldn't plant the seeds outside when the first frost was only weeks away.

When Sergeant John Walter first asked her about the woman, Stahl had trouble remembering what she looked like—not surprisingly, since she waited on so many customers every day. But this sale had stood out. Stahl didn't sell that many castor beans, even in spring; this was a special order for seeds that were exotic, deadly poisonous, and out of season. And Stahl was able to will her memory back to that day in September when she saw the woman who had special-ordered castor beans. The customer had probably been in her mid-forties, Stahl remembered, of medium build but leaning toward the heavyset side. Her hair was medium dark and chin length.

Stahl said Earl May's cash register tapes could offer even more precise information about the sale itself: its time and date, the department, the number of items, the total amount of the sale, and whether the customer had paid by cash, check, or charge card. At Detective Rod Smith's request, Stahl asked to have the tapes returned to her from the home office in Iowa, where they were stored. She pored over them and found the transaction she recalled. She also remembered that the cash register used at the time of the sale was off by one day. Although the tape read "September 21, 1995," it should have been either "September 22, 1995," or "September 20, 1995." The time was correct, however: 3:27 P.M.

The tape showed 10 packets of seeds sold at $1.29 apiece, for a total of $12.90 plus 83 cents' tax. The woman had paid with a $20 bill and received $6.27 in change. The price of castor beans was $1.29, but Stahl could not prove that the ten packets of seeds had actually been castor beans because the tape did not specify the type of seed. She could tell detectives only that her memory was that this was the castor-bean sale.

As for identifying the woman who had bought the castor beans, Stahl looked at a photo laydown of eight women that Sergeant Walter showed her. Was one of them her customer? She sighed and finally pointed to a picture of Debora Green. "I told him I had about a seventy percent chance that I was sure it was that person," she said, "but there were a few differences in hair, possibly in weight."

Stahl had seen news coverage of the fire in Prairie Village before she looked at the laydown, but she had seen only pictures of Tim and Kelly Farrar and the burning house. She had never seen a picture of Debora Green. And she had no idea that Debora's husband had suffered four agonizing bouts of nausea and diarrhea during the late summer of 1995, and had experienced the exact symptoms of castor-bean poisoning.

The Earl May store where Leighann Stahl worked in the fall of 1995 was in Missouri, some distance from where Debora lived in Prairie Village. The other four stores in the Kansas City area were in Lee's Summit, Olathe, Overland Park, and on 169th and Barry Road; two of those were much closer to Canterbury Court. If the middle-aged, heavyset woman with short dark brown hair who bought the castor beans *was* Debora Green, it was certainly judicious for her to travel as far away from home as possible to buy the beans. And this was probably at least her second such purchase: Mike had first become ill on August 11.

But within three days or so of Debora's latest purchase of castor beans, Mike had found them. Debora responded to his questions by saying she was going to use them to commit suicide. *Was* she? Or had she been planning to try once more to poison Mike?

Whatever Debora's plans were, they were foiled by her commitment to Menninger's that same day. And by the time she came home, Mike would eat nothing she *served* to him. It wasn't so much a matter of Debora's *cooking*; she rarely cooked, preferring to bring in fast food. But Tim liked to cook, and if they had home-cooked meals that summer of 1995, it was usually Tim who cooked them. Even though the police had the castor-bean packets in evidence, Mike had not felt safe. He moved out within days of Debora's release from the Menninger Clinic.

Chapter 26

Celeste Walker had a long interview with Rod Smith and two Metro Squad members on Halloween. They watched the animated woman with the soft voice, and saw that she had a femininity and an effervescent manner so totally unlike Debora's demeanor. Both women were talkers, however, and Celeste was not at all hesitant about going back over her life, her marriage, her husband's suicide, and her relationship with Dr. Michael Farrar.

Wearing a long-sleeved white sweater and a gold charm on a long golden chain, Celeste was a very attractive woman. Her nervousness was revealed only by her frequent gestures: brushing back her shiny wedge-cut hair, sinking her chin into her hands, sighing, grimacing, and looking up at her questioners from lowered eyelids. She laughed often, although the laugh was more ironic than amused. She seemed surprised to find herself caught in the middle of this tumbling-down of lives. She did not deny her affair with Mike, and blushed only a little when she was asked to recall their first meeting, her attraction to him on the Peru trip, and, finally, the first time they had made love.

Celeste said she had kept a record of almost everything on her calendar at home. She asked for a calendar now, and tapped her fingernail on certain dates that she thought were important. She explained that she was aware early on in Peru that Debora did not like her. Debora's eyes, Celeste said, slid over her as if she were invisible, and she always directed her hilarious stories to someone else, never to her.

Celeste's memory and record keeping were very helpful in the police probe. If she didn't always provide new information, she certainly verified information that Mike—and even Debora—had given them. Celeste knew the very day when Mike had first become ill, and the dates and symptoms of his subsequent relapses. She believed absolutely that Debora had been trying to poison him, although she hadn't any idea with what—at least, not until Mike found the castor beans.

In a strange kind of way, Celeste was happy. She had lost her husband, a man she'd cared for but who had drained joy from her life. Now, she remained a woman in love, despite her sister's misgivings about Mike and the tragedies on Canterbury Court. She obviously felt terrible about the way her husband had chosen to give up on life, and her voice dropped as she described finding him dead in the garage. She regretted the loss of Tim and Kelly Farrar, although she seemed oddly unconnected to that tragedy. Perhaps it was simply too much for her to deal with—so many catastrophes in such a short space in time.

Celeste told the investigators that Debora was crazy, nuts, bizarre. No, she had not seen her in the throes of a temper tantrum, but Mike had told her about them. And she had seen Mike come close to death for no explainable medical reason. The investigators hadn't really expected that Celeste would have much good to say about Debora. She was "the other woman," and she had no more liking for Debora than Debora had for her. But they saw that, if anything, Celeste was afraid of Debora. They also saw that she had no intention of walking away from Mike, especially not now, when she needed her.

She talked to the detectives for more than an hour, and

then apologized, saying she had to leave to pick her sons up at school.

And then it was November, and the bright yellow and apri-cot-tinted leaves had blown away in the relentless Kansas wind. Now the hawks were visible again as they perched on bare, black limbs. They had been there all along, watching for vulnerable prey far below.

Everyone connected to the Farrar-Green case seemed to be in stasis. Debora and her parents still lived in the tempo-rary apartment; Mike lived in his apartment in Merriam; and Lissa visited back and forth. She was practicing with the Missouri State Ballet almost every day. The adult members of the *Nutcracker* cast had taken her under their protection, too.

On November 1, the Metro Squad announced that its list of suspects in the arson murders on Canterbury Court had narrowed to persons close to the family who had access to the house. That pretty well eliminated strangers running through the yard at night, or some passing itinerant who happened to be a pyromaniac. Then, on November 3, the news from the Metro Squad was more electrifying. The press was told that the investigation had now isolated one suspect only. That person was not named.

Curious media buffs in the Kansas City area were getting their news in slivers, just enough to keep them at bay. On November 8, the Metro Squad finally acknowledged that it was investigating more than the arson. Members of the squad were also looking into the possibility that Dr. Michael Farrar had been poisoned at least three times, and that he had come close to death in one of his hospitalizations. Friends who had known the Farrar-Greens were aghast at the news. Strangers who had long considered life in Prairie Village all that anyone might hope for shook their heads in bewilderment.

*

Debora was devoting almost all her time to Lissa. She sat for hours in a darkened theater in Kansas City, Missouri, while Lissa rehearsed the part of Clara. She fussed over Lissa's hair, making sure it was just right for a fledgling ballerina. Lissa loved her costume, and she looked like a professional dancer, only in miniature. Debora watched avidly, caught up in the music and her child's talent.

Flo Klenklen, the Missouri State Ballet School administrator, told reporters that Lissa was one of the youngest ballet students ever to be cast as Clara. She felt that Lissa had the strength and drive to become a professional dancer. "She is not timid when it comes to things she's interested in," Klenklen said. "To excel in ballet, you can't be shy."

Both Debora's daughters should have been dancing in *The Nutcracker*—Lissa as the star, and Kelly as an angel. Debora did not comment on that, but neighbors and passersby noticed that several times she had shown up outside the burned-out wreck that had once been her home. One Sunday, she came with Ellen Ryan. Waiting television crews filmed Debora in a bright yellow rough-weather jacket and pants, as if to ward off the least smudge of soot from her clothing. What was she thinking?

Ellen said she knew what Debora was thinking. "She asked me to take her back inside the house. She said she could never accept that Tim and Kelly were dead unless she saw where they had been found. So I took her, and I led her around by the hand. I showed her where Tim's body had fallen onto the beams holding up the living room floor, and I took her into the kitchen and told her that we couldn't get up to Kelly's room anymore, but that that was where Kelly had been found, in her own bed."

According to Ellen, the whole scene had been surreal. Dennis Moore, who had not yet acknowledged that he was representing Debora in anything more than her divorce from Mike, came along with Ellen and Debora. Moore had brought a wine expert to put a price on Mike's wine collection. *Mike* and his divorce attorney, Norman Beal, were also there. All the men were in the comparatively undamaged basement level of the house.

"They were tasting wine downstairs," Ellen remembered, rolling her eyes. "And Deb and I were walking through the upstairs part of the house, where it looked as though an explosion had hit it. It was like something out of a Fellini movie. She was sobbing, just hanging on to me, sobbing, frightened, confused . . ."

Debora apparently accepted finally that her children *were* dead. Once, however, she went to a soccer game in which Tim's team played, she sat on the sidelines, and wept. She was an odd, lonely figure. No one rushed over to comfort her, not at her blackened house or at the soccer match. She had become a pariah, someone to be whispered about. No one wanted to talk to her; she was a little frightening. She had only her daughter, her parents, and her lawyer.

Ellen kept running into facets of the case that either puzzled or angered her. Now, when it was far too late, she heard about all the suspicions that people in the medical community or at Pembroke Hill School or in the neighborhood had had about Debora's fitness as a mother. "All they had to do was pick up a phone," she said vehemently, "if they were concerned. Why didn't someone report Debora—*if* they thought there was child abuse going on? Nobody did. They just gossiped about it. Maybe a tragedy could have been averted—but no one wanted to get involved."

Not one of the gossips *had* called. Mike was the only one who had tried to get help for Debora and for his family. He had called the Prairie Village police to help him commit his drunken, abusive wife. She had checked herself out of Menninger's within a few days. And, despite Mike's belief that his call would raise red flags, no one had reported Debora to child protection authorities.

"I wanted the children," Mike said fervently, "but I was told I could not get them away from her—that a father wouldn't have much of a chance of winning custody." And Debora had seemed so much better after Menninger's that

Mike dared to hope they could share in raising their children, even if they were divorced. But she had hidden her anger so well. Now, Tim and Kelly were gone, and no amount of finger-pointing was going to change that.

There was a feeling of foreboding in the air in the early weeks of November, more palpable than the chill of an early winter. The Metro Squad had announced that there was only one suspect. Now the case had either to be dropped or it had to move ahead.

Chapter 27

Mike had enjoyed only a few weeks of moderately good health. But after the fatal fire, his condition declined again. Debora had always maintained that his illness was all in his mind, that he was overreacting to every little symptom; he hadn't been really ill in the first place, not with anything anyone could diagnose. *She* was the one who had been under so much stress that she had actually vomited up blood, if only a minute amount.

In November, sensing something was wrong, Mike asked for an echocardiogram to see what was happening in his chest. The test showed he had a severely leaking mitral valve, caused by a bacterial infection of the heart. His physicians had feared this might happen. Once again *Strep viridans* showed up in his blood culture. Mike was hospitalized with endocarditis just before Thanksgiving, scheduled for surgery to insert a Groshong catheter into his subclavian vein so that he could receive intravenous antibiotics at home.

Two days before his surgery, Gary Dirks, the forensic chemist from the Johnson County Criminalistics Lab, received a vial of Mike's blood from Gary Baker. Dirks locked it in the evidence freezer and kept it there until he was instructed to mail it to the FBI laboratory in Quantico, Virginia, in early December. He sent it, along with a packet

of castor beans, to Dr. Drew Richardson. Dirks also sent samples of Mike's blood to forensic serologists at the U.S. Naval
Academy. He printed the Johnson County Lab number on
the sealed evidence: L–95–2941.

Although she was not aware of it, Debora's activities were
being closely monitored in the week before Thanksgiving.
She spent some of her time on the Kansas side of the state
line in Johnson County, but she was living south of the river,
in Missouri; Lissa's dance rehearsals at the Missouri State
Ballet took place in Kansas City, Missouri. Ellen Ryan practiced in Missouri, too.

The Prairie Village police, the Metro Squad, and D.A.
Paul Morrison and Rick Guinn were convinced that there
was only one logical suspect in the deaths of Tim and Kelly
Farrar. And that suspect was Debora Green. They also
believed that she had poisoned her estranged husband,
either to prevent him from leaving her or to keep him
from being with another woman. With all the physical evidence they had gathered, with the circumstantial evidence
that had evolved from the enormous number of interviews
the Metro Squad had conducted, the case had come down
to a scenario like the Greek myth of Medea. Medea's husband, Jason, had left her for another woman; and to
punish him for his treachery, she killed their beloved children. It was the harshest revenge she could mete out to
him.

To investigators, it appeared that Debora had done the
same thing. She had set a fire with the deliberate intention
of killing her own children. Her last phone call before the
fire roared had been to the man she both hated and wanted:
her husband. He was leaving her for another woman. Worst
of all, he had shouted at her that she was an unfit mother,
that people were talking about her and threatening to call
the authorities. She was in danger of losing her children,
her beautiful house—everything that gave her life meaning.

And, investigators believed, she had destroyed it all in a vengeful rage.

All the men and women who had been working on the arson murders and the suspected poisonings for four weeks had come to a consensus: their prime suspect—their *only* suspect—was Debora Green. Despite her IQ and her vast knowledge of so many subjects, the investigative teams were convinced she had made a number of clumsy errors as she set out to destroy what she loved most.

"We felt good about going for an arrest," Gary Baker said. "Because Paul Morrison was so confident. He wouldn't have ordered the arrest warrant if he hadn't felt he could get a conviction."

"He was with us all the way," Rod Smith agreed. "All the police departments in Johnson County believed in Morrison. He and Rick were there every day, evaluating, planning strategy. If he said it was time to move in and arrest her, then it was time."

Dennis Moore and Ellen Ryan had told Morrison that if an arrest was coming down, they preferred not to have Debora picked up; instead, they would bring her in to surrender. However, the police and the district attorney's office saw a gaping flaw in that plan. They trusted Moore and Ryan, but they had no idea what Debora might do if she knew she was going to be arrested. They had seen her be cooperative and accommodating; and they had seen her so angry that she was completely out of control. If she *knew* she was being charged with the murders of two of her children, there was no telling what she might do. In fact, there would be four charges listed on the arrest warrant: aggravated arson, murder, and two counts of attempted murder (against Lissa and her father, Mike Farrar).

Debora had been overtly suicidal in the past. If she had a warning of what was coming, she might choose to kill herself rather than turn herself in. Or she might run—and take

Lissa with her. The authorities' biggest fear was that she would include Lissa in her plans to avoid arrest. They believed she had meant Lissa to die on the night of the fire, and they were afraid she now might kill Lissa in a suicide-murder plan.

No, they did not dare give Debora time to formulate a plan that might end in disaster. They kept in constant touch with those who cared for Lissa. They wanted to know where she was at all times. And, if at all possible, they did not want Lissa to witness her mother's arrest.

Wednesday, November 22, 1995, was the thirty-second anniversary of President John F. Kennedy's assassination. It was also the day of the *Nutcracker* dress rehearsal at the Midland Theater in Kansas City, Missouri. The detectives trailing Debora knew that they would find her at the theater that afternoon and they planned to arrest her there. They knew she would not miss seeing Lissa dance the part of Clara in her diaphanous white costume, her dark hair pulled back and caught up with shiny ribbons.

Unknown to the arrest squad, Channel 41, the NBC affiliate in Kansas City, had also staked out the Midland. The word was that someone had leaked them the information that an arrest was coming down. But it may have been that the reporters, knowing that the suspect list was down to one, were just keeping close track of police activity. Earlier in the afternoon, cameramen had filmed Lissa, Debora, and a relative as they walked into the theater. Debora then drove away alone.

Gary Baker and Trish Campbell were stationed inside the theater, while Rod Smith and Greg Burnetta waited in the parking lot outside. The squad set up to arrest Debora did not want to involve Lissa in that scene. They would approach Debora only when they were sure Lissa was safely onstage. A half-dozen cars from the Kansas City, Missouri, police Fugitive Apprehension Unit were parked where they could watch cars in the parking lot.

It was November and it was dark when the officers spotted Debora's car approaching. As she pulled in and parked, they saw an older couple with her. Instantly the car was surrounded; Smith and Burnetta told her she was under arrest. At that moment, Debora's face was a study in fleeting, unreadable emotions. She barely changed expression, but her eyes, caught by Channel 41's cameras, looked trapped.

"She was nonchalant," Smith recalled. "She didn't break down or anything."

It was a great scoop for Channel 41, and misinformed people said that its cameramen had gotten the footage because District Attorney Paul Morrison's wife worked there. It wasn't true. Morrison was handling everything by the book. And Joyce Morrison didn't work for Channel 41; she was an assignment editor for Channel 5. Her husband had not breathed a word about the upcoming arrest. "My wife wouldn't speak to me when I got home," Morrison recalled with a wry grin. "Things were pretty frosty around my house for a while. Channel 41 was a *competitor*. But I couldn't even tell *Joyce* before it happened."

Debora was wearing a long-sleeved black dress with an unflattering round neckline when she was arrested. Her hair was very short. If not for the enormity of the crimes she was accused of, it would have been easy for an observer to feel sorry for this plain, stoic woman, who would not see her daughter dance after all.

Debora asked the officers what would happen to her car, and she kept repeating that she had to get in touch with Ellen Ryan. She was taken to the Jackson County, Missouri, jail where she was booked, fingerprinted, and photographed. She was given a jail uniform that resembled the "scrubs" she had worn in her days as a physician, only it was far too large for her and mismatched: the top was blue and the pants were gray. And as a final ignominy, she was handcuffed to other prisoners and led past media cameras.

Unaware of what had happened to her mother, Lissa danced wonderfully onstage with the Missouri State Ballet

company. Her father hadn't been able to come to the dress
rehearsal. Mike lay in the recovery room at North Kansas
City Hospital after his surgery to implant the Groshong
catheter.

Now, while his estranged wife was being arrested, Mike
slept a drugged sleep. He had survived the strain on his
heart, and doctors were cautiously optimistic that he had
made it—at least this time. But now they knew that the
septic shock had left behind deadly bacteria, which could
attach to any organ in the body. Mike was far from being out
of the woods. He almost certainly faced more surgery to
repair the leaking mitral valve in his heart.

He learned only later that his wife had been formally
accused of poisoning him as well as of killing their children.
Mike had suspected her for some time. But could prosecutors prove the charge? If his condition was, in fact, due to
castor-bean poisoning, it might be possible that advanced
forensic techniques could isolate antibodies developed after
ricin poisoning from the blood samples he had given.

When the news broke that Dr. Debora Green had been
arrested and charged with murder, arson, and two counts of
attempted murder, Paul Morrison gave a press conference.
Reporters, voracious for details, went away unsatisfied.
Without tipping the investigation's conclusion about the
motive for murder, the Johnson County D.A. would say only,
"It's a domestic situation and that's where I'm going to leave
it." Asked whether he would seek the death penalty, he
shook his head and said it was too early to speculate.

Morrison spoke of the dilemma that he and the investigators had faced. First of all, in every case they had to be
sure the public was safe and that the suspect or suspects
didn't flee. But balanced against that consideration was
another: they could not make an arrest before they had
enough evidence to feel confident of winning a conviction.
If they jumped the gun, they would surely lose. Morrison did

not say what an agony waiting had been for everyone who had worked around the clock while the public was clamoring for an arrest. But finally, on the day before Thanksgiving, 1995, Morrison, Rick Guinn, the Metro Squad, and the Prairie Village detectives had agreed that they had enough evidence for a conviction. What that evidence was, the press would have to guess.

Debora's parents had been present at her arrest. And Mike's sisters, Karen Beal and Vicki Farrar, were at the theater to help break the news to Lissa—but they told her that her mother would be in jail for just a little while. Actually, Debora would stay in the Jackson County Jail for at least thirty-six hours. Jackson County did not hold hearings on Thanksgiving. The courts were closed.

Debora later described her terror at being arrested. "Michael planned it that way," she insisted. "He got together with the district attorney and they planned to arrest me at Lissa's ballet theater—right before Thanksgiving."

She said she was horrified at being thrown into a crowded jail cell full of women unlike any she had seen since the days when she was an intern in the ER. She did not mention her children or the fire. She spoke only of what *she* had to endure.

Debora was locked in a square cage that had been designed to hold eight women. She counted fifty prisoners. "It was so crowded, and there were no mattresses on the iron bunks—just the wire and the metal edge. If you sat on the 'bed,' you would get deep marks on your legs. When we tried to sleep, three of us would lie down on one bunk on the bare wire. But they never turned off the lights. They would feed us whenever they felt like it. Once, they fed us at two A.M. All we ever got was bologna sandwiches and water."

Debora was often given to hyperbole. But no one could argue that the Jackson County Jail would not seem like a descent into the bowels of hell for a woman who had so recently resided in an eighteen-room mansion with a four-car garage. Debora had dreaded even a minor stepdown in her lifestyle if Mike left her. Indeed, loss of face, loss of prestige for herself and her children, and having to live in a less grand house were the reasons she gave for fighting the divorce.

Now, on Thanksgiving Eve, as Lissa danced at the Midland Theater and Mike slowly came to in North Kansas City Hospital, Debora sat amid the cacophony of jail: the shrill voices and sometimes maniacal laughter of her fellow prisoners; the sound of the omnipresent television set turned to peak volume. She had always hated noise, and now she was surrounded by it, enveloped in it.

Ellen Ryan was livid when she heard that Debora had been arrested in Jackson County, Missouri. She still believed that Debora would willingly have turned herself in to the Johnson County, Kansas, authorities—if they had only warned her that she was about to be arrested. Had Debora been taken to the Johnson County Adult Detention Center in Olathe, Ellen was sure she could have bailed her out immediately. Now, Debora would be locked up until Friday morning at the very earliest, in a holding facility that Ellen described as "built at the turn of the century. It is unbelievable."

Ellen and her fiancé, who was both a physician and an attorney, went down to the holding facility the night of November 22. She wanted to get Debora's medication to her, and she wanted her fiancé to make sure Debora was okay, not about to lapse into another of those strange states in which she seemed to lose touch with reality.

The jail was so overcrowded that night before Thanksgiving that there was no one to escort them on the elevator to the eighth floor. Visitors were not allowed on the elevators without an escort, so "We walked the eight flights of stairs," Ellen recalled. "I had her eyeglasses and her meds. I wanted her to be able to sleep, at least. But she was in a cage with people who were screaming, and some who were so out of it that they had to be chained to a bed. They had the television going all the time, to try to calm the prisoners down. There is no sleep in that jail."

Debora asked Ellen to be sure that Lissa knew she was okay, and Ellen promised to pass on that message. That was about all she could do. Debora would not have an extradition hearing until sometime on Friday, November 24.

Ellen went to see Lissa at her aunt Karen's house and assured her that her mother was okay. "They are being very kind to her at the jail. It's not a very nice place, but they're treating her kindly."

Ellen had a message for Lissa: "Your mother wants you to hold your head up and dance like a queen."

Lissa straightened up, holding her head at a ballerina's tilt. "I will," she said. "Tell her I promise."

Chapter 28

As soon as Jackson County opened for business after the Thanksgiving holiday, Dennis Moore and Kevin Moriarty, a member of his firm who would join in Debora Green's defense, appeared at an extradition hearing before a Missouri circuit judge. Debora sat in a holding area with several other prisoners, occasionally laughing as she talked quietly with her attorneys. Moore and Moriarty told the judge that their client would waive extradition and return willingly to Johnson County, Kansas, where her arrest warrant had been issued.

In court, Debora herself stared straight ahead. She seemed stunned, unbelieving. That may have been because she had not slept since Wednesday night. She wore the same long-sleeved black dress she'd had on when she was arrested. Although she had the smudgy, drawn look of extreme fatigue, the video cameras in the courtroom caught the intelligence in her eyes. Exhausted, shocked, disheartened, fearful, yes—but it was not possible for a woman of Debora's intelligence to look stupid.

After the hearing, Ellen told reporters that Debora was in a state of "profound grief. All she talks about is worry about Lissa, and what the pressure is doing to Lissa," she said. "I think she is still somewhat dazed and confused. She's very surprised that she would be charged with these kinds of crimes. She lost everything in this fire—including her children, *everything*, and she's astounded."

Ellen had arranged Debora's finances so that she could bail her client out of jail, but she had not foreseen the tremendously high bail that would be set by judge Peter Ruddick when Debora was arraigned in Johnson County. *$3 million.* That was the highest bail ever asked in Johnson County, and Debora didn't have nearly enough money set aside. She would have to stay in jail until the preliminary hearing to determine whether Paul Morrison had presented enough evidence to warrant a trial.

Debora's quarters in the 270-bed Johnson County Adult Detention Center in Olathe were palatial compared to the Jackson County holding cell. She occasionally had visitors from a small group of women she had known before. Lissa did not visit her mother in jail, but she did speak to her on the phone. Debora had no radio or television, but she did have books to read. Books had always been her refuge.

Johnson County's courthouse, administration building, and jail were mostly new, built of stone and red brick and set on a full-city block-sized square of manicured grass with trees, lights, a clock tower, and a huge stone circle filled with flowers in season. It could well have been a movie set, a pleasant spot to linger—unless you had business there. Olathe, the county seat, where Debora's preliminary hearing would be held, has about 70,000 citizens. The county buildings are located in the original part of Olathe, which dates back a hundred years or more. The businesses there are not thriving. Aside from lawyers' offices, supermarkets, craft stores, and tiny strip malls, nothing much seems to be happening downtown; many storefronts are boarded up or papered over. Olathe's citizens have not yet realized the worth of historic buildings. The newer half of Olathe was not nearly as endearing. Upscale—but quickly constructed—housing developments and apartments have sprung up, and franchises line the main drag for miles.

In the jail in Olathe, Debora had a cell to herself and there was quiet. She later remembered that she was heavily dosed with Prozac and Klonopin, her mind so fogged over that she moved through the next few months in a haze. There was one other prisoner in her section, an Asian woman who spoke little English. "But we were never allowed in the common room together, so I never talked to her," Debora said. This was just as well. The woman was also charged with child murder. She had decapitated her child and was later judged insane.

Debora would complain that Dennis Moore and Kevin Moriarty rarely came to see her. "They told my mother they came three times a week," she said, "but it was more like every ten days—and then they only stayed for ten minutes."

Ellen Ryan, who had little to do with Debora's criminal defense, would be remembered a bit more favorably. She had promised Debora that she would be there, beside her, if she had to go to trial, and that she would sit with her at the preliminary hearing scheduled for late January 1996. Even so, Joan Jones would say bitterly that Ellen didn't do enough for her daughter. "She just took all her money and gave it to those *lawyers*." Indeed, in her mother's view, Debora had been victimized by the whole world. If, in her desire to see her daughter succeed, Joan had railed at the child Debora and the teenage Debora, she now found no fault with her at all.

Celeste visited Mike in the hospital, and not a day went by that they didn't talk by phone at least four times. Celeste stubbornly refused to believe that they could not wrest some

kind of future out of, quite literally, the ashes of their lives.
She knew that Mike's family did not approve of her. Once,
when they met at the hospital, his mother was frank in suggesting that Celeste should not be there. Celeste saw the
distaste in Velma Farrar's eyes. Still, she lingered in Mike's
room.

But what did it matter anymore how things looked?
Celeste knew the truth. She had seen John waste years of his
life in gray depression, and then rob himself of all the rest of
his life in a moment of despair. She loved Mike and she was
not going to stay away when he needed her. It may have
been that Celeste was the one who loved more in their relationship. Mike was too ill, too grief-stricken, and too
preoccupied by what new catastrophe the future might
hold; he scarcely had time or the strength for love. Nor did
he have time to listen to his parents' admonitions about
staying away from Celeste. He had to get well so that Lissa
would have at least one parent to take care of her. And,
somehow, he had to get strong enough to practice medicine
again. It had been so long that sometimes he didn't even
feel like a doctor anymore.

But without a sure diagnosis, Mike was in limbo. He knew
he had been sick enough to die during his illnesses, that he
had endocarditis and a leaking mitral valve in his heart, but
he still didn't know for sure why he had suddenly become so
ill. There was no definitive reason for it. Until some expert
could validate his feelings about what was wrong with him—
and why—he would never be truly well.

In the bitter cold of a Kansas winter, crews moved in and
tore down what was left of the house on Canterbury Court.
They hauled truckload after truckload of debris away until
nothing remained but cinders. The pool was gone, and
Tim's basketball hoop, the stone façade that would have
lasted a century, the four-car garage. Everything gone. And
soon the snow covered even those minute reminders of the

house that had stood there. The trees survived—even the slender white birches, although they had been scorched by the flames and nearly flattened by the firefighters' hoses.

Now, when the Jurdens looked to the west, they saw only the Formans' home. That was odd, but it was certainly better than seeing rain and snow invade the charred remains of 7517 Canterbury Court.

Chapter 29

The Debora Green case would not be the first in which Paul Morrison had come up against his old boss, Dennis Moore. The men respected one another, and both were extraordinarily impressive in a criminal trial. In the courtroom, each was entirely focused on presenting his side of the case at hand. As one newspaper columnist termed it, the Green trial would be "a battle of the titans." Debora might have the best in defense attorneys, but she also faced a prosecutor with a solid record of convictions. Both Morrison and Moore had graduated from Washburn Law School in Topeka, and between them, they had prosecuted several of East Kansas's most notorious cases.

Moore was a big man, very tall—a handsome man with dark silver-streaked hair, whose courtly manner made him seem more like a Southern lawyer than a Midwesterner. Whatever his feelings were, they lay beneath the surface; he betrayed none of them to court watchers. He seemed—always—unruffled and confident.

During his three terms as Johnson County district attorney—from January 1977 until December 1989—Moore had prosecuted a number of high-profile cases. Among them was that of Danny Crump, who was convicted of planting a bomb that killed six members of an Olathe family. Another newsworthy case in which Moore won a conviction was that of Sue Ann Hobson, whose manipulations convinced her son and his friend to murder her stepson. Two books were written about the Hobson case; Danny Crump's crime also received national attention.

Now, besieged by the media, Moore gave a number of interviews, not just to the Kansas City press and TV, but to tabloid shows such as *Inside Edition*. He hinted at a defense, rather than coming out with any absolute statements. He mentioned a run-in Tim had had with the Prairie Village police for lighting a Molotov cocktail in his neighbors' yard. He managed to raise the question of a possible connection between Tim's fascination with fire and the tragedy that killed him. Asked if Dr. John Walker's death was truly a suicide, Moore said that his defense team was looking into that. He obviously wanted to leave the impression that his client was *not* the only suspect in the case. And he did that while adroitly managing to stay within the guidelines of Judge Ruddick's gag order.

On December 5, there was, finally, a conclusive report on Dr. John Walker's death. J. Michael Boles, M.D., the coroner of the Tenth Judicial District of Kansas, released his conclusions about the suspected suicide. Boles's review of Bonita Peterson's autopsy explained why the Pentothal found at Walker's death scene had not been recovered from venous blood in his body. The chief question raised by Dr. Peterson's postmortem was why it appeared that Walker had chosen to be awake when he would have known he could not breathe voluntarily. Surely no anesthesiologist would choose suffocation as a manner of death.

And, mercifully, Walker hadn't. Dr. Boles's autopsy review verified that he had been an extremely intelligent and well-informed anesthesiologist. His choice of drugs and the way he administered them to himself showed that he was fully cognizant of what he was doing when he chose a final escape from his constant depression.

"The most probable reason Pentothal could not be recovered from the venous blood is as follows," Boles wrote. "The subject first injected the paralytic agent (Pancuronium). As he began to feel the effects of this agent (inability to breathe), he then injected the Pentothal. At this time the subject would have been in a state of respiratory acidosis with associated high CO_2 (Hypercapnia) and also would have large levels of circulatory endogenous adrenalin[e] [normally present in the body, to help humans respond to danger]. Both Hypercapnia and high adrenalin[e] levels have been associated with Sudden Cardiac Death during the induction of anesthesia with Pentothal. In this scenario, one would expect to recover little, if any, Pentothal from the blood stream, since the heart has no time to recirculate the small amount available back to the tissues. . . . Thus death in this case was due to sudden cardiac arrest secondary to Pentothal administration."

John Walker had not wanted to risk waking up from an insufficient dosage of anesthesia. He had made sure that his heart would stop instantly. And it had. For those who loved him, it was a small comfort. He had not suffered for a moment.

The whispers that had cast Celeste Walker as a clever murderess who had killed her husband so that she could inherit millions and run away with her lover were silenced. But there were those who still suspected that Debora had played some part in driving John Walker to suicide. There always would be.

It was on that same day, December 5, 1995, that Drew Richardson, Supervisory Special Agent of the FBI, received the request from the Johnson County criminalist, Gary Dirks. Richardson examined the two containers of evidence that Dirks had sent him. One was a sealed plastic envelope containing a packet of Earl May castor beans. The other was a sample of blood from Dr. Mike Farrar.

Richardson knew that antibodies to ricin do not appear in the blood and tissue within a week or two of ingestion.

Therefore, there is no way to test for ricin poisoning early in the treatment. The condition masquerades as a number of other illnesses. However, the human body has a remarkable ability to fight "enemies" that attack it. Months after poisoning with ricin, antibodies to this deadly poison *do* appear.

If he could find ricin antibodies in the blood and tissue samples taken from Mike Farrar, and if Debora Green should be bound over for trial, Richardson would be a powerful witness for the prosecution. His findings would also vindicate Mike, who had suffered so gravely from what had seemed to be a phantom illness.

Two weeks after Richardson received the ricin exemplars from Dirks, an incident in Arkansas demonstrated that ricin/castor-bean poisoning was not the uncommon weapon that it seemed. Thomas Lavy, fifty-four, was arrested on his Onia, Arkansas, farm and charged under the federal Biological Weapons Anti-Terrorism Act with possession of a toxic substance—ricin—with intent to use it as a weapon.

Canadian customs agents had searched Lavy's car at a border crossing between Alaska and Canada two years earlier and found $89,000 in cash, four guns, more than 20,000 rounds of ammunition, and a quantity of white powder. An analysis of the powder proved that it was not cocaine; it was ricin. FBI Agent Thomas Lynch said that because of a communications mix-up, he had not learned of the incident until early 1995. He had traced Lavy, who had earlier been indicted in Alaska on a federal charge of possession of a toxic substance with intent to use it as a weapon, to his Onia farm.

Agent Lynch knew a lot about ricin. He explained to the press that it is the third-deadliest toxin in the world; only plutonium and botulism are more deadly. "It has no known antidote," Lynch said.

Investigators who searched Lavy's farm found a copy of *The Poisoner's Handbook*, which describes how to extract ricin from castor beans, and *Silent Death*, which discusses ways to use toxic compounds to poison people. When Lavy explained that he was carrying 130 grams of the poison from Alaska into Canada only because he wanted to bring it to Arkansas to kill coyotes that were preying on his chickens, prosecutors looked doubtful. U.S. Prosecutor Robert Govar explained, "It would be tantamount to saying you can use a thermonuclear device to protect your property from break-in or burglary."

But there would never be a trial for Thomas Lavy. He was found hanging in his jail cell in Little Rock on December 23, 1995, and pronounced dead. The Associated Press dispatch on Lavy's arrest and suicide ended by describing the Debora Green case in Kansas and the contention by prosecutors there that she had attempted to kill her husband with ricin.

By December 1995, Mike was ill again, suffering from severe frontal headaches. He called his doctor and said he was afraid he needed a CAT scan. After evaluating the results of a cerebral angiogram (where dye is introduced into arteries in the brain), his physician agreed that he had an abscess that had bled. "I was a walking time-bomb," Mike recalled.

On December 11, he underwent a craniotomy. The clump of bacteria originating from his heart valve had found its way to the right front part of his brain. The surgeon who operated on him, Dr. Stephan Reintges, knew it had broken loose from the heart to roam through the bloodstream unchecked until it began building a potentially fatal abscess in Mike's brain. "He may have had a stroke," the surgeon told reporters. "Or the bacteria itself may have simply broken through."

Mike's brain surgery would involve drilling burr holes in the right frontal portion of his skull until a "lid" of bone could be removed, exposing the brain beneath. Then the abscess could be drained. Because the original cause of the sepsis—the reason that bacteria had flooded Mike's body organs and bloodstream—had yet to be isolated, Dr. Reintges took yet another sample of body fluid to be analyzed in the FBI lab.

The critical nature of Mike's condition had not escaped Paul Morrison. The husband who was in the process of divorcing Debora Green was slated to be one of the prime witnesses against her. Mike had been there, behind the walls that hid their tumultuous family situation, for years. Morrison had to get his testimony first before a judge in a pretrial hearing and then in front of a jury if he was to have a prayer of winning a case that was mostly circumstantial.

Knowing that Mike could very well die during the surgery to drain his abscess, Morrison had asked him if he would agree to having his testimony videotaped. Both Morrison and Moore would examine him and cross-examine him before his surgery. Of course, Morrison had not said, "We need this in case you die before trial or in case you end up a vegetable," but Mike was a physician himself; he knew the odds. If his surgery was successful, that videotape would never be used. If things went badly, at least his image and his voice would be there in the courtroom. He believed that Debora had killed two of their children and had meant to kill him. He felt strongly that she must not be allowed to escape retribution. So, with a nurse accompanying him, he gave his testimony before a video camera.

Mike had more wrong with his brain than an abscess, however. The cerebral angiogram showed that he also had a mycotic aneurysm in a main blood vessel in his brain. The vessel was thinning and weakening, assaulted by the bacteria spewed out during his attack of endocarditis. He would have four more brain angiograms over the next four months. His doctors wanted to keep track of the condition of the bulging artery. If anything, this was more dangerous than his infected heart and the abscess in his brain. The poison he had ingested was not static; it continued to do silent damage inside his body. Even the tests were so dangerous that he had to be hospitalized overnight each time. A small percentage of patients suffer strokes from the angiogram itself.

*

Christmas 1995 was a holiday that the principals in the Farrar-Green case would have to get through somehow. There were too many losses, too many memories, and no one knew what the new year would bring. Among the hundreds of photographs now kept in the district attorney's office, there were scores showing Christmases past that Mike, Debora, and their children had shared: Debora decorating a succession of trees; Kelly gleefully unwrapping a present; Tim posing in his Kansas City Chiefs sweatshirt and pants while Mike looked on proudly; Tim, Lissa, and Kelly smiling as they cuddled on a sofa, their cheeks pink with excitement; Boomer happily sitting in a morass of crumpled wrapping paper. Looking at those pictures long after they had been snapped, it did not seem possible that this family could have been so tragically destroyed.

Kansas City, Missouri, once again celebrated Christmas by decorating the already picturesque County Club Plaza with thousands of tiny white lights. Their sparkling silver reflections on the snow and the old-fashioned streetlights slightly dimmed by yet another profusion of snowflakes make the city especially beautiful during Christmas. And so it still was, of course, in 1995—for most families.

Debora remained in jail, while her daughter held her head high and danced in *The Nutcracker Suite*. It was a beautiful performance. Lissa celebrated Christmas with her father and his family, but she was sad because her mother was not in the audience watching her dance. Celeste was trying to help her sons have a good Christmas despite the fact that their father was gone. People in both Johnson and Jackson counties—indeed in all of Kansas and Missouri—clamored for news of the case, but there was none. Neither the prosecution nor the defense intended to reveal its cards. For Paul Morrison, Rick Guinn, Dennis Moore, and Kevin Moriarty, the holidays had to be short; they were girding up for one of the biggest legal battles the Kansas City area had ever known.

Part III

And fire and ice within me fight
Beneath the suffocating night.

—A. E. HOUSMAN

Part III

Chapter 30

Suspected arson, murder, and poisoning and the Debora-Mike-Celeste triangle made the case going into a pretrial hearing a barn-burner. It was a case any criminal defense attorney or prosecutor would be eager to try, and one any reporter would fight to cover. But reporters had been given the barest tidbits of information. Debora's pretrial hearing would be open to the press and public, but would be held in a very small courtroom and seats would be at a premium. Morrison planned to present a startling item of evidence to Judge Peter Ruddick; the press could see and hear it, but would be forbidden to tape or film it before trial—that is, of course, if the Green case did go to trial.

Long before the preliminary hearing, court officials began preparing for the mass of reporters, producers, and writers expected to descend on the Johnson County Courthouse. Judge Ruddick asked for help from a specialist from the Kansas Supreme Court to keep track of the media and arrange the courtroom seating. Ron Keefover served as the Supreme Court's education and information officer. He had experience in keeping a lid on Kansas trials that sparked national attention. The Debora Green trial promised to be the biggest thing to hit Olathe, and Ruddick needed Keefover. They both intended to keep it from becoming a circus.

Ironically, it had been another marital quartet murder that had demanded the most of Ron Keefover. In 1985, the Reverend Thomas Bird of Emporia stood trial for the murder of his wife, who was first thought to have perished in a car accident, *and* his mistress was charged with the shooting death of her husband. Mrs. Bird's car had plunged off a bridge and Kansas State Trooper John Rule had become suspicious about the accident. Convicted, Thomas Bird and his lover became the subjects of a book and miniseries called *By Murder Ordained*.

Johnson County's biggest trial to date had been that of serial killer Richard Grissom, Jr. In a face-off with Kevin Moriarty, Paul Morrison had won a conviction. During that trial, which ended on November 4, 1990, a hundred people or more had stood in line every morning, waiting to get into the courtroom. And, as at all sensational trials, there were outbursts of temper when reporters or others with reserved seats were allowed into the courtroom before people who had been in line for hours.

This time, Keefover advised Judge Ruddick to set up an "overflow room" with closed-circuit television sets and chairs for sixty people. The room, one floor below Ruddick's third-floor courtroom, would double as a press room. There would be no still cameras or interviews on the third floor. This technique had worked remarkably well in many high-profile trials, beginning with Ted Bundy's first trial in Miami, Florida, in the summer of 1979. Technology and the psychology of trial watchers had come to little Olathe in 1996.

Press credentials alone were not enough to get you into the Green preliminary hearing; what mattered was that your name was on Ron Keefover's list. He was a friendly, laid-back man, but he believed in organization. There would be no "musical chair" seating at the Green hearing.

During the preliminary—or show cause—hearing, Paul Morrison and Rick Guinn would have to convince Judge Ruddick that they had enough evidence to move on to trial. And Dennis Moore and Kevin Moriarty would fight to suggest that the wrong person had been arrested, that Debora Green was an innocent and grieving mother unjustly accused of arson and murder.

The hearing was scheduled for the last week in January

1996, and Olathe was icy cold—normal weather for natives, shocking to reporters who had flown in from more moderate climates. It was too cold and dry for Santa Fe Street, the main east–west thoroughfare that ran between the new and the old in Olathe, even to be slippery. The snow only feathered over Santa Fe. But there were drifts left by earlier storms around the parking strips of all the streets near the Johnson County Courthouse; the piles of old snow were four feet high and iced over. Navigating the diagonal sidewalks that led to the steps of the courthouse without the sense that noses, ears, and even lungs were actually freezing was a challenge. And, then, once you were through the many doors of the building, heat trapped in the outer lobby made coats unbearable.

Reporters, clutching their credentials but still nervous lest they might not find their names on Ron Keefover's list, jogged down long corridors and snagged elevators headed for Judge Ruddick's courtroom. There were only three rows of twenty seats, room for sixty people, in the courtroom. They were comfortable, theater-like seats, but the media and the fascinated spectators who had lined up to get in would not have cared if they had to sit on cement blocks. Witnesses were excluded from the courtroom before they gave their testimony, but as the week progressed, many of them would return after testifying to watch the rest of the case unfold. Paul Morrison was dealing with a mostly circumstantial case and he had predicted that "there won't be many surprises left" after the preliminary hearing.

The courtroom was modern and almost sumptuous. Everything was curved: the shining wood in front of the jurors' box; the tables where the prosecutors would sit on the left and where Debora Green and her defense team would sit on the right. Even the judge's "bench" was curved. Ruddick, who looked too young and too benign to be a judge, was both—but courthouse regulars knew that he was very, very good at his job.

A television camera was mounted on "sticks" in front of

the empty jury box; the cameraman of the day would dis-
tribute the film in a pool to Kansas City television stations.
There would be no jury, of course, during this preliminary
hearing. And it might prove difficult to select a jury if the
case proceeded to trial. Every television station in the
greater Kansas City area planned to feature the Green hearing at the top of the news at noon, at five, and at ten P.M.

Even with a press pass, it was not easy to get into the courtroom. Johnson County deputies searched purses and
briefcases, and everyone had to pass through a metal detector. Every trip down the hall to the phone or the restroom
meant another search and another slow walk through the
scanner.

Tony Rizzo of the Kansas City *Star* and Andy Hoffman of
the Olathe *Daily News* were in the courtroom. Mark Lorber,
a producer from Hollywood, attended, and there were at
least a dozen women who were about Debora's age. Some of
them said they had known her; one woman was eager to
tell the rest of the gallery that she and Debora had been
"very close" and often played tennis together. Others were
there because this case mesmerized them.

Everyone wanted to see Dr. Debora Green, who had been
invisible to the public for two months. It was rumored that
her husband, Dr. Michael Farrar, would testify against her,
and that his alleged mistress, Celeste Walker, would testify
too.

And then, suddenly, Debora emerged from a room
beyond the jury box, accompanied by Ellen Ryan. She wore
a white sweater that was clearly too large for her over a pink
turtleneck top and a pleated white skirt. She had obviously
lost twenty pounds or more since her arrest. Without seeming even to glance at the spectators in the room, she moved
quickly to her chair at the defense table. She had a faintly
clumsy, almost masculine stride.

Once she took her seat, Debora looked only forward. She
had to have been aware that every pair of eyes behind her
was focused on her, but she never looked around to check

out the gallery. Her hair was probably her best feature; chestnut brown and gleaming, it fell naturally into thick waves. She wore makeup, but very subtle makeup—a touch of eye shadow, a little lip gloss. Pearl stud earrings were her only jewelry.

Like most defendants, Debora had a yellow legal pad on the table in front of her, and she clutched a pen as if she planned to take notes. Her expression was alert, even wary, but she didn't look worried. Ellen Ryan, sitting close beside her—for moral support only; she was not a criminal lawyer—*did* look worried, and she often glanced anxiously at Debora. The male attorneys, on both sides, looked businesslike.

No one outside the inner sanctum of the district attorney's office and the Metro Squad knew for sure what evidence the State of Kansas might have against Dr. Debora Green. Ninety days after the fire that killed two of her children, the rest of the world was about to find out. There was a good chance they would also get some idea of what Dennis Moore and Kevin Moriarty would counter with in her defense.

The proceedings began with Paul Morrison asking Judge Ruddick if he might make an opening statement. He would not be talking to a jury; in this phase he had only the judge to convince. And, for the first time, step by step, in perfect chronological order, Judge Ruddick and the court watchers learned of the events that led up to the catastrophic inferno on Canterbury Court. In his deep calm voice, Morrison described the strange fire that happened on West Sixty-first Terrace after Dr. Michael Farrar left Debora Green the first time, and after he had reneged on the deal to buy 7517 Canterbury Court and on a reconciliation.

"Within a couple of days after that, Judge," Morrison said, "their house in Kansas City, Missouri, burned, suffering severe damage, and it burned just a few minutes after

Debora Green left one day with the children while Dr.
Farrar was at work. Well, now the family had nowhere to go
and that sort of forced a reconciliation. They moved in with
him. And as part of that they went ahead and bought that
house on Canterbury Court in Prairie Village."

Morrison went on to explain that the couple had made
an attempt to be happy together. But that attempt was short-
lived. Michael Farrar wanted a divorce.

"After he told her that," Morrison said, "Dr. Michael
Farrar and others will document for this court a series of
very bizarre, very obsessive, strange behavior by Dr. Debora
Green. . . . [She] began to drink very heavily. . . . She
began to make threats—mainly threats to commit suicide,
but at times threats against other people, specifically Dr.
Farrar. Sometimes, she would lay in bed for days and refuse
to get up, causing a lot of problems within the family, particularly with the kids. The kids were scared. Dr. Farrar was
scared."

Morrison told about the time Debora had hidden in her
own home and pretended to be calling her husband from
someplace else. Those in the gallery stared at the back of
Debora's head, obviously curious about her reactions to
Morrison's accusations. But those who could see her face in
profile saw that her expression never changed. Morrison
might as well have been talking about someone else.

"In early August, Dr. Michael Farrar began to get sick,"
Morrison said. "And it wasn't just a minor illness, Judge." He
related the symptoms of Mike's illness and the doctors' puz-
zlement over what could be wrong with their colleague. "He
was hospitalized for several days," Morrison said. "He got
better. . . . He went home. He ate food prepared by Debora
Green. He got sick again. . . . He was eventually released on
September eleventh after three fairly long hospitalizations,
and the doctors could not figure out what was wrong with
him—finally diagnosed him as having some sort of a tropical
sprue syndrome because they'll tell you that they really
couldn't figure out what else it could have been. . . ."

Debora continued to look straight ahead, watching Morrison as he spoke.

"The bizarre behavior continued," Morrison said. "It got so bad, Judge, that Michael Farrar on September 25, 1995, attempted to have his wife committed involuntarily to a mental institution. . . ."

When Morrison said that Mike had found castor beans in his wife's purse at about this time, reporters began to scribble furiously. What did castor beans have to do with the deadly fire? The few newspaper reports that mentioned castor beans and ricin had been tantalizingly brief.

Paul Morrison then described the strange night when the Prairie Village police had taken Debora to the KU Medical Center. She had been quite cooperative with her acquaintance, Dr. Pam McCoy—until Dr. Farrar had arrived. "As soon as he walked in that room, Pam McCoy will tell you that Debora Green turned around, spun around, assumed some kind of assaultive posture toward him, *spit* at him, screamed at him, 'You fuckhole. . . . You will get those kids over our dead bodies!'"

Morrison moved next to the night of October 23–24. He detailed all the pages, the phone calls, the arguments as Mike phoned Debora first from Celeste Walker's home, and then from his apartment. "He gets home, he calls her back. They have a heated conversation between . . . eleven-forty-five and probably five minutes until twelve. In that heated conversation, he will tell you that Debora Green was drunk, and that made him mad. He will tell you that he was angry because of the fact that the neighbors had complained to him about what had been going on over in his house during his absence. He was tired of dealing with the drunkenness of Debora Green. She wasn't taking care of the house. He was worried about the kids.

"And he said to her, 'I think you're poisoning me. I think you're poisoning me, you're drunk, you're abusive, you're not taking care of those kids, people are threatening to call SRS. Get your act together.'"

Morrison told Judge Ruddick that Mike had received one last phone call from Debora. She had obviously not expected him to be home; she had thought he was calling her back from his car phone. "And Debora Green said to him, 'Oh, I didn't know you were home. I was just going to leave a message.' *Click.* Several minutes after that last call, Your Honor, the house at 7517 Canterbury was an inferno. . . . Kelly Farrar and Tim Farrar died in that fire. Ten-year-old Lissa Farrar, their middle child, got out through the window of her bedroom."

Morrison promised the judge that over the next few days he would produce witnesses who would prove that Mike's illness was neither a virus nor tropical sprue but something far more sinister. Morrison said he would put witnesses on the stand who would testify that the fire that killed Kelly and Tim Farrar had been deliberately set by someone who had poured accelerants around the house and then set fire to them. "And most importantly, Judge, in their opinion, based on the accelerant patterns in that house, the fire started from the defendant's bedroom, which was the *only* room on the main floor of that house that was not heavily poured with accelerants and not heavily damaged. . . . Judge, Debora Green set that fire intentionally, knowing that it would kill all those children in that house."

Dennis Moore rose to make an opening statement for the Defense. He assured Judge Ruddick that he would be brief. "As the Court well knows," he began, "under Kansas law, the evidence in this case presented at this probable cause hearing has to be construed in the light most favorable to the State. So this is basically the State's chance to show the Court . . . what they have."

Moore said that the Defense might present some evidence, but he viewed probable cause as a "very low standard" compared to what would later be a "beyond a reasonable doubt" jury trial. He would present only that evidence he deemed necessary at this time.

Moore allowed that Mike and Debora had not had a happy home for a long time. But he struck out at Mike for deciding he wanted a divorce without telling Debora before the trip to Peru in June, 1995. "He thought it wouldn't be a happy occasion if he told her prior to that time that he wanted a divorce, that he wanted to leave the family, leave her and the children. So he kept a pretense up and basically lived a lie."

Moore also hit at Mike for the "close relationship" he had developed with Celeste Walker on the Peru trip. "Well, it was more than just a friendship. The evidence will be that it was a very, very, close friendship. . . . Dr. Farrar came back and told various people that, in fact, the friendship had not turned sexual, romantic, until Dr. Walker's death—Celeste Walker's husband—which was on September 5. That was a lie. Dr. Farrar will admit that he lied to the police about that."

Moore did not deny that Debora had begun to drink heavily, but he added that she was on medication and also seeing a psychiatrist. He insisted that she had "tried to maintain stability during that period of time." As for the alleged poisoning of her husband, Moore said that medical reports had said the final diagnosis *was* tropical sprue. "They also said it could be some sort of typhoid—and noted the fact that during the trip to Peru, Dr. Farrar swam in the Amazon River, he ate food prepared by local people, and some of the symptoms that he had could have been caused by those things and [by] the so-called tropical sprue."

As for the fire, Moore said that the defense would not dispute some of the evidence gleaned from the gutted house. But then he pulled out his trump card. He would name as the arsonist one of the fire's victims: Tim Farrar.

"There's going to be evidence presented that Tim Farrar, thirteen-year-old Tim Farrar, had an unnatural fascination with fire. He liked to strike matches. In fact, back in March of 1995, just a few months before the fire that took the lives of Tim and Kelly Farrar, Tim and another boy were caught by the Prairie Village police with a Molotov cocktail one or two houses down from where Tim Farrar lived. . . . Tim Farrar hated his father. Tim Farrar had a very, very, ugly relationship with Michael Farrar. In fact, the relationship turned violent."

The spectators were electrified by Moore's accusation, and frankly puzzled. This defense tactic was repugnant. Experienced court watchers suspected that Debora's case was so weak that her attorneys were willing to risk the backlash that would surely come when they accused a dead boy of starting the fire that killed him and his little sister. Moore went on to explain to the judge that Tim had been a "very disturbed young man," who disliked his father but feared his parents' divorcing more than anything else. Still, it would require nimble rhetoric, indeed, for Moore to paint Tim as villain and victim at once.

Next, Moore told Judge Ruddick that Debora had been the sole suspect from the very beginning—that the investigators had ignored the possibility of other suspects. "The police had Michael Farrar *drive* over to the police station in Prairie Village," he said. "The police *transported* Debora Green over to the police station in Prairie Village."

But, of course, Debora had no other way to get there. The $40,000 Toyota Land Cruiser that she had wanted so much was sitting on melted tires in one of the parking bays in her burning home.

"Judge," Moore said in conclusion, "I'm going to ask the Court, even at this probable-cause hearing, to keep an open mind and listen to *all* the evidence. There are at least two sides to every story. . . ."

Paul Morrison's jaw muscles tightened when he heard Dennis Moore accuse a dead boy of setting the fire that killed him, and, for a fleeting moment, Debora looked distressed. Tim had been the child who was closest to her, the son she counted on. Had she agreed to this betrayal in order to save herself? Or was she as shocked as the murmuring gallery to hear her attorney shift the blame for the crimes she was accused of to her lost son?

Chapter 31

Dr. Michael Farrar, the first witness for the State, was very thin and pale as he stood to take the oath. Debora Green shifted and turned slightly toward her estranged husband, whom she had not seen for months. Now she stared at him. Did she still love him? Was she uneasy about what he was going to say about her in front of the judge and the spectators?

Mike's hair had just begun to grow out after his December brain surgery, and a long scar was visible on the right side of his forehead and back into his hairline. He looked as if he had just had a very close crew cut, and it made him appear much younger than his forty years. It seemed almost impossible that the man in the witness chair and the woman at the defense table had ever been in love, let alone married for sixteen years; it seemed impossible that they had conceived three children together. Although Debora was only four years older than Mike, there looked to be a decade's disparity in their ages.

Mike had spent the day before forcing himself to go over the events of the previous two years, from the time when his marriage and his family's lives had dissolved into macabre soap opera. He had kept his composure when he videotaped his testimony eight weeks before, and now he did not want to break down on the witness stand when he would have to again recall the last terrible days of his children's lives.

When he answered Paul Morrison's and Dennis Moore's questions, Mike would seem at times almost clinical, a demeanor those in his profession often assume when they have to give bad news or face the certain death of patients. He showed his emotion by the way he clenched and unclenched his hands on the rail in front of him. Rarely would he glance at Debora, and then only with a sidelong shift of his eyes skimming over the defense table.

"Doctor," Morrison asked, "was your marriage to Debora Green a happy one?"

Debora seemed to be holding her breath, waiting for the answer. When it came, she flinched almost imperceptibly.

"In my eyes it was not," Mike answered. "It was a long-term loveless marriage that was characterized by a lack of care, compassion, understanding. There was no mutual respect, no outward affection."

" . . . Is that from both of you or is that one way?"

"Well, I think it was mostly on her part."

Debora's eyes stayed fixed on her husband. She didn't shake her head, or open her mouth to protest, or look to Ellen Ryan for comfort. If she had done what the State asserted, set fire to "her babies" in a storm of jealous, possessive rage, she had done it to take revenge on a man who spoke now of the ordeal of being married to her.

Mike said he had stayed in the marriage because he didn't want his children to grow up in a broken home. He added that he was not a man who liked to fail, and that failure at marriage seemed to him the worst kind. "I tried to stick it out for their [the children's] sake. And then I think later I was worried that when we did get a divorce—because of the nature of Debora's behavior—I thought it would be a horrible divorce. . . ."

"What about the nature of her behavior made you feel that way?" Morrison asked.

"She was an extremely volatile person," Mike said, "had temper tantrums characterized by particularly foul language— oftentimes in public. She was chronically depressed. She felt ill all the time. . . . Her mood was always dark and pessimistic. She was a very difficult person to deal with, very unpleasant."

Debora frowned and turned slightly toward Ellen Ryan, who whispered something to her. She barely shook her head, her eyes still fixed on her husband.

In response to Morrison's questions, Mike described the sixteen years of his marriage to Debora. He spoke of the failure of her medical practice, and of how, when she finally realized that private practice was not for her, he had urged her to stay home. "I said that was fine. I encouraged her to do anything that I thought would make her happy. The problem was she was never happy at doing anything she ever did."

Mike went on to describe the first fire, his tentative reconciliation with Debora, their final decision to buy the house on Canterbury Court, and the long-planned trip to Peru. Before the trip, and for a month after their return on July 6, he said he had been in good health.

Mike said he had never changed his mind after deciding to ask Debora for a divorce in midsummer of 1995, although he dreaded her reaction. It was, as he expected, a temper tantrum.

"Did her behavior change after you announced those divorce plans to her?" Morrison questioned.

"Her depression became more severe," Mike answered. "She started drinking heavily. She would go on alcoholic binges where she could drink a liter and a half of vodka or gin over a couple of days. I found her passed out on the basement floor. There were days when she had to stay in bed all day because she was too drunk. She would also say horrible, vile things to the children about me. . . . She told the children one day that I was out fucking three women. . . . She told the children that I was running around Peru chasing women with my dick hanging out."

"Those are quotes?"

"Absolute quotes. In front of the children . . ."

"How did the children take this impending divorce?" Paul Morrison asked.

"Tim and Lissa reacted to it very negatively," Mike said. "They were both very angry, very hostile. Their behavior deteriorated significantly. They became defiant. They repeated a lot of the foul language that their mother said. . . . They wanted me to move back in. They were very angry with me for moving out."

It was obvious that this had become a marriage made in hell, the most combative marriage the majority of those listening in the courtroom had ever contemplated. Mike also testified that much of the worst arguing and profanity—and Debora's drinking—took place after he became violently sick with the illness no one could diagnose. For the first few weeks, he had tried to keep going. After that, he was either ill at home or ill in the hospital.

Paul Morrison now changed gears. He produced several scale drawings of the house on Canterbury Court and asked Mike to describe it. Testimony about the progress of the fire through that house would be crucial to the case against Debora. Although the house no longer existed, Mike had a strong visual memory that allowed him to recall each room, each piece of furniture. The building had been L-shaped, with the four-car garage forming the short leg of the "L."

Mike described the dining room table and the oriental rug that had once been beneath it, both incinerated now.

"What about the great room?" Morrison asked. "Did it have carpet or did it have a hardwood floor?"

"Carpet."

"Okay. And what all did you have in there?"

"There was a couch along the north wall—a sleeper couch. There was an oak-and-glass coffee table in front of it. On each side of that there were oak-and-glass end tables with lamps on both of them. . . ."

Mike frequently closed his eyes as he re-created these rooms, gone forever. It was almost as if by bringing the house back, he could bring his children back, too.

Morrison pointed to the formal living room, and Mike said they had used it as a music room. "We had a baby grand in there, and a couple of chairs and a curio cabinet again, a small desk."

"Whose piano was that?"

"Well, I think it was a piano for the entire family, but it was actually a Christmas gift to me one year. On Christmas morning, Debora told me to stay in bed and I heard a bunch of noise downstairs. Somebody was obviously delivering something, and it was a baby grand Steinert piano." Arson investigators had seen that piano; so much accelerant had been poured around it that its legs had burned away. (If Debora was the arsonist, this was odd. It was she who played the piano; Mike played the clarinet, oboe, flute, and tuba— but not the piano.)

Together, Paul Morrison and Mike Farrar moved through each room of the lost home. Debora watched Mike, her eyes darting like birds' eyes, as she was forced to remember every detail of the house that was supposed to save their marriage. The loss of such a house would have been sad under any circumstances, but in the end, it would have been nothing compared to suffering the ineffable grief of seeing one's children die.

The unspoken question in this packed courtroom was, *Who* had set the flaming horror in motion? The prosecution contended that the culprit was the woman who sat almost motionless at the defense table. Her attorney suggested that her dead son had been responsible. Both possibilities seemed beyond belief.

Chapter 32

Celeste Walker was not allowed in the courtroom: she was a potential witness. But unlike many other potential witnesses, who waited in the corridor outside the courtroom, she passed the hours, instead, in the lunchroom of the county office building across the quad, nursing cups of coffee. She didn't want to be recognized and she certainly didn't want to have her picture taken. She knew that her name was bound to come up in testimony. She didn't know yet if she would be called to testify; she devoutly hoped not. But she wanted to be close by, to give Mike moral support.

On the witness stand, Mike continued the story of his sinking marriage and of Debora's increasingly odd behavior. He told of the frantic calls he had received from his children, begging him to come home because their mother was so drunk she would not wake up. He recounted the occasion when Lissa called because her mother had passed out. He described that afternoon and night: how he had raced home, taken the girls to his sister Karen's house, and come back to find that Debora had vanished; how he had spent hours searching for her, expecting to find her a suicide; how he finally concluded that she had left the house; and how, late that night, she phoned him repeatedly, arguing with him until he finally unplugged the phone and went to sleep. He did not know, he said, that Debora was still in the house, calling from the children's phone. He did not know that she was moving through the house quietly as he slept. That might have annoyed him, but he would have had no fear. He had not yet become ill; he had no idea that someone might be trying to kill him. "She told me that all that time she had been hiding under the bed or behind the bed in the basement bedroom."

The gallery murmured. If Mike's testimony was to be believed, the woman in soft pink and white who sat at the defense table was strange indeed.

Paul Morrison knew that Mike's affair with Celeste Walker would come up. He decided to meet it head-on rather than wait for the defense to bring it in.

"Now, you had developed a romantic relationship over this period of time, Doctor?"

"Yes, I did."

"What is that person's name?"

"Celeste Walker."

"Was that a romantic physical relationship?"

"Yes, it was."

Debora's dark eyes were fastened on Mike's face. Of all the testimony thus far, this clearly interested her most.

"And when was that begun?"

"Well, a strong friendship started on the Peru trip. But the romantic relationship started on July 8, after the Peru trip."

Morrison had his direct examination perfectly choreographed. He wanted to be so familiar with the events of this case that he could arrange and present them in such a way that Judge Ruddick—and later, surely, a jury—could follow the course of Debora's despondency and rage until she reached a flash point.

After the testimony about Mike's affair with Celeste, Morrison moved forward on to Mike's illness. Mike testified that he had first become ill on August 11. He was initially hospitalized on August 18, released on the twenty-fifth, hospitalized eight hours later, released on August 30, and hospitalized again on September 4. On September 11, Mike had been released once more from the hospital, with the understanding that his wife would oversee his intravenous feeding and try to build him up from the 125 pounds he then weighed. He testified that he had not had further episodes of vomiting, torrential diarrhea, fever, or stomach pain.

But five months later, Mike was far from well. Even those who had not known him before they saw him on the witness stand could see that he was still a very sick man.

"Have you been hospitalized since then [September 11]?" Morrison asked.

"Correct."

"And is that as a result of some further complications?"

"I've developed bacterial endocarditis, which is a serious heart valve infection," Mike answered. "As a complication of that I developed a brain abscess which had to be surgically evacuated."

"And do you face further medical procedures in the future?"

Although Moore objected to Mike's "medical expert" testimony, it was difficult for him to ignore his medical education and even more years in practice as he described his condition. It was ironic that Debora, who stood accused of the series of poisonings that had allegedly necessitated the very serious operations her husband had faced and would face again was perhaps the only one in the courtroom who truly understood the medical terms Mike used.

The prosecutor was blunt. Asking about Mike's thoughts as he lay weak and helpless in his own bed while his wife administered the multivitamin- and nutrition-packed intravenous feeding, Morrison said, "At that time, did you think your wife was poisoning you?"

"I had some concerns early on because every time I'd go home, I'd get sick," Mike answered. "But I did not really believe she was poisoning me. I just couldn't imagine she would do such a thing."

Debora's face was inscrutable, but her eyes never left her husband. Except for occasionally crossing and recrossing her legs, she did not change position.

"Had there been discussions with some of your co-workers and friends about that?" Morrison asked.

"Yes, I had discussed it with Carolyn Stafford and Celeste Walker who were both convinced she was poisoning me."

"Objection! Hearsay, Your Honor."

"Sustained."

"Just so we're clear," Morrison continued. "You did not indicate that [the possibility of poisoning] to your doctors?"

"Not at that point."

But Mike testified that on September 25, he had been forced to have Debora committed because her behavior had become so bizarre. The day before, he had found the castor-bean packets and the empty potassium chloride vials in her purse. Only after his research into castor beans did he begin to wonder if Debora *had* been trying to kill him—or to commit suicide herself.

It had been a terribly hard decision, to have his own wife committed. But Mike said he had to force Debora to see a psychiatrist and get treatment. He described the scene at the KU hospital that night, and Debora's eventual voluntary commitment to the Menninger Clinic.

"Did you move out of that house?" Morrison asked.

"Yes, I did."

"After she got back?"

"Yes. About the first week of October . . . Initially, I stayed with my parents, for two or three nights. And then I moved ultimately on October fifth to the Georgetown Apartments."

"Did the kids stay at the family home on Canterbury, or did they go with you?"

"No, they stayed at the family home."

"Were you concerned about the kids?"

This was a very painful question for Mike. How many times had he berated himself for his belief that the children would be better off at home, that their mother would not harm them?

"I was concerned about their psychological well-being," he said.

"Were you concerned about their physical safety?" Morrison pressed.

"Mildly. I did not think that there was a high likelihood that there would be any physical danger to them, because clearly Deb had improved after she came home from Menninger's. Substantially improved."

"Why did you move out?"

"I moved out, obviously, ultimately, because I wanted to be separated and divorced. But I felt that it was time to move out because whenever I was home, the situation was so volatile. Debora was saying horrible things to the kids in front of me, and I thought it would be better if I was out of the house. It was clearly better for the kids."

"Was Debora still saying things to you that indicated her unhappiness with the divorce . . . ?" Morrison asked.

"She expressed feelings of unhappiness all along, yes."

"Going into the future—did those activities with her continue?"

"They clearly improved for a period of time."

"Did they get bad again?"

"They did toward the end. Just before the fire, her behavior started to deteriorate again—although I never saw her as drunk as she was before."

Morrison then led Mike through the most difficult portion of his testimony; step by step through the weekend before the fire, and, finally, the events of Monday, October 23.

His last evening with Tim and Kelly had been a good one, Mike testified. The hockey game had been one of Tim's best. "Tim was in a great mood," he said. "He was very pumped up from the game. He played a great game. The coach came out and complimented him. He said, 'He played out of his head. This is the greatest game I've seen this kid play!' He was in a great mood on the way home—he was laughing and joking and he and I had a wonderful time."

"How was Kelly acting that night?"

"Fine. She was in a good mood—like she always was."

"Happy little girl?" Morrison asked. Few observers knew that Morrison was the father of three children exactly the same age as Tim, Lissa, and Kelly were—or would have been. He could not allow himself to make comparisons, but at this stage of his questioning, it was hard not to.

"Happy little girl," Mike agreed.

"What time did you get home?"

"About eight-forty-five."

There had been better evenings in the house on Canterbury Court, and there certainly had been worse. Mike testified that he had stayed only about five minutes— long enough to glance through his mail and talk to Lissa. Debora seemed uninterested and vaguely annoyed that he was there. But she wasn't in a rage. There was no yelling or swearing. Mike had said good night to his children and walked out into the blustery, cold wind.

He had no warning that he would never see two of them again.

Mike identified pictures of Tim and Kelly as they had been in life, school photographs taken just two months before their deaths. He had fixed Kelly's hair for her picture, and he blinked hard at the memory, managing to keep his composure. And now, for the first time, Debora wiped tears from her eyes.

Chapter 33

After lunch that Monday, Dennis Moore rose to cross-examine Mike. He needed to rehabilitate his client and he had his work cut out for him. Moore wanted to show that Mike was less than a perfect husband.

"You said the marriage was not happy—there was no mutual respect? There was a lack of care and compassion? Is that right?"

"That's correct."

"You said basically that was one-sided on Debora Green's part. Is that what you testified?"

"I said that *most* of it was on her part."

"Are you perfect?"

"No, obviously, I'm not, counselor."

"Did you contribute, do you think, in any way to the lack of care and compassion in the marriage and the lack of mutual respect?"

"I'm sure, as in any marriage, I did."

Moore stressed how often Mike had been away from the house, working long hours; how, in the final three weeks, he had been completely absent. He was obviously going to paint Mike as a bad father, as well as a bad husband. He derided Mike's decision not to tell Debora he wanted a divorce until after the Peru trip.

"So that trip was extremely important to you, wasn't it?" Moore prodded.

"Well, I think to all three of us it was."

"But you were willing to basically live a lie to keep the trip going, weren't you?"

Mike would not back down. "I thought it was reasonable to postpone announcing the divorce."

"You said Debora Green, on occasion, threw horrendous tantrums—she used foul and abusive language?"

"That is correct."

"Did *you* ever use foul and abusive language?"

"Sure I did."

"In your relationship with Debora Green?"

"Sure."

"So it's not, again, all one-sided, is it?"

"No. But I think hers was much more to the extreme."

Moore elicited testimony from Mike that suggested that Debora's *physical* attacks were directed against herself, not others. She had hit her head with a book and her thighs with her fists. No, she had not hit Mike with a book.

"Did she ever hit Tim or Lissa or Kelly with a book?"

"I don't recall seeing her do that."

Moore then moved on to Mike's difficulties with his son. "You didn't have a great relationship with Tim Farrar, did you?" he asked.

"Not recently—not the last few months."

"The last few months before his death on October twenty-fourth?"

"Yes . . ."

"You testified he was angry and upset when you left in January of 1994—the first separation?"

"That is correct."

"And presumably he became happier when you came home?"

"He did," Mike answered. "And that initial anger was fairly short-lived."

"And he was angry again at you for the last several months before his death. Isn't that correct?"

"The last couple of months."

"He was angry at you when you went to Peru, wasn't he?"

"I don't know that that is true."

"Didn't he tell you, in fact, that he didn't like you going around with your dick hanging out after Celeste Walker?"

"After he heard it from Debora, yes."

Mike could not deny that his son had been disappointed and angry when he asked Debora for a divorce the second time, and he didn't try. He braced for what he knew was coming.

"Were you ever violent in your relationship with him?" Moore asked.

"Unfortunately, yes. I was."

"Tell me about that, sir."

"One time," Mike said, "when he was particularly obnoxious—it was a particularly awful evening—I grabbed him and pushed him to the floor and held him. And then he used very foul and abusive language and I hauled him into the other room. And as I was hauling him—it was pitch black in the room—he let out a punch and hit me in the nose."

"Did you, in fact, push his head against the wallboard and knock a hole in the wall?"

"Not his *head*," Mike Farrar said. "I held him up against the wallboard and knocked a hole in the wall."

"Was that the same occasion when Tim hit you in the face?"

"No, that was a different occasion."

Moore jumped on that, stressing that there had been violence between Mike and his son on at least three occasions.

"He broke your nose?" Moore asked.

"He did."

Once that point was established, Moore began to ask questions about the activities that might have caused Mike's puzzling illnesses.

"Did you, in fact, Dr. Farrar, swim in the Amazon?"

"I did swim in the Amazon."

"And did you, in fact, eat meals and food prepared by local people in Peru?"

"Yes, I did."

"Including fruits?"

"Yes, that's probably how we got the traveler's diarrhea."

The defense was using a scattershot technique, switching from topic to topic, working deftly to hit Mike where he might be the weakest. "And you said she said horrible vile things to your children—such as 'Your father is out fucking three women' . . . was it true what she said?"

Morrison objected that this was irrelevant to the case at hand.

"Overruled."

"Was it true?" Mike repeated. "No, it wasn't true."

Again, Moore switched subjects. Did Tim have access to a computer? Most particularly, "Was the Internet available?"

"I don't think so."

"Do you know if Tim had the Internet available at school?"

"I don't know."

"In science class?"

Mike didn't know. The gallery was curious about what the Internet might have to do with the fire—or, for that matter, with poisoning.

Moore then began to grill Mike about his affair with Celeste. "The friendship was so fast forming that you had sex with Celeste Walker, you testified, on July eighth. Is that correct?"

"That is correct."

"Two days after you returned from Peru?"

"That is correct."

At the defense table, Debora gazed at Mike, her face as washed of emotion as it had been all day except for her brief spate of tears when photos of Tim and Kelly were introduced into evidence.

"During that period of time—three or four weeks—you and the Walkers went to parties in each other's home[s], didn't you?"

"Yes, we did."

"And did you steal kisses from Celeste Walker at one of those parties?"

"Once, yes."

"And this is when you had still not told your wife that there was a relationship with another woman?"

"That is correct."

"You weren't being terribly honest with your wife, were you?"

"I would say that's absolutely true," Mike answered. Of course he had not confessed to Debora—nor, for that matter, had he told anyone else—about his affair with Celeste.

"Is the truth important to you, Dr. Farrar?"

"Yes, the truth is important to me."

Moore had backed Mike into a corner, and now he pounced. "Is it important to you whether you're under oath or whether you're just talking to anybody that's asking you questions in an official investigation?"

Mike had not told the Prairie Village police about his affair—not at first. He regretted it now. But Moore had already moved on: to the first allegedly tainted food Mike had eaten, the chicken salad sandwich. "Did you see Debora Green prepare that chicken salad sandwich?"

"No, I did not. She said she had saved it for me when I got home."

"Where did it come from?"

"It came from chicken salad that someone prepared."

"That *someone* prepared, right?"

"That's correct."

"You don't know who prepared it, do you?"

"I did not see anyone prepare it."

On August 25, Mike had spent only eight hours at home before he had to return to the hospital, suffering the same symptoms he'd had after eating the chicken sandwich.

"You testified you were served a spaghetti dinner by Debora Green," Moore said.

"That is correct."

"Who prepared that spaghetti dinner? Do you know?"

"Timothy did."

"You also testified on a third occasion that you were down in the basement watching the Chiefs and that Debora Green brought down ham and beans and cornbread?"

"That is correct."

"Do you know who prepared that?"

"Debora did."

"Did you see her prepare it?"

"I did."

"Okay. Where was Tim?"

"I don't know where Tim was."

Although Moore peppered Mike with questions about where Tim might have been, he could not remember. "He was not sitting there watching the ball game with me. . . . I don't know where he was."

"You don't know that he wasn't up there in the kitchen with Debora Green, do you?"

"He may have been in the kitchen some."

Moore had already suggested in his opening statement that Tim might have set fire to his house; he had characterized Tim as "a very disturbed young man." Might a very disturbed young man who hated his father, who had broken his father's nose in a fistfight, who had, perhaps, been whipped into a frenzy of anxiety about the need to protect his mother—might such a young man set out to *poison* that father? That was the question Moore seemed about to ask.

Mike was coldly angry. He had lost his son and his daughter. Sadly, he had just begun to repair his relationship with Tim when the boy died. He could not bear the thought that Kansas City and the world might believe that his own son had deliberately tried to kill him with slow, agonizing poison. It wasn't true. Mike knew it wasn't true. Debora had had castor beans in her purse. Not Tim.

Moore asked Mike about tropical sprue. Although he had objected earlier when Paul Morrison sought Mike's testimony as an expert medical witness on his own illness, now, during cross-examination, he had no objection to Mike's use of medical terms. Moore wanted to emphasize that Mike's symptoms were quite similar to those of tropical sprue. The fact that he had so recently returned from Peru, the defense hoped, made a good argument for a benign cause of his illness.

"What *is* tropical sprue," Moore asked, "as you understand it?"

"Tropical sprue is a malabsorption syndrome that's thought to be caused by an infectious agent, although the precise cause is often uncertain," Mike explained. "It occurs generally in parts of Central America, sporadic parts of northern South America, and it also occurs in Asia. It's generally characterized by an onset of an acute diarrheal illness followed by a chronic diarrheal illness."

Moore had managed a coup: he was eliciting the information he wanted Judge Ruddick to hear from an expert witness—and the expert witness was the victim.

"Is it bacteriological in nature?"

"It's unclear, unclear," Mike said. "Probably is, but it's unclear."

"When did you first think that she might be poisoning you?"

"I first thought about the possibility early on—during August or September. I'm not exact; I'm not exactly sure where in the entire scenario, but sometime during those three hospitalizations I wondered if Deb might not be poisoning me."

"Did you wonder about what she might be using . . . ?"

"Sure I did."

"Did you wonder enough to go down and get a blood test to see if you could locate any kind of poison in your system?"

"No, it would be useless," Mike answered.

"Dr. Farrar, you testified that on the twenty-fourth of September, you decided to secretly get into Deb Green's purse. Is that correct?"

"That is correct."

"Did you *ask* her if you could do that?"

"Absolutely not."

"Did you search anyplace besides her purse for whatever you were looking for?"

"Yes," Mike answered. "I looked in the bottom drawer of the bedside stand next to the bed in the basement."

"What were you looking for when you went into her purse?"

"I was looking for anything that she might use to kill herself."

Moore returned again to the affair between Mike and Celeste Walker. "During this trip to Peru, Dr. Farrar, when you struck up this close friendship with Celeste Walker, her husband wasn't along, was he?"

"No, he was not."

"Her husband's name was John Walker?"

"That is correct."

"John Walker is now deceased. Is that correct?"

"That is correct."

"In fact, he was found dead on September 5, 1995."

"That's my understanding."

"It was your testimony that after you got back [from Peru], that Deb began to drink and act crazy?"

"After I told her that I wanted a divorce, yes."

"You testified you could listen to her voice and tell that sometimes when her words were slurred that she had been drinking or on medication?"

"Yes, that's correct."

"Do you know what kind of effect Klonopin would have on a person?"

Once more, Moore was treating Mike like a doctor, urging him to give medical opinions when it suited the defense. Morrison noted this, but said nothing.

"If someone takes too much Klonopin," Mike answered, "it can have that sort of effect."

Moore especially wanted to end his cross-examination

with the suggestion that Mike had been living a life of subterfuge and clandestine meetings. "Do you recall telling Detective Burnetta that you had a romantic involvement with Celeste Walker but it began after her husband's death?"

"Yes, I do remember that," Mike answered.

"That was a lie, wasn't it?"

"It was a lie, yes."

"And we've established that your sexual involvement with Celeste Walker began, in fact, almost two months prior to September 5. Isn't that correct? On July eighth?"

"That is correct."

"Did you ever tell John Walker that you were having sex with his wife?"

"Of course not."

"You were at that time living a lie, weren't you, Dr. Farrar? . . . You weren't being honest with, certainly, Debora Green . . . [about] your relationship with Celeste Walker, were you?"

"That's correct."

Morrison sat, poised to object. Moore was close to exhausting this line of questioning. Mike had admitted several times now that he had chosen not to tell the police how long he and Celeste had been lovers, and Moore was beating it into the ground.

"Did you and Celeste Walker talk about what story you should tell the police as far as to when your sexual relationship began, if they ever asked?"

"We discussed it. I don't think we phrased it quite like that."

"Well, I'm sure you didn't," Moore said, with just a trace of sarcasm in his voice. "You didn't say, 'We're going to conspire and lie to the police,' did you?"

"No."

"But you did, in fact, talk about what you would tell the police—and what you were going to tell the police was not the truth, was it?"

"Well, it wasn't quite the truth."

Morrison objected. The questions from the defense were becoming convoluted; he wanted to be sure just what Moore was asking about. Judge Ruddick admonished Moore to confine his question to the date the affair between Mike and Celeste began.

Mike admitted that they had hoped to portray their affair as beginning after Dr. John Walker's death. Neither of them had known how pervasive, how *invasive*, a murder probe is. In sudden, violent, deliberately planned murders, everyone around the dead is eventually pulled into the vortex of the investigation. Moore was going for something. What? Was he looking for a motive? To make Mike out to be a liar about everything? Probably.

Moore tried once again to link Tim to the poisonings and to the fire. He seemed to be planting the possibility that Tim might have been the instigator of both crimes, and a device to draw attention away from Debora.

Finally, Moore finished.

Paul Morrison had only two points to make on redirect. First, he wanted to be sure Judge Ruddick understood that although Mike was first hospitalized on August 18, his symptoms had begun a full week before. Second, he asked Mike questions that pointed up the fact that it didn't matter who had *cooked* the allegedly poisonous meals; what mattered was who had *served* them.

Finally, after almost five grueling hours on the witness stand, Mike was allowed to step down. Some in the gallery complained that he hadn't been emotional enough for their taste; they would have felt better if he had cried on the stand. He had admitted to being unfaithful at the end of his marriage; but on the other hand, the marriage sounded like something out of a madhouse. One man in the gallery whispered, "Who would blame him?" and got a sharp look from the woman sitting next to him.

Chapter 34

Monday, January 29, was a very long day in court. The State put on a succession of witnesses who would verify its premise that Debora was a woman whose behavior made her the prime suspect not only in the fiery deaths of her own children, but in the repeated poisoning of her husband. Sergeant Wes Jordan and Officer Kyle Shipps testified about the night of September 25, 1995, when they saw Debora highly intoxicated, and her family distraught and weeping. Shipps had taken her to the KU Medical Center ER, and waited with Mike while she was examined. Later, he'd had to go out and look for her when she walked away against medical advice.

Mike had given Shipps a plastic bag containing several packets of seeds, vials of potassium chloride, iodine, and some syringes; Shipps kept the bag in his possession until he returned to the Prairie Village Police Department at six the next morning. He had marked the police evidence bags with his initials. He identified his mark on evidence exhibits 6-B, 6-C, and 6-D. Shipps had also taken a statement from Mike in the waiting room of the KU Medical Center.

Paul Morrison asked Officer Shipps about Debora's behavior after she was found walking toward Prairie Village in the early hours of the morning. "What was her mood—was she calm?"

"Very sporadic between calm and irate."

"Why don't you tell the judge some of the physical behavior that you witnessed from Debora Green while she was sitting in that waiting room?"

"At times," Shipps said, "Dr. Green would become very upset with how long the process was taking. . . . Committals in general take quite a bit of time."

"What would she do when she became frustrated?"

"She beat her fists against her head. She bit her hands,

and she banged her head against the wall." Shipps said that
Debora had then begun to yell "very loudly" and call her
husband the same vulgar names she had used before: "asshole" and "fuckhole."

Leighann Stahl, the assistant manager of the Earl May
Garden Center, testified next, about her encounter with the
woman she had identified as Dr. Debora Green. The woman
was memorable to Stahl because she had come in to pick up
a large order for out-of-planting-season seeds.

"What did she say [they were for]?" Morrison asked.

"She said they were for a school project."

"And how old was this person?"

"Probably, I don't know—mid-forties maybe."

"Skinny, heavyset, fat, medium build?"

"Medium build, a little bit heavyset, perhaps."

"Light or dark hair? Medium hair?"

"Kind of medium dark."

"Hair long? Hair short?"

"About chin level."

"If you saw that individual again, would you be able to recognize her?"

"I feel pretty confident I would."

"Is that individual in the courtroom today?"

"Yes."

"Would you point her out for us, please?"

Leighann Stahl pointed to Debora, and Kevin Moriarty
rose to object, calling the identification "a charade." He
went on, "They've shown her pictures of this individual previously. It is noted in the report she was not able to identify
our client in those photos. They've shown her photos. Why
in the world would she not be able to identify our client
today? This is ridiculous!"

"Judge," Morrison countered, "I'm going to try to maintain a non-editorial and appropriate commentary during
my response to that. But, for the record, this witness was

shown a photo lineup back in early October, at which time she picked out a photograph of the defendant—but stated, 'Because of the hair being different, I'm not sure that's her—' And she has been shown no other photographs since then, Judge. And I play my IDs straight up."

Judge Ruddick overruled Moriarty's objection.

The cash-register tape was entered into evidence: ten packages of garden seeds at $1.29 each. There were no other sales of that many packages on the tape. Although the tape did not specify what kind of seeds had been purchased, Stahl remembered the sale. Castor beans were poison, and castor beans were out of season.

Moriarty worked hard to shake Stahl's testimony. She did not remember the exact day the investigators from the Metro Squad had come to interview her. It might have been late October or early November.

"The police report . . . stated they made contacts with individuals on the thirtieth of October, 1995," Moriarty said. "So it's at least consistent with your time frame?"

"Yes."

Stahl admitted that when the police first got in touch with her she had not remembered the sale, but as she forced herself to think back, she had recalled the woman who wanted castor beans. On the second police contact—from Officer John Walter—she did remember.

"What does John Walter look like?" Moriarty asked.

"He was tall, he had short hair, he was medium build— not at all heavyset," Stahl answered, correctly.

"Were you asked to give a description of the person purchasing those seeds?"

"Yes."

"And if I were to say that description that was given was somebody between the late thirties to early forties, five foot three to five foot five, 160 to 170 pounds, dark hair, top-of-the-shoulder-length hair, loosely curled on top—would that be consistent with what you told police officers that day?"

"Probably, yes."

Stahl was a good witness and she could not be shaken. She knew all the markings on her cash register receipts. She knew that a "z" signified her store out of all the Earl May stores. She had not seen any news about the fire in Prairie Village *or* a picture of Debora until after she had picked her out of the photo laydown.

"I saw her arrested on TV," she said.

"Have you sold any other castor beans in lots of one or greater in the month of August of 1995 that you recall?"

"Not in August . . ."

"How many seeds are in each envelope?" Moriarty asked.

"I would estimate maybe fifteen."

"Have you ever seen a castor bean?"

"Yes."

"Can you tell us what they look like?"

"They look—I don't know. I think they look like a chili bean—"

"If I were to say," Moriarty offered, "they were light brown, about the size of a dime, and had brown spots on it, would that be about right—darker brown spots?"

"I would almost consider them a purple spot, rather than brown—yes."

"Are you familiar with the plant?"

"Yes."

"I would assume that this plant is like any other plant— that it could grow indoors?"

"I suppose it would be possible."

"Is there any reason why it would not be possible?"

"It would be difficult," Stahl said, "to put it in a pot that would stay upright because of the large height of the plant. You'd have to have a very large pot."

"Aside from that?"

"Possible light requirements, but—"

"I don't have anything additional," Kevin Moriarty cut in. "Thank you."

The gallery was left to wonder if Tim had intended to grow castor-bean plants for a school project. His mother had bought enough seeds to grow 300 plants—plants that would have grown higher than the ceiling of his room. Had his mother purchased Gro-Lights, too, for this strange experiment? Or had she bought those seeds to grind them up and release the deadly poison at their center?

Kansas hearings and trials are brisk and efficient, totally unlike the endless delays and ponderous day upon day of testimony from single witnesses that have come to be regarded as standard in California pretrial hearings and trials. On this, the first day of the State of Kansas's show-cause hearing, four important witnesses, including Mike, had finished their testimony by late afternoon. Morrison called the last witness of the day: Velma Farrar, Mike's mother.

Velma Farrar, a retired grade school teacher, was old enough to have a forty-year-old son, but she scarcely looked it. Tall, with her brown hair perfectly coiffed, she had the figure of a much younger woman. It would be an easy bet that Velma and her daughter-in-law had little in common except for having each given birth to one son and two daughters. Mike said that they had made an effort to get along, but never at the same time.

Morrison asked Velma the names of her children.

"Michael Farrar . . . Vicki Farrar, and Karen Beal," she replied.

Both her daughters were married; Velma and William Farrar had been married for forty-two years. They lived, she testified, "North of the river."

"First of all," Morrison began, "did you receive a telephone call on September twenty-fifth of last year to help with some child care?"

"Yes. . . . I was in bed reading. . . . It was between eight o'clock or nine o'clock or so."

"Who was on the phone?"

"Michael. . . . He told us he needed help and that he needed us immediately."

"Did he say why?"

"He told us that he was going to have Debbie committed against her will."

"What was his demeanor like when he called you?"

"He was crying. . . . He was very upset."

Velma said that she and Bill had gone to take care of Tim, Lissa, and Kelly and spent the night in their son's home. By the time they got there, Debora and Mike had already left; Karen Beal was with the children. A doctor had called from the hospital to talk to Tim. "I took the telephone up to him," Velma said.

She had not heard the conversation. Tim mostly said, "Yes," "No," or "What?" "He was answering questions," Velma said. That would have been the call from Dr. Pam McCoy, trying to determine how Debora had been behaving lately.

"I'm going to change gears now," Morrison said, "if I might. Did you read anything that was laying [sic] on the counter in the kitchen of that home that night?"

"Yes, I read a letter that was laying there," she answered.

"Was that a letter that was machine made, if you will, or printed on a machine?"

"No, it was written on stationery like you pick up in a hotel or motel. . . ."

"Did you recognize the handwriting?"

"Yes I did . . . it was Debbie's."

Velma had read the letter. "I cannot remember all of it, but the letter was supposedly from a friend. It said, 'To Dr. Farrar,' and it was signed, 'From a friend.' And the letter was trying to convince Mike that he should not divorce Debbie."

"And do you remember any specific lines in it?"

"One of the things that this person—this friend—had written was that the children would not have a chance to be BOTARs or escorts. This person who wrote this letter was on one of the committees who helped select the people for this—that they normally did not take children from broken homes. . . ."

Velma remembered another of the letter's arguments against divorce. "It said that it was probably a midlife crisis and that more romantic times would follow." She had found the letter odd, but that night everything was odd. She had left it on the kitchen counter.

Dennis Moore cross-examined Mike's mother. "Had Mike told you prior to this time that he and Debbie were having marital problems?"

"I did not know before that night. Is that what you're asking me?"

"Yes, ma'am."

"No," Velma said. "I did not know about this."

"So Mike had never called you prior to September twenty-fifth when you were there that evening, when you found this letter, and told you that he and Debbie were having problems?"

"He told us on the phone that they were having problems."

"But that was the night of September twenty-fifth? Prior to that night, had he ever told you that he told Debbie that he wanted to divorce her?"

"No. But my parents were very, very ill. You know, they both have since died. And—"

Moore interrupted and Paul Morrison asked that Mrs. Farrar be allowed to finish her answer.

"Go ahead," Judge Ruddick said, smiling at Velma.

"And they were protecting me because I was spending most of my time with my father. Both of my parents died within—well, twelve weeks."

"Mrs. Farrar," Dennis Moore asked, "did Mike tell you that after his return from his trip to Peru . . . he was having an affair with another woman?"

"No, he did not."

"I believe you indicated that you told one of the police officers that Debbie had a very bad temper. Is that correct?"

"Yes."

"But you also told the police officers that she never touched the children in anger. Is that correct?"

"Not that I know of. She never touched them that I knew of."

Velma Farrar was excused. Although she had kept her dignity on the witness stand, it was obvious that she was humiliated and grieving, caught up in this tragedy, which had erupted so ferociously without warning. She had expected to lose her aged parents; she had never dreamed she would lose two of her grandchildren.

It was almost five P.M. The streets outside the Johnson County Courthouse were dark and snow threatened. Some of the reporters and spectators on their way home pondered what a bad year 1995 had been for the Farrar and Jones families and those close to them: divorce, suicide, cancer, murder, fire, poisoning. Mike had lost two grandparents and two children within three months, and had nearly died himself. Debora's mother was ill but was trying to stand beside her daughter nevertheless. And Debora herself was accused of crimes almost impossible to comprehend.

Celeste Walker waited for Mike to tell her what had gone on in court. Everyone else saw the proceedings on the evening news. Sound bites from Paul Morrison, Dennis Moore, and Kevin Moriarty; file film of the actual fire, broadcast for the dozenth time; and film taken that very day in the court-room, showing a stolid, almost expressionless Debora Green as she sat at the defense table.

Chapter 35

It was 2 degrees in Olathe at dawn on Tuesday, January 30. A high of 11 was expected. That morning was devoted to medical testimony. Dr. Regina Beth Henry, the specialist in infectious diseases, was a small, pretty young woman. She answered Paul Morrison's questions about Mike's treatment and the puzzling aspects of his illness. He had come close to dying on the night of August 18.

"On August 18," she testified, "the nurse reported that he had a profound weakness—in fact, almost passed out—and his blood pressure had dropped some. And they also did a white blood cell count at the time of this incident in the evening. And previously in the day, it had been markedly elevated—approximately 17,000. And then that evening . . . his white count had dropped to less than 3,000, which is a tremendous difference, and basically a sign of sepsis."

The crux of Dr. Henry's lengthy testimony was that "we never felt perfectly comfortable with any of the considerations that we had as far as the actual diagnosis of his symptoms and his problems because, quite honestly, it didn't fit perfectly into any of the disease states we were considering."

"Did you look at any issues of whether or not Dr. Farrar was being poisoned?"

"No, we did not. We had no reason to think that."

"Because nobody brought that up to you?"

"No, we had no idea that there were any problems that would suggest that." Besides, as she pointed out later in her testimony, she was not an expert on poison.

Dr. Henry testified that Peru was not mentioned in papers on tropical sprue, and that even where the disease was common, those who contracted it had lived in the area for a long time, at least a year.

Typhoid fever didn't fit either. "Even though it's an acute infection, [it] does not cause a tremendous elevation of the white blood cell count."

Dr. Henry believed that Mike had been septic more than once during his three hospitalizations.

Dr. Pam McCoy, the ER physician at the UK Medical Center, testified next. "I work with residents and medical students. I teach them how to work in an emergency department. And usually . . . I go see patients, they go see patients with me; we talk about how you see a patient in the emergency department, how you take care of people, how you put in stitches, that sort of thing."

The KU emergency room is a very busy facility, but Dr. McCoy remembered the night of September 25 very well. That was when her former colleague from Trinity Lutheran Hospital had been brought in for possible mental commitment. At first, Dr. McCoy said, although Dr. Green had looked "bad" and smelled of alcohol, she didn't seem any more upset than the average wife who was fighting over a divorce and had had too much to drink.

Dr. McCoy could not force Debora to see a psychiatrist; she had to follow the same rules as the police. Was Debora dangerous to herself or others? "It's not necessarily wrong to get into a knock-down, drag-out fight with your husband," she said, "to be very angry and upset, and to have half a bottle of wine. . . . If we had somebody in the emergency department every time they had a fight with their husband, we'd be overloaded. . . ."

But when Mike arrived, Debora had begun spitting at him and calling him a "fuckhole. I was trying to kind of pull her back because I actually was sort of afraid she was going to physically assault him. . . ."

It was Pam McCoy who had heard the terrible threat Debora screamed at her husband: "And then she said to him, 'You're going to get these kids over our dead bodies.'"

"Did you ever look at those castor-bean packets?" Morrison asked.

"Yeah."

"Did you show any of those packets to Debora Green at any time during that evening?"

"We had a discussion about it, because I was asking her why Dr. Farrar would think she was suicidal. She kind of dismissed the fact of the medications. Then, when we talked about castor beans, there was some comment to the effect of, 'Well, for heaven's sakes, you can't even buy plant seeds anymore without somebody saying something about it.'"

Castor beans are commonplace in Kansas. Dr. McCoy testified that, while they are poisonous, it is very hard to extract the poison. "When someone calls and says, 'My child has swallowed a castor bean,' we don't get too excited because it has a fairly hard coating on it. . . . It just passes through the system whole—kind of like if you swallow a pit from a plum. . . ."

No, unless a child really bit down on a castor bean, it was not a serious problem. "And another thing," Dr. McCoy said. "What I was thinking is that that kind of poisoning is a lot of vomiting and diarrhea and who'd ever want to kill themselves by 'stooling' themselves to death? I mean—to puke and vomit and stool yourself would be no way to kill yourself. A physician wouldn't do that. . . . A doctor would figure out something smarter than that to do."

Dr. McCoy had auburn hair, a lovely complexion, and a no-nonsense manner. She had spent too much time in the emergency room to be surprised by anything she saw there. She had learned to seek out a neutral—or as close to neutral as possible—third party when she was confronted by two warring factions. That was why she had called Tim, the couple's oldest child. He had admitted that he was a little scared and a little worried.

"What *did* Tim tell you?" Morrison asked, over Kevin Moriarty's objections about hearsay.

"Well," Dr. McCoy testified, "when I said, 'What's going on with your mom?,' he said, 'She's been very sad and upset lately—that she hasn't gotten out of bed for several days, just been laying around.' And he said, 'She's been drinking a lot,' that he actually hid bottles of alcohol from her because she was drinking whole bottles of alcohol, and he said, 'The big kind like you get from the wholesale club.'"

"'Tim, do you think your mother could hurt herself?'" Dr. McCoy recalled asking. "He said that he thought that she was so sad that she might be able to hurt herself. And said, 'I know she's been drinking so much that she could hurt herself.' And that he was worried about her because he was afraid when she went to the basement and hid, that he didn't understand why she was doing that. And that he knew she was very mad at his dad."

Dr. McCoy had asked Tim if he was ever afraid for himself and his younger sisters. She always asked that question, because she worried about kids caught up in domestic disputes: sometimes the grown-ups were so angry and so concerned about *their* feelings that they didn't realize the heavy load their children were carrying.

"And he said that right now they were okay because there was somebody there to take care of them. And I said, 'Well, are you afraid for yourself?' and he says, 'Well, sometimes I'm afraid.'"

Debora had denied that she was suicidal, but her son was afraid for her. That was enough to convince Dr. McCoy. She arranged for Debora to be evaluated.

"His [Tim's] concern was primarily geared toward Debora Green's hurting herself?" Moriarty asked Dr. McCoy on cross-examination.

"I didn't ask him exactly what he was afraid of," she replied. "I asked him *specifically*, Was he afraid his mother would kill herself? And he said he was afraid she could kill herself."

Moriarty ended his cross with a question, "When you asked Dr. Green if she was suicidal, she was very clear and she told you that she was not and that she had to stay around so she could make sure that she could take care of her children. Is that correct?"

"That's exactly what she said," Dr. McCoy agreed.

On redirect, Morrison asked about potassium chloride. "It is a common substance that you find around hospitals, correct?"

"It's very common. . . . It's an IV additive. When people become dehydrated or on certain other medications . . ."

"You wouldn't take a hit of potassium chloride to get high?"

"No. In fact, it burns a great deal if you put it into an IV.

It's very painful for a direct injection. So it has to be added to large bottles of fluid."

Morrison asked Dr. McCoy why she had taken careful notes after the episodes with Debora and Mike Farrar on the night of September 25. "I took those notes because I was worried about what had happened after Dr. Green eloped from the emergency department," she said. "I thought things were worse than I had initially interpreted her response to be when I first saw her. I thought—if she's left—that looked like a bad sign to me. And I thought, 'Well, maybe she *is* going to kill herself.' So I was really afraid about what would happen that night. . . . Frankly, I thought that I was going to get called into a really ugly divorce and custody thing. I wanted to be clear about what had happened, and what people had said."

"And, speaking of messy divorce," Morrison asked, "who was doing the yelling? Debora Green or Michael Farrar?"

"Dr. Green yelled at Dr. Farrar."

"Who was doing the cussing? Debora Green or Michael Farrar?"

"Dr. Green cussed at Dr. Farrar."

"Who made the threats about what's going to happen? Debora Green or Dr. Farrar?"

"Dr. Green."

"I have nothing further."

Kevin Moriarty returned for recross.

"The fact that she was yelling and calling him names is actually just a reflection of the frustration she was having that night? Is that correct?"

Of course, Paul Morrison objected. "That's outside the scope of her knowledge."

Judge Ruddick overruled him twice.

"Dr. Farrar was having an affair with another lady; he told his wife he wanted to get a divorce," Moriarty said. "I would assume that some people might think he's a fuckhole. Is that correct?"

Dr. McCoy gazed down at him. "I think that if Dr. Green

was very angry with Dr. Farrar for having an affair and wanting a divorce, that would be an appropriate response."

"And it was Dr. Farrar who actually set up this entire
evening to get her there to be committed? Is that correct?"

"To my knowledge; I was told by the police that Dr. Farrar
had called for assistance, yes."

At long last, Dr. McCoy was allowed to step down. She had
feared she might be involved in a messy divorce and custody
hearing. She had no idea she would be a prime witness in a
case of attempted and double murder.

The thirtieth of January was to be devoted to witnesses who
spoke in medicalese. Reporters spelled the long, unfamiliar
words as best they could; later they would look them up in a
medical dictionary. This clinical testimony was not surprising
in a trial that involved two medical doctors and an arcane
poisoning. The reporters were challenged even further when
Drew Campbell Richardson of the FBI laboratory explained,
finally, what ricin was and why it was so hard to identify in the
human body. But most important, would he testify that he
had isolated ricin antibodies in Dr. Michael Farrar's blood?

Richardson had advanced degrees in chemistry, forensic
science, physiology, and pharmacology and had worked in
the FBI lab since 1978, when he was assigned as an examiner
in the Bureau's chemistry and toxicology unit in
Washington, D.C. "I'm also employed as the program manager for the FBI laboratory's nuclear, biological, chemical,
and its counter-terrorism program."

"How long have you been program manager?" Morrison
asked.

"Approximately three or four months . . . I have been
involved in a leading role in the program since March of last
year, with the Tokyo subway poisoning [in which members
of the Aum Shinrikyo cult released nerve gas on a subway
train]. I went to Japan two times and have been involved
internationally and nationally in a variety of different

things. . . . I'm also involved in terms of threat assessments of chemical and biological terrorist incidents that would be potential violations of federal law."

Richardson had more than a passing knowledge of ricin. He had an insider's knowledge of the Arkansas case where the man accused of smuggling ricin killed himself in jail.

"What is ricin?" Morrison asked, knowing that the answer was going to sound like so much gobbledygook to almost everyone in the courtroom.

"Ricin is a protein," Richardson began. "It's a two-chain protein weighing approximately 65,000 Daltons or atomic mass units. You might wonder what '65,000 atomic mass units' mean. In order to get some relevance to that, drugs that we're familiar with, such as cocaine, heroin, marijuana, and so forth, have a molecular weight of about *300* atomic mass units. So we're talking about a very large compound. It's a compound that largely occurs and is present in castor-bean plants. . . ."

"Is ricin toxic to humans?" Morrison asked.

"Yes, it's very toxic."

"What does that mean?"

"The toxicity of ricin is route dependent. There are several ways that one might be exposed to ricin. One could inhale it, one could actually take it orally . . . intramuscularly . . . subcutaneously; the toxicity is on the order of a few micrograms. Oral ingestion is considerably less toxic, in the range of perhaps a milligram per kilogram of body weight."

There was no sound in the courtroom except Richardson's voice and the frantic scribbling of two dozen pens.

Richardson explained that if ricin was administered by a shot, a lot less of it was needed to kill a human being than if it was swallowed. He said the poison's only known source was the innocent-appearing castor bean.

"If I took a castor bean and just swallowed the whole bean and didn't chew on it, would that kill me?" Morrison asked.

"Quite likely not. . . . The bean itself has a rather hard coating—shell—which would essentially protect one from ricin toxicity."

"Ricin's not in the shell?"

"That's correct. It's in the pulp of the bean itself."

State's Exhibits No. 11 and No. 12—the sample of Michael Farrar's blood, and the packet of castor beans sent to the FBI lab—were shown to Richardson. He identified the sixteen beans in the Earl May packet—mottled reddish-brown seeds, shiny on the outside, with a white, pulpy, oily material inside—as castor beans. He had done a number of tests on them.

"And you performed some chemical assays to determine whether or not the insides of those beans contained ricin?"

"That's correct."

"And did they come up with a positive for that?"

"These were positive for containing ricin . . . in the percentage that the literature indicated should be in those beans."

"You said that the literature said those beans would have between one and five percent ricin?"

"That's correct. And those had two to three percent."

"Has ricin been used in mystery novels as an agent of death?" Morrison asked.

"Probably the most notable in terms of ricin," Richardson answered, "which could well have been a fictional account—but in fact turned out to be a *real* account—was one involving an individual named Markov, a . . . defector from Communist Bulgaria in 1979 or 1980. He was living in Great Britain at the time, was a writer and a speaker, and happened to be saying unkind things about the Communist regime in Belgrade on Radio Free Europe and the BBC. . . . He was poisoned by being stabbed in the thigh with a James Bond type of device, an umbrella that injected a combination of ingredients containing about half a milligram of ricin. He succumbed about three days later."

Richardson explained that one didn't need a scientific background to poison someone with ricin. "In the underground terrorist literature, there are simple cookbook solutions of how to do this."

"And one way to do it would be to mash the beans up?" Morrison asked.

Richardson said that would make it easy to administer ricin orally.

"What's going to happen to that person?"

"A variety of things—both at a biochemical and a molecular level . . . At a molecular level, the effects of ricin inhibit protein synthesis, which is important to cell function. It's also a lectin [a protein found in plant seeds] that is going to cause cell agglutination [clumping together] and breakdown of red blood cells at a tissue level. It's going to cause organ toxicity in the liver and pancreas. And the general toxic nature orally: vomiting, nausea, diarrhea, gastroenteritis, hemorrhagic enteritis, bleeding in the GI tract . . ."

Richardson testified that he had reviewed Dr. Michael Farrar's medical records, producing an instant flurry of objections from the defense. Moriarty objected on the grounds that Richardson was not a medical doctor and could not give a diagnosis on the basis of the 150-page stack of medical records.

"Judge," Morrison said. "I'm not going to ask him if he has an opinion whether or not . . . [Michael Farrar was] ricin poisoned, based on those records."

Ruddick nodded. "Well, I think we're ready for the next question."

"Do you," Morrison asked Richardson, "have an opinion on the symptomatology on those medical records? Is [it] consistent or inconsistent with ricin poisoning?"

"I found them to be consistent with ricin poisoning. I found nothing to be *inconsistent* with ricin poisoning."

The courtroom buzzed, but Debora, as usual, stared at the witness, her face a mask.

It was time for the noon recess. Frustrated, Morrison lapsed into the Kansas vernacular. "Judge, I'm not near close to being done with him." But whatever further questions he had for Richardson would have to wait.

*

Lunch hours were short. There was no time to leave the
county complex; spectators, lawyers—even the judge himself—walked across the quadrangle, heads bent against the
icy wind, toward the basement cafeteria in the administration building. If anyone who knew her recognized Celeste
Walker sitting in the least conspicuous corner of the cafeteria, nobody gave her away by acknowledging her. Mike had
not returned to the courtroom after his testimony the day
before—nor would he. Celeste did not yet know if she would
be called to testify, and so she waited.

At 1:15, Drew Richardson was back in the witness chair. His
morning testimony had shown him to be a scientist, who
often gave overlong answers while the gallery waited to hear
if he would answer the one question that truly mattered:
Had he found ricin antibodies in the samples of Mike's
blood sent to him from Johnson County, Kansas?

But Richardson would not be hurried. He testified that
ricin enters the victim's tissues rapidly and does damage
there, sometimes causing "cell death."

Morrison, patient, but anxious to translate Richardson's
testimony into lay terms, asked, "I guess what I'm getting at
is—let's say I was poisoned with ricin and I survived. If I was
brought to you or some other chemist or physician, let's say
a week or two weeks later, would you be able to perform
some sort of a test on me that would be able to tell you
whether or not ricin is present in my bloodstream or in my
tissue or whatever?"

"It's quite unlikely," Richardson said. Unless the ricin had
been injected. If it had been swallowed, ricin would remain
undetectable for a much longer time.

"Now," Morrison asked, "if it was a month or two after the
ricin had been administered—let's say orally, for example—
would it be fair to say that it would be difficult, if not
impossible, to find it?"

"Yes. Certainly in a nonlethal situation."

And, somehow, Mike had survived.

"Now, are there ways to analyze tissues of the body to detect whether ricin has been there?" Morrison asked.

"Yes."

"How would you do that?"

It was fascinating to watch these two men, both trying to present the same information to Judge Ruddick. Morrison was searching for lay terms; Richardson had difficulty speaking in anything but scientific jargon. They arrived at a system: Richardson would speak and Morrison would translate. It was so desperately important for the prosecution to show that Mike had been systematically poisoned by castor beans like those found in Debora's tote bag. Proof of that would reveal a heedless side of her personality, would show how far she would go for revenge.

Richardson began another long answer, explaining how he tested for ricin in the human body.

"One would indirectly analyze for ricin exposure by looking for antibodies. . . . Ricin . . . is a protein. It is a toxin. It is also known as an antigen. . . . An 'antigen' is actually an abbreviation for 'antibody genesis.' A compound the size of ricin, and with the structure, et cetera—the nature—of ricin, would produce an antibody response. *One*. Not only an antibody from a class of antibodies, but produce a very specific lock-and-key fit—an antibody specifically and uniquely designed and structured to fit the structure of ricin."

"Are antibodies in our blood?" Morrison asked.

"Yes."

"Pardon me for being so very, very, basic here," Morrison interrupted. "Would it be fair to say that an antibody is in the body to defend against attacking substances to the body—in the bloodstream? Correct?"

"That's correct. It's also a protein in nature, and a multi-charged protein."

That wasn't really information Morrison needed. Heads began to shake in the gallery, and Judge Ruddick was listening hard for what he needed to know.

"Let's say"—Morrison was trying to translate again—"I'm being poisoned with ricin and I survive. What you're telling me is that if ricin gets in my bloodstream . . . my body is going to build antibodies to defend against the invader. Correct?"

"That's correct."

"Those antibodies—do they disappear as soon as that invader's gone, or is it something that's going to stay with me forever?"

Richardson said that one dose of ricin would likely produce a very small amount of antibody. However, someone exposed a second time—and then a third—would produce more antibodies, which might last for months or even years. Furthermore, there was a way to test for specific antibodies, Richardson explained, using the ELISA test—the same process used in home pregnancy tests.

Now, Morrison asked about Mike's blood serum samples, which Richardson had tested. "And were you able to determine from the testing whether or not there was the presence of specific antibodies that reacted to ricin?"

"Yes, I was able to make the determination."

"And were they present?"

"Yes, they were."

Not only were antibodies to ricin present in Mike's blood serum, Richardson testified, they were present in such large quantities *two months* after the last episode of illness that he felt certain Mike had had "multiple exposures" to ricin. In lay terms, Richardson had just testified that, deliberately or accidentally, Mike had been fed ricin—not once but two or three times. Or more.

Moriarty rose to cross-examine, being deliberately folksy even though, for now, there was no jury listening. "Doctor," he said, "there are some in here that think I'm not as smart as you. But be that as it may, I'm going to try my best."

And try he did. Moriarty had boned up on ricin and the

ELISA test. He had researched articles on ricin with long, esoteric titles and he had also found on the Internet a "book" called *The Big Book of Mischief,* which seemed to have some relevance to this case—a rabbit, perhaps, for the defense to pull out of its hat later. Moriarty did an admirable job of cross-examining Richardson, but he could not shake the scientist's conviction that the antibodies in Mike's blood proved he had been poisoned with castor beans several times.

Chapter 36

With the tedious—but vital—scientific testimony on ricin antibodies out of the way, Morrison moved on to the night of October 23–24. Miriam Russell, the dispatcher from the Prairie Village Police Department, was first. It was Russell whose experience and quick thinking had resulted in the immediate dispatch of officers to Canterbury Court.

A hushed courtroom listened to a tape of the call Russell had taken at 12:21 on the morning of October 24. There were unidentifiable background noises and the sound of someone breathing into the phone, a ragged, panicky breathing. Then the line went dead. Either someone had hung up the phone, or the lines had been severed.

The "someone" had been Lissa, calling from her bedroom phone as black smoke oozed through her walls and around her door.

Steve Hunter was next. A field sergeant in charge of several patrol units in his sector, he was a trim man, well muscled, with a thick head of light brown hair. He had been the first officer on the scene of the fire, and memories of that night flickered across his face as he told how he had tried in vain to find Tim and Kelly and get them out of the burning house.

In clipped phrases, Hunter described for Morrison his first meeting with Debora and Lissa. "The juvenile was very frantic, sort of jumping up and down and screaming toward me that her brother and sister were inside the house trapped. 'Please don't let them die!'"

"Did she say that more than once?"

"She said, I believe, twice, 'Please save them! Please don't let them die!'"

"What was the other person doing?"

"Standing there. Did not make any comments. Did not say anything to me."

"Is that other person here today?"

"Yes, she is." Hunter pointed to Debora Green. "The second female at the defense table, in the white flowered top."

"So what did you do then?"

"The juvenile said that her sister was in the rear upstairs bedroom. I also advised the dispatcher that we did have people trapped in the house."

"All right. Did you know where Mom was—the mother of this girl?"

"No, I did not. . . . I asked, 'Where's Mom?' And the defendant said, 'Well, I'm Mom.'"

"Is that *all* she said?"

"Yes."

"What was her demeanor like?"

"If I can describe it best," Hunter replied, "about the same demeanor as I'm looking at her right now. Very unassuming. Very calm. Very cool."

Staring back at the officer who had tried so hard to save her children, Debora *was* very calm and very cool.

Hunter told Judge Ruddick that he had tried to get into the house again and again, only to find all the doors blocked. "The fire was growing immensely, faster moving than I've ever seen a house fire."

"Could you hear anybody at that point inside the house?" Morrison asked.

"No, I could not."

Over the fire's roar, it would have been difficult to hear

voices calling for help. Hunter estimated that he and his men reached the scene about five minutes before the fire units began to arrive.

"Did you talk to a neighbor, John Forman?"

"It was later on in the morning—approximately seven o'clock that morning."

"Did he give you something?"

"He gave me a typewritten letter, and Dr. Forman advised that he had found it in his yard."

Hunter told Dennis Moore during cross-examination that he had remained at the fire scene until sometime after noon—twelve hours later—when two bodies were removed from the burned house.

The defense had demanded the "field notes" of the officers who had been present at the fire scene, but that issue was put off until further proceedings. Now, Moore questioned Hunter closely about what he might have said to other officers at the scene. "You were, in fact, interviewed by members of the Metro Squad on October twenty-sixth?"

"Yes."

"How did you describe Debora Green when you were talking to the officers of the Metro Squad that interviewed you?"

"Well, since I don't have any notes to refer back to, to the best of my recollection as to how I testified: her demeanor was very calm, cool, and collected."

"Did you say to Officers Boyer and Perry that she had a look of indifference on her face?"

"That may be the word I used to describe her."

"Did you also say that she had a 'smug look on her face' and an expression like, 'You're not going in there. You're not going to save anybody'?"

"That may be, yes."

Hunter said he had not spoken to Dr. Mary Forman, except to say hello. The Formans had allowed him to use their bathroom. After he spoke to the Metro Squad, he had had no more input into the investigation.

*

Dr. John Forman, a thoracic surgeon—a heart and chest surgeon—took the stand next. He was a well-built man with high cheekbones and short hair. He looked young, although he had graduated from medical school seventeen years earlier. He also looked as though he would have preferred to be anywhere but on the witness stand in this hearing.

In response to Morrison's questions, John Forman recounted how his eleven-year-old son found a letter in their yard while he was raking leaves. The boy had been confused by a word on the page he found: "adultery."

"And I asked him where he'd found the letter and he took me outside and we found a second page and they seemed to go together."

"Were they weathered?"

"Not a bit. . . . They were easily read and quite fresh."

Over objections by the defense, Judge Ruddick allowed Forman to describe what he had read in the letter. "Well," Forman began, "the letter accused Mike Farrar and Celeste Walker of moral indiscretion. It also praised Debora Green as a paragon of virtue. And it dealt with some adult issues that we didn't think he [the Forman's son] ought to be reading."

"Did you find that letter—unusual?"

"It's the only letter like that I've ever found."

Dr. Forman testified that Debora had come to his house at about 12:20 or 12:25 A.M., asking him to call "111."

"Where could you see the fire from?" Morrison asked.

"I could see it blazing over the top of the garage. . . . flames and a glow and smoke."

"Did you recall anything unusual about Debora Green's hair when you first saw her that night?"

"It looked to me as though it had been wet and dried expeditiously."

"Was it wet?"

"It looked . . . The hair is wet—but it looked like it had been toweled off, dried quickly, but not dripping wet."

Kevin Moriarty tried to get Dr. Forman to say that he and his wife did not like Debora.

"I wouldn't say that."

"But you *have* said that before in this investigation."

"That we did not like her?"

"Yes."

"I don't think we said that."

Moriarty drew out the information that Dr. Forman had not remembered Debora's hair being wet until a day or so after the fire. But, Forman said, "When I made my realization about the hair, I called [Detective Burnetta] independently to see if that would be of interest to him."

"The night that Debora came over, she was yelling, 'Call the fire department' whether it was '111' or '911.' Is that correct?" Moriarty asked.

"Yes, that is correct."

"Did she make any comment about her children?"

"Yes, she did. . . . She said they were in the house and the house was burning."

The defense position here was obvious: Moriarty wanted to show that John and Mary Forman had deliberately added to the investigators' suspicions about Debora. "Did you tell the police that evening that you had concerns about Debora starting the fire?" Moriarty asked.

"I don't believe so."

"Do you know if your wife had concerns—and you can answer yes or no—first: the night of the fire and everything was going on, did she express concerns to you that she suspected Debora Green had started the fire?"

"I don't think there was much question in either of our minds about that," Dr. Forman answered evenly.

Moriarty was obviously beginning to annoy the State's witness, but he kept after Dr. Forman, trying to get him to say that he and the other neighbors and Mike Farrar had all talked to the police immediately, expressing their opinions on Debora's guilt.

"Did you communicate to Mike Farrar your concern that Debora Green had set the house on fire?" Moriarty asked Dr. Forman.

"That's a difficult question to answer. I guess we talked about it, but not so directly."

"Help me out," Moriarty said. "I don't understand what that means."

"I asked him if he thought their other fire was a random event in light of what was going on now."

Moriarty wondered why Dr. Forman had given the strange letter he found in his yard to the police at seven A.M. "You must have thought there was some significance of this letter and the house fire. Isn't that correct?"

"Sure, I did," Dr. Forman said, a tinge of anger in his voice.

"When did that strike you?"

"The moment I opened the door and saw the house burning down."

"But you chose not to share that information or your concern with any police officers?" Moriarty said, incredulously.

"I guess I was more concerned with Lissa and Kelly and Tim getting out and our kids getting out," Dr. Forman said with his jaw set. "I felt a little more concern about those things than trying to pin it on anyone at that point."

Perhaps Moriarty had gone a bit too far. He ended by asking Dr. Forman the effects of Klonopin, and Forman said he couldn't give those off the top of his head.

On redirect, Morrison asked Dr. Forman about his written statement of October 24. "Is that the one where you also said you did not believe Debora Green was genuinely hysterical?"

"That's correct."

"And it was at that time, and still is, your opinion that she did not exhibit any visceral concern in that situation?"

"I thought she was relatively devoid of emotion in what I considered to be a highly emotional situation."

"Was she cool?"

"Cool—or just distanced."

*

Moriarty tried again on recross. He clearly wanted to show Judge Ruddick that Debora's neighbors had not liked her to begin with, and that they had built a case against her even before the ashes of the deadly fire were cool. It was already clear that Debora had not been a contender for Ms. Congeniality of Canterbury Court, but there was no evidence that anyone had conspired against her. There was only Mike's testimony about Dr. Mary Forman's frantic, angry call to him just after the fire was discovered: "Your wife is a fucking arsonist!"

"Had you had any contact with Mike about Debora," Moriarty asked Dr. Forman, "before the fire and after he moved out?"

"I don't believe so."

"Do you know at the time of this evening that she was taking medication for depression?"

"No, I did not."

"Do you know if that type of medication can affect one's affect?"

"I was not familiar with what she was taking. I don't know that much about antidepressants."

"Can some medications affect one's affect?"

"I supposed they can."

"What does 'flat affect' mean?"

"Devoid of emotion."

Moriarty had what he wanted, and he turned away briskly with a "Thank you very much."

But Dr. Forman was a chest surgeon, not a psychiatrist. He had known Debora as a next-door neighbor, and that was how he was describing her for the judge. He had watched her as her children were trapped in a burning house and had seen not a scintilla of emotion on her face. If there were antidepressants *that* powerful, Dr. Forman didn't know which ones they might be.

Chapter 37

Paul Morrison had given Judge Ruddick and the gallery a crash course in how ricin poisoning affects the human body, and he had established that Mike Farrar still carried in his bloodstream the proof that he had been exposed to ricin several times. But the charges against Debora Green were bifurcated; Morrison maintained that she had tried to poison her husband, then gone on to set a fire that would trap her children. He now had to recreate what had happened inside the house on Canterbury Court just before the fire erupted and during the hour and forty-five minutes that it burned.

Except for the occasional movie with special effects that show what firefighters must do inside a burning building, the public tends to take them for granted—unless *they* are the ones who need help. Just as police risk their lives, so do firefighters. The jobs require slightly different mind-sets, although they both begin with the premise that the preservation of life is their most important duty.

Few of us would deliberately enter a burning building; for hundreds of years, firefighters have been running, crawling, and sliding into flaming, smoky structures that other people have fled. It is safer now than it used to be. Before the advent of masks and air tanks, firefighters, all unknowing, breathed in the by-products of burning chemicals and asbestos. As they pulled down ceilings with their picks, they often vomited over their shoulders from the effects of the poisonous gases they were forced to inhale. After years of exposure, any number of veteran firefighters contracted cancer—of the mouth, throat, lungs, and other organs damaged because they had no masks and no oxygen tanks. Nor did they have radios with which they could communicate with fellow firemen outside.

By 1995, Chief Maurice Mott and the men of his ladder company had the benefit of safety equipment. That meant they could breathe inside a burning structure, but it did not mean they were not in constant danger of becoming trapped in the fire themselves.

Mott, a compact man with black hair, took the witness stand and began to explain, with the help of slides, what he saw on the night of October 23–24. Along with three other firefighters, he had entered the house at the basement level on the south side, the opposite end from where Kelly and Tim were trapped. By the time Mott and his crew arrived, that was the only way left to get in. (The window he crawled through led into the basement bedroom where Debora had once spent the night hiding from her husband.)

Mott used a floor plan of the house to identify where they had been. "I think this is a hallway and this is a door here. . . . Across from that—this door here was closed. I opened the door, not knowing if it was a closet or whatever, and that's when I visualized this entire fitness room was on fire. I could see through the floor joists to the first floor of the residence."

"Up to this point, you saw no fire?" Morrison asked.

"No fire."

"And you open this door and it's like an inferno?"

"Yes. . . ."

The room above the fitness room was the living room; above *that* was Tim's room. All three rooms were burning, fully involved in flames.

Mott testified that he and his partner searched the playroom, but they found no one—only dolls, teddy bears, and dress-up clothes and hats. They recognized a pool table by feel, but as they worked their way around it, sweeping their gloved hands beneath it, the ceiling fell in on them.

Debora watched the light and shadows of the fire scene slides. This charred structure had been her home. She seemed very alert now, as if watching for something.

Moore's cross-examination of Chief Mott was basically a reprise of what Mott had already said. It is usually unwise for

a defense attorney to quibble over small points with someone who has risked his life for strangers. Moore wanted to
know if Mott remembered a fierce wind blowing that night;
Mott did not.

"While you were inside the house," Moore asked, "did
you smell anything unusual?"

"In the basement area, I did not. When I went into the
basement I had an air pack on, so once I made entry into
that house, I wouldn't be able to smell anything. Now, when
I yelled into the windows, I did not have my face mask on."

Mott had smelled nothing unusual. However, his job was
not to determine the cause of fires; his job was to put them
out and, if at all possible, save human beings trapped inside.

The next witness was someone who *did* determine the cause
of fires: Jeff Hudson of the Shawnee, Kansas, Fire
Department. Although Gary Lamons had been in charge of
the investigation into the fire's cause, Hudson represented
the Eastern Kansas Multi-County Task Force in this hearing.

Hudson testified that the arson investigators had gathered at the site of the fire at eleven the morning after.

"And what role did you play?" Morrison asked.

"I played a role with the origin and cause team in removing debris and assessing the origin and cause of the fire."

"How many of you were involved in the origin and cause
[team]?"

"Probably five or six people were assigned to that."

Hudson explained "layering"—how the arson investigators moved from the top down, tediously sifting through
the levels of a burned structure in search of the fire's cause.
"All the way along, we're documenting what we're doing
and photographing," he testified. "And then we remove the
contents of the room and get down to floor level."

"And is that sometimes important?"

"It's very important because you're looking at burn patterns and the most significant damage to the structure.

You're coming across different parts of furniture. We can use that for reconstruction purposes to determine which way the fire moved and what areas of the room are more damaged than the other areas."

"Is it important for you to be able to see whether or not there are the presence of burn patterns, for example, on a floor?"

"Yes."

"Does that relate to your investigation of what might have caused your start of that fire?"

"Yes—it relates directly to that."

"And is it important for you to know whether or not fires burn low or high in a room—and can you tell by looking at debris, walls, maybe pieces of furniture, the direction and path of travel of the fire?"

"Yes, you can."

Hudson looked only at Paul Morrison; his eyes never shifted to the defense table. Debora sat up straighter; she seemed fascinated with this testimony.

Again, Morrison began projecting slides while Hudson described what they depicted. There was the home's entry with its stone façade that rose toward the now ragged roof. The door was gone and the entryway resembled an open, toothless mouth. The camera moved in closer. Blackened windows. The window near the garage roof where Lissa had escaped. There was a shot of arson investigators shoveling debris into piles.

Using the slides, Morrison and Hudson took Judge Ruddick and the gallery around the outside of the house. Now you could see where Mott and his men had crawled into the lower-floor window; above that was the window that opened out from the Jacuzzi off the master bedroom.

The slides of the east side—the back of the house— showed the most damage. The roof was gone; the railings that ran along the back deck of the house were charred by flames that had shot out more than eight feet after the wall of windows and sliding glass doors shattered from the heat.

"Now, some of the charring around that one—that main set of sliding doors—I'll call it the hotter part of the house," Morrison said, "is that evident there on the right?"

"The wood is charred."

"Now, what's that just to the left of the wood?"

"That appears to be an intercom appliance."

Those in the courtroom who had heard Debora's recall of talking with her son through this intercom looked puzzled. If she had been able to stand there and converse with Tim in his room, there should have been plenty of time for him to jump out onto the roof and lower himself to the ground. Why hadn't she encouraged him to do that? Why had she told him to wait for someone to help him?

Debora watched the screen and whispered occasionally to Ellen Ryan. The cameras were in the basement now; here were the two furnaces, the two electrical panels, the water heaters—all perfectly intact. They had not caused the fire. The carousel shuffled ahead, each new slide dropping into place to reveal another basement room in ruined condition. Some were damaged by water, some by falldown.

"We're in the exercise room, a workout, weight room in the basement," Hudson testified. "And this debris in this photograph has fallen down through the floor joists from the floor in the living room directly above this exercise room. You can see that the drywall that's on the walls in this room is still intact. The dark part of the drywall is up high. The fire in this room moved from the top down. . . . The paint is still on the walls except up high where there was intense heat."

"And does that tell you anything about whether or not the fire started in that room?"

"Yes," Hudson said, directing a beam of light at the slide with a laser pointer. "This room was ruled out as an area of origin because it's obvious that the fire came down from the floor above. . . ."

Next, the two men, prosecutor and arson investigator, moved on to the rec room, where most of the damage had been caused by water. "The room for the most part is intact and has very little damage," Hudson testified. "With the exception of a burn pattern—an area of the carpet down low, right next to that bar stool. The floor is burned in that area."

Hudson explained that the carpet had melted and the fire had gone out. This fire had no connection to the others in the house. It had begun—or been set—separately.

"We've got an unconnected fire down there?"

"Certainly."

The slide projector threw another image on the screen. A fireman's glove held something, but it was impossible to discern what.

At the defense table, Debora turned her head away quickly and whispered urgently to Ellen Ryan, who then spoke to Dennis Moore and Kevin Moriarty.

"Judge," Moriarty said, "we'd like—the defendant would like to voluntarily absent herself at this time. . . ."

There was a sidebar discussion between Judge Ruddick and the defense team. Debora looked agitated for the first time since this hearing had begun.

Moore explained: "Judge, we would state for the record that we understand there may be a couple of slides in this presentation Mr. Morrison's making that would show some scenes that our client would not like to be present in the courtroom when they were shown. They are scenes that may be involving her children. . . ."

Debora was half out of her seat. "She understands she has the right to be present," Moore continued, "but she's giving up that right so she doesn't have to witness this."

"Is that correct, Debora?" Moore turned to his client.

"That's correct." For the first time, Debora spoke, and then she and Ellen hurried from the courtroom to the judge's chambers.

The image on the screen was still puzzling; then, suddenly recognition hit. The glove was holding some part of a human being.

"Tell us what this depicts," Morrison asked Hudson.

"This photograph was taken in the fitness-exercise room,"

Hudson testified, his voice professional still, but slightly hushed. "And that's a photograph of a foot that was found in the falldown debris as it was being removed from that room. It's a human foot."

There were gasps in the courtroom.

"The fitness room is below the living room on the main floor," Morrison said. "Was the floor of the living room still intact or was it gone?"

"The floor in the living room—the subfloor—was burned away and all that was left of the floor and structure were the floor joists."

"Now, my next question is, What room is above the living room?"

"It would be a bedroom that belonged to—to my understanding—to Tim."

"Was there any floor left other than joists between the two rooms?"

"No, there was not."

"In other words, Tim's floor was gone. . . . Did you find some other things down there—either in the basement or on the joists in the living room that had fallen down from Tim's bedroom?"

"Yes, we did. Bed parts and furniture debris. Clothing."

One more slide appeared; this time, the gallery recognized what it depicted. Hudson explained to the judge: "This photograph was taken in the fitness room and it's showing another human foot that was found in the debris in that fitness room."

"So you found two feet?" Morrison asked.

"Yes."

As the horrifying handful of slides showing the damage done to Tim's body ended, Debora was escorted back into the room. She half-smiled at Moore as she took her seat.

The direct examination continued; Hudson explained how his origin and cause team had made its way through the house to determine the origin of the fire. On the screen, the foyer of the house appeared.

"What's significant to you as a fire investigator about what you see in that picture?" Morrison asked.

"There were several significant things just inside the front door," Hudson said. "First of all, the floor in the foyer had varying degrees of damage . . . You could see the floor had been subjected to some significant heat down very low. There was a pattern on that floor that told me it was subjected to different temperatures right next to each other. That's an indicator of a liquid accelerant being poured on the floor. And that [pattern] ties into the wood that's around the stairs and the baseboard to the right and left of those stairs."

"Right here?" Morrison pointed to a portion of the slide.

"Yes," Hudson said. "Very heavy char. A lot of fire damage down low . . . Going up the stairway, you can see the back portions of the stairs—the risers, if you will—were burned away on the back portions, indicating a significant amount of heat right in that area. That's also consistent with low burn and a liquid accelerant being on that area."

"So if we had a fire going up on that stairway, it would be difficult, if not impossible, to get out if you were upstairs?"

"Yes," Hudson said quietly. "That's correct."

The slides clicked again and there was Kelly's little-girl bedroom. Her body was not there, but the imprint left behind on the bedding was almost harder to contemplate. All eyes in the room gravitated automatically toward Debora. She seemed to have regained her composure.

Past the foyer and the stairs leading up to the children's bedrooms, there was more liquid accelerant: "The pour pattern was continuous," Hudson said. "The pour pattern extended around from the stairs, along the floor, into the room on the left where the piano is, and then right into the hallway. Again, we have a very low burning in this area." The flames were most intense around the legs of the piano, which had collapsed.

"In a normal room fire," Hudson continued, now discussing the formal dining room, "you would be able to reconstruct the room by placing the burned parts of the furniture back in place, but, in this case, that furniture was not there. This is indicative of a very hot, very rapidly moving fire. Something was put on that furniture or underneath that furniture to make it burn rapidly." Hudson said a single cup of liquid accelerant tossed on the hard surface of even a large table would have sufficed.

By now, the lopsided pour patterns were clear even to neophytes. It was as if someone had taken a marker pencil and drawn a line around every spot where the arsonist had splashed accelerant on floors and furniture. For comparison, Hudson presented slides that showed even burning in the areas where the arson investigators had found no pour patterns. "This left part of this slide shows even burning across the floor. That's what you would see when you have even heat placed across the surface, where you don't have those splotchy patterns."

Morrison returned to the living room, where furniture and clothing from Tim's room clung to charred, half-gone joists. "Now I see over here some floor joists that appear to be cut," he said. "Is that due to the fire?"

"No, it's not. That's something that was done by the engine crews that were there."

"Why did they do that?"

"To remove a body that was located in that portion of the great room."

"Whose body was that?"

"That was Tim's body. . . . Tim's body was supported by those two floor joists. They had to remove the joists to remove the body."

Debora made no move to leave the courtroom this time. Ellen's head bent near hers, obviously whispering words of comfort.

Hudson continued to describe the huge "pool" of accelerant that had stoked the blaze so the living room floor burned through. How long, one wondered, had the arsonist moved through the house, sprinkling, dumping, pouring accelerant?

What kind of rage or hysteria could have compelled someone to do this, knowing that three children slept above?

Jeff Hudson had wondered about those questions too, but now he was the complete professional as he described the accelerant-saturated rooms along the hallway that led from the living room. And then, finally, he reached the end of the "trailer." The long "wick" of accelerant had led to the door of the master bedroom, the room where Debora said she had been sleeping. A new slide showed that door.

"What does that depict?" Morrison asked.

". . . the door to the master bedroom. This is prior to debris removal. You can see the debris covering the bottom part of that door, just as it was found."

"What's that tell you?"

"That tells me the position of that door during the fire." The door had, according to Hudson, been open. Yet Debora had said that when the alarm woke her up, she had opened the bedroom door and then immediately slammed it shut because there was so much smoke.

Three things convinced Hudson that the door had been open and that the fire had led right up to it. The debris, first; and second, the fire pattern. "It shows . . . the fire right there at floor level in that door, and you can see the pattern starting at the lower right portion of the door. It goes up and out in that 'V' or arrow, showing that the heat came up and out from that hall area and it was moving through that doorway."

But there was a third factor, one perhaps easier for a layperson to understand. When the debris was cleared, and the origin and cause investigators were able to open the door a little wider, they found a clean area on the carpet— a clean area the size and shape of the bottom of the door. In that thin bright strip of carpet was the proof that Debora's door had been open during the fire.

Hudson testified that all the pour patterns were connected, from the kitchen to the dining room to the entryway; to the stairs up to the children's bedrooms; to the living room; to the hallway, music room, den, and finally the master bedroom. The slide on the screen now showed charring in one single drawer of the vanity in the master bath. "That is a separate distinct fire of its own," Hudson explained. "That's a good photograph of how a fire starts and burns up and out. You can see the vanity to the left and to the right is undamaged by fire."

"Mr. Hudson," Morrison asked, "did you form an opinion as to whether or not this fire was intentionally set?"

"Yes."

"What is that opinion?"

"That it *was* intentionally set . . . that there were liquid accelerants used to accelerate this fire."

At the end of his long direct testimony, Hudson summed up: there had been "two big fires" and "two small fires." The big fires had been set by someone in the doorway of the master bedroom who lit the trailer's wick.

In cross-examining Hudson, Kevin Moriarty obviously intended to suggest that he had been influenced by conversations with other firefighters and with policemen, which might have tended to prejudice him toward an arson verdict. Hudson's bearing and obvious expertise quickly closed off that avenue. Moriarty then offered other scenarios that might have been responsible for the tell-tale patterns Hudson found. Perhaps cleaning solvent had been left after the carpets were professionally cleaned? Perhaps some portion of the house that was already on fire had fallen on the carpet and created the appearance that liquids had pooled there? Perhaps the "chimney effect" had caused the rapid burning Hudson had observed?

Arson investigation has its rules and its proven theories; none of Moriarty's diversionary tactics impressed Hudson. But most of all, Moriarty wanted to sway Hudson from his position that the door to the master bedroom had been open when the fire started.

It was a valiant effort, but Hudson knew fire and he knew arson, and this cross-examination was akin to attempting to sway Einstein from his belief in the theory of relativity. Unfailingly attentive and pleasant, sometimes baffled by the defense questions, Hudson was unmovable. He knew exactly how the fire on Canterbury Court had been started. He cited even more evidence that proved that the door to Debora's bedroom had been open during the fire. He pointed out that the top of the door would not have been charred had the door been closed. He showed the pattern of a fire traveling into the bedroom through a doorway, not across a closed door.

Moriarty asked Hudson what had become of the containers that would have held the liquid accelerant. It was difficult to say, Hudson replied. He had found what might have been a melted container in the breakfast area of the kitchen.

On redirect, Morrison asked Hudson about that object. A white circle less than a foot across, it could well have been the white plastic of a milk bottle or some similar container, Hudson said; no one could tell for sure. All they could do was speculate that someone had emptied a white plastic container of some liquid and set it on the floor of the breakfast room. Hudson could not say definitely what had been in that container—if, indeed, it had been a container.

Some containers would have virtually dissolved in the inferno; others—a liquor bottle, a perfume bottle—might have remained intact. The arsonist could even have removed the containers from the house before lighting the trailer. This *was* a puzzle, one that would never be solved.

"Even with all your experience, education, and training," Morrison said, ending his intense questioning of Hudson, "you cannot tell us who started the fire, other than you believe the fire was started. Is that correct?"

"That's correct."

*

No, Jeff Hudson could not prove who had started the horrific fire. But he had followed the trailer of that fire to the
open door of the master bedroom, and he had a private
opinion concerning who had lit the match that started fire
racing up the hall, into the rooms beside it, into the entryway and dining room, and finally up the stairs to block the
children's escape. "I didn't look at Ms. Green while I was testifying," he would recall months later. "But when I was done
and leaving the courtroom, I looked right at her. I wanted
her to know that I knew exactly what had happened. And no
matter what she said to anybody else, she and I knew exactly
what happened."

Debora must have been aware of Hudson's penetrating
blue eyes staring at her. She moved her head slightly and
looked directly at him as he stepped down from the witness
chair and walked to the door. It was over in mere moments,
but Hudson felt he had gotten his silent message across.

Chapter 38

There was a good chance that the State would finish presenting its witnesses and evidence by the end of this frigid
Wednesday in Olathe. Now, the Prairie Village detectives
and the criminalists would follow each other to the witness
chair.

Gary Baker was first. He had accompanied Mike to the
lab at the Shawnee Mission Medical center, and kept the
blood sample obtained there until he gave it to Lieutenant
Gary Dirks. But Baker's testimony chiefly concerned his
assignment to go to the site of a burning house on
Canterbury Court. When he got there, it was about 2:30; the
fire was out, the chill air was full of smoke and steam.
Sergeant Steve Hunter had briefed Baker and told him they
had found two fatalities.

"Did you have occasion to view the bodies of the two child
fatalities of that fire?" Morrison asked.

"Yes, sir," Baker said.

Again, Debora was on her feet, asking to be excused. The proceedings paused while once again Ellen led her from the courtroom.

"Where were the two bodies located?" Morrison asked as the door clicked shut behind the defendant.

"The first body was located about fifteen to twenty feet directly inside the front door. The second body was located in a northeast bedroom on the upper level."

A slide, "State's Exhibit 15–5," lit the screen.

"Can you identify that for us?"

"Yes, sir," Baker said. "As you can see in the middle there, you'll see a large iron daybed-type frame there. And then, just to the left of that, this is the body of Tim Farrar. . . . As you can see, there's no floor underneath. It's completely burnt out except for the joists, and Tim's body was resting on the floor joists there."

Another slide, so upsetting that most of the gallery looked away, showed Tim from the weight room below the floor beams where his body was caught.

It was so senseless. In all likelihood, Tim could easily have leaped onto the roof outside his bedroom window and dropped to the backyard. Why had his mother told him to stay inside? Had he tried to find his little sister, as she instructed, and never made it back to that window? It was hard to cope with the thought that this was the boy who, only hours before his fiery death, had been so gleeful about his hockey game.

Slide 15–7 was a picture of Kelly. She lay in her bed as if only asleep, on her back, her knees slightly drawn up. The covers were still tucked around her. She had gone to bed and never awakened.

Dennis Moore's cross-examination dealt with when Baker had first heard Debora Green named as a suspect.

"The day after the fire," Baker answered. "I heard Dr.

Farrar, Debora Green—and Tim Farrar's name also came up."

Yes, Baker agreed that the Metro Squad met each morning to discuss the case, but he was not familiar with all the tips and theories that had come in. "The tips that came in were assigned to the lead officer, and the lead officer assigned the tips out to various detectives who were assigned to the squad."

Lieutenant Gary Dirks of the Johnson County Criminalistics Laboratory testified to the intact chain of evidence—the evidence being the exemplars of Mike's blood and the single packet of castor beans—that had been sent to Drew Richardson at the FBI lab.

Detective Rod Smith was next. He had spent the critical hours after the fire interviewing Debora. She had seemed to like him at first; in the end, he had been the target of her wrath. Blond and affable, Smith was about to introduce the most startling evidence of this preliminary hearing: the videotape of his and Detective Greg Burnetta's interview with Debora, which took place about three and a half hours after she had rung her neighbors' doorbell and told them to call "111."

"Was Debora Green in custody at that time?" Morrison asked.

"No."

"And was she informed that she was not under arrest?"

"Yes."

"Was she informed whether or not she had the right to leave or not? In other words, that she was free to go at any time? Did she understand or at least relate to you that she understood what you were telling her?"

"Yes."

"What about her coherence? Did she appear to be under the influence of alcohol or drugs at that time?"

"To me—no."

"And how long did the interview last?"

"The first part of it lasted approximately fifty minutes,

and then there was a short break and about ten more minutes after that."

Morrison prepared to show the videotape of the interview but, as he'd expected, Moore objected—first on the ground that it was not relevant and second because, after this preliminary hearing, the defense intended to file a motion to suppress the tape. The attorneys moved forward to hold a sidebar discussion with Judge Ruddick. From their gestures and the intensity on their faces, it was clear that this was, perhaps, the most important argument of the hearing.

Moore noted that Judge Ruddick had already seen the tape, and he did not want to risk its being seen by the public for fear they would never get an unprejudiced jury. That was problematic. There were reporters in the courtroom, and there were reporters one floor down who could view the tape on closed-circuit TV. In the end, Judge Ruddick ruled that the videotape was relevant; it would be shown in the courtroom, but could not be broadcast through the news media. "The fact of the matter is—if we do it my way," the judge explained, "somebody that is clever enough can recite the whole thing in the paper if they want, but it would shield the public from an electronic broadcast of this tape. The text of what is said is going to be available. I just won't let it be broadcast."

The camera in the media room downstairs was pointed away from the television screens there. The camera in the courtroom was turned off. Those fortunate enough to be in the courtroom already, and the reporters watching on the closed-circuit television sets downstairs were about to hear *and* see Debora's interview with detectives. To retain as much of it as possible would not really be a matter of being "clever"; it would depend on who could write fast enough to capture Debora's words in scrawled sentence fragments on yellow legal pads. And that, of course, meant that they would be unable to watch the screen to study her body language and facial expressions as she talked to detectives. Quick trade-off arrangements were made among reporters. Some agreed to compare notes; others did not. About to embark on a peculiar kind of race, they sat, pens poised, as the tape began. For over an hour, there was no sound in the court- room but the voices of Rod Smith and Debora Green, with an occasional word or two from Greg Burnetta and Lieutenant Terry Young. It was as bizarre an interview as any reporter there had seen. Those assigned to capture the "text" listened and wrote, with only brief opportunities to look at the woman on the screen as she twisted and turned in her chair, tucking her bare feet beneath her. She laughed and chatted easily with Rod Smith, the sound of her merry voice in stark contrast to the proceedings. Occasionally, with their curiosity overwhelming them, the reporters glanced quickly at Debora, the three-dimensional woman in the courtroom, to check her reaction to the shadow Debora on the television screen.

But mostly, they wrote. They had to get this conversation down; the chances were excellent that they would never hear it again. The defense might very well manage to have it suppressed.

The woman on the screen was so different from the woman who sat at the defense table, watching herself on the videotape. The Debora Green in the dark pink nightie patterned with a flock of white sheep was witty, talkative, and friendly. She appeared to be a woman who was used to bantering with men, who might have been chatting with friends at a backyard barbecue—not flirtatious, but a "good old girl." Her affect was totally wrong for a mother who, in all likelihood, had just lost two of her children.

The Debora Green watching the tape in the courtroom varied her expression between two modes: a look of concern and a blank stare. This was the woman who had demon- strated neither humor nor charisma during the hearing. Most of the time she had had no expression at all, although sometimes the lines between her eyes had deepened into furrows of annoyance. Only once had she cried a single tear. Now her own image on the screen, her facile words, and especially her laugh, belied that façade.

Watching Debora's interview with the Prairie Village detectives during the pre-dawn hours of October 24, those in the gallery saw someone they had not seen before. She seemed entirely comfortable wearing only a nightgown, talking with two men she had just met, after a fire had destroyed her home and taken the lives of two of her children. She played with her feet, and she used phrases like "you guys," "crap," and "fuck" easily. As she spoke with Smith and Burnetta, she hardly seemed to fit the image of a doctor, much less the mother of future BOTARs and a BOTAR escort. She was coarse, but not unlikable.

Ellen Ryan watched the screen avidly, as if she, too, was seeing a Deb different from the dependent, sad "child" she had fought so hard to protect. From time to time, as she had all during the preliminary hearing, she whispered something to Debora. Occasionally, she nodded or shook her head.

Despite all the testimony about her use of drugs and alcohol, Debora seemed perfectly sober. Although she spoke rapidly in a nasal voice, her words made sense and she remembered the previous evening and the fire in detail. But she tended to relate her memory of the night in a dramatic way, putting her own and others' statements in quotes. "Tim said, 'Mom, what shall I do?' I said, 'Tim, wait where you are and I'm going to call 911 to come and save you.' And he said, 'Well, should I get one of the girls and try to come out?' I said, 'No'—which, I'm sure, was the kiss of death . . .'"

As, indeed, it was. But somehow Debora had managed to distance herself from the fire events, even though this tape had been made only three and a half hours after the first officer was dispatched to Canterbury Court. With her jolly attitude, she might well be talking about strangers and not her own family. Reporters noted—as Smith and Burnetta had—she did not refer to her children by name, but as "my thirteen-year-old" or my "ten-year-old." The impression she made was that she had been raising her children for her own gratification rather than loving them for themselves.

Every so often, Debora said something so outrageous that the sound of reporters' pens hurriedly writing down her words was synchronized. Although she had not learned of Tim's and Kelly's fate—and, shockingly, had not even asked about them—she referred to them in the past tense: "As I went around the corner to inform the neighbors to call 911, that's when I heard Tim on the intercom by the pool deck— *he used to be my thirteen-year-old.*"

She told the detectives she had picked her children up from their Pembroke Hill schools at three o'clock Monday afternoon. "They all go to Pembroke Hill," she said, speaking so fast it was hard to make out her words. "*At least, the living ones do. . . .*"

And still she did not ask which of her children were living.

When Debora recalled—reciting yet another dramatic dialogue—how she had saved Lissa, she took full credit for the rescue and she spoke of her daughter in a subtly deprecating way. "Lissa's afraid of heights—she's afraid of pretty much everything. I said, 'Jump!,' and she said, 'No, I can't do it,' and I said, 'You will! Jump to me now.' And she jumped—and I missed her totally. I'm sure she'll never trust anybody. And she fell down right at my feet, but she was not hurt. But I'm sure that's the only reason we have Lissa alive." This was true enough. But Debora, as witnesses testified, had made no effort to save her other children, nor had she expressed any concern for their safety. She had watched the fire that consumed them without a flicker of emotion on her face.

One striking trait of the Debora on the television screen was emerging: her selfishness and total self-absorption. Worried that *she* might "asphyxiate," she had fled the house in a panic for her own life. She spoke volubly about *her* plans for her future once her divorce was final. "A big deal in *my* life the last couple of weeks has been, 'What am I going to do? Now.' Because my life is changing whether I like it or not. So what I've decided I want to do is I want to do a psych residency, which will be a whole new deal for me . . . to live life the way I want." Although she surely knew that Tim and Kelly were dead, this interview was all about Debora.

Every bit of testimony in the preliminary hearing thus far had indicated that she had clung to Mike with a grip born of desperation, but in the interview, she denied that she even thought much about their looming divorce. Somehow, the "actress" on the screen was convincing when she brushed Mike away as a mere annoyance. Debora chuckled as she said, "I haven't been particularly upset—or really even terribly emotionally involved. That's not quite the truth. I felt a tremendous sense of relief when he moved out, which surprised him because he thought I'd be *devastated.*"

She waffled continually on vital times. She could not remember when she went to bed, or when she talked to Mike on the phone. Her estimates of when she went to sleep changed from "between nine-thirty and ten-thirty" to "But Tim was up until about eleven. I talked to him for quite a while in the kitchen." She had a "fuzzy" recall of when she had awakened to the sound of an insistent alarm. "Whenever. Maybe twelve-fifteen? It seems as if everything telescoped pretty close together. But I—honest to God— have no idea when the alarm went off. I didn't look at a clock. It could have been as early as midnight—or as late as twelve-thirty."

The tape seemed to be coming to an end. There were long spaces where no one was in the pale green room. But suddenly the pace picked up; Burnetta, Smith, and Debora reappeared. Burnetta was telling Debora that he had official notification that Tim and Kelly had died in the fire. She dropped her head to the table and sobbed, but only for a moment. And then she turned to the detectives—and a totally different woman emerged, a woman seething with

anger and accusation. It was as if she had three entirely separate personalities: the quiet woman at the defense table,
the talkative and friendly woman who had been on the
screen for over an hour, and now a furious and profane
woman. For those watching the videotape, the shock of her
metamorphosis was palpable.

"Oh Jesus Christ!" Debora said. "I should have let my—I
should have let Tim come out when he wanted to! Jesus
fucking Christ! . . . Oh God. Beautiful Tim and beautiful
Kelly are both *dead?* Jesus Christ! Did they make any attempt
at all to save 'em? *I* saved one of the kids. I could have gotten
the second one out and didn't. I'll never forgive myself for
that. . . ." She demanded to go back to Canterbury Court
and see her dead children, and she was enraged as Burnetta
and Smith told her that wasn't possible. This swearing, out-
of-control woman was the Debora her husband had spoken
of in his testimony; she had replaced the garrulous, affable
Debora in a heartbeat.

And then, very softly, Debora was asking, "Does my husband know? I would love to see my husband—even though
we're getting a divorce—because he and I will be the only
ones who can share in the mammoth grief. But I can't do
that. I can't go to my home. I can't see my dead children. I
can't see my husband. You people are pathetic."

Most of all, Debora wanted to be with Mike. "Jesus
Christ!" her taped voice rang out in the courtroom. "There
are two people here that care about what happened. So why
can't *we* be together? But apparently you don't have compassion for anyone else. . . . *I* want to tell him. *I want to tell my
husband that our babies are dead. . . .*"

The screen dissolved into a blur. The videotape was over.
In the press row, reporters were still writing as the screen
went blank, getting down the words that echoed in their
heads. Later, those who agreed to compare notes would
share an ominous suspicion. Debora had had one house
catch fire, after which her estranged husband had returned
to her. Could it be that she had set fire to the house on

Canterbury Court and destroyed her own children so that
her husband would take her back one more time? Although
she had continually denigrated Mike during the interview
on the night of the fire, in the end it was he she wanted to
be with. She wanted to be the first to tell him that Tim and
Kelly were dead. Was it so he could comfort her? Or, more
chillingly, having set the fire that killed them, did she want
to see Mike's face when he heard the news?

Chapter 39

The State rested on Wednesday. It had been an emotional
day in court, beginning with Jeff Hudson's testimony that
the fatal fire had been deliberately set, and concluding with
the videotape of Debora's bizarre interview with the police.
Frustrated television reporters who had hoped to get copies
and sound bites from that interview were left with only their
notes. But even those were dynamite.

What ammunition would the defense team have to refute
the damning testimony that Morrison had presented—the
most damning, perhaps, being the defendant's own words?
Moore and Moriarty had subpoenaed a number of witnesses, among them Celeste Walker, who would most
assuredly not be friendly to Debora's camp and who
dreaded going on the stand to discuss her affair with
Debora's husband.

Morrison knew what Moore and Moriarty intended to do
to save their client, and he was appalled. The person they
would attempt to indict, as it were, would never be subpoenaed. He could not be. He was dead. The defense planned
to accuse Tim Farrar as the arsonist.

It was a monstrous plan, one that would enrage Mike and
that Debora would later deplore, but there *was* a possibility
that the defense contention was true. Tim had been an
angry, troubled boy—and for good reason. He had been a
pawn between two desperately unhappy parents. Debora

had used him—the child who most resembled her in looks
and, she felt, in intelligence—as the "man of the house."
Mike and Tim had dealt with the usual father–teenage son
rivalry, but it had been exacerbated by Debora's deliberate
pitting of one against the other. If she could not have Mike,
she had apparently decided she would encourage the continued animosity between Mike and Tim. She was losing her
husband, but she was robbing Mike of his son.

Debora had ensured Tim's loyalty by demeaning his
father. He had obeyed her even in the last minutes of his
life. He could have saved himself from a fiery death, but he
had waited, just as she ordered, "until the professionals
come to get you out." He had waited as the floor disintegrated beneath him and the roof over his head burned away.
Whether Debora thought she was doing what was best for
Tim at the time didn't matter; what mattered was that Tim
had automatically followed whatever instructions a patently
disturbed mother threw at him.

Morrison argued that the defense's plan to dredge up
Tim's past behavior contravened Kansas case law, which
does not allow "prior bad acts" by a defendant to be introduced into trial, "the theory being that you can't just
present carte blanche bad acts of a witness or victim if they
were remote in time."

"All we're trying to do is present the theory of the defense,"
Moore insisted, "whether Mr. Morrison agrees with it or not.
We believe case law is abundantly clear as to what the defendant has a constitutional right to do, and the due-process law
gives that right under the United States Constitution."

Most states do not allow former arrests, convictions, or
other negative information about a defendant to come out
during the trial proper, just as most states *do* allow that information during the trial's penalty phase, once a jury has
found a defendant guilty and is deliberating over the punishment. The exception to be filed in Kansas was 60-455, a
legal loophole that would allow prior bad acts of a witness or
defendant or victim into a trial.

As he had with many other issues in this preliminary hearing, Judge Ruddick decided that since there was no jury listening, he would hear what the defense had to say about Tim. This did not mean, however, that he would rule similarly during an actual trial.

The first witness for the defense was a twelve-year-old boy, Todd Balsam,* who was in the seventh grade and had been Tim's friend. Todd testified that he had played on Tim's soccer team and then later Tim had moved onto his street, Canterbury Court. He had visited Tim's house and had seen the computer that he often used. Tim had talked to Todd about making bombs.

"What did Tim tell you about fires or bombs, Todd?" Moore asked.

"He told me that he had a book on his computer about how to make bombs and rockets—he said that he made them for his friends."

Todd could not remember the exact name of the book Tim had downloaded into his computer, but thought it was something like "The German Book of Bombs."

"Do you know if Tim had any interest in science?"

"No," Todd answered; he did not know.

"Do you know if he had any interest in fires and bombs?"

"Well, he talked about it a lot and he lit matches and stuff. . . . He lit matches inside his house, but he never lit anything on fire. And then outside, he lit stuff on fire like leaves and pine needles." Todd said he had seen Tim starting leaf fires in the yard "five or six times."

Under cross-examination, Todd told Morrison that he and Tim had lived fifteen houses apart. And although they had once been good friends, they seldom saw each other toward the end of Tim's life, because they attended different schools.

Len Jurden, whose family lived on the east side of the Farrar-Green house, took the stand next. Court watchers expected that he would be questioned about his former next-door neighbors, much as John Forman had been. But, with Jurden, the defense was about to spring a surprise.

Jurden testified that he—or rather, his wife—had had occasion to call the Prairie Village police on March 10, 1995, seven months before the fatal fire next door.

"I was walking from the kitchen to my dinner table and looked out the window," he said, continuing in his clipped, shorthand way of speaking, "saw a fire, two boys standing around it, went out the front door, asked them what was going on; they took off running."

Jurden testified that he had hurried to the fire—in the northeast corner of his yard—and put it out. It had involved no more than the grass, and he could not determine how it had started.

"What did you do after you put the fire out?" Moore asked.

"I saw one of the boys going around the corner through the neighbor's yard and went after him and caught him. . . . It turned out to be Tim Farrar."

Jurden had never met Tim before, and told the Court that he did not speak to the boy's parents about the fire. He knew the police were on the way and he took Tim back to his yard to wait for them. "The other boy returned voluntarily. . . . The police arrived, we went over and I showed him the spot, and the policeman began to question the boys."

Jurden, who appeared to be a reluctant witness, testified that he had seen a bottle of some sort in the burned area. His reason for calling the police was to impress upon Tim Farrar and his cohort how dangerous fire was and that it was not to be played with. Jurden said he had children aged four and two and wanted to protect them. He commented that the final fire had disrupted the whole neighborhood, frightening the children who lived there and had to look at the burned-out house.

*

Bob Thomas, a Prairie Village patrol officer, was the next defense witness. He recalled the incident in March.

"Did you see what was set on fire?" Moore questioned.

"It was a coffee can [jar] which had evidently been filled to some extent with gasoline."

"Okay. And what had actually caught on fire?"

"A small amount of grass."

Thomas said he had spoken with the boys' parents. Tim's mother, whom the officer referred to as "Mrs. Green," had appeared concerned at the time. The coffee jar had had some kind of cloth or vinyl rope fuse in it, which had been ignited. The resulting fire had burned a circle of grass that Thomas estimated as "a foot and a half" in diameter. Len Jurden had not wanted to prosecute the boys for arson and the case was closed.

So Tim had been playing with a rudimentary Molotov cocktail. The question naturally arose: Would he have set a fire that would almost certainly trap him, his little sisters, and his dogs on the top floor with no way to escape? Tim loved his sisters and he loved his pets. He had been angry but he was certainly not stupid. If he was going to set fire to something out of rage, would he not have destroyed something of his father's?

Two more boys waited to testify about Tim's fascination with fire and explosives. The first was thirteen-year-old Dane Wilson,* who attended Pembroke Hill. He said that Tim had been a "very close friend. [I knew him] through school. I'd often go over to his house . . . and one time I went on a trip with him . . . to Breckenridge, Colorado." Dane had also been in science class with Tim.

"Do you know what kind of a relationship Tim had with his dad?" Moore asked.

"It wasn't a very good relationship. In the times that I was over there they'd often get into arguments, yelling arguments. They'd go into the next room and argue about something as little as not taking out the trash . . ."

Over Morrison's vigorous objections, Judge Ruddick allowed Dane to discuss Tim's and Mike's problems with each other. "One day last year," Dane said, "Tim came to school with a black eye, and he told everybody that his dog caused this black eye. . . . [Later] he said his dad and him got into a fight and his dad caused the black eye."

However, Tim had given as good as he got, or better. "Tim told us," Dane testified, "about him constantly giving his dad bloody noses when they were fighting. And he even told us he broke his dad's nose one time."

"Dane," Moore asked, "did you ever hear Tim talk about fires or bombs?"

"Yes, once in a while. And I also saw drawings of them. He had made his own descriptions of bombs and rockets in his spiral notebook . . . His own drawings . . . They were good drawings. He had chemicals needed for it labeled on the side."

"Chemicals for what?"

"Making the bomb."

Tim had had access to computers both at home and in science class at Pembroke Hill.

"Have you ever heard of a book called *The Big Book of Mischief?*" Moore asked.

"I heard that through Tim."

"Did you ever see Tim with a copy of *The Big Book of Mischief?*"

"In Breckenridge . . . I looked at the contents page."

"What did you understand the table of contents to contain?"

"Explosives, descriptions of bombs, lock picking, rockets."

Moore attempted to enter *The Big Book of Mischief* into evidence, but Morrison objected on the grounds that there was no proof that the looseleaf book Moore held contained the same information as the book Dane Wilson had seen in Breckenridge, Colorado. The book, which resembled revolutionary underground "cookbooks," was full of recipes for all manner of destructive projects. (Once available on the Internet, it has since been removed.)

The first page of the book would be a natural draw for a teenage boy, smacking of forbidden secrets and programs like *The X-Files*.

! DANGER !

THE FOLLOWING DOCUMENT CONTAINS
INSECURE INFORMATIONS!
DO NOT FOLLOW ANY OF THE
DESCRIBED OPERATIONS IF
YOU ARE NOT FAMILIAR
WITH CHEMISTRY

GETTING
INJURED OR EVEN KILLED
BY TRYING ANY OF THESE
EXPERIMENTS IS EASY!

THINK BEFORE YOU ACT <u>OR</u> DEATH IS (CAN BE) IMMEDIATE!

The information published in the following pages are [*sic*] just for informational purposes. Neither for terrorists/anarchists nor for the unexperienced minds! Note that I am not the author of these pages and I will not take any respobilities [*sic*] for. Continue with care!

Mischief contained formulas for everything from harmless smoke bombs to tear gas to laughing gas to dynamite. They were, however, very complicated; anyone who wanted to duplicate them would have to be a rather sophisticated student of science. *Mischief* also had a chapter on poisons and drugs. Interestingly, there was no listing for ricin. The instructions were as riddled with grammatical and spelling errors as the warning page was.

Judge Ruddick said he would admit the pages downloaded from the Internet, with the exception of four early pages, which Dane did not recognize.

Morrison rose to cross-examine the boy. "Dane, you saw Tim Farrar the Monday before he died, right?"

"Yes."

"You had lunch with him at school?"

"Yes."

"He was in a good mood that day? He was upbeat?"

"Yes."

"Wasn't talking about bombs or rockets or blowing [up] anything or anything like that?"

"No," Dane said. "He usually didn't talk about that a lot. Just when he was looking at his drawings and stuff."

"He was a nice kid, wasn't he?"

"Yes."

"He was the kind of kid that stood up for other kids that got picked on in school, wasn't he?"

"Yes."

Thirteen-year-old witnesses are rarely spilling over with words, but Morrison kept trying—as Moore had. "And he had told you before that him and his dad didn't get along very good?"

"Yes."

"And, in fact, you knew about the trouble he got into over that can of gas at the next-door neighbor's. . . . He had told you that he learned from that and that was a onetime thing, didn't he?"

"Yes."

One more thirteen-year-old boy testified about Tim's interest in bombs. "I was a pretty close friend, I guess," Jed Trimble* said. "I just never went to his house, though."

"Did Tim ever talk to you about fire or bombs?" Moore asked.

"At a football game, he said that he knew how to make C-4 and he was going to make some and try to make a bomb out of it."

"When was this football game, if you know?"

"I know it was in September, but I'm not sure of the date."

"That would have been the month before his death in October of 1995?"

"Uh-huh."

"Jed," Moore continued, "have you ever heard of a book called *The Big Book of Mischief*?"

"Yes," Jed testified. "Bill Lee* talked about it and that's about it."

"Did you ever see the book?"

"No."

The point was, of course, to show that Tim had lit fires and played at making bombs. But a bomb would have left entirely different evidence for the arson team to evaluate. And the defense had been unable to elicit strong testimony from Tim's friends. Except for the primitive Molotov cocktail in Len Jurden's backyard, it sounded as though Tim had done more talking than acting out.

The boys who had been Tim's friends were neither photographed in court nor named in official records, but some television photographers waiting outside the courthouse caught them on film as they walked out after testifying.

Dennis Moore and Kevin Moriarty had another witness. Phyllis Grado had been employed by Debora and Mike as a nanny from 1989 to 1993. A sweet-faced, fiftyish woman who appeared to be of Hispanic descent, she testified that she had applied for the job after seeing an ad in the paper. Mike and Debora had interviewed her and hired her together. Phyllis Grado would prove to be an emotional woman, considerably more voluble than the last four defense witnesses.

"When you say you were a nanny for the Farrar children, how much time was involved?" Moore asked. "Can you give the court a sense of that?"

"Well, at the beginning it was like five hours a day, and that was only until she felt at ease with her children with me—that she could trust me enough with them. And then, a couple of months later, she started working her full eight hours."

"Do you know where she was working at that point?"

"At Trinity Lutheran Hospital—she was a physician there."

"After she started working full-time at Trinity, how much time were you working then?"

"Ten hours a day for her."

Grado said she had gotten to know her young charges well; she gave the impression that she and Tim were very close. She remembered an episode that took place some three years earlier: "He was upset one morning when I came and I had asked him what was the matter with him, and he just kept saying 'Nothing,' shying away. And I finally got to him and he said, 'My father was arguing with my mom again and he's asking for a divorce—he wants my mom to give him a divorce. And the girls are going to go live with [my father] . . . and I'm going to stay with my mom. But it's all my fault they're getting a divorce. He's always arguing and getting after her. I hate him. I hate him. I'm going to kill him.'"

Grado scarcely had to be asked a question, so eager was she to recreate a conversation that she insisted she had had with Tim. "He said he hated his dad for making his mother angry and sick," she testified. "He said, 'I can't stand him. He's not my father. I'm going to burn this house down and I'm going to burn everybody in it.' I says, 'Timmy, you're going to hurt yourself by talking this way.' He said, 'I don't care.' He says, 'If my dad's going to do that to my mom, I'm just going to kill him. I hate him. And I'm going to start a fire. I'm going to burn this whole house down, everybody in it. I don't care who gets hurt!'

"I said, 'Not even yourself?' He said, 'No, I don't care.' And this just kept going on every time he got angry. He always despised his father. . . ."

"When he got angry, how would he react physically?" Moore asked.

"He would throw his fist up in the air and shake and turn all red with a tantrum. And he'd start throwing and banging things in his room. He'd destroy his set of hats he had. He'd just toss them all over on the floor. And I'd go behind him and pick them up the next day. And he'd take his clothes all out of the drawer and he would mix them with the dirty clothes and I would have to pick them up after him again. And this went on after my second year I was there."

That would have been in 1990 or 1991, when Tim Farrar was only eight or nine years old.

"Mrs. Grado," Moore asked, "did you ever have any conversations with Tim Farrar about fires and bombs?"

One would have thought she had already delved into the topic of fire, but Phyllis Grado continued, breathlessly. "I asked him where he was getting all this about fires and stuff. He said he read a lot of books, that he was into science and he knew what he was doing. And he had a little wooden box—and he hammered down some nails on it and some wires—*electrical wires*—that were tied together. And he had them plugged into the outlet of the bedroom. And then he had like a little tapping thing on it. He said . . . 'If I want to, all I've got to do is tap this and that wall will burst into flames because that's the way I have it set for it to go off.'"

Moore wasn't keeping pace with his witness. His next question was almost comically late. "Did you ever see him with anything that concerned you . . . any kind of device, fire device, that concerned you?"

"Yeah," she said. "Matches. He was steady playing with matches. Just striking them, throwing them anywhere where they could catch on fire. Trash cans—"

"Did something ever happen with a trash can, Mrs. Grado?"

"In the basement of his home—he started a fire downstairs where he had his Nintendo."

"How do you know he started a fire?"

"Because he was awfully quiet," the witness continued with scarcely a pause for breath. "And I went to check on him . . . and he had started a fire in the trash can. And I . . . grabbed the can and I threw it into the shower room in the bathroom, and I told him, 'Look what you're doing to me,' and he says, 'I don't care.'"

"Did you ever have any kind of similar experience at your home with Tim?"

"Yes," Grado said firmly. "I used to take him to my house quite a bit when I cared for them during their summer vacation . . . and we'd wind up at my house. . . . One of those times, I left him in the kitchen, and I told Timothy, I said, 'There's pop and stuff in the refrigerator. You help yourself to whatever you like.'

"And I went into the living room to watch TV and then pretty soon I heard him laughing again. And I says, 'Well, what's he laughing about?' So I went in there and sure enough, there was my trash can just engulfed in flames. I thought it was going to catch my ceiling because my ceilings are pretty low. So then I just threw water in it and I tossed the can out onto the patio."

Grado testified that she had caught Tim with a Coke bottle that contained something strong-smelling and had a rag stuck in the neck. She had tried to get it away from him, but he grabbed it and dumped it in the backyard.

"Did he ever tell you what he could do with that bottle?"

"Yeah. He said that was a bomb. He could throw it against a wall and make it explode and start a fire with it—"

"Did he tell you where he learned how to do that?"

"No, he just said that he learned it by reading science books. And he liked to practice stuff like that."

While Moore had allowed Phyllis Grado to ramble on about Tim and bombs and fires, Morrison attempted to rein her in on cross-examination.

She remembered that she had last worked for the Farrar-Greens in 1991 or 1993. She was not sure now.

"Now, in fact, you had not seen Tim Farrar for a couple of years before this fire, correct?"

"No, I hadn't."

"And so, just right off the top here, you don't have any personal knowledge—"

"Well no, I did see him in the month of December . . ."

"Just bumped into them? All right. You don't have any personal knowledge of what happened on October 24, 1995, do you?"

"No—but I don't *need* to know, because—"

"You answered—"

"—I know *him*—"

"—the question. Thank you, ma'am." Morrison turned away, but Phyllis Grado was still talking:

"I know Tim."

"You've answered the question."

Judge Ruddick attempted to explain to the witness that she could not offer gratuitous statements.

Morrison got Mrs. Grado to admit that Tim had been eight when he was angry with his father and talking about setting fires. "Okay. All right," he cut in before she took up her monologue once more. "What did you do? Did you call the police department or the fire department when you had these fires over at your house?"

"I didn't call them at all."

"*Oh, you didn't?*"

"No," she said, slightly subdued. "I took care of it myself . . . but my husband said that in the near future 'Just make sure that he doesn't get ahold of matches and stuff when he's here.'"

"And, in fact," Morrison continued, "you didn't even tell his parents about that, did you?"

"No, I didn't tell them. No."

Phyllis Grado stepped down. How odd that she would not have consulted the parents of an eight-year-old boy who was experimenting with fire. She had not been a believable witness. What she said about Tim was upsetting, but her manner blunted the effect of her testimony.

The courtroom waited. Celeste Walker would naturally be the next witness. People glanced at the double doors to the hall. No one came through them. Moore told Judge Ruddick that the defense was resting. Celeste would not have to answer the subpoena the defense had issued. Moore would not explore her relationship with Mike, which the prosecution contended was Debora's primary motive for setting the fire that had killed her children. Nor would Moore offer any evidence that it was Tim who had poisoned his father.

The preliminary hearing was over. And now it was up to Judge Ruddick. If he found there was not enough evidence against Debora Green to bind her over for trial, she could walk free. If there should be a trial, Paul Morrison wanted to include all the charges against Debora as part of a pattern. As he saw it, the poisoning and the arson murders were "inexorably entwined," evolving from a single motive, and therefore should be tried as one case. "It's our theory," Morrison told the judge, "that, frankly, those children were killed by Debora Green because Mike Farrar was no longer available to her. We're arguing, Judge, and in fact have pled this case as such—these transactions are all related to one another by motive, if not by plan."

Moore wanted to sever the poisonings from the arson. "We intend to challenge that," he told the judge. "But the evidence the State produced is that Debora Green, they say, attempted to murder Michael Farrar by poisoning, a *wholly* different method and manner of murder, if you will, than arson and a person burning to death in a fire. . . ."

Judge Ruddick had listened carefully to both the prosecution and the defense for almost four days and he was ready to make his ruling. "Based on the evidence that's been presented at preliminary hearing," he said, "I *do* find that the crime of capital murder as defined in K.S.A. 21-3439(a)(6) *was* committed in Johnson County, Kansas, on or about the twenty-fourth day of October, 1995. That is Count I of the Amended Complaint. There is probable cause to believe that the defendant in this case committed that crime, and she is therefore bound over under Count I." (This was the charge of killing Kelly.)

Debora allowed no emotion to cross her face as she heard she would be tried for murder. Ellen, however, looked stricken. She had promised Lissa that she would take care of her mother; a murder trial meant this would be increasingly more difficult.

There was more. Judge Ruddick also found probable cause to try Debora on four other charges: a second charge of capital murder, (for killing Tim) and charges of aggravated arson, attempted murder, and attempted capital murder. The State would now have to prove to a jury of Debora's peers that she had deliberately set fire to her own house, thus killing two of her children, and attempting to kill a third—and that she had meant to kill her husband with poison.

Judge Ruddick had done his best to keep potential jurors from being prejudiced by hearing or reading everything that had been presented in the preliminary hearing. But there was no way of knowing in February who might receive a jury summons in June or July. The public had not heard Debora's voice or seen her alternately blasé and furious image on the videotape recorded the morning of the fire in the Prairie Village police station. Judge Ruddick had not prevented reporters from printing or repeating those phrases they had captured in their notes, but without the sound of Debora's voice, and her facial expressions, they would not be nearly as prejudicial as the tape itself.

Judge Ruddick said he would delay his decision about whether there would be separate trials—one for murder by arson, another for attempted murder by poisoning. Morrison was not prepared to say whether he would seek the death penalty if the defendant were found guilty.

Ellen Ryan rose from her seat at the defense table and asked Judge Ruddick to allow her to withdraw as a defense attorney. "I am Dr. Green's divorce attorney. I am not her criminal counsel. I have not signed off on any of the pleadings. But in order to be available to testify . . . I would request that I be allowed to officially withdraw from Dr. Green's case, the criminal part of the case, today. I have discussed this with my client and she is in agreement with that."

Judge Ruddick granted Ellen's request but advised her that she would remain subject to the gag order that bound all the attorneys.

Debora Green would be arraigned in one week, on February 8, 1996. If all went smoothly, her trial would take place in the hot summer of 1996. Those in the gallery who had stayed for the last motions straggled out of the Johnson County Courthouse into a depressing, frigid dusk. It was six degrees above zero, and summer seemed years away.

Chapter 40

Tony Rizzo, who covered high-profile cases in Johnson County for the Kansas City *Star*, commented on how the feeling of electricity vanished overnight in the courthouse. By Friday, February 2, 1996, those who had come to the preliminary hearing had scattered; some had flown home to one coast or another, and Kansas City residents who were curious about the case no longer had to rise early and drive over icy streets to Olathe. Court TV and *A Current Affair* had moved on to other sensational stories. However, courthouse habitués knew this was only the calm before the storm. "We can relax for about twenty-four hours," one courthouse employee commented to Rizzo, "and then we have to start getting ready for the next step."

Paul Morrison characterized the defense's plan to blame the arson fire on Tim as "obscene," as "character assassination." Tim's father felt the same way. "Tim was a strong-minded kid," Mike said through tears, "but I don't believe he would ever do those things. The defense exaggerated the situation. I don't want people to believe that about Tim, and I want them to understand that I loved him and we were getting along much better at the time of the fire."

It was hard enough on Mike to lose two of his children, without having people who had not been inside his home declare him the kind of father a son wanted to kill. It was not Tim who had brought him the plates of food that made him ill; it was Debora. And it was Debora who offered him the cup of cappuccino at the soccer match, insisting he drink it lest he hurt Tim's feelings. Mike knew who had poisoned him, and it had not been his dead son.

One authority who grew angry at the defense's insistence that Tim had not only poisoned his father but set the fire he himself died in was Jeff Hudson, the Shawnee fire marshal. "That fire didn't start anyplace but in the south end of the main floor—in or near the master bedroom," he explained, once again. "There was simply too much damage on the main floor. Fire burns up. Tim could not have set it on the first floor and made it back upstairs to his bedroom. It's impossible."

Conversely, Hudson said, if Tim had poured accelerant throughout the house and up the stairs, then lit it from the top of the stairs, the fire would have done more damage to the children's upstairs bedrooms. But Hudson would stake his reputation on it: that had not happened. The fire that killed Tim came, he said, from the blazing living room directly beneath his bedroom. The flames from the large pool of accelerant there had flared up high enough to burn away the floor of Tim's room completely, causing his bed, his furniture, and Tim himself to fall down into the living room.

Debora was once more shut away from the world in the Johnson County Adult Detention Center. Ellen visited her often. She had begun as Debora's divorce attorney, and technically she still was, but Ellen was more: she was a caretaker. It was Ellen who had husbanded money for Debora from the marital estate, and Ellen who made out the checks to Debora's defense lawyers. Now, having been so visible in the television coverage of Debora's preliminary hearing, she began to get hate mail and angry phone calls. She was defending "that woman—the baby killer," and one sector of the Kansas City public was furious with her.

"Then I had calls from businesswomen who had known Deb and they said she was innocent—that she was being set up," Ellen said. "Associates of mine said I was risking my reputation as a lawyer by continuing to be concerned about Debora. Even my children were being teased at school. The teachers were asking if I wasn't spending too much time on the case, and had I considered what it was doing to my children? Of course, they would never say that to a *male* lawyer. . . .

"I finally sat my children down and told them that I was helping a woman that a lot of people didn't like, but that I had always tried to find the truth—and that's what I was doing. They told me that I should keep on until I found out the truth."

Surprisingly, Ellen's children grew more attached to Debora from talking to her on the phone. She often called Ellen's home in the evening now. "It was like the boys who had been Tim's friends," Ellen said. "They hugged Debora at the funeral; they really liked her. They and my own children told me, 'You have to help that mom.'"

While she had always had difficulty establishing adult friendships, no one disputed that Debora was able to establish warm relationships with children. Youngsters who had grown fond of Tim and Kelly's easygoing mom still refused to believe that she could have killed them.

Within weeks of the preliminary hearing, Paul Morrison had decided to ask for the death penalty if Debora should be convicted at trial. It was a risky decision, but one that he could not, in good conscience, avoid. Under Kansas statute, certain criteria must be met before the State can seek the death penalty. A capital murder has to be intentional and premeditated, *and* has to include one of several additional elements: A single act must have had more than one victim. Or a "common scheme" must have resulted in the deaths of more than two victims. Or the killing must have been committed as part of a kidnapping with intent to hold the victim for ransom, or a contract killing, or committed in the course of—or subsequent to—an act of rape or sodomy of the victim. Or, lastly, the killing must have been committed in the kidnapping of a child under the age of fourteen with the intent to commit a sex offense.

Morrison believed that Debora had intentionally set the fire that killed her children; and she also qualified for a death sentence because there was more than one victim. However, he did not make his decision alone. "Most big decisions up here," he explained, including his entire office in a sweep of his hand, "we usually 'staff.' With this case, we did some whole-office staffing; we had about twenty people in here. A lot of staff lawyers that might not necessarily have a whole lot of experience were great for bouncing things off of—to see what they thought."

Morrison was lucky enough to have several excellent trial lawyers on his staff. "A half a dozen *superb* trial lawyers," he said. "We run decisions by them. . . . On the death penalty, we talked about it a lot with them.

"Finally," Morrison said, "for me, the decision came down that if you were not going to do it on this case, I don't think you could do it on any case. You really work hard to be fair and try to treat everybody equal. And I just thought, 'If we don't do this, what are we going to do five years from now when some black guy or some Hispanic woman walks in and kills three or four people in an armed robbery?' What are you going to say that's different about them from Debora Green? In fact, you could almost argue that someone like Debora who's had all the advantages—apparently—makes it even more inexcusable."

If Debora's jury should find her guilty of deliberately setting fire to a house in which her children were sleeping, of
deliberately poisoning her own husband, no one could
argue these were not heinous crimes. It should not matter
that she was a physician, a wealthy woman who lived in a
posh suburb.

"Plus," Morrison said, his face turning sadly reflective, "I
went to those posts, and I remember—when you see that
little girl, who was just the cutest little girl in the world,
laying there on that autopsy table, because Mom wants to
get back at Dad. That adds a little fuel to the fire, too, on a
personal level. . . ."

And district attorneys, for all the bleak side of the population that they must deal with, are human, too. Morrison's
children were the same ages as Debora and Mike's children;
he could not help but feel this case on a personal level.

With the death penalty hanging over Debora, both Dennis
Moore and Ellen Ryan had the same thought: Sean O'Brien.
O'Brien was an attorney with the Missouri Capital
Punishment Resource Center, a gentle man opposed to the
death penalty. His philosophy and his career were devoted
to the premise that capital punishment should not exist in
America. Ellen went to see O'Brien, whom she remembered
from law school.

"I spent a long time talking with him," she said. "I
explained to him that I didn't know what had happened,
that I had all these rumors that kept coming up, that I had
a client who couldn't participate in telling me what happened, and that I didn't know what to do to save her. But I
told him too, 'If she did it, I want to know that she did it'—
because I promised her I would find out and tell her if I
thought she did it."

O'Brien agreed to join the defense team. He started
hiring investigators and suggested bringing in Bev
Marchbank, a skilled mediator. The criminal defense

attorneys began meeting every Monday to discuss what they would do, what motions they would file.

Debora knew she was going to be tried for murder. She also knew that she would be facing the death penalty. No matter that the death penalty had not been carried out for decades in Kansas; she was frightened. Her parents made plans to return to Texas; there was no longer any reason to help her keep an apartment, and they hated the cold weather and were nervous driving on icy roads.

As she waited for trial, Debora grew very quiet and seemingly very depressed. "She became almost catatonic," Ellen recalled. "She could not initiate conversations. That was when her mother became concerned and I became concerned."

Debora seemed to respond better to women; the male part of her defense team overpowered her. Alone in jail, she became convinced that her attorneys were not working hard enough. They didn't come to see her often enough, and when they did, she felt they didn't pay attention to what she had to say. She was not used to dealing with their brusque, businesslike manner. They were trying to protect her from the death penalty; they were not there to make small talk or to comfort her. She had problems dealing with men anyway, and Dennis Moore and Kevin Moriarty couldn't be handled the way she had treated Mike and the detectives, Rod Smith and Greg Burnetta. She could not shout and swear at them or stamp her feet. They stood between her and the death chamber.

By court order, Debora's phone conversations with Lissa had to be monitored by a psychiatrist. But on February 10, when the monitor, Dr. Rutger Weiss,* was out of town, Debora managed to get a call through. And afterward Lissa was once again preoccupied with what was going to happen to her mother. Debora had urged her not to tell anyone that they had talked. Either she was the "confused, out-of-it child" whom Ellen perceived most of the time, or she was a scheming murderess who didn't care that she was upsetting Lissa once again, giving her mixed signals.

Or perhaps she was both.

Trying to cheer Debora up, Marchbank spent time with her, while Ellen tried to double her visits. As soon as she felt that someone was paying attention to her, Debora started to perk up. She was taking antidepressants; the doses were adjusted, too. She still claimed that she had no memory of the night of the fire, that she could not have torched her own house. And she certainly had not poisoned Mike.

The defense hired Marilyn Hutchinson, a psychologist, to examine Debora, administer some personality tests, and give the lawyers some idea of the woman they were representing. Debora enjoyed Hutchinson's long visits.

Moore and Moriarty had pursued a number of avenues in Debora's defense. During the preliminary hearing, Moore had kept Celeste Walker on hand as a possible witness. Moore let it slip that he was thinking of having John Walker's body exhumed for yet another autopsy. "I was a murder suspect again," Celeste said bitterly. "John's picture was back on the news. People who didn't even know us were wondering if there was some conspiracy between Mike and me to wipe out everyone who was in our way. It was terrible for John's mother—for his brothers."

In the end, neither the defense team nor Paul Morrison chose to call Celeste. She was the "other woman," but there was absolutely no indication that she had any guilty knowledge of either her husband's death or the killing of Mike's children.

Now, the defense team pursued the possibility that Debora herself had no guilty knowledge about the fire. They hired a fire chief in North Kansas City, who said that the rumor was that there was *no* trace of accelerants in the house on Canterbury Court. There had been pour marks, yes—but according to the defense's first arson expert, a lot of different things could cause pour marks. He did not feel the State had enough evidence to prove arson.

Despite Debora's protestations of flawed memory, some facts disturbed her defense team. There was the matter of her hair. According to the Formans, her hair had been wet when she ran to pound on their door and beg them to call "111." If she had gone to bed and was sound asleep when the fire alarm sounded, why would her hair have been wet? Was it possible that she had accidentally set her own hair on fire? Moore had been present when Rod Smith served the search warrant on Debora to obtain clippings of her hair. The hair had showed singe marks—a common finding in people who set accelerant-enhanced fires—and Debora had had two haircuts in the week following the deadly conflagration.

Physical evidence—which can often free a defendant— did not look promising for Debora. Her lawyers wanted to know the truth. If they knew the truth, they could work with it; if she continued to stonewall them with a failed memory, they would be defending her with one hand tied behind their backs. But when they were forceful with Debora, she fell silent. When they told her time was growing short, she didn't speak. The insanity defense works in the movies; it rarely flies in real life. Debora was happiest talking to Ellen and Bev and Marilyn, but her happiness wasn't the goal of her male lawyers.

Ellen, the most patient and understanding of all, could see that something had to be done. There had to be some way of confronting Debora with the emerging truth. If they did that, she might go to prison for the rest of her life, but she wouldn't go to the death chamber.

Chapter 41

Mike and Lissa were living together again, in an apartment instead of a huge house. They spent a lot of time together. When Kelly's classmates dedicated "Kelly's Corner" in their

classroom, her father and sister were the special guests. The
children had designed ceramic tiles with their drawings of
all the things that Kelly had loved. There was Kelly swinging,
Kelly with Boomer, Kelly with her friends, a tiny pair of pink
ballerina shoes like the ones Kelly would have worn as an
angel in *The Nutcracker Suite*, hearts, sunshine, clouds and
stars. Her classmates could sit in that quiet corner of the
classroom, among the memories of Kelly, and read. She had
loved to read.

Mike and Lissa took a vacation trip to Mexico that March,
just the two of them. One seriously ill man and one little
girl. They were all that was left of the family that had been.
Even if Debora were acquitted of the charges against her,
she and Mike and Lissa would never again live together.
Mike and Lissa could not help but think of other trips they
had taken to Mexico, with Kelly and Tim along.

Lissa was still fiercely loyal to her mother—she had not
told even her father that Debora had made forbidden
phone calls to her from jail. Ellen had then explained to
Lissa that she must never lie to her dad, and the girl had
promised that she wouldn't. But she still worried about her
mother.

Slowly, tentatively, Lissa and Mike began to form a real
father-and-daughter relationship—something they had never
been able to enjoy before. Debora had always made Mike out
to be a villain; the children believed what their mother told
them. And it was true that he had been away at work from
before breakfast until after supper. He *had* been uncomfortable in his own home, waiting for another storm to erupt.

And he *had* been unfaithful to Debora, although only
after a dozen years of marriage had not brought them any
closer together than they had been on their wedding night,
when she chose to read a book rather than make love. Still,
no reasonable wife and mother would have pitted her children against their father. But now, beginning to doubt her
mother's many horror stories about him, Lissa wanted to
feel closer to her father and to trust him.

Lissa did not like Celeste Walker. That was predictable. The transition had been too fast, and Debora had called Celeste all manner of obscene names, blaming her for the breakup of their family. Mike's mother didn't care for Celeste either, something Lissa was aware of. So asking Celeste along on the trip to Mexico would have been a bad idea.

Celeste understood, just as she understood that Mike was having a rough time emotionally in late February and early March. He faced the prospect of another operation on his brain; he was having headaches and felt unwell. Neither of them had been anywhere near ready for a new relationship, and that became more apparent as the immediate stress of Debora's preliminary hearing receded. The reality that Tim and Kelly were gone sank in. The horror of the past five months would not go away soon. It would never go away completely.

Celeste's boys, too, had problems dealing with the upheaval in their family. Initially, Celeste and Mike had been drawn together to escape their unhappy marriages. But Mike, at least, realized that their attraction for each other might not survive all the tragedies that had scarred their lives. They shared many interests, but whether that would be enough to keep them together was questionable. There were so many ghosts that haunted them.

Celeste had begun to worry about their relationship in February after the hearing. "Mike had a lot of cards from people all the time. These were people from his past—some of them women friends," she said, "and he called them back and I thought that was really weird. He even went out to lunch with one of them. He told me all this stuff about going to lunch with her. And some secretary of some department in Cincinnati. He called her after she sent him a sympathy card. And he told me all about her life and that she was attractive."

Whether his response was "weird" or not, Mike wasn't keeping secrets from Celeste. But she reacted to his conversations about women friends with suspicion and insecurity. Although he was still calling Celeste at least four times a day, she grew anxious. She felt he was using what she called "his doctorness" to attract other women. Perhaps she shouldn't have felt inadequate—but she had been married to John all those years and been unable to make him happy. She needed a man who needed her, who loved her and made her feel attractive, and she cringed when she heard about any other woman in Mike's life, even if their relationship was platonic.

The trip to Mexico had helped solidify Mike's relationship with Lissa. She enjoyed living with her dad. She had friends who lived close by; she had her ballet lessons; and everyone in her extended family was prepared to help shield her from the scandal of the upcoming trial. She had no further personal contact with her mother, who was waiting in jail as her attorneys planned her defense. And Debora continued to see Marilyn Hutchinson, who was evaluating her competence to participate in her own defense at a trial.

In another hearing, on Thursday, March 7, 1996, Dennis Moore discussed one of his main concerns: the publicity fiesta he expected at any further pretrial hearings as well as at the trial itself. The amount of coverage the preliminary hearing drew left him troubled, he asserted. Even though Moore had given innumerable interviews to the press and television, he now said there could be no justice with cameras and microphones poking into every aspect of Debora Green's legal proceedings. The defense asked that all cameras, still and videotape, be banned from the courtroom. They also wanted to limit public access to legal documents.

Under Kansas statute, Judge Ruddick was allowed wide discretion in deciding what he would permit to be photographed in his courtroom. As in the preliminary hearing, witnesses had the right to request that they not be photographed. Moore was worried that jurors—yet to be selected—might be exposed to further pretrial arguments. During the actual trial, jurors could be sequestered; their reading and television watching would be censored. But the chances were that they might not be sequestered. Hotel rooms and meals for a jury in a long trial can be a tremendous expense for a county. But, in the meantime, no one knew who the jurors might be. The pool would be drawn from registered voters in Johnson County, any of whom might be watching pretrial hearing coverage on the evening news.

Paul Morrison said that media coverage of future hearings would undoubtedly be heavy whether cameras were allowed or not. "I think the public has the right to know what's going on in the courtroom," he argued.

Moore and Moriarty also requested a face-to-face meeting with Lissa Farrar, without the prosecuting team being present. "We just want the same opportunity as the State," Moore said. But Morrison said that he had not talked to Lissa either. The only interview the investigation team had had with Lissa was the one which took place on October 25, when she talked with several members of the task force. "Everyone has been careful to keep her out of this as much as possible," Morrison said.

His real concern was that if the defense had a meeting with Lissa, Debora might be present. He did not want that kind of pressure put on a little girl. His motion objecting to the defense's request included a letter from Dr. Weiss, who recommended against Lissa being interviewed by either the State or the Defense: "It would compromise her present condition and place her in the midst of becoming either the savior of her mother or an important witness to her demise."

Under the law, the defense team could not compel any witness to speak with them before trial. Judge Ruddick denied Moore's request.

Judge Ruddick, having read two confidential reports by

psychologists, also ruled that Debora Green was competent to stand trial. Moore had requested the mental evaluations to be sure she comprehended the charges against her and would be able to participate in her own defense; he said that his defense team was untroubled by the judge's decision.

Judge Ruddick postponed Debora's arraignment until March 28 and denied the defense request to lower her bail from $3 million to $500,000. She would remain in jail where she had been for three and a half months. The judge let stand an order allowing television cameras in the courtroom and permitting the public to view legal documents. But he said he might approve a defense proposal to seal certain information in the case at some time in the future.

On March 13, Judge Ruddick handed down another decision. He refused the defense motion to try Debora separately on each set of charges. He said he did not see how the arson and murder cases could be presented to a jury without also presenting evidence concerning the alleged ricin poisoning of Michael Farrar. "It is clear, based on the evidence presented at preliminary examination, that evidence related to the various offenses will, at the very least, overlap," Ruddick wrote. And that was true. Several dozen of the State's witnesses were prepared to testify on both the arson and poisoning charges.

Judge Ruddick also said that there was a very "real possibility" that a jury would have to be sequestered. His jury trial docket was jammed, with thirty other cases that needed to be heard over the next three months. If Debora were to be granted two separate trials, justice in Johnson County would have to wait on her.

Mike's health remained fragile in the spring of 1996. His most recent angiogram showed that the aneurysm in his brain was not improving. It could be likened to a bulging, worn spot on a tire, foreshadowing a blowout. The sepsis that had raced through his body after the repeated ricin poisonings had so weakened the blood vessels in the right frontal portion of his brain that he was a prime candidate for a stroke unless he had very delicate surgery. The weakened vessel could break at any moment and drown his brain with blood.

Dr. Reintges did extensive research into Mike's chances of surviving brain aneurysm surgery. After looking all over America for the best neurosurgeon available and talking to neurosurgeons and neuroradiologists on both coasts and in the heartland, Reintges told Mike that he thought his best chance would be with Dr. Charles Wilson of the University of California Medical School in San Francisco.

Wilson, arguably the best brain surgeon in the country, was a man whose life revolved around the operating room and his solitary jogs through the hills of the Golden Gate city. Featured on a number of medical documentaries, "Charlie" Wilson was revered by fledgling neurosurgeons, whose dream was to study on his service. He could work inside the human brain with an incredibly deft touch. Coincidentally, the doctor who needed this risky surgery and the doctor who would perform it were both Missouri boys. "The first thing Dr. Wilson told me," Mike recalled, "was he was from Neosho, Missouri."

Arrangements were made for Mike to undergo brain surgery in San Francisco on April 12, 1996. Celeste would accompany him to California, and Stella and Mike Wilson, two of Mike's closest friends, would come down from Portland, Oregon, to lend their support during this arduous time. If Mike didn't make it, he didn't want Celeste to be alone in a strange city. If he did survive, his recovery would take a while and friends would help.

Sometimes Celeste felt as if Mike kept her around because she was a nurse and he was so ill. But those thoughts only taunted her during those periods when she was filled with doubt about their relationship. They still saw each other often and talked on the phone several times a day.

They both dreaded Debora's trial. Until that was over, no one connected to this case could breathe easy.

Chapter 42

There wasn't much news in the papers about Debora Green anymore. Everyone who would be involved in her trial was gearing up, but quietly. Paul Morrison contracted to have a computerized multidimensional model constructed of the house on Canterbury Court. The model could be turned and opened up onscreen so that a jury could truly "see" the house. This up-to-the-minute exhibit of trial technology would even "catch fire" so that the jurors could follow the precise progression from the first match struck, to the inferno the death scene had become. Morrison had his witnesses ready. To say he was looking forward to the trial would probably be an exaggeration; it would mean weeks, perhaps months, of intense courtroom work. And yet the case was so convoluted and challenging that he prepared for it eagerly, as an athlete would prepare for a marathon. He suspected that the Debora Green case would be remembered in Kansas just as the Grissom trial was, and long before that, the Clutter family massacre in Garden City, which Truman Capote had turned into the classic *In Cold Blood*.

Dennis Moore, Kevin Moriarty, and Sean O'Brien worked feverishly to save Debora from the death penalty. This would be a go-for-broke trial for the defendant. If she was convicted, there was every indication that one day in the next few years, Debora would be executed. They might proceed with the "Tim did it" defense, but the trial balloon they had sent up at the preliminary hearing had brought the defense team more disapproval than anything else. Johnson County citizens interviewed by the press had been frank in saying they found that line of defense distasteful—it wasn't fair to blame everything on a kid who could no longer speak for himself. Moreover, they criticized even the tremendously popular former D.A. Dennis Moore for doing so. If the man on the street felt uneasy about blaming a fire on a boy who had died in the flames, what would a jury think?

More than anything else, the defense team wanted to hear the true story of the night of October 23–24 from Debora herself. Reassured now that she was competent and rational, Moore and Moriarty pushed harder to get her to talk to them. Although Debora seemed cowed by Moriarty, his steady, pounding questions elicited some information from her. He made it difficult for her to draw into herself and shut her attorneys out.

Debora was emotionally dependent on Ellen Ryan. Ellen had a compassionate heart and she felt sorry for Debora, but she still wanted to know the facts. Whether she meant it or not, Debora had asked Ellen over and over again to find out the truth. Now, with each new piece of information the defense attorneys uncovered either through discovery or through their own investigators, Ellen sensed trouble. There was a tornado brewing and Debora was caught in its eye. The intelligence coming in did nothing to draw guilt away from her, and much to incriminate her further.

"I think it was on a Thursday when our arson expert's report came in," Ellen recalled. "Sean called me and said, 'Our expert says there was not as much accelerant used as they said—but there was *some* accelerant used.'"

That was not good news.

A short while later, Sean O'Brien called Ellen again and asked her to go with him to the jail. "I think you'd better come out. The guys are there now." "The guys" were Dennis Moore and Kevin Moriarty.

O'Brien picked Ellen up. On the drive south to Olathe, he told her about the damning evidence found on Debora's robe. She had been wearing only a nightgown when she escaped through the master bedroom door, but the arson team had found her robe, with a semicircular hole burned in it, on the floor of the master bathroom. It lay in a jumble in front of the vanity sink where there had been a fire in one drawer. The hole in the robe could not have been made by flaming objects falling from the ceiling in the bathroom, because the fabric was folded over, the exposed fabric was not burned, and the scorched half-moon was *inside* the crumpled robe. The fire in the bathroom drawer had been one of the "unconnected" fires the arson investigators for the State had located in the house.

"Okay, it's time," Ellen said to O'Brien. "I know what happened now."

When they arrived at the Johnson County Adult Detention Center, they found Debora in an interview room with Moore and Moriarty. In their discussions of Debora's defense, the thought had gradually emerged that going to trial might not be a good idea. Now, given the newest incriminating physical evidence, her attorneys were urging her to plead no contest instead of risking a conviction at trial and a sentence of death. A plea bargain might save her life.

"Kevin was hammering on her hard," Ellen remembered. "He can be like a harsh Hallmark card when he needs to be."

Debora sat there, silent; she was the frightened Deb— not the witty, charming Deb, not the in-charge physician Deb, and not the raging harridan Deb. Some corner had been turned, but she was not yet ready to commit to a plan.

Now, Ellen saw that Debora was listening intently to Moriarty's argument that she had to tell them the truth. "She was listening but she wasn't saying anything." Ellen moved close to Debora. "I touched her arm, and I said, 'Deb, you always asked me to find out what happened to your children. You told me that you wanted me to tell you if I thought you did it. Today,'"—Ellen paused before she said the words— "'today, I believe that *you* did that. I believe that *you* set the fire, Deb.'

Bitter Harvest   379

"She looked at me, and, finally, she said, 'Yes, Ellen—I set the fire.'"

"And I said, 'Tell me what happened. Tell me what you did.'"

But Debora insisted she had no clear memories. "She said, 'I don't know why I did that. You know I never meant to hurt my *children*. I was drinking and I can't remember anything. I was lying down on the bed and I went back to get the kids and there was a fire everywhere. I did not use accelerant. I didn't do it.'"

Debora was admitting that she had set the fire, but denying that she used accelerants. And they knew that she had used some flammable liquid to speed the flames along. But, again, she sought refuge in her insistence that she was extremely intoxicated and not responsible for her actions.

Still, she *was* talking, so Ellen asked her about the poisoning. "Deb," she said, "I've also suspected for a long time that you and Tim were involved together in this poisoning. What happened? And she said, 'You're right. Tim did it. Tim poisoned his dad. . . . Do we have to get that out? Do we have to let people know that happened?'"

Ellen had no problem with keeping that part of Debora's confession secret. It would make no difference in her sentence if she decided to plead guilty or take an *Alford* (no contest) plea. Of course, the suggestion that Tim was interested in fire and bombs and poison had already been raised in the preliminary hearing, so Debora's sudden protectiveness came rather late.

"Deb," Ellen said, "before you are a human, you are a mother. I've always believed you were a good mother. You have to try to survive now as a way to protect your daughter. And you have to try to survive to help Lissa put together—when she's an adult—what happened in this family. There may be nobody else who will help her put that all together as much as you will."

"Okay," Debora said. "I'm going to do it [plead no contest]."

Caught in what were either her lies, or her delusions, or
her deliberate plans to kill, depending on who was evaluating her, Debora began to list aloud the things that she could
never again do if she went to prison. They were all about
milestones in Lissa's life. It was as if she now existed only
through the little girl she had almost killed.

"She was very sad," Ellen remembered. "She said, 'If I
could just one time before I die be able to watch my daughter dance again. Or be able to be there at her wedding. If I
could just be there for that . . .'"

Ellen left the room and found a quiet spot in the courthouse square. Quite possibly, she had become far too
emotionally involved in this case; hearing what she had just
heard was very painful to her. She wanted to be alone and to
think about what had just happened. If anyone had wished
for Debora to somehow be proved innocent, it was Ellen.
Her whole career has been dedicated to helping families
and children. "This was such a horrible tragedy for that
whole family," she would say later. "And it reflected the cul-
tural expectations that we have about relationships that
don't make sense. I was so angry and frustrated that we have
all these mechanisms in place to help families in trouble and
they didn't get used."

Unaware that Debora had admitted to her attorneys that
she had set the fire that destroyed their home and killed two
of their children, Mike, accompanied by Celeste, flew to San
Francisco for his brain surgery. They went a few days early,
and to judge by the snapshots they took, they might have
been any couple on a romantic vacation. With Mike's
friends from Oregon, they visited Fisherman's Wharf, took
the cable cars, and explored Golden Gate Park.

It was a bittersweet time. They could not be sure that
Mike would survive the surgery. If the aneurysm burst
before it was sealed off, Mike might die on the operating
table. And he was going into surgery in a weakened condi-

tion. Although he had put on some weight, he still carried the afteraffects of the ricin poisonings within his body. Mike would need heart surgery too. But the damage to his heart was not as immediate a threat as the aneurysm.

Mike was pragmatic about his marathon surgeries. He had studied up on all the procedures and chosen the surgeons he trusted most; he evinced little anxiety. It was harder for Celeste. She didn't want to lose him. And by the time they were in San Francisco, she felt that she might lose Mike in either of two ways. As a nurse, she knew the odds of surviving brain surgery for an aneurysm; they weren't great. As a woman, she still sensed that he was pulling back. But the second fear was somewhat assuaged by their carefree days in California before the surgery. She liked Mike's friends from Portland; the four of them had a good time together. And she began to feel that once they weathered Mike's surgeries, once the trial was behind them, she and Mike really would get married.

She tried to ignore the warning signs. She knew Lissa didn't like her and neither did Velma Farrar. Her own sons were angry and depressed; their father had been dead less than eight months. Celeste wanted so much to be happy, and she loved Mike; she remembered his telling her she was "the love of his life." She didn't believe that kind of love could ever disappear. And in San Francisco, in the spring of 1996, it seemed that she had been right.

But Mike had yet to realize that promises are not to be made lightly. Living with Debora, he had often been coerced into making promises to keep the peace. He had promised his children that he would stay with their mother always, and that the reconciliation after the first fire would last. He had promised Celeste that theirs was more than a transient affair, that he would always love her. He may well have meant it at the time, unaware of what wildly seesawing emotions could follow the numbness of almost unbearable tragedy.

Chapter 43

Ellen Ryan had characterized Debora as a "baby," dependent and confused. Even after the confession, she still felt that Debora was a good mother, in the sense that she truly loved her children. But Ellen, who *was* a good mother, may have become so caught up in Debora's case that her perception was clouded—or, rather, divided—so that she could see the love there even though she knew what Debora had done to her children.

During the investigation into the murderous fire on Canterbury Court, a stray mother cat in Brooklyn, New York, made every wire service when she returned time after time to a burning parking garage to save her kittens. Although badly burned and temporarily blinded, the cat did not give up until she had her kittens safely across the street from the building. One observer recalled that he saw her touch each kitten with her nose. "She was counting them," he told reporters in awe. "She couldn't see them but she was counting to make sure they were all out."

To many observers of the Debora Green case, that cat was a good mother, and she was not.

The task force investigators, working with Paul Morrison's office, had fanned out as far as Ohio to learn as much as they could about Mike and Debora, and particularly about Debora's past behavior. One of the people they spoke to was Norma Wallace, a kind, grandmotherly Jamaican who lived in Ohio. She had worked as a nanny for Mike and Debora in the early years of their marriage, when Tim and Lissa were babies. "She told us," Morrison recalled, "that Debora had confided in her that she didn't want kids; she never had—she was doing it for Mike."

Norma Wallace said she had seen Debora abuse Tim both

mentally and physically. With that information, the picture of Debora as a caring, devoted mother in the early years of her marriage was seriously smudged.

More than one former nanny said that when Debora had her medical practice, she worked long hours and, when she came home, often went right to her room with a book instead of visiting with the children. The one consistent interest, passion, and obsession of her life was books—even on the night of the fire. While people had often disappointed her, books never did. She was seldom without a stack of ten or more unread library books, a hedge against the reality she could not face.

Paul Morrison was revving up for the trial. Aware that his case was largely circumstantial, he did not expect that Dennis Moore and Kevin Moriarty would approach him about a plea bargain. The State's case was coming together, each aspect dovetailing. Paul Morrison was ready. Rick Guinn was ready. But then Moore, Moriarty, and O'Brien notified the district attorney's office that they wanted to talk.

The Kansas City public knew nothing at all about the discussions being held behind closed doors, nor did the press.

On April 12, 1996, Mike spent most of the day in surgery and the rest of the time unconscious. With strange synchronicity, he had been hospitalized at almost every major turn in the case. He was in the hospital when John Walker committed suicide, and his first Groshong tube surgery took place on November 22, the day Debora was arrested on murder and arson charges. On April 13, while Mike struggled back to consciousness in San Francisco, negotiations that would shock the Kansas City area took place back home.

"I woke up to a call from Paul Morrison," Mike said. "He was calling me to tell me that Debora was ready to plead no contest to the arson charges, but not to the poison charges. Paul said, 'That's not good enough for me, Mike, but I wanted to be sure you agreed.'"

Mike did agree. He urged Morrison to go for a plea on all the charges Debora faced. "Then he called me on Monday night, April 15," Mike said. "He said their [the defense's] whole case had broken down."

Morrison asked Mike to be in the courtroom when Debora entered her no-contest pleas. He also wanted Mike to appear at a press conference afterward. "Can you do it?"

"I'll be there," Mike answered, although he had undergone brain surgery only three days earlier. He knew that the public was crying out for Debora to be tried and to receive the death penalty for what she had done to her own children. Morrison's decision to accept a plea bargain would not sit well with popular opinion. Mike prepared to fly back to Kansas to back up Morrison on his stance.

There would be no trial now, and that was a tremendous relief for Mike and Celeste. It was finally over.

On April 17, Case Number 95 CR 5387, *The State of Kansas* versus *Debora J. Green*, was about to be adjudicated. And there would be no need now for any more rulings about cameras, or crowd control, or jury selection. What had begun with headlines would end in an hour.

Judge Ruddick looked at Dennis Moore. "I am advised by counsel that this matter is now for plea," he said. "Is that correct?"

"That is correct, Your Honor."

"Would one of you then state for the record the basis of any plea negotiations which are going to apply?"

Paul Morrison stepped forward. "Judge, I will. The negotiations are as follows: It's my understanding that the defendant today will enter a plea of no contest to all five counts of the Amended Complaint. Those counts are: Count I, the capital murder of Kelly Farrar; Count II, the capital murder of Timothy Farrar; Count III, aggravated arson; Count IV, attempted first-degree murder of Michael Farrar; and Count V, the attempted capital murder of Lissa Farrar.

"In exchange for this, Judge, the State agrees [that] at the time of the plea being entered, the State will withdraw its request for the death penalty in this case.

"Both parties will recommend that the defendant be sentenced to hard forty counts on Counts I and II, and in conformance with the sentencing guidelines on Counts III, IV, and V, and on the sentencing date, both parties will recommend to the Court that the Court sentence the defendant to those terms of confinement.

"Both parties will also recommend to the Court that those counts be run concurrent with one another so that the defendant will be serving a substantive hard forty sentence. . . ."

A "hard forty" in Kansas means just that. Debora Green would serve forty years in prison, with no possibility of parole. She was forty-five years old. If she lived that long, she would be in prison until she was eighty-five.

But she had escaped the death penalty.

It was necessary now for Debora herself to listen to Judge Ruddick read the counts against her. He asked her first whether she understood the terms of the plea bargain.

"Yes."

"In Count I," Judge Ruddick intoned, "on or about the twenty-fourth of October, 1995, in Prairie Village, Johnson County, Kansas, you did then and there unlawfully, feloniously, intentionally, and with premeditation kill a person, to wit: Kelly Farrar, and that the premeditated killing of Kelly Farrar and Timothy Farrar was a part of the same transaction. . . . This is a crime of capital murder and the sentence provided by law is life imprisonment. . . ."

It took Judge Ruddick a long time to read all the legal

language of each count. And somehow, the dry words of
the law were more terrible than soaring rhetoric. The names
sandwiched in between the "to wit"s and the "premeditated
killing"s were the people who had seemingly meant the
most to Debora. But she stood there, calmly, as Ruddick
read all of it—the fire setting, the "did place ricin, a poison,
in the food of Michael Farrar," and, finally, "to wit: set a fire
in a residence located at 7517 Canterbury Court, Prairie
Village, Johnson County, Kansas, in which Lissa Farrar was
sleeping, toward the perpetration of the crime of capital
murder . . ."

"Dr. Green," Judge Ruddick asked when he had finished,
"you understand both the nature of all these charges against
you and you understand the punishments which are provided by law?"

"Yes, I do."

Debora answered yes repeatedly as the judge explained
that she could still have a trial and asked if she had discussed all aspects of her case with her attorneys. Did she
understand that she had a continuing right to counsel?

"Yes."

"Have any promises or threats been made to you with
regard to this plea . . . ?"

"No."

"Are you presently under the influence of any sort of
drug? Are you taking anything that would affect your ability
to understand these proceedings?"

"I am taking Prozac, Desyrel, and Klonopin," Debora said.

". . . And do they affect your ability to understand what's
going on here in court?"

"No, sir."

Moore said that his client had read and understood the
allegations in the State's case and that the defense would
accept it for filing without its being read. "And we're willing
to—*not* to agree with all the evidence or the allegations in
that statement, but certainly understand that would be the
State's case."

Morrison wanted to read the State's case into the record, and Judge Ruddick agreed. The case had been wonderfully prepared; Morrison had dammed up each slightest chink in his arguments. He had witnesses waiting all over America who were prepared to testify. Now, he read aloud the summary of the State's case against Dr. Debora J. Green. It did not take that long; the bare bones of the case could be summed up in twenty-three double-spaced pages. But those twenty-three pages described vengeful, deliberate acts of planned cruelty and the evidence that would point to Debora Green as the perpetrator.

Once again, Morrison recounted the significant events in the marriage of Dr. Michael Farrar and Dr. Debora Green; the births of Tim, Lissa, and Kelly; the homes they had shared; the breakups and reconciliations. He included the danger signals, the crimes, the attempts to cover up. He listed the dates of Debora's drunken rages and her voluntary commitment, Mike's illnesses and hospitalizations, and, finally, the date of the fire on Canterbury Court. It was a hellish chronology.

Morrison also read the results of the arson investigators' probe. The fire that killed Tim and Kelly Farrar had been deliberately set on the main floor by someone who had poured out "substantial amounts" of accelerants. They had also found other small fires which were far removed from the main-floor holocaust. "Investigators also determined," he said, "that the accelerant pour pattern and burns *inside* the doorway of Green's room are absolutely inconsistent with her statement as to how the fire occurred. . . .

"Criminalist William Chapin of the Johnson County Crime Laboratory, with the aid of experts from the federal Bureau of Alcohol, Tobacco and Firearms . . . was able to discern at least two samples of isoparaffins . . . commonly used in charcoal lighter fluid . . . from the debris. Investigators found at least one empty lighter fluid bottle in the garage area at the fire scene. Arson investigators also believed that more than one accelerant was used to fuel the fire." And there was also a "definite amount" of singeing of Debora Green's hair.

Had Debora attempted to save her children? Morrison said no. "Investigators noted that except for when Lissa Farrar had escaped through her window and was out over the roof in full view of everyone, Debora Green made *no* attempt whatsoever at any time to rescue any of the children from the house.

"During the interview with Prairie Village police officers after the fire, Debora Green waited until approximately one hour into the interview to ask the officers if her children were alive or dead. During the early part of the interview, she appeared to be casual and almost nonchalant about the fire, expressing little emotion. When officers finally told Debora Green that two of her children had perished in the fire, she appeared to grieve for approximately one minute, then became angry and demanding with the officers."

Debora had been reading a book minutes before the fire began. "Analysis at the arson scene resulted in a book being found by Debora Green's bed," Morrison read. "The book was entitled *Necessary Lies*. The plot in *Necessary Lies* involves several children burning to death in a house fire which was intentionally set. The female protagonist in the book is accused of the crime. . . ."

Morrison ended with the information that shortly before the fire, Debora checked out of the Corinth Library, in Prairie Village, and the Johnson County Library several books that "dealt with the subject of intrafamilial homicide."

It was a grim recitation of damning circumstantial and physical evidence. "Judge," Morrison said, "that would be the bulk of the evidence that we would present in trial."

Judge Ruddick asked Debora if she understood the summary of facts just made.

"Judge," Dennis Moore answered for her, "she has heard—she read, as I've indicated before, the entire statement that Mr. Morrison just took several minutes to read here in court. She understands that would be the State's evidence were this case to go to trial. I would advise the Court that we would certainly challenge some of that evidence, but we understand that would be the State's evidence. Is that correct, Debora?"

"That would be—" she said quietly. "It's correct."

Dr. Debora Green, who had been a mystery woman to the public and the press, seemed fully competent now as she acknowledged that she understood the State's case against her. She asked that she be allowed to read a statement.

"After counseling with my attorneys," she began, "I plead no contest to all charges. I understand the court will find me guilty on all counts. I am aware that the State can produce substantial evidence that I set the fire that caused the death of my children. My attorneys are ready, willing, and able to present evidence that I was not in control of myself when Tim and Kelly died."

The courtroom was very quiet. Each word dropped like a stone into water, sinking to the bottom. Debora was very thin, her complexion sallow from months behind bars; the pinkish sweater she had worn to her preliminary hearing in January hung on her now.

"However true that may be," she continued, "defending myself at trial on these charges would only compound the suffering of my family, and my daughter, Lissa. I love my family very much. I never meant to harm my children, but I accept the fact that I will be punished harshly. I believe that it is best to end this now, so that we can begin to heal from our horrible loss."

Debora had not actually admitted her guilt; she had only acknowledged that she believed there was enough evidence against her to result in a conviction.

"Dr. Green," Judge Ruddick asked, "is your plea of no contest entered as to each and every count of the Amended Complaint, which is five counts?"

"Yes," she said softly.

"Dr. Green, I accept your plea as to each count. I find that plea to be voluntarily entered. I find that plea to be intelligently given and I find a factual basis exists for your plea on each count. I therefore find you guilty on each count of the Amended Complaint."

And then it was over. Although formal sentencing would come next, the murder and arson and poisoning trial of Debora Green had shrunk to this short hearing.

The man who had been her husband for so many years watched silently from the back of the courtroom, his head swathed in bandages, his right eye purple and swollen. Although Mike was only five days past his surgery, he had flown home so that he might be present to hear Debora's plea. Beyond keeping his promise to Paul Morrison, it was vital, somehow, that he hear her say the words that came as close to admitting she had killed their oldest child and their youngest child as she would allow herself to do.

A subdued press conference took place after Debora's *Alford* plea. Answering reporters' questions, Mike obviously felt no sense of triumph. The losses were still losses. "Despite what she did," he said quietly, "this is still a human being. I was married to her for sixteen years. . . ."

Paul Morrison said he had talked with Mike about accepting the plea agreement. "We decided this would be the best way to protect Lissa and still punish Mrs. Green." Dennis Moore said that, although Debora had seemed calm in the courtroom, she had sobbed as she walked out. "Debora Green," he said, "is a caring, living, breathing, human being. She's not the monster that comes out of the stuff the prosecution was presenting."

Paul Morrison was disciplined about keeping in shape, although most nights it was ten or later when he got to the gym. On this night, of all nights, he felt the need to work off the tension that had built steadily over the past six months. In a sense, he had trained hard for a race he would never run. No one but a trial lawyer would understand that feeling.

On that night in April, Morrison was at the gym, and

possibly putting himself through a stiffer sequence of exercises than usual. He saw one of the firefighters who had been at the fire on Canterbury Court. "He came up to me and said, 'My God, Morrison—what are you doing here *tonight?* Why aren't you out boozin' it up or something? Why aren't you celebrating?'

"I told him, 'Well, it's nice that we've got a fair completion on this thing—but *I'm* really disappointed.' I'm not sure if he understood that.

"My staff and I went back and forth with that plea. You don't know if it's going to happen or not, and then it happens," Morrison recalled with a grimace, "and a pall kind of settles over you for a couple of days. You were ready to go, ready to go into battle. You're a racehorse at the starting gate. And then it's over—and it's 'Stand down.'"

In all probability, Morrison would have won his case. It was for Lissa's sake that he agreed to the plea bargain. What was important was that Debora Green was going to prison for a hard forty.

Chapter 44

When unthinkable crimes are committed, the question of why? always arises. What was it about Debora Green that made her violate one of the strongest human instincts: mother love? A partial answer to that question came during her sentencing, on May 30, 1996.

Nothing that was said would make any difference in Debora's sentence. She had agreed to serve forty years in a Kansas penitentiary rather than go to trial. She wasn't insane; she had been interviewed and tested by psychiatrists and psychologists to determine whether she met the legal definition of insanity. Had she known the difference between right and wrong at the time of her alleged crime? Did she know the difference in the months after her children perished? The answer was yes.

Marilyn Hutchinson, the defense psychologist, had spent
a great deal of time with Debora during her incarceration in
the Johnson County Adult Detention Center. In large part,
it was her evaluation of Debora's state of mind that had convinced the defense to plea-bargain. Now she tried to explain
what had driven Debora to arson, murder, and poisoning.
Sean O'Brien, the defense lawyer who specialized in clients
who faced the death penalty, questioned her.

"Have you had contact with Dr. Debora Green in this
case?" O'Brien asked.

"I certainly have," Dr. Hutchinson replied. "My first contact with her was on a court-appointed competency-to-
stand-trial evaluation. I met with her for about two to two
and a half hours on February 27, 1996. Subsequently, I met
with her again for another two and a half hours on April 13
at the request of her private attorneys when they were asking
me to evaluate her competency to plead . . . Since that time,
I have met with her twice weekly conducting psychotherapy
for her at her request, for a total of eighteen hours that I've
met with her."

Dr. Hutchinson testified that she had not had access to
Debora's medical records, but that she had spoken with Dr.
Stamati of Menninger's regarding her brief commitment
there. "That had been initiated by her husband because he
was concerned about the possibility of her either harming
herself or her children. At the time she was admitted to
Menninger's, however, because she was not expressing anything of a verbal nature about that aggressiveness, there was
not a commitment past the initial twenty-four hours. It did
not meet the legal criteria for involuntary commitment."

Dr. Hutchinson said that in assessing Debora's competency she administered a number of tests, including the
Wechsler Adult Intelligence Scale and subscales from the
Wechsler Memory Scale. Debora, of course, had scored
almost off the scale on intelligence. "I also used the compe-
tencies as defined by the Department of Health, Education,
and Welfare," Dr. Hutchinson testified, "to determine what

her competency to stand trial was. I did that through both verbal and paper and pencil instruments."

The DHEW definition of competency included thirteen factors. The person being evaluated has to: "realistically consider possible defenses to the crime charged; manage his/her own behavior at a trial setting; be able to relate to his/her attorney; be able to participate with his/her attorney in planning a defense; understand the roles of the participants in the trial (know who the judge, jury, prosecutor, witnesses, defense attorney, etc., are); understand typical court procedures; appreciate the charges that he/she faces; appreciate the nature and range of possible penalties; perceive realistically the likely outcome of a trial; provide his/her attorney with available pertinent facts; be able to testify relevantly; and be motivated toward self-defense."

"Can you briefly describe your findings as a result of that first competency evaluation?" O'Brien asked.

"About fifty percent of those criteria are really cognitive tasks," Dr. Hutchinson said. "What does a judge do? What happens after you get a direct examination? The kind of thing that people pick up from watching television and reading accounts in the newspaper—just a common working knowledge of what is a trial like."

Dr. Hutchinson explained that some competency questions are "purely emotional. Can the person manage their behavior during the trial? Are they likely to get up and scream or are they going to be unable to stop crying[?]. . . The other one that I see as purely emotional is: Is the person motivated toward self-defense? And I found that in both of those purely emotional ones and in the ones that were purely cognitive, she was competent."

However, some aspects of Debora's personality disturbed Dr. Hutchinson during the assessment of her competency to stand trial. All these troubling areas came back to a level of emotional capability that Debora seemed to lack. "When I asked an emotional question, she was never able to give more than a minimal yes or no response, without any kind of elaboration. She described to me that when she begins to get emotional, her long-term strategy is to shut down or tune out—really not even to listen to what is being said—so that she wouldn't become overwhelmed with emotion."

Would Debora be able to participate in planning legal strategy? If she "shut down" her mind while they were testifying, could she challenge prosecution witnesses? In the same vein, could she herself testify with any relevance? Although the vast majority of murder defendants never take the stand—to avoid probing questions from the prosecution—Dr. Hutchinson wondered what would happen if Debora was faced with questions that evoked feelings she wanted to shut out.

In the end, she had concluded that Debora was competent to stand trial, within the prescribed parameters. Later, when Dennis Moore, Kevin Moriarty, and Sean O'Brien were discussing the possibility of a no-contest plea with Debora, they asked Dr. Hutchinson to examine her again. "They needed another opinion about whether she was emotionally getting this—well enough to make such a plea."

And so Dr. Hutchinson had come back into Debora's life. "I met with her again for about two and a half hours, and we talked about the consequences that she saw to her relationship with Lissa [if she pled no contest]. About the consequences of it [her plea], really meaning that her life as she had known it, as she had thought about her life in the future, would be coming to an end. I observed that she was still very emotionally blunted, emotionally flat, that during the entire time there were only . . . ten to fifteen seconds of breakthrough crying. That was pretty minimal considering the topic. . . . However, she was intellectually understanding it, and, to the best of her ability, she was processing it emotionally."

By the time of this second evaluation, Dr. Hutchinson had an affidavit from Dr. Stamati at Menninger's, along with Debora's records from her brief stay there. "I found that she was admitted to Menninger's with a diagnosis of either major depression or possibly bipolar depression, with suicidal impulses. It was noted that she was doing a great deal of binge drinking. . . . She was given medicine for gastrointestinal problems that were the result of the intense drinking she had done."

Debora had told Dr. Stamati that the violence between her son and her husband had made life very difficult for her. But probably the most compelling information to come from Dr. Hutchinson's testimony was about Debora's score on a GAF (Global Assessment Function), a test of an individual's ability to exist, interact, *cope* with the world he or she lives in.

"It was noted," Dr. Hutchinson said, "that she had a Global Assessment Function of 35. And this is on a scale of 1 to 100. Short of normal, walking-around functioning for most people is 80 to 85. And she was given a rating of 35. That kind of rating [indicates] there were either gross reality disturbances [or] gross impairment in communication and/or most aspects of functioning. . . ." That meant that at the time of Debora's brief sojourn at Menninger's in late September, a month before she set fire to her own home, she was functioning "minimally" on a daily basis.

But why? She was not the first—or the last—woman whose husband wanted a divorce. She was assured of an income with which she could maintain an upscale lifestyle, even if she didn't go back to work. She had a medical degree, her children were all in school, and she had the ability, seemingly, to make a handsome living on her own. She could even have made the mortgage payments on the Canterbury Court home.

Sean O'Brien asked Dr. Hutchinson what her psychological findings about Debora were. "I find that Debora has a very limited internal self—or ego," she said. "Whatever it is inside that makes us a person, who we are—that comes from her childhood and comes from our genetics, that really is the driving force of our personality—I found that ego or self within Debora is a very, very, immature person. She is really quite unable to handle most emotional experiences, or to handle those things that require emotional responses. So she has the emotional capabilities of a very young child— even younger than a toddler, perhaps—in her ability to process or sustain emotion."

That was a shocker. Could a woman with an IQ of 165 and a biting, facetious wit, a woman who had zipped through college and medical school, be a child emotionally?

Hutchinson's diagnosis was that Debora had a "schizoid personality. And it's really the 'empty inside' diagnosis," she explained. "There is no self in there. And consequently, people learn to imitate what it's like to be a human being. They imitate what it's like to have relationships. They imitate or pretend to be like the people they see around them.

"I also learned that because of some life experiences that happened to her as a preadolescent, that at that age, her ability to imitate became further compromised," Dr. Hutchinson further testified. "So, overall, although she was pretending to be an adult, really she had the sort of outside social skills of a ten-year-old, and the inside emotional capability of a one-year-old. And we have those two trying to walk around and pretend to be a grown-up.

"Unfortunately and fortunately *both*," Dr. Hutchinson continued, "because of her intellect, she was able to mask and able to get along in the world. She was not a trouble-maker. People didn't recognize . . . the intense amount of emotional difficulty she was having."

When O'Brien asked what external factors had affected Debora's mental condition, Dr. Hutchinson cited the problems in the marriage, the "violence" between Mike and Tim, and the fact that Mike was leaving her. "It was her understanding that Dr. Farrar had promised he would never leave again the last time that he had left the marriage. And so when he began coming back and then leaving again . . . she became extremely distressed. . . . Her emotions about the end of that marriage were more than she could handle."

"In performing your evaluation of Debora's competence,

did you discuss her decision to enter a plea of no contest?"
O'Brien asked.

"I did."

"And what did you find her motivation to be?"

"Predominantly, her motivation was to end the trauma
and drama for her daughter, Lissa. She felt that things
needed to settle down so Lissa could have her life again.
Secondly, I think she had given a great deal of thought
about what it would be like if she were convicted to a death
sentence—what that would be like for her daughter. I think
she had some information about other children whose parents were in that situation and how difficult it was for them.
And," Dr. Hutchinson continued, "I also saw some healthy
self-preservation operating, which is the fear of facing a
death penalty for herself. She was aware that there were certainly some mental health defenses that could have been
advanced . . . and she also understood that juries don't usually listen or respond favorably to mental health defenses
regarding the killing of children."

"Doctor, in your examination of Debora, did you uncover
any factor that would cause you to believe that she couldn't
knowingly and voluntarily enter into this agreement?"

"I certainly had some concerns when I first met her—
that were mitigated a bit at the time of my second
evaluation," Dr. Hutchinson said. "For the first several
months after the fire, it was her fairly standard coping mechanism to pretend the fire hadn't ever existed. And I find that
on some occasions, she still copes with this tragedy that way.
So she was pretty numb—and although not fully catatonic,
was close to that state prior to some of our regular contacts."

"What do you mean by 'catatonic'?"

"Catatonic [catatonia] is a defense an individual will use
where they become deaf and dumb and are literally unable
to respond to the world externally because the . . . situation
they're in is just too overwhelming for them. Debora, at
times, had that kind of feel about her, although she *was*
minimally responsive.

"Since then . . . I find that she is able to express some very brief moments of emotions. She is experiencing emotions of profound grief. She was terribly confused about how this all happened. She's very remorseful about her daughter's suffering and about the loss of her other two children in this tragedy. And she's very guilty that she wasn't somehow able to stop the terrible downward spiral that her family was in— to predict how it might end up."

Marilyn Hutchinson, like Ellen Ryan, perceived Debora as a nearly helpless "child." She ended her testimony by saying that Debora was as healthy at that moment as she had been at any time in the last year. "It's clear to me that she is not sociopathic and it's certainly clear to me that she's not an evil person. I see her struggling . . . to come to terms with her emotions and that she's moved from a time of being out of control prior to the fire to being numb and disconnected after the fire, and now she's in a very profound state of remorse and grief, trying to deal with what all happened."

O'Brien thanked Dr. Hutchinson for her diagnosis of what had gone wrong in Debora's life, or rather, for her diagnosis of the result of some early trauma.

At that moment, Dennis Moore rose to say that Debora had a statement that she wanted to read at an "appropriate time" before her sentence was pronounced.

"You're welcome to go ahead," Judge Peter Ruddick said.

All eyes in the courtroom were focused on Debora as she began to read her statement. She looked twenty years older than she had five months earlier. "The death of a child," she began, "*any* child, under *any* circumstances, is a terrible human tragedy. The death of these children under these circumstances is a tragedy almost too great to bear. It is nevertheless a tragedy that I must bear for the rest of my life, and one for which I also must bear responsibility. Nothing that I can do or that can be done to me can bring my children back. In accepting responsibility for this crime, I recognize that I must face and accept the punishment as judged by the court and must also face the sorrow of the loss of my children and the reality of my role in their deaths.

"For many, the administration of punishment for crimes is the primary role of the criminal court system. Others see deterrence of future crimes as the most important result of criminal punishment. I ask that you look beyond even this basic aspect of deterrence and somehow the lesson that can be learned from this tragedy is that these deaths might well have been prevented.

"Alcohol, psychiatric illness and, even more, basic communications failure that were in our family set the stage for this tragedy. I do not seek to use this fact to escape my personal responsibility. I do hope—I *do* hope, however, that the recognition of these problems and the fact that the signs of these problems could have led to earlier intervention will be a lesson learned from these tragic deaths.

"Alcohol abuse and the psychiatric problems that both lead to alcohol abuse, and spring from it, are treatable diseases. They are not, however, diseases for which the afflicted person will readily seek help on their own. Many of you know in your own lives of persons in danger from these illnesses.

"It is never easy to intervene in the life of another. I would ask that you look at these opportunities for intervention in your own lives and take the steps that must be taken to salvage those lives in danger before it is too late—as it has become for me and my family.

"My desire in taking this course of action is to spare Lissa and the rest of my family any further trauma. Two members of my family are gone forever and those who survive will never be the same. It is my hope that today marks a new beginning for all, and, as I said, that we can all begin the process of healing."

Debora was crying as she finished her statement, and she brought her hand up to cover her face. It was an important statement, and a beautifully written one. She had not, however, written it herself; it was a product of a collaboration, not with Ellen Ryan, but with another attorney whose philosophies were in line with Ellen's. Only time would tell if Debora truly believed in the sentiments she had expressed.

Judge Ruddick was now ready to sentence Debora. He ordered her to serve two forty-year prison terms, to run concurrently but without possibility of parole. He added an "aggravating circumstances" clause: "I specifically find that the defendant knowingly or purposely killed or created a great risk of death to more than one person and that the defendant committed the crime in an especially heinous, atrocious or cruel manner." He also added two sentences of ninety-seven months each, and one of forty-nine months for the crimes against Lissa and Mike, which were moot because they would run concurrently with the "hard forty."

Judge Ruddick subtracted 191 days for time Debora had already spent in jail. That meant she now faced imprisonment of thirty-nine years, five months, and nineteen days. She was ordered into the custody of the Kansas Department of Corrections and would soon be transferred to the Topeka Correctional Institute in Topeka, Kansas, to begin the rest of her life.

Chapter 45

Mike was in the courtroom the day Debora was sentenced to prison. His eye was no longer discolored, but he had a deep scar on the right side of his forehead and his shaved head was just beginning to show a bit of stubble. He, too, had prepared a statement—one he had written himself—but in the end, he decided not to read it. It had been cathartic enough for him to write it, and he didn't want to "pile on" Debora. Listening to Dr. Hutchinson's evaluation of her personality, seeing her so diminished, he folded his statement and put it away. But he kept it; in a way, it was his own memorial to his lost children.

"Approximately one year ago," it began, "my wife, Debora Green, and my son, Tim, and I all looked forward to a school trip visiting the Amazon River in Peru and Inca ruins in the Peruvian Andes. It was truly the trip of a lifetime and enjoyed by all. Unfortunately, it was the last great adventure in life for both Tim and Debora. While the trip itself had really very little to do with subsequent events, it now stands as an icon for a tragedy that will never be fully understood.

"October 24, 1995, took two innocent, promising young lives from all of us. Tim was a strong young man, both mentally and physically. He lived his life with vigor and the orneriness of a young teenaged boy, yet he had the courage to stand up to his peers when necessary and defend weaker children. This was surely an unusual and admirable trait in a young man. He came by his strong will honestly and because of this and my own similar attitudes, a stormy relationship between us was sometimes present. Regrettably, physical altercations occurred on a few occasions. For this, I take full responsibility. I am very proud of who Tim was. There is no credible evidence that he was ever involved in any part of the tragic events that ultimately cost him his life, and I will never believe that he was in any way responsible.

"Kelly was a beautiful, loving child with tremendous maturity and insight despite her age. She was able to intellectually understand the turmoil of divorce and family discord, and served as the sole calming influence in a very dysfunctional situation. I have no doubt that Kelly would have lived to be a great person, a leader among humankind, someone who would have been kind and generous. The extent of her loss will never be fully realized.

"Perhaps the tragedy most overlooked in all of this is the person Debora Green has come to be. She is exceedingly bright and can be witty and vivacious. However, despite her brilliance, she was unable to manage the usual stresses of being a wife and mother, let alone those of being a physician. Her performance should have been exemplary, but serious—yet undefined—psychological flaws resulted in deadly behavior. Life is not easy for any of us and clearly I have made my fair share of mistakes as a husband and father. Nevertheless, these mistakes and pursuance of a divorce do not justify attempted murder and murder.

"I will never know for sure if Debora truly intended to kill me, either as a punishment or for insurance reasons, or if she simply meant only to physically torture me for my actions and desire for divorce. She may have simply wished to gain sympathy as a doting and loving wife, caring for me while I was critically ill.

"It is, however, clear to me that during a few hours on October 24, 1995, Debora intended to kill our children in order to prevent me from taking them from her. It was more acceptable for her to lose her children by her own hand than have them taken away by someone else due to her failure as a mother. I also strongly suspect that she again wished to punish me by killing those most dear to me. I do not believe that the children's murders were premeditated. At this point, I do believe that she feels remorse for her actions and I do believe that she genuinely loves Lissa. It is therefore, despicable and incomprehensible that Debora would allow or encourage her attorneys to blame these crimes on Tim in order to absolve herself."

Mike had written far into the night, finally putting his feelings down. "Predicting criminal human behavior is one of the most difficult tasks our society tries to perform. Few people thought Debora was likely to murder her children. Despite some apparent mental illness that Debora suffered, I certainly never anticipated a homicidal predisposition. Obviously, neither did professionals trained to identify, evaluate, and treat psychiatric disorders. Debora is truly a victim in that the system failed by not being able to force her to remain hospitalized and obtain desperately needed, intensive psychiatric evaluation and care, therapy that could have potentially averted this disaster.

"Of course, the most important question of all is what will happen to Lissa as a result of all of this? How will she deal with her adolescent and teenage years? Later in life, how will she function when she is contemplating marriage, a family, a career? Will she ever be able to love a man openly and experience the intimacy necessary to sustain a lasting relationship? Will she ever be able to nurture her children?"

For Mike, a healer by profession, any discussions of the morality of capital punishment had been merely philosophical—until now. He had always been a proponent of harsh punishment for crimes, and of the death penalty. But he was glad that Debora would not be executed, although some of his friends had told him, "This is too good for her." Others had felt that a forty-year sentence was too severe.

"Harsher punishment to exact vengeance," Mike wrote, "serves no real purpose. . . . Tim and Kelly are still dead, the potential that should have been realized in Debora's life is still lost, and Lissa will still struggle. A lesser punishment, however, is not fair to society. Ultimately, I will recover from my health problems and hopefully resume a reasonably normal life. I hope that Debora can find a new beginning. I know that I can forgive her if she does. Although I hate what she has done, I do not hate her. Mostly, I feel sorry for her. However, at some point, I do expect Debora to say that she is sorry for what she has done; that she made a terrible mistake; that Timothy was an honorable young man and that blaming him for her actions was morally wrong. I expect the manipulation, the lying, and the evil that have become her primary method of dealing with life to end.

"Debora told me on several occasions prior to the fire that I would be sorry and unhappy forever if I left her. She is correct in that I am sad and unhappy because of the ensuing tragedy, but I refuse to remain paralyzed by sorrow and grief, and I will not allow my life and Lissa's life to be destroyed.

"There is still some good that comes from any situation, however horrific. I feel that I have matured and gained certain unique perspectives that will make me a better human

being. I have grown to know and understand Lissa better
than ever before. There is certainly little adversity left in life
that Lissa will have to face that matches what she has been
through already. I have witnessed our government,
represented by Mr. Morrison and his staff, and the Prairie
Village police and others, exhibit thoroughness, integrity,
sensitivity, and professionalism. . . .

"Finally,"—Mike had written these last lines doubting he
could read them in court without crying— "it appears that
Tim's suffering at the end was short-lived, and that Kelly
never awakened to experience pain and panic. Thankfully,
neither knew that their mother killed them. . . ."

By the time Mike wrote that statement, he had made some
difficult and important decisions about his life. He and
Celeste were no longer together, and the parting had not
been a friendly one. "He told me that he wanted to break up
on May eighteenth," Celeste recalled with bitterness, "the
day before Mother's Day. Right up until that day, he had still
been calling me four times a day."

Celeste, who felt burned by Mike's decision, would insist
that the breakup was sudden, and it was, but she had long
had some sense that Mike was pulling away. She had been
suspicious of women he mentioned to her, of any female
friend he saw, and she had not really trusted him or his
love. "I began to think that I was only good to use through
the trial, and he was tired of me," she said.

Of course, the trial had never taken place. But if it had,
Celeste might have been more a detriment to Mike's image
than an enhancement. She was a "scarlet woman," in many
people's eyes, and she probably would have been one of the
Defense's star witnesses.

Since coming to live with Mike, Lissa had been upset by
Celeste's presence. Celeste was a reminder of the bad days
when Debora told Lissa that Celeste had taken their father
away. And Debora had also told Lissa that Celeste had killed

her own husband. That was untrue, but it was imprinted on Lissa's mind. The situation was intolerable; when Mike wanted to see Celeste, he felt he was betraying Lissa. But in the end, their breakup probably came down to Mike's need to rid himself of pain and loss. It is doubtful that he and Celeste could ever have looked at each other without remembering Tim and Kelly—and John.

Celeste's legion of friends supported her, and so did her sister, who had never approved of Mike in the first place. "The only one who completely believed that Mike was right for me was Carolyn Stafford," Celeste remembered. "She and I thought it was the perfect romance. After it was over, my other friends said that it was better this way."

Better, perhaps, but heartbreaking. Celeste decided that she could no longer stay in Johnson County—or in Kansas at all. If she did, she would always be watching for Mike. She would have to force herself not to glance over from the freeway to see if his red truck was parked in front of his town house. In a way, losing Mike had thrown her into delayed grief for John. Until now, she had managed to blunt the worst pain because Mike needed her. Now, for the first time in two decades, she had no man in her life.

It was difficult for Celeste to leave her mother and her friends. She spent time in her backyard, wondering if she could take along cuttings of the plants she had cared for. It didn't matter; she and her sons needed to leave. She put her house on the market.

Debora was transferred to an "isolation pod" in the I-MAX section of the Topeka Correctional Facility. Perhaps her last glimpse of freedom came along the Kansas Turnpike, Route 70, during the trip of some 60 miles from Olathe. The route passed through Lawrence, site of the University of Kansas, and the city where Mike was born.

The Kansas Turnpike is not particularly scenic. Travelers can stop at combination fast-food restaurants and gas stations,

but, of course, the vehicle that carried Debora to prison did
not stop. She had been to Topeka only eight months before,
when she voluntarily committed herself to the Menninger
Clinic. Her new living quarters would be far less plush.

The prisoner van went through the last toll booth before
Topeka and almost immediately turned right. The route to
the women's section of the Topeka Correctional Facility led
away from the Beltway that circles Topeka, through scrubby
trees, and then turned left onto Southeast Rice Road.

The prison itself sat on the left side of the road, across
from a neighborhood of small, nondescript houses. Close to
the road were picnic tables and swings, and, beyond that, a
reception building. But the van bringing Debora followed a
meandering prison road that cut off to the right, past massive reddish stone buildings that had weathered decade after
decade of Kansas winters and summers, up to a low building
with fences and cages and razor wire and a tower where a
guard watched. Dr. Debora Jones Green was now Prisoner
#63205.

Her hard forty began in isolation. She could have no visitors as she acclimated to prison, took the mental and
physical tests required of all those in the "fish tank," and prepared for her time in the most secure facility on the prison's
grounds.

If the Peru trip had been an "icon," as Mike had called it
in his unread statement, it was a marker too. Just a year ago,
Debora and Mike had appeared to be totally "married," and
Debora had been so witty and hilarious that she kept everyone on the "dream trip" laughing. In isolation, she must
have dwelled on thoughts of all she had thrown away, and
dreamed about her other life as she slept.

In every sense, her life had turned to ashes.

Mike faced yet another surgery. In June, he had journeyed
to the Mayo Clinic in Rochester, Minnesota, to undergo tests
on his heart and brain. Some of the results had been

encouraging. The neurological tests, the neuropsychiatric tests, and the CAT scans of his brain were all normal. However, the treadmill test for oxygen consumption and the echocardiogram reconfirmed that his heart's mitral valve was damaged. Mike knew the inevitable progression of such a condition. Without open-heart surgery to close the damaged valve, he would develop congestive heart failure, which would result in irreversible heart damage. But he had to recover from his brain surgery before he could undergo the mitral valve repair. He was weak, but he was impatient. He wanted to get back to work; it had been eight months now, and he missed his practice.

Two months later, Mike was admitted to the Mayo Clinic; and on August 2, he underwent surgery for mitral valve repair. The operation seemed to go well and Mike was released to return home. But back in Kansas then he suffered a frightening and often fatal complication: cardiac tamponade.

The heart is surrounded by a sac called the pericardium. Surgery, or an accident, or even the wound of a slim-bladed knife can nick the heart, allowing blood or fluid to seep into the pericardium. With every beat, the heart is compressed more tightly as the space between it and the pericardium fills with an increasing amount of fluid.

After Mike's heart surgery, the seepage was not apparent right away, and Mike was given Coumadin to thin his blood and to prevent clotting. The drug increased the fluid building up in his pericardial sac.

A week after the mitral valve surgery, Mike noticed that he was short of breath and becoming very weak. He knew what was wrong. He was suffering from pericardial effusion; the sac that held his heart was literally strangling it. He called for help and was admitted to North Kansas City Hospital after an emergency run.

There was one more surgery. Under general anesthetic, the blood compressing Mike's heart was drained and the leak into his pericardium was repaired; but he remained hospitalized, with indwelling chest tubes to carry off excess blood. "I am hopeful," he wrote a friend, "that this represents my last medical problem and that I will return to work in October or November."

In exactly one year, Mike had been hospitalized eleven times. He realized that he had diagnosed himself—correctly—at the onset of each critical episode. He had called his doctors and asked for the tests that would confirm his sense of illness: the septic shock, the brain abscess, the aneurysm, the hole in his mitral valve, and, finally, the cardiac tamponade. Even so, he had come close to dying twice. "It's strange," he commented. "I almost died during my first hospitalization and my last. And then, finally, it was over."

This time, no shocking event coincided with his surgery. Mike began to get better in earnest. Debora was in prison, and it was time for him to begin putting his life back together.

Chapter 46

Locked away in I-MAX, Debora wrote a number of letters. She could not see Lissa while she was in isolation, and even when she returned to the general prison population, she would have to find someone to bring her daughter to Topeka on visitors' days: Saturday and Sunday. She could not really expect Mike to do that, and her parents were in El Paso. They would visit as often as they could, and, when they were in Kansas, they, of course, would bring Lissa to see her.

Debora had always had beautiful handwriting, and even though she sometimes had to write in pencil on plain lined paper, her letters were perfect. She set about mending fences.

Debora wrote to Mike's sister Karen Beal, to apologize. She was not able yet to apologize to William and Velma Farrar. "But that letter will be even harder to write," she confided. ". . . But all I can do is apologize to those I have hurt and hope you will forgive me.

"I've been working on getting in touch (?back in touch) with my spiritual self. . . . I have been studying the New Testament plus Proverbs. As soon as I'm out of this orientation unit and in the general population, I'll be able to attend church services several times a week and join a Bible study group. Getting in touch with God has helped me accept my situation with some degree of peace. Of course I'm still devastated with grief for Tim and Kelly, but I'm starting to come to terms with it a little bit."

Learning that her divorce would be final in July, Debora told her ex-sister-in-law that she hoped Mike would remarry before too long, so that Lissa would have a stepmother. It sounded like a whole new Debora, but Karen viewed the letter with some wariness. Debora urging Mike to take a new wife was hard to believe.

While she was still in isolation, Debora talked to Lissa once a week on the phone. Mike didn't listen in; he wanted Lissa to have some contact with her mother. It would be too cruel to her to break the tenuous connection abruptly. As long as Lissa handled her contacts with her mother well, he would not interfere.

In July, Debora wrote her eleven-year-old daughter a letter that began appropriately enough: she talked about her hope to become a helper–dog trainer and said how much she looked forward to visits from Lissa. But then, as if writing to another grown woman, she discussed Mike's faults and her own need to drink. "I drank until I started to have 'blackouts' which are times when I had no idea what I was doing or had done. I didn't do a very good job of taking care of you kids, but you never stopped being the most important thing on earth to me."

Heedless of the fact that Mike was doing his best to raise Lissa, Debora reminded her daughter that Tim had hated his father and had threatened to kill him with his bare hands "when he bulked up." Perhaps she was only trying to ensure that she would be first in Lissa's heart. Perhaps she was laying the groundwork for a legal appeal. "Tim was even close enough to you," she wrote to Lissa, "that he told you that he decided to kill your father by poisoning him. I took the blame for this to spare Tim's reputation."

But Debora had allowed her attorneys to ruin Tim's reputation.

Now she explained that she had had many, many drinks the night of the fire and that she had taken far more of her "medicines from Dr. Stamati" than she should have. It was all because she had argued with Mike. "The first thing I remember was being at the Formans' door and seeing you on the garage roof. I was in total shock."

But Debora had given Detectives Rod Smith and Greg Burnetta a precise account of her actions from the time the fire alarm went off.

"The police questioned me that night and I was totally inappropriate. I lied about my drinking and my drugs (medicines). I seemed not to care about Tim and Kelly, but this was the alcohol, the drugs, and the shock. There is a tape of this session. If you see it someday, keep this in mind."

But Debora probably would not have awakened at all that night if she had as many drinks and had taken as many antidepressants as she said she had. In the taped interview with police after the fire, she appeared perfectly sober.

Finally, Debora again told Lissa that she was the most important thing on earth to her. "Words can't tell you how much I love you. Please forgive me and continue to love me."

When Lissa left the letter lying out, Mike read it and was appalled. Despite all that had happened, he had believed that he could trust Debora to protect Lissa from any more disturbing accusations against her dead brother. He informed Debora that he would have to monitor her phone conversations with Lissa and read any letter she sent before Lissa did.

Debora responded on August 7 with an abject apology and told Mike she hoped his heart surgery had gone well. "I really am very sorry you have to endure all this. I pray for your complete recovery so you and Lissa can lead a normal life."

Mike had arranged for a woman from his office to take Lissa to Topeka to see her mother. Considering that Debora had sent him to the hospital eleven times and brought him near death more than once, considering that she had admitted setting the fire that killed two of his children, he was being remarkably civilized. But he refused to let her hurt Lissa anymore. He continued to let Lissa visit Debora, but he was watchful. Mike could see that Debora was distancing herself from the crime and speaking of his surgery almost as if she had no part in the problem.

"It was very wrong to have sent that letter to Lissa," Debora wrote to Mike. "I realize this isn't appropriate material for Lissa—she's just a little girl. I promise you I won't do such a thing ever again. I will continue to write to Lissa as often as I can and I will assume that you will read the letters. Please accept my apology and my promise that this won't happen again."

Mike wanted to believe Debora when she wrote, "Let's work together to make Lissa's life the best it can be?"

A month later, Debora wrote Mike three letters, again presenting a revisionist version of the night of October 23–24, 1995, very similar to the explanation she had written to Lissa in July. Again, she remembered, the night as being "fuzzy" in her mind. "I was drunk and over-medicated." After talking to Mike the last time, she wrote, she drank straight gin. "I passed out from drinking in exactly the way I did every night for about a month and a half. . . . Mike, you witnessed me passed out from booze and drugs on multiple occasions. Do you really think I could have thought any such plans out—let alone carried them out?

"As far as the poisoning is concerned, I have to ask you to accept what I have to say. I'm afraid I was responsible for Tim's hatred of you. Even so, I don't believe he was really trying to kill you. I think he saw that as long as you were sick, you were still here. I told a lot of lies in the county jail about a lot of things and tried to influence Lissa, but one fact remains. Lissa told Ellen the day I decided to accept the plea bargain that she knew Tim had done the poisoning and was trying to kill you. I didn't plant that specific idea!"

And now, Debora turned her back on Ellen Ryan. "She seems to have a need for me to be guilty. I discussed the possibility of an appeal with her and with Sean O'Brien and it's clear to me they both think I'm completely guilty."

She felt greater animosity toward Dennis Moore, whom she blamed for talking her into implicating Tim. "I am totally sorry and ashamed. . . . Please believe me. I am not just trying to exonerate myself—I have no plans or intentions of any further legal fal de ral [*sic*]. I wish I'd never met any of the attorneys who were involved in my case."

Debora pleaded with Mike to write back and answer her question: "Do you really think I could have thought any such plans out—let alone carried them out?" She needed him to tell her that he did not believe she could have set the fire or have had any part in poisoning him.

The next day's letter was filled with new revelations that Debora had finally remembered. "I accept the punishment which goes with my plea of 'no contest.' I pleaded that way out of fear of Paul Morrison and the death penalty, and to stop all the publicity and let Lissa (and you and my parents) settle back to a more normal life. I have no intention of re-opening that legal can of worms.

"Mike," she nevertheless wrote, "I *remember* that night. (I think!) I did not set that fire! I could *never* have endangered the children's lives like that and you know that is one fault I never had. I am trying to figure out for my own peace of mind what must have happened. Celeste is a very determined and self-directed woman and you were obviously her goal. Two major impediments to her having what she wanted—John and your family—were eliminated. Could she have been responsible?"

On Monday, September 9, Debora wrote to Mike once more, though she had told him she would not write him a letter a day, or call him as she had said she would. This third letter distanced her a bit further still from the crimes she had been convicted of.

"I would love to hear back from you concerning my questions—but that will have to be at your discretion. Please answer me if you feel you can. . . . I am totally ashamed of the month and half of wallowing in self-pity and I'll never forgive myself for not saving my (our) children. As far as the poisoning is concerned, I bought Tim the seeds and if I hadn't been so caught up in *me*, I might have realized what was going on. Wittingly or not, I was an accessory to all that and words cannot adequately convey how sorry I am. I'm sure Tim loved you—he was just going through an adolescent hate phase. . . . I never believed Tim had anything to do with the fire and I'm ashamed that I let Dennis Moore talk me into implying that at the preliminary hearing. I'm equally sure that I could and would never have endangered the lives of my children in setting the fire. I had settled into a very passive relationship with life and booze—shameful, but not evil. I know equally well that you were in no way involved in the death of your children, Mike. I'm left with only one possibility. I know it would be way too late to try to investigate this, but for my peace of mind, would you tell me whether you think it's remotely possible?"

Once more, Debora asked Mike to agree with her on a theory of the fire that would exclude her as the arsonist: "Celeste struck me as being pretty ruthless. And I was putting an obstacle in the way of her having what she wanted."

As the months passed, she would cling to this theory and refine it. But as brilliant as she was, Debora did not see the tiny flaws and inconsistencies in her letters. The more desperately she tried to back away from the horror of what even her attorneys believed she had done, the more she boxed herself into another corner.

Ironically, Mike received all three of Debora's letters on the one-year anniversary of his first ricin poisoning. The year of horror had come full circle, from the moment he bit into an innocuous-looking chicken salad sandwich, to the reading of these three letters from prison. He did not reply to Debora's pleas to help her as she constructed a new rationale to explain why their children were dead and he was fighting to regain his health.

He could not do that.

Epilogue

Although I was in the courtroom with Dr. Debora Green during her preliminary hearing, I had never heard her voice except on the extraordinary videotape of her police interview on October 24, 1995. I had talked to Debora's ex-husband, to her attorney, to D.A. Paul Morrison, to the Prairie Village detectives, to her acquaintances, and to her mother, and I had read voluminous files, but I still did not know who she was.

Was Debora Green like Diane Downs, who shot her own children so that her married lover would return? Was she like Susan Smith, who drowned her baby sons so that *her* lover would return? Or was Debora more like Betty Broderick, who could not give up her marriage or her status and finally murdered, not her children, but her ex-husband and his new wife? The list of infamous homicidal wives and mothers is not long, but we tend to remember the women who violate the mother instinct that is bone-deep in most of us.

The only possible way I could draw an informed picture of Debora was to meet her. Would she talk to me? And, if she was willing, would I be permitted to visit her in prison? These questions were moot for the moment; Debora could have no visitors until she was out of orientation.

I wrote to Debora in September 1996, suggesting that we exchange letters or attempt to arrange a visit. (Mike had already explained to her that I was writing a book and urged her to speak with me.) Because I do not believe in flying under false colors, I told Debora in my first letter that I believed that she had set fire to her home, although I was not convinced that she remembered doing it. I wanted her to understand my feelings before we met in person; I was not offering to write a "Debora Green is innocent" book, and she needed to know that. If she still wanted to talk to me, given that knowledge, I thought we would have a more meaningful dialogue. I also asked her about her childhood. What did she remember from the early years in Havana and Metamora, Illinois?

Debora wrote back to me on September 23, saying that she preferred a face-to-face interview to letters. I did not know of her barrage of letters to Mike just two weeks earlier. She had already begun her search for the "real killer" and hoped to file an appeal.

"You asked me about my childhood until age 10," she wrote in her first letter. "My childhood was extremely happy. I had one sister who was 19 months older than me and we were best friends. I excelled in school, athletics, and music. I really have no specific recollections to share with you, but my memories are all good. My parents have been very supportive of me throughout this entire ordeal and I have nothing but love and gratitude for them."

How odd, I thought, that Debora had no specific memories of her childhood, and yet she was sure those memories were all good. In her first letter, I saw again the dichotomy of reason that seemed to mark all of Debora's arguments.

My statement that I believed she was the arsonist had upset her. "I find it very distressing that you say you believe I set fire to my home," she wrote. "While I was in the county jail I was so frightened I didn't know what I remembered and what I didn't. I pleaded 'no contest' to the various charges in order to stop the publicity and enable Lissa to get on with her life—not because I was guilty."

With me, as with Mike and Lissa, Debora blamed her drinking for her inability to save her children. She would never forgive herself for that, she said. "I did not, however, have the wherewithal to set a fire with liquid accelerants which was started at four or five places at once. I also would *never* have done *anything* to put my beautiful children in harm's way. I loved those children more than life itself."

Debora explained to me that she had "behaved badly" because of the divorce, but that she had never neglected her children. Here, again, was her inability to understand that a drunken mother, passed out in bed while her little girls sob and her son tries to empty her liquor bottles down the sink, *is* a neglectful mother.

Debora knew that I had interviewed Celeste Walker; now she set forth her scenario of what had really happened during August, September, and October 1995. "You've met and interviewed Celeste Walker. She is an extremely determined woman. In the summer of 1995, she set her cap for my husband. I feel there were two major impediments to her having what she wanted—her husband John and myself and my family. Within less than a two-month period, these impediments were removed. In August, Celeste had told me she wanted to be rid of John—presumably by divorce—but not of the lifestyle his salary afforded."

Debora then explained the sequence of tragedies that began with John Walker's suicide. She told me that the fire was the work of a "professional arsonist" (it was not), and "certainly beyond the scope of my knowledge. The magnitude of the fire would make one think Lissa and I were supposed to perish in the fire as well. The prosecutor and even my own attorneys declined to look into this set of circumstances any further."

Debora wrote she also wished to discuss Mike's poisoning with me when we met in person.

Obtaining a visitor's pass to the Topeka Correctional Facility's I-MAX unit is not an overnight process, but within two months, I received word that I would be allowed into the maximum-security visiting area. The circumstances would be far from ideal for a writer. I could not take a tape recorder, a camera (which I had not requested), a pen—or even a pencil—or paper. Once I was inside, I could not leave and come back the same day. Debora urged me to eat a big

breakfast, because the only food available was from vending
machines.

For a writer accustomed to both taping interviews and
taking notes for backup, these restrictions were frustrating.
I planned to leave my tape recorder in my car, parked outside I-MAX, and record my memories of each interview
while they were still fresh as I drove back to my hotel, which
was, coincidentally, down the street from the Menninger
Clinic. Although I could have visited for six hours at a time,
such long sessions would swamp me with a tremendous
amount of information before I could get to my tape
recorder. Two four-hour sessions seemed a better idea.

In the end, because of holidays and blizzards, it was
March 14, 1997, before I flew into KCI, Kansas City
International Airport. I planned to drive to Topeka early
the next morning and meet with Debora from eleven to
three.

March in Topeka is a brown month. The grass, bushes, trees,
and even the constant wind seem to be the same shade of
dull brown. The wind sings as it slides around buildings, a
constant thrumming that I suspect natives no longer hear. It
whipped my hair and caught my car door as I set out on
Saturday, March 15, for the women's prison on Southeast
Rice Road.

I have been in innumerable jails and prisons for interviews. Sometimes I have talked to a prisoner on the phone
through double glass panes; sometimes we had "contact
visits" across a table, and, once, when I visited with Ted
Bundy in the Utah State Prison, we sat on two wooden chairs
in a cramped hallway between two electrically controlled
barred doors. I should long since have become used to the
feeling of being closed in and worse, the sense of not being
trusted that is the lot of prison visitors.

I would have to pass the "Security Access Control" building and follow a rutted road off to the right, toward where

the maximum-security prisoners were housed. The road between the redbrick medium-security buildings and the maximum-security pods was long and winding. The I-MAX grounds were surrounded by eighteen-foot-tall metal fences topped by three feet of razor wire.

Once I had found a spot in the I-MAX parking lot, I locked my purse in the trunk of my car, taking only my ID and keys. A solemn-faced guard checked through his list of approved visitors. Happily, my name was there. I surrendered my car keys and my drivers' license, and was turned over to another guard, whose hair was cut as short as a Marine recruit's and who wore mirrored sunglasses. He and I left the small I-MAX reception building and stepped into a cage—a literal cage—where we were surrounded by wire mesh on both sides and above our heads. I soon realized that small talk was discouraged; we walked in silence.

Even though I didn't know how to negotiate the maze of passages to get out of this cage, my armed escort had me walk in front of him, instructing me to "Push," "Pull," and "Enter" a series of cage doors until we finally turned onto a walkway that led through the sweep of green lawn surrounding the I-MAX pod. The tower guard, armed with a shotgun, watched us until we went inside.

The I-MAX visiting area looked like a grade school dining room, minus the food line. There were eight tables with chairs, and two vending machines. A matronly female guard sat at a desk just inside the entrance to the I-MAX building; clearly, she was overseeing the visiting area, but she did so cheerfully and without appearing to be watching.

Two rooms opened off the large room. These, I found out later, were for parent prisoners and their children, places where they could play and talk away from the direct gaze of guards and other prisoners and their families. There was a single uni-sex restroom.

I waited for several minutes, wondering if Debora had changed her mind about talking to me. When she finally

emerged from a corridor somewhere behind the female
guard, I was not sure it was really she. She seemed much
smaller than she had in the courtroom. She looked about
five foot three or four, and probably weighed 130 to 140
pounds. Nearsighted, she wore thick glasses. Her hair was
longer than when I last saw her, and quite curly. She was
dressed in the prison uniform: blue jeans, a blue denim
shirt, and athletic shoes.

When she held out her hand, it was damp and cold. She
was nervous, but she looked me directly in the eye and was
far more animated than I had ever seen her. I had inadver-
tently interrupted her lunch, but she hastened to tell me
that she had taken time to gulp it down.

How do you ask someone if she has killed her children
and poisoned her husband? You don't. At least, I don't. I
had told Debora in my first letter what I believed to be true,
and she had countered that she was innocent. Now, she
seemed eager to talk, choosing those subjects she wanted to
discuss. I let her lead the way.

The first thing Debora told me about was her terror the
night she was arrested, and the inhumane conditions in the
Jackson County, Missouri, jail. "We were packed into a cell
meant for far fewer people," she said. "They fed us when
they felt like it, and gave us water and bologna sandwiches at
three A.M. We had no mattresses on our bunks, only
springs."

She blamed Mike for "deliberately getting me arrested at
the ballet. He wanted to embarrass me. He didn't care about
Lissa. He expected she would be there too—but he didn't
care." Did she not know that Mike had been undergoing
surgery that day? He had no connection at all to the time
and place of her arrest.

Asked her criteria for being attracted to a man, Debora
told me that she felt a great sense of humor was important.
"Because you have to be really intelligent to have a sense of
humor." But Mike had "turned out to be no fun. He's meticulous, and a nitpicker. . . . He plans everything too much."

In spite of the conciliatory letters Debora had written Mike, asking his forgiveness, wishing him well, and promising to work together with him to help Lissa, she was obviously still very angry with him. "I think Lissa's safe with him," she said. "But he's not fun. Lissa has no fun with him. And Lissa loves to have fun."

Mike had been, Debora said, not just a bad father but no father at all. He left for work between six and six-thirty and didn't come home until between eight and ten. She felt he had been thrilled when Tim was born, less thrilled at Lissa's birth, and with Kelly, "an accident," not interested at all. She, on the other hand, had always put her children first. "My children are my life," she said—a remark she was to repeat many times during the interview. "When I talked to Mike that last night," she told me, "he threatened to take them away from me. That really scared me."

I asked Debora why she had not simply let Mike go. "You could have started a new practice. You could have supported yourself and the children. Why didn't you?"

"He was going to take our beautiful house for himself, and the children and I would have had to live in a smaller house. We had a place, a place in society. . . . I didn't want to give that up. And the children wanted me to be home. Tim said to me, 'Mom, we want you to be our mother and pick us up and go to our games and be there. We don't want you to start your practice again.'"

Debora had written to me of her belief that Celeste was the arsonist. Now, six months later, she thought *both* Celeste and Mike had been involved.

"Are you saying that they actually set the fire?" I asked.

"No—no, they wouldn't do that. I think they paid someone to set it. They never do anything themselves. They always hired people to do what they wanted. Celeste always gets what she wants. Things weren't happening quick enough for her."

Debora recalled John Walker from their days as anatomy partners in medical school in 1972. "He was very nice, very shy. . . . I knew he was depressed last year."

"Do you still think Celeste killed him?"

Debora shook her head. "No. She didn't murder him— but she drove him to suicide. He and I talked a lot around the pool after we came back from Peru."

"Did you and John talk about Mike's affair with Celeste?"

"Oh no," she answered quickly. "John didn't *know* about that."

Finally, Debora was ready to talk about the details of the night of October 23–24. She had been reading, she said, and she heard Tim in the kitchen. She had gone to see what he was up to and found him getting something to eat. She recalled that he had been dressed in just his pajama bottoms. They had talked and she had hugged him good night.

That was the last time she ever saw her son.

Back in her room, Debora had a late conversation with Mike, one that ended in angry words and his threat to take the children away from her. She told me she had swallowed a full glass of straight gin after that phone call. "And I passed out."

She no longer remembered anything about the alarms going off. She didn't remember if she had locked the doors, or even if she had turned the burglar alarm on that night.

I asked her if she had taken a lie-detector test about that night and she shook her head. "I'm afraid to. In college, we did these physiological studies using lie detectors. I'm the kind of person, that if they ask me what my name is, I'll be so nervous that even if I give my own name, it will look as though I'm lying."

In the videotaped interview, Debora had told the police that she had opened her bedroom door and been confronted by smoke. She said she had slammed the door, afraid that she would "asphyxiate" right there. Never, in any statement, had she mentioned going into the flaming hall. Now she told me: "I started down the hall into the flames to save my children. There was so much fire and smoke that I was forced back. That was when my hair got burned. I went to the Jones Store with my mother to get my hair cut because I wanted to look nice for the funeral. It was a bad haircut, so days later I went and got another haircut—to fix up that bad one."

I tried to keep my expression neutral, although I wondered if my eyes betrayed me. I knew about her singed hair and the haircuts; this story seemed a deliberate attempt to explain away some of the strongest physical evidence against her.

"I just can't understand why Paul Morrison was so concerned about my haircuts," she said. "He kept going back and forth, too. He wanted me to be drunk that night but he didn't want me to be so drunk I couldn't set the fire."

When Debora talked about what Tim had suffered, and the thought that Lissa had heard him calling, "Help me . . . help me," she started to cry. Even though I could not believe she was innocent, I thought her tears were genuine.

However, Debora told me that Tim had poisoned his father.

I was not interrogating her, I was only listening, but, as she piled the blame on her dead son, she changed her own participation in the ricin poisonings with each sentence. "I bought the castor beans for Tim," she said. "It was for a school project. Tim was always coming up with interesting projects. He wanted to try growing the castor beans using different pH levels in the soil, and where he could control the climate—but Tim *was* poisoning his father. I was so drunk I just wasn't paying attention to what he was doing. . . ."

I said nothing.

"You know," she said slowly, "I may have been helping Tim poison Michael. If I hadn't been drinking, I wouldn't have done it. . . . I was angry with my attorneys for making it look like Tim set the fire. He wouldn't have done it."

Debora said she was no longer taking Prozac and her thinking was clearer. Her whole time in jail in Johnson County, she confided, was a blur. She blamed this on the Klonopin and the Prozac. She blamed Dennis Moore and Kevin Moriarty for never coming to see her. As for Ellen Ryan and Sean O'Brien, "They think I should be content where I am because of the threat of the death penalty," she said angrily.

She was not content where she was. Debora said she had written to Legal Services for Prisoners in Topeka but they couldn't help her file an appeal. She had also contacted the National Organization for Women. "They expressed interest in helping me, but their funds are all earmarked for other things." NOW had suggested that Debora write to Alan Dershowitz, and she had done that, but he had not yet responded to her.

"I think Ellen thought I was guilty from day one," she said with some bitterness.

"But she fought so hard for you," I said, surprised. "Why do you say that?"

"Because she went and got Moore and Moriarty."

"They're the best criminal defense attorneys around. Whether she thought you were innocent or guilty, she got the best she could for you."

"Maybe that's right."

Except for her parents and Lissa, Debora felt that everyone had deserted her. When I asked about her sister Pam, she said sardonically, "I got a Christmas card from her. She's pulled away from me."

Debora hated being in prison, but she was no longer frightened. She felt safer, somehow, in prison. She said she had managed to get the best room in I-MAX, a corner room with a plastic window, in the MAX Swan Pod. Most of the rooms had only a bed, a toilet, and a metal desk. "*My* room has a little space at the end of my bed," she told me, "and in the other rooms, the beds go from wall to wall. I have a television set in my room. I've never liked television, but they have two sets out in the main room and they're always on MTV or PET stations."

The irony of her being happy to have a foot or two of space at the end of her bed when she had once lived in a luxurious mansion was stunning, but Debora did not seem to notice. She said she did not spend much time in her room, however. She usually went out in the main room and crocheted. "I have a lot of friends," she said. "They are people I would never have gotten to know otherwise. I get along fine with everyone."

As Debora had written to Lissa, she had achieved her hope of becoming a trainer for the Helper Dog program. This seemed an invitation to heartbreak because she was only allowed to keep a dog for seven weeks, after which it went on to the next step of its training. She admitted that she was dreading the day her current dog moved on, but she enjoyed her job. "I get to be outside when I work with the dogs." She worked with the dog each morning and again in the afternoon. Her days were regimented, divided into predictable segments. The food in prison wasn't very good and the portions were small. There weren't enough stools to sit on in the dining hall, so if all the inmates showed up, some had to wait a turn to sit down.

Most of all, Debora said, she hated the noise of so many women living together—and the lights. She said she had been delighted when the light in the hall outside her room burned out. "I could sleep in the dark for a week—until they put in a new bulb."

She said she had eight years to serve before she could hope to be moved into medium security. "I can't stand this now," she murmured. "How can I stand eight years?" We didn't talk about the real sentence. The "hard forty." That was too long to contemplate.

Debora gave me an overview of her life, beginning in high school. She felt that she had never really loved Duane

Green. She met Mike when she was still legally married to Green, and she was attracted to him because he was "calm and a nice guy." She was looking, she said, for security. Not financial security chiefly, but emotional security. She spoke of security a great deal. I wondered if Debora had been looking not for a husband but for a father.

Perhaps the most difficult subject of all to get Debora to talk about was her childhood and her family. It was as if her life had begun in high school. Pressed, she repeated what she had told me in her first letter. She had had a perfect childhood.

"Who was the boss in your family?" I asked.

"My mother," she answered immediately. "My mother runs the family. She's the strong person in the family. My father is a nice guy who's a lot of fun. He plays with the kids."

My letter from Joan Jones had been full of vitriol about Mike Farrar, particularly about the ghastly post-Mother's Day dinner when Mike and Tim fought. Now Debora agreed with Mike's account of that day. She recalled that Tim had been misbehaving badly and that her parents *had* sided with her husband, saying they would not have put up with such behavior as long as he had.

Debora said that her family had lived in modest circumstances when she was a child, but that they always had enough to be comfortable and happy. She knew her dad had driven a bread truck, but, unlike Mike, she could not name the company he worked for. She said she had always had the things that were important to her. Except for pets. "I could never have enough pets," she commented. Her mother had allowed only one dog and a few cats over the years, because she felt that generally pets were too much trouble.

I asked Debora if she remembered anything traumatic in her childhood, and she said no at once. Everything had been "idyllic." She could play the piano. She could play the violin. She was the top student in her school—always. She was good at tennis and soccer.

If she had been traumatized or sexually molested as a child, either she did not remember or she would not tell me. Something had happened to her, I was sure, but the troubled woman in front of me would not say what it was.

"Did your parents drink?" I asked. It was a reasonable assumption: Her sister was a drug and alcohol counselor, and Debora was blaming the fire and the poisonings on her own alcoholic haze.

"No, they never drank to excess," she answered quickly. "Neither one."

It was 3:30 on Sunday afternoon, March 16, 1997, and visiting hours were over on this last day I would spend with Debora. I had promised her to have my editor send her some books directly from the publisher—the only route by which prisons will accept books from outside. As always, she could lose herself in a book, but the prison library was sparse compared to what she was used to.

I could not promise Debora that I would write a book that proved her innocent. Even in talking to me, she had slipped and changed her story. I think it is necessary for the survival of her personality that she construct an elaborate scenario that allows her to believe she did not pour the fluid, strike the match, light the fire that destroyed her children. It is vital that she remembers that she "saved" Lissa. It may be just as important—or more important—for her to believe Tim poisoned Mike.

In the end, I think Mike may have been the most important thing on earth to Debora, perhaps even more important than her children. He was the father who would not stay home, and she was the little girl who threw tantrums to keep him there. When that didn't work, she punished him by taking away what he loved the most: his children.

The guards herded us into a manageable group—parents, husbands, children, and me—while the prisoners stood on the other side of the rail and watched us as we

prepared to walk the gauntlet past the guard tower. Debora
stood apart from the group, and she seemed the loneliest
person I had ever seen. And just for that moment, my last
glimpse of her, I could see the "child" whom Dr. Marilyn
Hutchinson had described.

And still, I was left with questions to ponder. Debora had
been convicted of two vastly diverse crimes. Setting the
deadly fire might have been an impulsive act—horrible to
contemplate, yes, but done in a rage fueled by a temporary
alcoholic psychosis and Mike's angry accusations. To poison
her husband, however, required an entirely different mind-
set. She had to research methods of poisoning and decide to
use ricin (certainly), and potassium chloride (quite possibly). No one in an alcoholic fog would have been capable of
the intricate planning it took to locate, purchase, and grind
up the deadly castor beans.

How Debora must have hated Mike as she carried him
plates of food with a smile—and then watched him become
desperately ill again and again. Poison, traditionally a
woman's weapon, has always struck me as the most cold-
hearted way to kill. Debora knew the symptoms of ricin
poisoning; she knew that her husband would soon be on his
hands and knees vomiting in the shower, and that he would
suffer terribly before he finally succumbed. This attempt at
murder was deliberate, premeditated, and prolonged. A
plan designed by a monstrously cruel woman.

Why did she hate him that much? I doubt that anyone—
perhaps not even Debora herself—could explain her
motivation. Mike had betrayed her with another woman,
but many wives forgive an unfaithful husband. Those who
cannot forgive seek divorces; rarely do spurned wives set
out to destroy the men they once loved. No, Debora truly
wanted Mike to die in agony.

In a sense, her hatred for her husband was self-hatred.
Mike had failed to make Debora happy, and she had long

since placed the burden of her self-esteem on his shoulders. At the same time, she had submerged her own personality so completely in her role of wife and mother that if she allowed him to leave her, she would be a woman made of air. By killing Mike with slow poison, Debora would wreak her revenge. And, quite simply, she would save her ego. Mike wouldn't leave her for a blonde who was pretty and slender; instead, he would die in her arms.

What Debora did not consciously realize was that as she acted out her rage, she would die, too. Had she succeeded in administering one more dose of poison to Mike, he would certainly have died. When that failed, she destroyed her children, which was also an act of self-destruction, and she became a woman who was not a wife, not a mother, not a doctor, nobody.

Even if she had escaped the death penalty, Debora Green received a terrible punishment. In essence, she has been condemned to spend the rest of her life alone with the person she most despises—herself.

That is, I think, worse than dying in an execution chamber.

Celeste Walker sold her home in Overland Park and spent her last Christmas in Kansas in 1995. She has moved her sons to the West Coast, 2,000 miles away from tragic memories.

Dr. Michael Farrar's divorce from Dr. Debora Green was final on July 25, 1996. He has regained his health, and is practicing medicine full-time again. He makes arrangements for Lissa to visit her mother regularly. Mike married Gillian Matthews,* an attorney, in May 1997. They live with Lissa and Gillian's child in a new house on the Missouri side of the state line.

Greg Burnetta has left the Prairie Village Police Department and works for federal law enforcement in Kansas City.

Detective Gary Baker has also left the Prairie Village Police Department. He now works as an investigator for the public defender's office.

Detective Rod Smith is still working for the Prairie Village Police Department. He will remember the Debora Green case, as will his fellow investigators, for the rest of his life.

Jeff Hudson is still the Fire Marshal for the Shawnee, Kansas, Fire Department.

Paul Morrison was reelected as district attorney of Johnson County in the 1996 elections.

Ellen Ryan is still practicing domestic law in Kansas City, Missouri—a field which she finds "more dangerous today than criminal law," given the emotions that divorce can unleash.

Debora Green did not write to me after our visits in mid-March, 1996. Reportedly, she is increasingly sorry that she pleaded no contest and is seeking a new trial—one that could cost her her life.

In what I knew would be my last visit to 7517 Canterbury Court, I took photographs to help me remember the street and the trees that had once surrounded the house where Mike, Debora, Tim, Lissa, and Kelly had lived. I knew that the lot where that house once stood would never again be a homesite. It had long since been leveled and planted in grass. And the neighbors on either side purchased it from Mike Farrar in 1997. Still, it was hard to forget the lives that had been lost and the hopes that had been buried there.

Then I saw two small creatures scampering across the grass—a wild rabbit and a squirrel. They seemed unafraid, and that somehow made me feel better. I could hear the noise of a lawn mower several lots away, and the *thunk, thunk* of boys shooting baskets. Although nothing would ever be the same again, life on Canterbury Court had not ended for everyone.

Acknowledgments

When I arrived in Kansas City in January of 1996, I was a complete stranger. I soon found that Kansas and Missouri are friendly states indeed.

Many people helped me in my efforts to unravel the puzzle that is Debora Green. Some were instrumental in convicting her. Others, I know, will not agree with my conclusions—yet I hope that, whenever I could, I gave them a voice.

I would like to thank everyone who spoke with me about their areas of expertise and/or their personal connections to this tragic story: Johnson County District Attorney Paul Morrison; Assistant District Attorney Rick Guinn; Terry Issa, Morrison's assistant; court reporter Kris Waggoner; Jeff Hudson, Shawnee, Kansas, Fire Marshal; Charles Grover, chief of police of Prairie Village; Detectives Rod Smith and Gary Baker; Ellen Ryan; Joan Jones; Dr. Debora Green; Gordon Purdy; Dr. Michael Farrar; Dr. Jeanne Hermens; Celeste Walker; Tony Rizzo and James Fussell of the *Kansas City Star*; Andy Hoffman of the *Olathe Daily News*; Dave Kaup, Marc Lorber, Nancy Glick, Janna Pettet, Illinois Prairie Library, Metamora, Illinois; Luis Wells, and the rest of the staff of the Topeka Correctional Institute.

Ruth Adams of the Flutterby, Carla Redburn, Ann Slegel, Karen Metcalf, Cary L. Swofford, Sue Jones, Janice Mccollum, Linda Meierhoffer, and Kay Waldo, and Kelly Waldo Dillman all helped immeasurably to make me feel at home in Kansas City and its environs.

As always, I thank my first reader, Gerry Brittingham, my friend and fellow author Donna Anders, Marni Campbell, Mike Rule, my office manager, and Leslie Rule, my photographer and audio-video specialist (who took time out from writing her own book to help). The rest of my family pitched in often: Laura, Andy, Kevin, Matt, Rebecca, Bruce, Machel, and Luke, Nancy, and Lucas Fiorante.

I have been blessed with what, albeit arguably, may be the best editorial team in the publishing world: Fred Hills, Burton Beals, and Hilary Black. Thank you, Fred, for your calm head in the midst of what seemed chaos at the moment, and thank you again, Burton, for the gentle green ink with which you deftly marked up my pages. Hilary, bless you for the nights you stayed overtime to piece together all the pages.

Joan and Joe Foley took a chance on me more than twenty years ago, and I still appreciate you both as agents and friends. Mary Alice Kier and Anna Cottle, I'm grateful that you storm the gates of Hollywood so that I won't have to.

Finally, because I wrote this book while my hill was sliding away in a continuous, frightening sea of mud, I thank my contractor, Martin Woodcock, for conquering one catastrophe after another and allowing me to keep my eyes on my computer and Puget Sound. I felt so confident that I hardly ever had to look over my shoulder at the mud creeping down the slope behind me. One day soon, I am confident that I will no longer have mud on my shoes, knees, elbows, and earlobes.

Time Warner Paperback titles available by post:

☐	A Rose for Her Grave	Ann Rule	£7.99
☐	You Belong to Me	Ann Rule	£7.99
☐	If You Really Loved Me	Ann Rule	£7.99
☐	Everything She Ever Wanted	Ann Rule	£7.99
☐	The Stranger Beside Me	Ann Rule	£7.99
☐	A Fever in the Heart	Ann Rule	£7.99
☐	In the Name of Love	Ann Rule	£7.99

The prices shown above are correct at time of going to press. However, the publishers reserve the right to increase prices on covers from those previously advertised without prior notice.

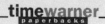

TIME WARNER PAPERBACKS
P.O. Box 121, Kettering, Northants NN14 4ZQ
Tel: 01832 737525, Fax: 01832 733076
Email: aspenhouse@FSBDial.co.uk

POST AND PACKING:
Payments can be made as follows: cheque, postal order (payable to Time Warner Books) or by credit cards. Do not send cash or currency.

All U.K. Orders	**FREE OF CHARGE**
E.E.C. & Overseas	25% of order value

Name (Block Letters) _____

Address _____

_____

Post/zip code: _____

☐ Please keep me in touch with future Time Warner publications

☐ I enclose my remittance £_____

☐ I wish to pay by Visa/Access/Mastercard/Eurocard

Card Expiry Date

_____